Changing the Language of the Abortion Debate

◆ ◆ ◆

John C. Rankin

TEI Publishing House
www.teii.org; www.teipublishinghouse.com

All biblical translations are the author's own.

Cover design by David Clarkin.

Other books by John C. Rankin:

- *The Six Pillars of Biblical Power*
- *The Six Pillars of Honest Politics*
- *Jesus, in the Face of His Enemies*
- *Genesis and the Power of True Assumptions*
- *The Real Muḥammad: In the Eyes of Ibn Isḥāq*
- *The Judas Economy: And What to Do About It*
- *Moses and Jesus in the face of Muhammad*

♦ ♦ ♦

Content

♦ ♦ ♦

Introduction

As the abortion debate goes, so goes the nation. It is the linchpin.

We, in the remnant church, need to learn a lived biblical theology that starts in the opening chapters of Genesis; one where love, a sound mind and the power of the Holy Spirit equips us to reach into a broken world.

Accordingly, we need to redefine the language of the abortion debate, gain the driver's seat and finally win the legal protection for women and their unborn equally.

There are three realities that can change the language, tested for several decades, here summed up in 400 pages, and I am satisfied they hit the mark. They starve the self-justifying oxygen of any pro-abortion ideology, and allow freedom for truth and mercy to rise.

1. Informed choice, rooted in an honest definition of terms, serves human life; *Roe* v. *Wade* is the opposite, based on a pretension of ignorance (tracing back to Cain and the enemies of Jesus).
2. Human abortion is the ultimate male chauvinism.
3. Pro-abortion advocates silence themselves in the presence of honest questions.

A simple and doable strategy is thus proposed.

These pages are written for a biblical and pro-life people, those who are committed to rigorous and honest thinking. As well, eavesdroppers are most welcome, especially the most qualified dissenters possible. Let's have a good debate.

◆ ◆ ◆

Chapter One

What About Rape and Incest?

To address any tough and painful questions, we must tackle them head-on, for in so doing we honestly gain the driver's seat in defining the terms and realities of the debate. To flee or sidestep them is to be tackled, and wind up face down in the mud of the playing field.

Baptism into the Debate

In the fall of 1972, I was baptized into the debate over human abortion.

In a religion class at Denison University – just several months before the U.S. Supreme Court *Roe* v. *Wade* decision – we read several articles on the subject, which was new to me.

The class had about thirty students, and when it came time for discussion, I was the only one who said no to human abortion. As I did, I was met with overwhelming opposition from my classmates. The most serious challenge was from a guy who asked me what I would do if my wife were raped and made pregnant – would I "force" her to keep the baby? (A reversal ploy – the rapist is the one who "forces" himself). The classroom was hushed, and I sought to give answer, never having thought about it before.

My instincts were rooted in the assumptions of a) a Christian marriage, where b) the humanity of the unborn child is affirmed, c) my simultaneous support for both my wife and her child, and d) how we would together pray through such an evil. My words were not this well composed, but this does reflect the content.

Also, it would be easy for me to argue for the abortion, since the child would not be mine. Nonetheless, I would be there every step of the way, affirm the most life-giving option possible, willing to help raise and love the child accordingly. This is still her biological child, and abortion only adds violence to violence. Good triumphs over evil.

The class broke out in a caustic and mocking laughter. The professor, Dr. Lee Scott, then said something pretty close to "Shut up." He probably did not use these words, as he was a gentle and gracious man, but his emotions carried the same force. He rebuked the class and told them to be quiet unless they were willing to be as consistent as I was, or able to make a better argument.

Thus, my initial encounter presented the toughest of questions. And such tough case scenarios have always been the fallback position for pro-abortion advocates. This is their strategy to define the terms of the debate, and avoid questions they do not want to address.

For those of us who claim to be biblical, we affirm the equal humanity and dignity of all women and their unborn children. We also address conflict and hard questions in the goal to intrinsically humanize those who oppose us, which also makes it easier for them to humanize the unborn.

The University of Massachusetts: A Woman Conceived in the Rape of an Eleven-Year Old

On September 19, 1985, I was addressing a forum in front of the Student Union at the University of Massachusetts (UMass), Amherst. Toward the end of a two-hour event that saw many people come and go, with about 100 people still there, a woman student asked me about rape and incest.

As I began to try and give answer, she interjected and stated, in the presence of everyone there, that she herself was conceived though an act of rape. I was stunned.

So I asked why she of all people would argue for abortion in the case of rape. "Would you rather have been aborted?" She was astonished, for she had never thought of it this way. Her concerns had been quite selfless, for the raped woman, her very mother. The forum ended shortly thereafter, and I walked over to her. We then went to the Student Union, sat down at a cafeteria table, and she shared her story.

6

She was a freshman or sophomore, thus about nineteen-years old. Her mother was raised in a West Virginia coal mining town, where everyone knows everyone, and where in the Baptist culture, abortion is opposed except in such cases as this. Her mother was eleven-years old when raped, and the rapist was known. Perhaps, as I read between the lines without probing inappropriately, by a member of the extended family, and thus the interface with incest as well.

When her mother was known to be pregnant, her family exerted severe pressure on her to get an abortion. The shame factor was huge, and a child born of rape would serve as a constant reminder of the evil act committed. This courageous girl resisted, carried the child and gave birth.

This twelve-year old mother was thus treated as "dirt" by the town, and her daughter was accordingly treated as "double dirt." Because she saw her mother's pain and wanted to stand up for her, the daughter uncritically accepted the abortion rationale in college – until she happened on the forum.

At this juncture, I looked straight at her and said something like, "It doesn't matter that you were conceived in rape – you are just as loved by God as anyone else, including those conceived in a loving marriage, or where there is great wealth."

I saw these words touch her soul in a fashion she had never experienced, affirming her as an equal image-bearer of God. They were received like water through the parched lips of a severely dehydrated person. So dehydrated that I ended the conversation there, realizing that such Good News is so radical that she needed time to process it. This encounter produced a number of signal "aha" moments for both of us.

Brown University: A Hushed Audience as the Question is Posed Then Addressed

In April, 1989, I was invited to address an abortion debate at Brown University in Providence, Rhode Island. My interlocutor was Mary Ann Sorrentino, immediate past president of Planned Parenthood of Rhode Island, in Providence. She had been excommunicated several years earlier by the Roman Catholic Church for her work, and it became national news.

Thus, Mary Ann was a heroine to the pro-abortion movement, and it was a packed auditorium in Sayles Hall that evening. She and I, along with the student organizer, had a pleasant dinner ahead of time.

The audience was overwhelmingly on her side. But in her opening comments Mary Ann spoke of how proud she was to stand in the tradition of Margaret Sanger, the founder of Planned Parenthood. In our time of interaction, I thus asked her how she could say that, given Sanger's very public support for eugenics, even praising Adolf Hitler once in this regard. Mary Ann could not give a defensible answer, and her stature in the sight of the audience thus suffered.

During the question and answer period, a young woman raised her hand, to my right, about seven rows deep. She said, "What about rape and incest?" as she found it justifiable in such an instance.

The whole auditorium came to an immediate hush. The hall had been built in 1881, and here, 108 years later, the seats, bolted to the floor, had been creaking and groaning all evening under the weight of shifting bodies. But not now – a dynamic anticipatory quiet. A "gotcha" moment pending as it were.

I began to frame my response by looking directly at her and saying: "In your life, are you like me, seeking the qualities of peace, order, stability and hope?" As I spoke these words, I had her eyeball-to-eyeball attention, and likewise with the hundreds of students and faculty. She said, "Yes." The gotcha moment for some was being transformed into an aha moment for all.

I continued, "Is it also fair for me to assume, that like me, you also seek to live, to love, to laugh and to learn?" Again, the same focus of intensity defined the audience, the seats unmoving, and again she said, "Yes."

So I added, "Then there is far more that unites us than divides us – we are seeking the same qualities. The question is, in the face of the hell of rape and incest: Does abortion unrape the woman and restore to her the lost qualities of peace, order, stability and hope? Or does the abortion only add further brokenness?" And I was using the term "hell" with theological accuracy.

The room continued its quiet, and I could have left it there. I knew that the resonation with the image of God, as represented by these qualities, was so complete in that moment that most students and faculty could answer the question themselves and deduce from there the reality I was addressing. I call them the POSH Ls – peace, order, stability and hope; to live, to love, to laugh and to learn.

One cardinal poison in political and top-down media life is the adversarial pursuit of the gotcha moments, seeking to entrap opposing partisan advocates and political candidates, et al. In this I have no interest.

Rather, as a minister of the Gospel, my entire interest is in serving reconciled relationships in the face of brokenness, in pursuing the wholeness of loving God and neighbor. Gotcha moments can be planned and maneuvered into existence. Aha moments, on the other hand, cannot be planned – they only happen spontaneously and unpredictably if there are healthy communicative qualities first in place. I have labored for years for those surprising 90-second slices in time where aha happens, and real humanity happily interrupts conflict.

WGAN Radio: Abortion Marketed on the Backs of Raped Women

In the fall of 1989, I was interviewed on WGAN radio in Portland, Maine. The topic of rape and incest was raised, and I sought to give answer.

Then a woman called and stated on the air that she had once been raped. Though this was radio, the stillness of the air permeated as her authority and emotions were evident. The talk show host looked at me as though I were trapped.

9

But she then said I was the first man she ever heard who understood her pain. And in listening to me, the hatred she had held against all men for years, drained out of her heart. Wow – I was not prepared for this. And I was later told, by friends in both Maine and New Hampshire, that this segment was aired many times thereafter.

The woman caller also stated that it is incredible for a woman who has been raped and impregnated by a man, to then allow another man to scrape out her uterus (thought she did not say so, she spoke with the painful authority of one so violated). And this hit me hard. How often is the topic of rape and incest used by "feminists" to justify abortion-on-demand? On the backs of raped women?

Surprising Response of an Abortion Advocate

In 1996, I addressed a group of public high school students where my second eldest son attended. The school was sponsoring an "in service" day where outside speakers would come to address various issues for tenth graders. A dialogue was set up with me and a woman representing a "women's rights" educational and political organization in Hartford, Connecticut. We addressed two separate sessions on the general topic of abortion, one of which my son attended.

Questions were elicited from the students, and in the first session, the issue of rape and incest was raised. I gave a brief synopsis of my understanding, including the stories of the women at UMass and on WGAN.

The resonance among the students was deep, but even more so, the feminist representing the women's rights group did not try to dispute me. Instead she gave compliment, stating how hard it was for her to follow up after such an "eloquent and moving" answer. During the second session, her presentation of abortion-rights was muted, and much less confident than her presentation in the first session. And during the question and answer period in the second session, she deferred to me repeatedly.

I treated her graciously from the outset, and in the first session before the rape and incest question was brought up, I likewise challenged some of her assertions, especially the rhetoric of calling pro-life people "anti-choice" and "anti-women," as well as erroneous data. I noted how none of my language involved such an accusatory nature toward abortion-rights partisans, and she responded well.

The Power of the Proactive in the Face of Lead Abortion Advocates

On a number of public occasions, I proactively raised the question of rape and incest. For example, in January, 1996, at All Saints Episcopal Church in Chevy Chase, Maryland, I was addressing one in my series of Mars Hill Forums. My guest was the Rev. Katherine Hancock Ragsdale, then president of the Religious Coalition for Abortion Rights (RCAR), which had recently changed its name to the Religious Coalition for Reproductive Choices (RCRC). We had also addressed a forum two years earlier at Yale Law School. Then, in February, 1996, I addressed a forum at Dartmouth College with Ann Stone, chairman of Republicans for Choice. In both cases, I was not thereafter challenged on the matter of rape and incest.

In other words, if we define terms honestly and proactively, and especially in face of the toughest questions, we earn the driver's seat in any debate. At present in American political, media and university life, pro-abortion advocates think they own the driver's seat. It is easy to reverse this reality if a biblically literate church arises.

No! Says the "Pro-Choice" Physician

In 2009, I was in a social gathering, and met a woman physician whose husband is an internationally leading academic (whom I had also just met, and whose work I admire). She and I had a delightful conversation, and talked theology in the midst of a whole range of other liberal arts subjects. At one point, I was about to give definition to the image of God in wide context, using the example of the POSH Ls. Before doing so, I mentioned the context of the abortion debate at Brown, and she interjected, "I am pro-choice."

11

I said no problem – this was not my focus. Then, when I came to the part of the story where I raised the question of whether or not abortion "unrapes" a woman, she jumped in energetically and graciously, "No!" She knew that an abortion does not remedy such an evil act.

In other words, and as the conversation continued, the common reality of the image of God between us is evident.

The Set-Up of These Anecdotes

We will return to this topic formally later on. Writ large, it turns out that a) abortion destroys a discrete human life, b) it is not "a woman's right to choose," but b) "a man's right to abuse." Hopefully, by means of sharing these stories, the confidence I have learned can be exported.

♦ ♦ ♦

Chapter Two

The Idolatry of the Religious Coalition for Abortion Rights

There are competing extremes in the debate over human abortion. On the one hand there is the idolatry of "choice" as found in the Religious Coalition for Abortion Rights (RCAR). On the other hand, we can note the idolatry of "life" as found in Operation Rescue (OR).

Idolatry is the worshiping of something good instead of the God who makes it good. We worship God alone, and none of his gifts instead. Both life and choice are God's gifts, they have their true biblical definitions, which we will examine, but to replace them with false definitions only multiplies human pain. To makes gifts into idols is to destroy the gifts.

Here we look at the former idolatry, and in Chapter Seven we will look at the latter.

1984 Debate at Gordon College: Can You Imagine Jesus Performing an Abortion?

My first public debate on human abortion was at Gordon College in Wenham, Massachusetts, November, 1984. The abortion-rights advocate was the Rev. Spencer Parsons, a minister with the American Baptist Churches (ABC), and lead spokesman for the Massachusetts chapter of RCAR.

During our interaction, he tried to argue for the permission for abortions in certain cases, leading the way with instances of rape and incest, along with child deformity and maternal age. He believed that "the fertilized egg" has some value, but is not fully a "person," and cited how "millions of Christians agreed with him," but did not attempt any biblical reasoning.

He also mentioned the rare hydatidiform mole cancer (an intrauterine growth at the beginning of pregnancy). This can threaten the pregnancy, but not always, and the Rev. Parsons automatically chose abortion (via dilatation and curettage) as the remedy ahead of the possibility, maybe risky maybe not, of a successful pregnancy and birth.

Not only is the idolatry of abortion choice here evident, but also an idolatry of maternal life, as it were. A biblical ethics of life and choice always honors mother and child equally, regardless of intrinsic or extrinsic suffering. Biblical ethics do everything to save the life of both mother and child, and if a medical intervention were necessary in the case of the cancerous mole, it would aim at the cancer, not the unborn child. The child could die in such an intervention, but not deliberately, and only because both mother and child could not be simultaneously saved. Hard cases make bad law and injure or kill many, many people.

(In those rare cases where an abortion is honestly judged as the only means to save the mother's life, where otherwise both would die, then it is not an "active" abortion, but an intervention to prevent a "passive" death to the mother when the child cannot otherwise live. As I oppose abortion in these pages, this is the only exception assumed. Far better to save the mother and restore her to her husband and other children, as it may be, than to lose both.)

At one juncture in the debate, I spontaneously asked "Spencer, can you ever imagine Jesus performing an abortion?"

He was taken aback, and he tried in several attempts to say yes, but in the final analysis he could not do so. Then he asked me, "Is this an ordination exam?" And I replied, "Maybe it should be." I have yet to meet anyone who has answered yes to this question with a straight face, and the inability to imagine Jesus performing an abortion sums up the nature of the Redeemer's perspective on this matter.

But we need to be careful not to be too simplistic here. Neither can we properly imagine Jesus leading an armed revolt against Roman occupation. But this focuses on the distinction between his two comings. In the first servant song of Isaiah 42:2-3, the Messiah does not snuff out a smoldering wick or break a bruised reed. So too his attitude toward the unborn. And, in the fourth servant song of Isaiah 52:13-53:12, he comes as the suffering

14

servant. But in his second coming, Jesus will lead an army of heaven against his enemies (see Revelation 19:11-21), now that they have given final rejection to his love. He will come as the Judge, and in this capacity he will also vindicate the unborn.

1986: The American Baptist Churches Eject the Religious Coalition for Abortion Rights

In May of 1986, I was asked to present a biblical pro-life position at a meeting outside Hartford, Connecticut. The leaders from the national ABC and in New England were there, along with two of the national leaders of RCAR in Washington, D.C.

Because of alphabetic reality, the ABC was always listed at the top of RCAR's member organizations (though it was only one committee in the ABC that had joined). Many in the denomination did not like this. So the ABC set up a task force to reconsider its affiliation with RCAR through a series of similar meetings across the nation.

It was a tense gathering despite the best attempts by the organizers to make it pleasant. In my presentation, following that of the RCAR leaders, I gave a theological sketch rooted in Genesis 1-2, part of which involved defining the relationship between life and choice. Namely, both are given us by God, but choice is designed to be in service to life, not employed to destroy it. We cannot make choices unless we are first alive. And I defined how the unborn fully qualify as human life, made in God's image. The RCAR representatives did not engage the substance in the slightest, but in turn, repeatedly called me "anti-choice."

So I asked them to define how choice relates to life, and they were unable or unwilling. I stated how I was truly "pro-informed choice" in my position, which means that an honest definition of terms is prerequisite for people to make sound decisions. They did not refute me, instead falling back to the language of calling me "anti-choice." I was so appalled by this poor thinking and amorality, that I wrote a critique of RCAR following the meeting, sent them a copy, and likewise to the ABC task force.

In it, I diagnosed three aspects of RCAR: 1) their idolatry of "individual choice" as supreme to obedience to God's definition of human life, thus reversing the boundaries of freedom which God defines for us in Genesis 2:15-17 (a subject to be addressed in the next chapter); 2) they operate in hiddenness and refuse to be publicly accountable to defend their position in the face of any pro-life challenge; and 3) they seek to motivate by appeals to fear and hyperbole.

RCAR was furious that I dare write such a critique, complaining bitterly to the ABC task force, saying how it was not my place to do so. Nonetheless, in my critique, I stated that if I were in error in any substance or nuance, I would be pleased to be corrected. After four months there was no reply until the chairperson of the ABC task force wrote me tersely, asking that I not mention them in my critique. Then there followed a letter from a pro-life minister on the task force, dissociating himself from the "embarrassing and insulting" nature of the chairperson's letter; he had not known of it until after the fact.

In Deuteronomy 29:18, Moses speaks of how the worship of false gods – idolatry – produces a "root" of "wormwood" (a bitter poison) in the souls of those who do so. I had not encountered such a reality until this time. Namely, the bitterness was rooted in a reaction to chauvinistic evil, where unforgiveness unchecked only poisons the humanity as substitute gods are de facto chosen. In this case, the god of a false choice to kill nascent humanity is chosen, as opposed to seeking the true God of informed choice, and thus serve all human life.

And as it turns out, the ABC subsequently rescinded its membership in RCAR.

1986 Massachusetts Council of Churches Pro-Abortion Conference, and the Relentless Percolation of a Pro-Life Ethic

I crossed paths with Spencer Parsons on several occasions, including a radio debate on WEZE, Boston, and where the same territory was covered. Then I chanced to cross paths with him at an abortion-rights conference sponsored by the Massachusetts Council of Churches, some weeks after my meeting with the ABC and RCAR.

The featured speaker was the Rev. Dr. Beverly Wildung Harrison, professor at Union Theological Seminary in New York City, and author of *Our Right to Choose*. This book is the most ardent I have read that advances the idolatry of choice in the name of theology – erudite on the surface, but underneath full of so much reactive anger against male chauvinism. She phrases the question as "who shall control the power to reproduce the species?" aiming to "eliminate misogyny from Christian abortion teaching." It is always hard for me so see such pain in a human soul, but too, we all make our choices in how to address it. How much of her pain is understood and addressed by the biblically committed church?

At that conference I also joined in and listened to a group discussion meant to be a sounding board for abortion-rights sympathies. It was remarkable. One man, whose politics used to be in favor of abortion, shared how he had been converted by the work of the Sojourners magazine and community in Washington, D.C. This was clearly an unexpected turn for many in the circle of discussion of some twenty or more people. But too, it was readily affirmed by others and a surprise for even more.

Then a woman told a painful story of having been pregnant in the 1950s, when her husband decided to leave her. She had four children, and she told of the humiliation she went through trying to get a hospital to grant her a "therapeutic" abortion – and not being able to get one in the days before legalized abortion. She was very emotional, and her pain was palpable – she was winning people's empathy. I was expecting to then hear the horror of a tragic end in some fashion with a "back-alley" abortionist.

But it was a spontaneous sharing on her part, and she even surprised herself. For once she had testified about the humiliation, she suddenly concluded by saying that she gave birth to a boy, her husband returned to her, and this son was the greatest joy of her five children. We were all surprised not only by how she concluded, but how abrupt is was. (And surprise is the essence of "aha").

17

After the conference, I talked with Spencer in the parking lot. I was answering various questions he had for me at a more personal level than formal debate allows, and he concluded by saying that I was right about the Bible's opposition to human abortion. He just did not believe we should impose pro-life laws on others, in his concern for church/state balances. I sought to address this concern and allay his fears, speaking about my commitment to the power of informed choice within political process.

In our conversation he also remarked off-handedly that my critique of RCAR hit the nail on the head (I had mailed him a copy the week prior). I was astounded. I asked him point-blank if there were even any nuance of my critique that was unfair, and he said, "I can't think of any."

Spencer then thanked me for talking with him, saying that I was the first pro-life advocate he ever met who listened to him and respected him as a human being. He also shared some personal bitterness he had in this regard from other encounters. I remember thinking as I drove away: *What is so difficult about listening to someone? Is that not the nature of Christian love? What would happen if we in the church did show such love, instead of a condescension into dehumanizing political rhetoric?*

1986 Debate at Beaver Country Day School: Should Two Men Address a Woman's Issue?

The next time I crossed paths with Spencer was again a surprise. Also in 1986, I was invited to speak to a school assembly at Beaver Country Day in Chestnut Hill, outside Boston. My sponsor, mother of a student there, saw how deeply the pro-abortion ethos was etched into the school's culture and curriculum. There had been pro-abortion presentations, but not pro-life. So she approached the school, and gained approved for me to come.

As soon as the invitation become public, some pro-abortion advocates at the school strenuously objected. They demanded equal representation, the school yielded, called the Planned Parenthood League of Massachusetts (PPLM), and they sent – Spencer Parsons. My sponsor told me about the rescheduling for a debate, and I was delighted. I always prefer to have a public dialogue with someone who disagrees with me in such a setting. But I had no idea who the interlocutor would be.

So when I saw Spencer that morning, I smiled and we shook hands. The fun part was his opening quip. He said how ironic it is that two men are addressing a woman's subject. The students and faculty roared with approval at the gotcha. But it easily turned into an aha, for I replied something like: "Then why did Planned Parenthood, with their executive director being a woman, send a man to do a woman's work?" The audience response was also raucous. So the stage was set. In my comments I explained the intrinsic nature of the abortion industry being rooted in male chauvinism, and I do not recollect any challenge on this point, certainly not from Spencer.

1989 Debate at the University of New Hampshire: No Biblical Exegesis Please

As I will further detail in Chapter Nine, I participated in an October 1989 debate at the University of New Hampshire (UNH). There were three of us on each side.

A Methodist minister represented RCAR. At one juncture I mentioned Psalm 139, where the presence of *Yahweh* is with the unformed child in the womb, and even before. The RCAR minister began to ridicule my interpretation of the text. He said it was "poetry" and had no relevance to the biology or moral status of the unborn. He evidenced his argument by asking me if I seriously thought we were "woven together in the depths of the earth" as the text says descriptively about the mother's womb. He said such a phrase reflects the primitive and unscientific basis of Israelite society, and as influenced by pagan religion. It was clearly the poetry of an unsophisticated society, he said.

I responded by asking if his seminary training included Hebrew, and thus, knowledge of parallelistic structure in poetry. He said no. I then asked how he could make such an observation about a psalm written in a genre he knew nothing about. He did not respond. His question to me was both sarcastic and mocking in tone, as clearly evident to the audience and other panelists. I did

not return any such attitude. Rather I treated him as an intellectual equal –
since he brought up the question of poetry as a genre.

I then explained the nature of Hebrew parallelisms in poetic structure, and
summed up the nature of the psalm's focus on the presence of *Yahweh*, along
with the reason why David is looking at the subject of the womb. In so doing,
I explained that all Hebrew poetry is in service to the assumptions of
verifiable history, science and the scientific method. Accordingly, David is
free to use a literary device, here with metaphor and hyperbole, to underscore
such realities. He considers the remoteness of the literal womb where his
inner being has been fashioned by *Yahweh*, the "hidden place" as a parallel
expression to the womb, and finally, the remoteness of "the depths of the
earth" as a parallel expression to the "hidden place" and the womb. The
image is one of a place below the depths of a volcano – utterly remote – and
David can neither travel inside the womb nor under a volcano, but *Yahweh* is
present in both. In other words:

> "The hidden place" and the "depths of the earth" are parallel to "the
> womb" in terms of remoteness, not scientific description.

Thus, too:

> This literary image is invoked to say that *Yahweh* chooses to abide
> with the unborn child through all pregnancy, and thus, to abort a child
> is to abort the presence of the Creator.

The RCAR minister was stumped. Later on in the evening, in response to
something else he said, I began to refer to some exegetical background to
frame my thoughts, and he interrupted. He complained that it was unfair for
me to "get academic" again. True academic pursuit will always ratify the
Gospel even if it questions it. The Gospel is coextensive with reality.

We will look at Psalm 139 structurally in Chapter Two.

1994 and 1996: President of RCAR: No Biblical Exegesis Please

As mentioned earlier in the context of rape and incest, I addressed two forums with then president of the national RCAR, in 1994 and 1996, the Rev. Katherine Hancock Ragsdale. She also later served as dean of students at the Episcopal Divinity School, Cambridge, Massachusetts. In her presentations, and more fully in subsequent talks and writings, Katherine developed a "liturgy" that treats abortion as a "sacrament," saying "abortion is a blessing" at one point. So, alongside Beverly Wildung Harrison, we see the idolatry of choice *in extremis*. What human suffering at the hands of male chauvinism must be at play, that such a posture willing to twist Scripture comes to pass?

Too, in both of our forums, Katherine did not want Psalm 139 or Exodus 21 to even be addressed. She and others use the Exodus passage as an eisegetical proof-text in favor of human abortion, but the biblical exegesis shows the opposite. Thus we have a disagreement. But when I started to explain my understanding of the Exodus text, she forcibly interjected to cut off the subject, nervously mocking the possibility of an alternative interpretation. She was not interested in my sense of how to exegete the text, and this is why up front, her attempt to eisegete it was evident. (To exegete is to discover what is in the text; to eisegete is to put into the text what you want to be there, "discover" it, and pretend it was there all along.)

Also, in Chapter Two, we will exegete the text of Exodus 21:22-25.

The Idolatry of Choice

It is one thing to identify the idolatry of choice that perverts the biblical language of freedom in service to human abortion. It is another thing to witness it in action, and this I experienced in depth with RCAR. As Jesus says: "By their fruit you will recognize them" (Matthew 7:20). I have identified some cardinal encounters with RCAR, and some more will also percolate in other contexts as we progress. And their theology, as it proves out, is a doctrine of demons – the destruction of the image of God.

◆ ◆ ◆

21

Chapter Three

Biblical Theology 101

I Once Took a Shower

In the 1970s, my sense of calling in ministry was to share the Gospel in some dynamic way within a skeptical age, but I had no real idea what that meant specifically.

One morning in May, 1982, in the years while working my way through Gordon-Conwell Theological Seminary, I took a shower. Which is not to say I have not done so in the meantime. I was having a shadow-box debate with then Massachusetts Governor Edward J. King, and the once and twice future Governor Michael S. Dukakis. They were competing in the Democratic Party primary.

Though not politically wired, the issues mattered, and I did pay attention. After a lull in the debate, I said to them: "Gentlemen, don't you realize that for everything you say you care about, the answers are in the Gospel of Jesus Christ?" Silence.

So I prayed: "Lord, don't these gentlemen realize that everything they say they care about is found in the Gospel of Jesus Christ?" As if the Lord had any other opinion – I was just ratifying it in the conversation of prayer.

So I continued, in a life changing surprise turn: "Lord, you need some theologically educated people in politics." His answer came to the depth of my soul at one of those moments of utter clarity. The reply: "John – good idea. Any suggestions?"

Now translation is an art, and not a mathematical science. So I could translate what I heard the Lord say to me: "Any volunteers?"

I threw my hands in the air and said, "Lord, you know I would never go anywhere where I would have to compromise my faith." I had some deep

22

assumptions on how politics continually swallow up the integrity of people who join its world. But the Lord answered with the same clarity: "Maybe your faith is not big enough."

In the intervening decades, I have sought to grow my faith enough to make it "first the Gospel, then politics ..." And the word "politics," from the Greek *polis*, refers to the walled city in which culture and social order is maintained against external threats and disorder. Far more than just government, but fully inclusive of it.

The Call to Christian Pro-Life Ministry

In 1983 I did a summer-long independent research on Darwinian science and its theological, sociological and political impact. During that time, I was also in prayer about ministry trajectory. I was set to resign my church position on Labor Day and study full-time that fall, after which I would be broke and in need of landing in a vocation.

In prayerful reflection, I was pursuing a) what the Lord was calling me to do, which b) I was equipped to do, that which c) no one else was doing, and which d) needed to be done.

I remember, during many a study break, reclining on the couch and proposing to the Lord various ideas. He listens well. Finally, I said at one juncture: "Maybe I should check out Christian pro-life possibilities." And he spoke clearly to my soul: "Good idea. Check it out." And for me, it is "Christian" that modifies "pro-life" and not vice versa.

So I did, and traveled to Washington, D.C., that fall for a conference of the Christian Action Council (CAC), an evangelical pro-life initiative started by evangelist Billy Graham, C. Everett Koop, M.D. (later the U.S. Surgeon General) and Harold O.J. Brown, professor at Trinity Evangelical Divinity School. I thus founded the Massachusetts Bay Christian Action Council (soon renamed the New England Christian Action Council [NECAC] as I was quickly called on to teach across New England).

The CAC also began its Crisis Pregnancy Centers (CPCs) nationwide, caring for pregnant women in need. This initiative bore, and still bears, great fruit. However, the political side of the CAC was comparatively short-lived on Capitol Hill, and so too with the various chapters started across the country.

Theological and Street-Level Learning Curve

In the spring of 1984, I began teaching the "Sanctity of Human Life Seminars" (SOHLS). The first one was in my home church, Pigeon Cove Chapel, Rockport, Massachusetts, and some fifty people. Having no prior no prior experience in teaching on the subject, I simply started in Genesis 1-3, and went from there.

My second seminar, shortly thereafter, was at the College Church in Northampton, Massachusetts. About forty people attended. Afterward, I received a letter from the associate pastor who attended. He said he came to the seminar expecting to learn about how the Bible addresses the abortion debate, but left having been equipped to address "any and every issue." This was a great surprise to me, for I thought I was only focusing on the abortion debate. But in later reflection I realized that indeed, Genesis 1-3 sets the table to address any issue, and this reality must have clearly shown itself.

As I surveyed the pro-life landscape, I immediately noticed several elements. First, whereas certain biblical assumptions were in place, I saw little if any strategic theological thinking and consequent action. Second, the language of "choice" was greatly feared. And third, and as I wrote in my first newsletter for the NECAC, I saw human abortion as the ultimate male chauvinism – men getting women pregnant, then fleeing responsibility.

Also, I began to receive invitations to debate the subject on various university campuses. I was interested in making my case persuasively, but too, I also noted how I was more interested in real communication with those who disagreed with me. We can win a debate, but lose a relationship. This is pyrrhic, disserves the Gospel, and only leaves hardened positions in its wake. Or we can win an honest relationship in the face of a real debate, seeking always to honor the humanity of the other, and thus serve the work of the Holy Spirit in allowing people to think in new ways. And we too can learn to think in new ways. The pursuit of the aha not the gotcha. Rigorous thinking is dangerous to the devil, and always serves the Gospel.

"Theology" can be an obtuse word for many in the church, thinking of it in terms of theoretical and arcane ideas. But for me, "theology" (Greek *theos* for God and *logos* for word – literally "God's Word") is dynamic. If lived out at the street-level, it becomes alive and far more powerful. And this is what happened to me. I did do a post-graduate degree at Harvard Divinity School in the process – in ethics and public policy – but it also served my work of street-level ministry. It is only now, in my advancing years, that I have found time, purpose and focus to pursue a Ph.D., in political theology, at the Oxford Centre for Mission Studies. And as I do, I see how my theology was shaped by ministry at the street-level – confronting questions and realities easy to miss within academic silos.

The Theology of God → Life → Choice → Sex

With this question of defining life and choice in mind, I was invited to speak at a Crisis Pregnancy Center banquet in Ithaca, New York, March, 1989, in conjunction with a debate at Cornell University. In the banquet address, I was defining the language of life and choice in Genesis 2, honing further what had been roundly tested in the opposition of the Religious Coalition for Abortion Rights. As I was speaking, I moved from an implicit clarity to an explicit one, namely, that the theological order of Genesis 1-2 starts with the sovereign God, then it defines the purpose of creation as the making of human life in God's image, followed by God's first words to Adam which equals the gift of choice.

I also noted that "pro-life" people are overwhelmingly rooted in a biblical sense of the nature of God, and that "pro-choice" people are overwhelmingly rooted in a sense of approving, or at least not disapproving, of sex outside of marriage. It hit me – so simple:

God → Life → Choice.

The three basic elements of the order of creation, I thought. The three basic issues surrounding the abortion debate, it appeared. By extension, the reversal of this order was:

Choice → *Life* →/ *God.*

However, the next week I set to reviewing Genesis 1-2 with this newly observed paradigm. As I did, I realized I had not considered the fourth and final defining subject of Genesis 1-2, that of human sexuality.

This inclusion of course reveals how the idolatry of choice, while powerful, is energized by the prior and more powerful idolatry of sex outside of marriage. The conflict between "pro-choice" and "pro-life," in the language of the abortion debate today, only exists because of a reversal of the order of creation, when choice is used to destroy life. Thus, the full paradigm is this:

God → *Life* → *Choice* → *Sex.*

The self-defining terms of "pro-life" and "pro-choice" are thus in the middle of this paradigm, and in a graphic sense which identifies the locus of the conflict over human abortion:

God → *Life* → | ← *Choice* ← *Sex.*

In other words, it is fidelity to God that defines life, and should properly motivate the political language of "pro-life." And it is sexuality in promiscuous context that in truth defines the idolatry of choice, and thus motivates the political language of "pro-choice." "Pro-life" thus reflects the order of creation, and "pro-choice" reflects the reversal. A false dichotomy is set up: sex/choice versus God/life, and thus yields the reversal order:

Sex → *Choice* → *Life* →/ *God.*

Sex outside of marriage employs atomistic choice to destroy the life of the unborn in the act of human abortion, and in an affront against God – the Creator of life, choice and sex. The idolatry of "choice."

Thus, we have a profile of the contest of the ages, between the biblical and pagan views of the four subjects in the order of creation:

God → *life* → *choice* → *sex*, on the one hand, versus
Sex → *choice* → *life* → */God*, on the other.

As we set the table for the larger and necessary theological structure, these four subjects remain central and always percolate, in the face of any and every issue, and especially that of human abortion.

And as specifically applicable here:

Pro-life = pro-informed choice, versus
Anti-life = anti-informed choice.

Thus, Male Chauvinism as Idolatry

In other words, abortion justifies sexual promiscuity and infidelity, and as such it is the ramrod of male chauvinism where the man who gets the woman pregnant outside of marriage is able to take off and leave her to face the pregnancy alone.

According to the Alan Guttmacher Institute, the research arm of Planned Parenthood Federation (PPF), International, the statistics from the late 1970s to the present show consistently that some 82 percent of all abortions are done on unmarried women. Then there is the reality shared with me among a number of women I know who run, or have run, CPCs, those who have personally counseled tens of thousands of abortion-minded women. Of the nearly all of the remaining 18 percent (excepting the extreme cases of health and life concerns), the child is conceived in adultery in three-quarters of the cases. In the other one-quarter, nearly all the men are on the way out the door. Only rarely does a stable married couple seek an abortion.

In 1999, I spoke with a volunteer at a CPC. She had personally counseled 250 abortion-minded women at that point, and her words are these: "100 percent of these women do what the man wants." A woman's freedom to choose?

Creation, Sin and Redemption

This autobiographical profile paves the way to how, following two graduate degrees in theology, it matured through being tested in such a street-level context. In other words, apart from such relentless grass-roots ministry, so much of my biblical exegesis and theology would not have had occasion to rise. Happily, I was wired to test biblical theology in the real world, and thus arrived at what I call Biblical Theology 101. Let's take a look.

The storyline of the entire Bible is based on Genesis 1-3 and its three all-defining doctrines of:

Creation → sin → redemption.

The word "fall" can be inserted in place of "sin," as it describes what the first sin does to man and woman – we fell from God's original place, and need to be lifted back. But too, the word "sin" describes both the original fall and its consequences, so I use it as the primary term. "Sin" is a word that is easily misunderstood. It essentially means brokenness of trust, and we all know that from one or many angles.

There are two ways we can describe these doctrines. The first is directional in nature:

The order of creation → the reversal → the reversal of the reversal.

The second is organic in nature:

The wholeness of creation → the brokenness of sin → the restoration to wholeness.

The order of creation is the root of all truth and reality in time and space:

28

From the beginning, God establishes the order of creation, and our lives, according to a set plan that is intended for our greatest joy as his image-bearers. But through a disobedient act of the will, Adam and Eve and the whole human race have submitted to a reversal of that order, and we reap the painful consequences. Sin can thus be understood as a reversal, as brokenness. It is a reversal in that it goes in the wrong direction. It is brokenness in that it breaks relationship with God, with one another and the wholeness of his creation, i.e., broken trust. Following the inception of human sin, God institutes the reversal of the reversal, the redemptive process designed to purchase us back from the slavery of sin, and to restore to us the original purposes, trajectory and wholeness of the order of creation.

The word "redemption" means to buy back out of slavery (e.g., the whole purpose of the exodus from Egypt, cf. Exodus 20:2). Slavery, by definition, is the loss of an original freedom. Thus, we can also define the doctrines of creation, sin and redemption a third way:

Freedom → slavery → return to freedom.

The Eleven Positive Assumptions of Only Genesis

A Biblical Theology 101 begins with the biblical order of creation, what I call "Only Genesis," and there are eleven positive assumptions:

1. Only Genesis has a positive view of God's nature (the power to give).
2. Only Genesis has a positive view of the heavenly court.
3. Only Genesis has a positive view of communication (the power to live in the light).
4. Only Genesis has a positive view of human nature.
5. Only Genesis has a positive view of human freedom (the power of informed choice).
6. Only Genesis has a positive view of hard questions (the power to love hard questions).
7. Only Genesis has a positive view of human sexuality.

29

8. Only Genesis has a positive view of science and the scientific method.
9. Only Genesis has a positive view of verifiable history.
10. Only Genesis has a positive view of covenantal law.
11. Only Genesis has a positive view of unalienable rights.

These eleven positive assumptions reflect the integrity of the biblical content introduced in the order of creation in Genesis 1-2, define virtually every subject in the universe, and as infused with the concerns for *God →life → choice → sex*. These eleven assumptions also equal the basis for a fully genuine and rigorous liberal arts education.

The Six Pillars of Biblical Power

There are six pillars of biblical power distilled from the eleven positive assumptions. Both these assumptions and the six pillars of biblical power are unique, and in their essence and wholeness, they are not found in any pagan origin text or secular construct. These assumptions and pillars are at the core of all that is good in human civilization.

These pillars are ethical in nature. "Ethics" comes from the Greek terms *ethos* and *ethikos*, for "social customs or habits," for how we treat people. And depending on context, "ethics" can be used either as a singular or plural term. "Ethics" as a term, apart from context, is by definition neutral – there are good ethics and there are evil ethics.

The six pillars equal the basis for the most Spirit-filled doctrine possible, doctrine that leads to transformed lives and a transformable world. In fact, these pillars, as believed and lived, lead to the highest standards and accountability to the work of the Holy Spirit in our lives, and in the presence of skeptics.

The first four pillars are distilled from the eleven positive assumptions, and are placed in parentheses in the listing of the eleven assumptions above. The last two pillars are drawn from the order of redemption (specifically rooted in the Sermon on the Mount), which is to say, as a remedy for the broken trust of sin that assaulted the goodness of the first four pillars.

Thus, the six pillars are below, and they literally sum up the whole Bible ethically. Jesus repeatedly says that the whole Law is summed up in loving God with all our heart, soul, mind and strength, and thus, in loving our neighbors as ourselves. And as the rabbis say across the millennia, all else is commentary. The six pillars are my commentary, distilled through my studies and experiences of sharing the Gospel in the face of a skeptical age:

1. The power to give.
2. The power to live in the light.
3. The power of informed choice.
4. The power to love hard questions.
5. The power to love enemies.
6. The power to forgive.

As we proceed, we will touch on each of the eleven positive assumptions, and accordingly, as they generate the six pillar extrusion. Our focus in so doing, and in depth in setting the foundation, is on how to change the language of the abortion debate. The subject of *God* is easy to define up front, and the realities of → *life* → *choice* → *sex* will receive the most appropriate attention against the larger backdrop.

First: God's Nature

Bereshith bara elohim eth ha'shamayim w'eth ha'eretz are the first words in Genesis – 1) in the beginning; 2) the unique verb for God's creating power; 3) God; and 4) his creation, the heavens and the earth. In Hebrew, the verb precedes the noun, thus we translate it: "In the beginning God created the heavens and the earth." The object is *Elohim*, God, and hence God is the first assumption in the Bible. The nature of God is that he creates, he is the Creator. And to create is the essence of goodness.

31

When pagan religious texts are read, no such assumption is in place. In fact, the gods and goddesses are finite and petty, and what is assumed is a preceding undefined yet hostile cosmos.

The Compound Name for God in Genesis 1-2

The Hebrew word for God in the first sentence in the Bible is *Elohim*. The English word "God" comes from proto-Germanic roots that interface with the idea of creating, of the Creator.

In Genesis 1, we have the grand design of creation, and in Genesis 2 we have the first covenant between the Creator and man. Genesis 2 actually takes place within the theological structure of Genesis 1, on the sixth day.

In Genesis 1:

Elohim as the Creator of all mankind is used as a title.

Across the Hebrew Bible:

The use of *Elohim* carries with it this assumption, namely, the one true Creator that all people recognize, including polytheistic Gentiles.

In Genesis 2:

The compound *Yahweh Elohim* is introduced, where *Yahweh* is the personal name of the covenant keeping Creator.

Across the Hebrew Bible:

The stand-alone personal name of *Yahweh* refers to his specific covenant-keeping identity, as the Hebrew people recognize, but not by the Gentiles as they migrate away from the assumptions of Genesis 1-2.

Across the Hebrew Bible:

With the great frequency of the compound name, *Yahweh Elohim*, in the minds of the Hebrew peoples, both factors combine – personal name and title.

Space, Time and Number

Yahweh is the third person form of the verb for "I am," thus translated, "He is." That is, *Yahweh* is the I AM, which in the first person is *Ehyeh*, the original Existence and Presence who is greater to and prior to, and thus defines, space and time.

Elohim is grammatically a unique term. It is a masculine plural (known also as the honorific plural in contrast to the singular *el*). But *Elohim* is overwhelmingly used with the singular case. This means the singular *Elohim* is greater than the concept of number. In the few cases when the singular case is not used, the reference is to the plurality of pagan gods.

Thus, the name *Yahweh Elohim* in totality means the One who is greater than space, time and number – a concept found nowhere else in history.

The Power to Give

In sum, God's nature and person, as *Yahweh Elohim* who is greater than space, time and number, is rooted in unlimited power and goodness, and his purpose is to bless all people equally. His nature is the power to give – the first pillar. He gives us life, liberty, human sexuality and the power to build civilization. This is the starting assumption in Genesis 1-2, where all is declared good (*tov*).

This is also where the "Gospel" is rooted (the Greek term here is *euangelion* for "good news," from whence "evangelical" comes). Namely, Genesis 1-2 is good news, and Jesus in preaching the Good News restores us to its promises.

Human Abortion

Human abortion is not congruent with the Creator, the power to create nor the power to give.

Second: The Heavenly Court

In Genesis 1:1, as we have already noted, it reads: "In the beginning *Elohim* created the heavens and the earth." These are two domains, with the heavens being the domain of *Yahweh Elohim*, and the earth being the given stewardship for man and woman.

Yet, in Genesis 2:1, the text reads: "Thus the heavens and the earth were completed in all their armies." Many translations render the end of this sentence as "in their vast array" or "in all their hosts." Why, in a statement of the summary goodness of the created order do we have armies? It is a noun rooted in the Hebrew verb *tsaba* for making warfare.

The term "host" refers to armies, but it is so antiquated in usage for many, that it loses its accurate edge. In English Bible translations, we see at least 250 times where the words are translated as the "LORD Almighty." In Hebrew, it literally means *"Yahweh* of armies," and the soldiers in *Yahweh*'s armies are the holy angels.

The heavenly court is a positive assumption, that which includes the idea of a guarding army, even before the rebellion of the angel Lucifer, which is a subject too large for these pages. When Adam is made, his first charge is to "to work and guard (*shamar*)" the garden from intrusion.

Thus, and perhaps more properly, this positive assumption of the armies of *Yahweh* is part of the domain of the heavens in Genesis 1:1, being a principal reference to his heavenly court, or assembly. This is also the original locale of *Yahweh Elohim*'s freedom, a freedom given first to the heavenly host, and especially then to man and woman as his image-bearers to govern the domain of the earth, and to whom the heavenly armies are to be Adam and Eve's servants. And given the rebellion of a high-ranking cherub in the heavenly court, Lucifer, who thus transmogrifies into *Satan* or the devil, Adam and Eve are called to guard the Garden from the devil's intrusion.

The use of *shamar*, to guard, is strategically found across the Hebrew Bible. usually in this context, in both Genesis 3 and 4, later in Genesis 17, Exodus 20 and 23, Leviticus 25, Deuteronomy 11, Judges 6, Joshua 23, early in the book of Job, Psalms 91 and 121, the end of David's life, the end of Ecclesiastes, Malachi 2 and elsewhere.

The original freedom *Yahweh Elohim* gives to man is the language of informed choice. The devil hates informed choice at the deepest level of his perverted soul, for he tries to destroy it in his narcissism and solipsism, and in the end it destroys him. Which is to say, the original positive freedom in the order of creation given to the angels is the underlying reality, and in the end slavery cannot conquer freedom.

Also here, the names for *Satan* in the Hebrew (*ha'satan*), and in the Greek (*tou diabolos*), the devil, mean the same – "the *satan*" (but usually used as a proper name) and "the devil," both mean "the accuser," "the slanderer." And in Revelation 9:11, the devil is the angel of the abyss, whose Hebrew name *abaddon* and Greek name *apollyon* both mean the "destroyer."

Human Abortion

Human abortion is a quintessential act of destruction (from the Latin *ab* + *oriri*, "to stop from rising," "to cut off from being born"). The work of the Destroyer.

Third: Communication

In two sequentially parallel texts, Genesis 1:1-5 and John 1:1-5, we see the immediate assumption of communication:

> In the beginning *Elohim* created the heavens and the earth. Now the earth was formless and empty, darkness was over the surface of the abyss, and the Spirit of *Elohim* brooded over the waters. And *Elohim*

said, "Let there be light," and there was light. *Elohim* saw that the light was good, and *Elohim* separated the light from the darkness. *Elohim* called the light "day," and the darkness he called "night." And there was evening, and there was morning – the first day.

In the beginning was the Word, and the Word was with God, and the Word was God. He was with God in the beginning. All things were made through him, without him nothing was made that has been made. In him was life, and that life was the light of men. And the light shines in the darkness, but the darkness cannot understand and overcome it.

The apostle John deliberately makes the opening words of his gospel parallel to and building upon the opening words of Genesis. The presence of the Father, Son and Holy Spirit infuse these two texts together. Jesus is the one true Creator in human form – and the epitome of communication in the face of a darkened world.

At the simplest threshold, the language of light defines the nature of honest communication. Light reveals what is truly there: "Let there be light." And prior to that is sound: "*Elohim* said." Sound is also essential to communication. And light is the language of revelation, of God's nature and purposes.

To ponder, for a moment, the scientific theory of the Hot Big Bang – sound and light define it. Who or what put the mass there to being with, and who or what prepared the fuse and ignited it? Intellectually, logically, aesthetically and in the joy of sheer wonder, only the One who is greater than space, time and number. Sound and light are the most basic elements in the universe. "And *Elohim said*, let there be *light*." Think of the language of observation and discovery – it starts with light. Biblical theology is the queen of all the sciences.

Three Domains

Starting in Genesis 1, the biblical theme of light versus darkness is a commanding one across all Scripture. Light, full communication and honesty, on the one hand, are co-extensive. Darkness, broken communication and deceit, on the other, are likewise co-extensive. There are three domains where we see this.

First is that of physics. Wherever light is present, by definition darkness cannot exist. Light has an atomic weight, and darkness has none, which means darkness does not exist. We are speaking of absolute darkness, just as with absolute cold (-459 Fahrenheit) where life cannot exist because no chemical reactions can occur. Darkness it is the absence of light. So when the light appears, darkness immediately dissipates.

This observational reality is assumed throughout the Bible. Not in terms of modern calculations, but that modern calculations are made possible because of biblical assumptions about the inanimate and observable nature of the physical universe.

Second is that of ethics. Consider the averted gaze where Cain looks away from the face of *Yahweh*, in his anger for not being able to deceive him (Genesis 4:1-7). Whereas Abel's offering is from the best of his livestock, Cain's offering from his grains is not said to be of the best – rather, almost as a grudging afterthought.

And as well, we can look at a contrast between two responses to the coming of the kingdom of God. In Luke 21:25-28, the words of Jesus point past the destruction of the temple and Jerusalem in 70 A.D., to his Second Coming. He commends his disciples to stand up and lift their heads – alluding to the Jewish posture of prayer – eyes fixed heavenward with arms outstretched to God. Jesus refers to an eyeball-to-eyeball yearning for the soon coming King.

In Revelation 6:15-17, in response to the opening of the sixth seal, the peoples of the earth call on the mountains and rocks to fall on them and "conceal us from the face of him who sits on the throne and from the wrath of the Lamb!"

These two snapshots reflect a constant theme in the Bible, where those who choose to live in the light see God as a Friend who rescues them from judgment; and those who choose to live in the darkness see God as an enemy, the one who puts on them a wrath they have chosen. The eyeball language is again in place – unrepentant persons fear the face of God, and would rather be crushed to dust under the weight of the mountains than to look at Jesus, seek and receive forgiveness.

To believe in Jesus is to live in the light. Here the language of John 1:1-5 links with Genesis 1:1-5. Jesus is the Word (from the Greek *logos* for word, thought, expression, idea, communication), the very communication of *Yahweh* in our midst. He is also the light and the life. And when we consider the reality in physics that darkness and absolute zero have no existence, we see the contrast dramatically. Jesus calls himself "the light of the world" in John 8:12, and in the Sermon on the Mount he calls his disciples the same (Matthew 5:14-16), where we have nothing to hide. Jesus calls himself the "life" in John 14:6, and he comes to give us that life (John 10:10).

In John 3:19-21, as Jesus addresses Nicodemus, he concludes:

> This is the judgment: Light has come into the cosmos, but men loved darkness instead of light because their deeds were evil. Everyone who does what is bad hates the light, and will not come into the light for fear that his deeds will be revealed. But whoever does the truth embraces the light, so that it may be manifest that what he has done has been done through God.

John further addresses the ethics of living in the darkness versus the light in 1 John 1:5-10. Here there is no darkness in God, we lie if we walk in the darkness, but we can live in the light through the candor of confessing our sins.

The third domain, spiritual territory, leads us back to John 1:1-5, and the parallel to Genesis 1:1-5. It is also a cognate to the reality of the heavenly court.

Thus, just as *Elohim*'s first words in Scripture are "Let there be light," and the light is separated from darkness, here we see that Jesus as the Word is the "light" – defining John's constant theme of light versus darkness. The physics and ethics are in place in this parallel between Genesis and John, and now we gain introduction to the spiritual war between light and darkness.

In John 1:5, as the light shines into the darkness, the Greek term at the very end is *katalambano*. It is the metaethics of learning, of grasping – it most fully means to reach up, seize hold, pull down, dethrone and trample – to conquer. Thus, another translation here is that the darkness has not "overcome" the light. "Metaethics" here refers to the larger context of word usage.

Or to flesh it out a little more, we cannot overcome what we do not understand. Darkness cannot know or comprehend the light, and light knows darkness will flee its presence by definition. *Satan* is "the prince of darkness," in the words of Martin Luther as he reflects on biblical reality, and in the face of Jesus who is the Light of the world, the devil cannot understand and overcome Jesus. *Satan* is, literally, the "prince of nothing." The power to live in the light resonates here in the language of James: "Accordingly, submit to God, resist the devil, and he will flee from you. Come near to God and he will come near to you" (4:7-8).

So, what is the speed of darkness? It has none, but only eviscerates in the presence of light. Just as slavery has no power in the face of freedom.

The Power to Live in the Light

The assumption of communication in Genesis 1 and John 1 can be summed up in the power to live in the light – the second pillar. Light reveals what is there, reality, and along with sound, makes communication possible. If we embrace light in all of its permutations, and eschew darkness, we are a free people.

Human Abortion

Human abortion governs a domain of darkness, in its facilities, resources, and strategies of deceit. It cuts off honest communications and breaks trust in relationships. It drives women from the joy of light into the struggle with a darkness having invaded their souls.

Fourth: Human Nature

In Genesis 1, the created order begins with the most remote up to the most accessible, from the lowest forms of life up to the highest. As creation reaches its apex with man and woman, we have descriptive reality defined. In Genesis 2, we encounter the storyline of exactly how *Yahweh Elohim* does this creation work. Genesis 1:26-28 defines man and woman being made in *Yahweh Elohim*'s image. There are many elements to what this all entails: 1) reflecting *Yahweh Elohim*'s infinite character in our finite capacities; 2) being given the commission to govern the good creation under him; 3) man and woman are made after *Yahweh Elohim*'s own kind, not after any animal or other species; 4) man and woman are male and female, equals and complements; and 5) they are called to fill and bring the earth under their stewardship and control.

Then, a sixth element proves central to our present focus.

Nephesh (Soul)

In the debate over human abortion, the question of "ensoulment" comes into play in determining human nature and how it relates to the status of the unborn. In Jewish history, the soul relates to the "breath" in Genesis 2:7, and thus there are two basic views: 1) the soul begins at "quickening" or movement in the womb that can be related to in utero "breathing," or 2) when born and breathes in the air. For Plato, and his influence on the Alexandrian school in the early church (Origen), the soul is pre-existent and "transmigrates" into the body. But when does this "embodiment" happen? The Eastern Church (e.g., Jerome) believes that God creates a new soul at the birth of each individual ("creationism"). The Western Church (e.g.,

Turtullian) are Traducianists, believing that the soul is inherited from the parents. Again, the question of the time of ensoulment. The debate continues between these last two positions until the Reformation, then splits between Luther (Traducianist) and John Calvin ("creationist").

The operative concern is when or if the unborn becomes a "living soul" (Genesis 2:7). If at birth, then no abortion kills a human soul, and thus is not a high moral concern. If at quickening, then late-term abortions are problematic, but early abortions are not.

I believe this whole question of ensoulment is completely off the mark, and only an exegesis of the Hebrew in Genesis 2:7 can ground us in biblical and scientific reality. The text reads: "*Yahweh Elohim* formed the man from the dust of the ground and breathed into his nostrils the breath of life, and the man became a living soul."

The Hebrew for "the man" is *ha'adam*, from which Adam derives his name. He is made directly from the dust, or dry earth, but he is not merely material stuff. *Yahweh Elohim* sets him apart as he breathes his own Spirit into him, and thus he comes alive.

The words translated "living soul" are *nephesh hayyah* in the Hebrew, or "soul alive," where in the Hebrew the adjective follows the noun. *Nephesh* is the biblical term for human nature and personhood, and its definitive nature will become clear as we progress.

There are two principal sources that define the term – Edmund Jacob's article in the *Theological Dictionary of the New Testament* (TDNT), where he examines the Hebrew background for the Greek parallel term *psuche*; and Hans Walter Wolff in *The Anthropology of the Old Testament*. *Psuche* is our root for the "psyche," for psychological wholeness.

Jacob says, "*Nephesh* is the usual term for a man's total nature, for what he is and not just what he has. This gives the term priority in the anthropological vocabulary ... The classical text in Gn. 2:7 clearly expresses this when it calls man in his totality a *nephesh hayyah* ... The *nephesh* is almost always

41

connected with a form. It has no existence apart from a body. Hence the best translation in many instances is "person" comprised in corporeal reality (IX:620, Hebrew transliterated).

There are seven observations to be made, where the first five depend on Jacob, and the last two on Wolff.

1. Maturity at the Beginning

Adam is created as a whole, mature male adult, and the same is true for Eve as a female adult, as *Yahweh* draws her out of Adam's mature body. The idea of wholeness is rooted in the Hebrew *shalom*, where the common translation of "peace" is rooted in a prior integrity of the soul. The language here is clear in terms of *Yahweh Elohim's* active work in creation. Every form of life is made by him, mature and ready to procreate. And likewise with man and woman in his image – they are mature and ready to govern the creation, to have children and build civilization. Adam and Eve are of necessity unique as our first parents – they do not go through infancy and the maturing process to become adults, as we all have. The fruit of such a process is built into them at the outset. It is in every fiber of their beings and instincts. This is the reality of greater order producing lesser order.

Which comes first – the chicken or the egg? Well, an egg cannot hatch, nurture and protect itself. The chicken and the rooster together come first. The predicate in Genesis 1-2 is that maturity precedes and provides for subsequent generations to grow into maturity. As well, how can the theory of the origins of the universe and life posit something coming out of nothing, a non-order producing order, or a lesser order producing a greater order?

All the assumptions and statements in Genesis 1-2 are by definition proactive. There is no brokenness of the body, trust or the environment in place – there is nothing negative present, so there is no reactive language. This is interpretively central. Namely, living in a broken world, millennia later, it is easy to put certain assumptions into the Genesis text that are not there.

2. The Breath of God

I am daily thankful for every breath I take – it is the gift of God. And I think too that any of us who acknowledge the same, regardless of theological or cultural background, are reflecting the image of God, and are open to the work of the Spirit in our lives. As *nephesh* is introduced, it is *Yahweh's* breath that is primary, not that of *ha'adam*. It is *Yahweh* who breathes the breath of life into Adam's nostrils, this creation who takes on life from the dust. Man is not sufficient to himself, he is not his own creator, he is not something that derives from nothing. *Yahweh Elohim* gives and man receives. The text presents to us a fully formed man, but lifeless, nothing more than beautifully organized material stuff – until the breath of *Yahweh Elohim* is given.

Once Adam and Eve receive *Yahweh Elohim*'s breath, being made after his own kind, they are set to pass on that breath to their children. This we see in Genesis 5:1-3 where man and woman are in the image of *Yahweh Elohim*, and Seth is born in the image of Adam (representing both man and woman in the Hebrew use of his name).

The opening pages of Genesis, and the teaching power of biblical stories, are very economic. There are no wasted words. Thus, for the Hebrew reader of Genesis 1:26-28, 2:7 and 5:1-3, the teaching is clear: The breath of *Yahweh Elohim* given to man and woman is the signature of his image, which we are empowered to pass along to our children.

Thus, in the face of this reality, any honest person is grateful for *Yahweh Elohim*'s creative breath that sustains all of us – including the ecosphere. And any honest person will honor his parents who pass along that breath. Even in spite of sin, and as such, we also anticipate the fifth of the Ten Commandments: "Honor your father and your mother, so that you may live long in the land *Yahweh* your *Elohim* is giving you" (Exodus 20:12). Yet, what of the parents who do not honor the breath of their unborn children?

43

Simply, the whole procreative process from the beginning is "very good" (Genesis 1:31), as *Yahweh Elohim* declares after man and woman are created and set in place.

3. Essence not Achievement

As Jacob points out, *nephesh* is a matter of what we are, not what we have. We do not possess soul or personhood – we are souls, we are persons. We are what God has given us to be, not what we achieve by some other means (e.g. a godless and chance driven macroevolution). Essence not achievement is thus central to a universal humanity, with an assumption of equality of worth.

Adam and Eve, created as mature adults, then have children, and pass along the same humanity. This assumes that the whole procreative process – along with the human intellect and moral sense to steward the creation and build civilization – is not one of a secular achievement ethic. It is not where a definition of personhood is "achieved" somewhere in the process, by human effort, but rather, is there from the outset.

4. Unity of Body and Soul

Since *nephesh* does not exist apart from the corporeal (bodily) reality, we do not possess our bodies; rather, our bodies are good and integral parts of our whole identities. "Soul" sums it all up – heart, mind, spirit, body. Not just one aspect or another. Adam and Eve are created to live forever, and thus the resurrection body is an assumption for what redemption is all about.

The nature of *nephesh* and its uniqueness in Genesis 1-2 stands in stark contrast to Gnostic dualisms – a Greek manner of thought that eventually traces back to Babylonian dualisms. Most simply, Gnostic dualism sets up a war between the body and the spirit, where the body is evil and the spirit is good. When it infects the early church it leads to asceticism on the one hand (hatred of the body and human sexuality) and sexual licentiousness on the other (since the body is viewed as evil, just let loose). In Hindu and Buddhist dualisms (which are historically derivative), there is no understanding of Genesis 1-2 and the goodness of the human body, being entrapped in the samsara struggle of karma and dharma, with no hope of a resurrection body and identity.

5. Personhood and Biology

Jacob concludes with the observation that *nephesh* in its primary sense is best translated as "person," rooted in bodily reality.

We each physically begin at the specific moment of biological fertilization. The spermatozoon (sperm) and the ovum (egg) are gametes, both "haploid" cells. This means they are incapable of cell division, incapable of reproduction in and of themselves. Cell division is necessary to qualify as biological life, as well as fully sufficient to define it. The sperm and egg each carry the necessary and complementary components of biological life. But these components are only "potential" ingredients apart from their union at fertilization. Biological life becomes an "actuality" when the sperm fertilizes the egg, which in general terms is called "conception" (technical differences between the two, but not in focus here). Apart from conception, these haploid cells have no possibility but to die in their incompleteness. In and of itself, a haploid cell can never become a human being. In the prior and defining reality, Adam has no future apart from Eve.

At the moment of fertilization, a dramatic and immediate change occurs. These two complementary haploid cells form a "diploid" cell, which is otherwise known biologically as a "whole body." This diploid cell has a genetic uniqueness, completeness and wholeness as a one-celled "zygote." Such a zygote has all the genetic identity and programming necessary to mature into an embryo, a fetus (from the Latin *foetus* for "young person"), a baby, a child, a teenager and an adult. None of this is possible or in actual existence apart from the moment of fertilization, after which the genetic code for each human individual is fixed. Thereafter, no new genetic information is added or taken away. The one-celled zygote is a fully human life. This is not just a "potential life" as though there is the potential to be other than human, to be other than who he or she is, or who they are in the case of twins et al. The one-celled zygote is the offspring of two human parents, and human beings can procreate nothing else but other human beings.

45

In other words, I was once a one-celled zygote – as with all of us. We were never just an egg or sperm, but came from a specific sperm that fertilized a specific egg. In genetic terms, our individuality begins at fertilization, and thus the biology of conception is an unqualified good assumption in the biblical order of creation. *Yahweh Elohim* makes us corporeal beings – we have no identity, no existence, no *nephesh* apart from the human body. Before conception there is no existing identity for a given person in the human world, before *Yahweh Elohim*'s breath there is no identity.

We are made in *Yahweh Elohim*'s likeness, and we procreate after our likeness which is after his likeness. The assumptions in Genesis 1-2 provide for biological reality. Thus, in grasping *nephesh*, we see that the body is good as defined by the biblical order of creation, meant to live forever until sin intrudes, and remedy is needed.

In terms of the biology of conception, we can take a light hearted approach. If you are ever having a lousy day, and thinking poorly of yourself, remember this (absent the manipulations of in vitro technologies which involve arbitrary selection): The sperm you come from places ahead of as many as a half-billion other spermatozoa racing up your mother's fallopian tubes to fertilize the egg you also come from. Which is to say: You have a solid track record of winning that produces who you are.

6. Needfulness

The nature of *nephesh* involves needfulness or dependency. Wolff says that *nephesh*:

> stands for needy man per se ... *nephesh* therefore does not say what a man has, but who the person is who receives life (*hayyim*): "person," "individual," "being" ... If we survey the wide context in which the *nephesh* of man and man as *nephesh* can be observed, we see above all man marked out as the individual being who has neither acquired, nor can preserve, life by himself, but who is eager for life, spurred on by vital desire, as the throat (the organ for receiving the nourishment and for breathing) and the neck (as the part of the body which is especially

at risk) make clear. Although in this way *nephesh* shows man primarily in his need and desire, that includes his emotional excitability and vulnerability ..." (pp. 21, 24-25; Hebrew transliteration my own).

Wolff's chapter on *nephesh* focuses on the etymology, or word history, of the term. It is rooted in proto-Semitic languages concerning the anatomy of the throat and neck. It denotes a physical vulnerability, or needfulness, around the capacity to breathe. *Nephesh* is found some 700 primary times, with 350 cognates, in the Hebrew Bible, where this "corporeal needfulness" is always in place. Adam's breath and ability to continue breathing is dependent on *Yahweh Elohim*'s original breath and the ecosphere he creates for us.

And as breathing is incessant, so our moral character is created and purposed to be continually eager and passionate for life. As well, the area of the neck and throat involves hunger and thirst. This assumption is in place as Genesis 2:8-9 identifies the pleasing nature of the fruit to the eye (artistic elements also assumed), and the goodness of food. It is also in place when Jesus speaks of those who hunger and thirst after righteousness (Matthew 5:6), and at the end of Revelation where the restored tree of life is provided along with drinking from the water of life (19:7-9; 22:1-2, 14, 17).

Thus, *nephesh* is strength. Only when we acknowledge our need for God's good nature and his power to give, are we able to be nourished and have strength.

I have yet to meet anyone who does not like a good backrub (or "massage" as I once had to use the term in Singapore so they could understand my reference). Now, if any of us wish to be independent and do not acknowledge *nephesh*, and try to give ourselves that backrub – well, we can only imagine the unsatisfaction. If on the other hand, we know *nephesh* as given in human community, and we receive the backrub from someone we love and trust – well, we arrive at a happier imagination. Which produces true strength in heart, mind, spirit and body?

7. Salvation

What is the doctrine of salvation in Genesis 1-2?

Well, there is none. All is whole, all is *shalom*, all is good, and all human needs are met. But on the other side of the brokenness of sin, the nature of salvation returns us to the purposes and trajectory in the order of creation. It returns us to *nephesh*. The interpretive power of this assumptive reality will repeatedly surface. Salvation is simply the return to the *shalom* of *nephesh*, and thus, any effort we make to serve *shalom* and *nephesh* in all image-bearers of God, advances the Gospel of salvation.

Nephesh and the Unborn

Given the nature of *nephesh* as beginning with *Yahweh*'s breath, not human breath, the Jewish view is off the mark, which sadly serves a secular construct allowing abortion in the first half of pregnancy. Given the nature of *nephesh* as embodied needfulness, and with all the cognate realities, we can conclude that the Platonic (and Origen's) view of soul migration is neither biblical nor scientific. The soul is not a pre-existent thing, rather our persons are known to *Yahweh* before our conception (see Psalm 139:15-16) in his eternal mind, and there is no biblical concept of soul apart from the body (including the Greek term *psuche*, being the Septuagint (LXX) and New Testament parallel to *nephesh*). [The Septuagint is the translation of the Hebrew Bible into Greek in the third century B.C.]

The creationist view of Jerome (and Calvin) falls short, for whereas the individual creation of each soul is affirmed, it is located at birth, and thus contradicts the embodiment realities and needfulness that begin at conception. And finally, the Traducianist view of Turtullian (and Luther) falls short in that, while Seth is made in Adam's image, the "soul" is not a property or some sort of object passed along to him – similar in this sense to the Platonic error. Seth takes on the genetic influence of both parents pace the call for Adam and Eve to fill the earth, but does not exist as a soul until the biological moment of fertilization.

48

In all these views, the very idea of ensoulment misses the mark, for they are all concerned with a soul apart from the whole person as a starting concern, not the reality that the soul equals the whole person by definition. Thus, the etymology of *nephesh* shows that the unborn are fully human from the point of fertilization.

Indeed, this only ratifies the larger assumptions in Genesis 1-2. Human life is made in *Yahweh Elohim*'s image, is good, is passed along through procreation, and there is no death present. All is good until sin pollutes the Garden. Thus, to seek to find any putative logic in Genesis 2:7 for the possibility of human abortion, is an up-front and wholesale rejection of *Yahweh Elohim*'s nature, goodness and creation.

All of Scripture ratifies this, from these large themes to minute ones. For example, in Psalm 7:14, "pregnant," "conceives" and "give birth" are in sequence, and in Psalm 51:5, birth and conception are in parallel construct – different words making the same point. And in some two dozen biblical instances, conception and birth are paired together in the same sentence, in a sequential unity. One fun way to illustrate this functioning parallel to an abortion advocate is in two sequential questions. Are you a thinking person? Have you ever conceived a thought?

Human Abortion

Human life is good from the very beginning of biological reality, the fertilization of sperm and egg, with eternal value present, and thus human abortion destroys both life and the good.

Fifth: Informed Choice

In the Bible, the first words to Adam in Genesis 2:16 are often translated something like "The LORD God commanded the man, 'You are free to eat ...' " ("LORD" in capitals refers to *Yahweh*). The Hebrew is far more dynamic yet, as we will shortly review. The most important verb in the Bible is "to eat" (including the implicit and always present "drink"), at least when it comes to defining human nature, and as here the eagerness for life of *nephesh* finds bodily expression. This metaphor is also the basis for human freedom as "an unlimited menu of good choices." This menu is protected when we do not eat poison and die. There are boundaries to freedom, and this is the power of informed choice, the third of the six pillars on biblical power.

The Golden Rule

The Golden Rule is taken from Jesus's words in the Sermon on the Mount: "So in everything, treat others as you wish for them to treat you, for this sums up the Law and the Prophets" (Matthew 7:12). It is proactive, not reactive, for it hearkens back to the order of creation. This is also the same reality underlying the *shema* ("hear"), the greatest commandments of the Law of Moses:

> Jesus answered them, "The first is this: 'Hear O Israel, the Lord your God, the Lord is one. Love the Lord your God with your whole heart, your whole soul, your whole understanding and all your strength.' The second is this: 'Love your neighbor as yourself.' There is no greater commandment than these" (Mark 12:29-31).

But outside the Bible, the highest concept of freedom is reactive, a freedom from violation. And none of us want to be violated. Human abortion starts in the violation of women who are then pressured by the man to pass that violation on to the child, and the woman gets screwed in-between. What can break the cycle, especially in face of the political and judicial evil, and the pecuniary purposes of the abortion industry, that market it?

The First Words in Human History

Genesis 1:1 declares *Elohim*'s sovereign power. This is the first reality in the Bible. In Genesis 2:16-17, we have *Yahweh Elohim* speaking the first words recorded for human history.

Genesis 1 is the grand design of creation, and Genesis 2 takes place during the sixth day of the theological structure in Genesis 1, where the first covenant is given to the man, and prior to the creation of the woman. Thus the words in Genesis 2:16-17 precede those given in Genesis 1:28ff. *Elohim*'s sovereign nature (Genesis 1) precedes, and *Yahweh Elohim* defines human freedom (Genesis 2).

The text of Genesis 2:16-17 gives us the first recorded words of *Yahweh* to Adam:

> And *Yahweh Elohim* commanded the man, "In feasting you shall continually feast from any tree in the garden; but you must not eat from the tree of the knowledge of good and evil, for in the day you eat of it, in dying you shall continually die."

Interestingly, the word here for command (*tsawah*) is never used for calling people to heed (*shema*, "hear") the words of *Yahweh*; but here it is the authority to guarantee freedom.

An Unlimited Menu of Good Choices

The language in most translations, "You are free to eat," or "You may freely eat" do reflect a reality, but there are far greater depths. We need to understand the Hebrew idiom in use. The Hebrew words *akol tokel* are fully translated this way: "In feasting you shall continually feast." The grammatical idea is more powerful than an active particle in Romance languages – the sequential use of the infinitive absolute and imperfect tenses for the verb "to eat," a feast that never stops feasting. It is the idea of an unlimited menu of good choices – not only in terms of food options in the Garden of Eden, but also in the application of this metaphor to all practical, moral and aesthetic choices in life.

This language of eating and feasting, with implicit drink, permeates the rest of the Bible. Worship in the Law of Moses revolves around a series of feasts, the Messianic prophecy in Isaiah gives invitation to eat and drink without cost, Jesus celebrates the wedding supper at Cana, gives invitation to the wedding supper of the Lamb, institutes the Eucharist or Lord's Supper, prophesies that he will again drink wine in the kingdom of the heavens, eats fish as proof of his resurrection body, and the Holy Spirit beckons us to the wedding supper of the Lamb in Revelation as well. The final act of redemption, in the last chapter of Revelation, is the provision for the river of the water of life (22:1) and the tree of life (22:2). In Jesus' final words, he invites us to partake of the tree of life (22:14), and after the Spirit gives his final invitation of "Come!", the apostle John adds, "Whoever is thirsty let him come; and whoever wishes, let him take the free gift of the water of life" (22:17).

Feasting permeates Scripture from beginning to end, it is celebrated as the essence of the mountain of *Yahweh* in the *eschaton* (times of the end; see Isaiah 25:5-9); it is the metaphor of human freedom (*akol tokel*). This is the freedom to feast from an unlimited menu of good choices – to satisfy our eagerness, hunger and thirst for life (*nephesh*). Or to sum it up theologically: "Taste and see that *Yahweh* is good" (Psalm 34:8).

But access to this feast requires a moral understanding of the freedom to choose between good and evil, and the feast of Genesis 2:16 carries with it the caveat, boundaries and structures for the power of human freedom. All humanity knows protective boundaries in daily life, from gravity to a highway median strip to a thousand other examples.

In Genesis 2:17 we see the "but." The unlimited menu of good choices has a restriction that is in reality a boundary of protection. Namely, freedom cannot exist without boundaries. Thus, *Yahweh* defines the power of informed choice. The protection of an unlimited menu of good choices requires the prohibition of a singular evil choice – do not eat poison.

To understand the trees of Genesis 2:16-17, we must return to Genesis 2:9:

> And *Yahweh Elohim* made all kinds of trees grow out of the ground
> – trees that were desirable in appearance and good for food. The tree of
> life was in the middle of the garden, along with the tree of the
> knowledge of good and evil.

This phrase, "the knowledge of good and evil," refers to Adam's given authority on the one hand, and inclusive of a Hebrew idiom or *merism*, on the other. Adam and Eve are created to rule over the creation, under *Yahweh Elohim*, and thus in accordance with his definitions of good and evil. Their authority includes the power to name, for names carry identity, and terms are defined. But then, to eat of the forbidden fruit perverts such authority. It is for man and woman to say a) *Yahweh* is not good, that he must be withholding something good from us in the prohibition, that is to say, calling *Yahweh* evil; thus b) to rationalize the will to disobey *Yahweh*; c) to redefine good and evil; and thus d) to lift ourselves up to the level of *Yahweh Elohim*, if not actually seeking to transcend him.

To challenge *Yahweh*'s goodness is the basic nature of unbelief. In the letter to the Hebrews, the writer (I think it is Barnabas) speaks of faith as the quality of believing that God rewards those who earnestly seek him (see 11:1-6). God is good and worthy of invested faith, of trust.

Being limited within the good boundaries of space, time and number, how can we think we can redefine *Yahweh Elohim*'s terms and realities, and still live and prosper in his universe? To eat the forbidden fruit is to redefine good and evil over and against *Yahweh Elohim*. Instead, man is ordained to judge good and evil in the universe congruent with *Yahweh*'s definition of terms, recognizing the forbidden fruit as a test and a boundary.

Another factor is a Hebrew *merism* for that which is comprehensive, covering the ends and means of the spectrum. Namely, the polar opposites of "good and evil" can refer literally to the knowledge of everything. Everything there is to know lies in the spectrum between good and evil. The polar opposites of beginning and end are likewise comprehensive in defining time (see Isaiah 44:6; 48:12; Revelation 1:8; 21:6; 22:16). The polar opposites of height and depth, of east and west, are likewise comprehensive in defining space (see Psalm 103:11-12).

Therefore, "the knowledge of good and evil" is a concept that equals a whole unit. It is knowledge only *Yahweh Elohim* as the uncreated Creator can possess. As well, only *Yahweh* can know the totality of intrinsic evil without being tempted or polluted by it. Evil is ethically the absence of *Yahweh Elohim*'s holy presence, the absence of true ethics, which means the absence of true relationships. Just as darkness is the absence of light in physics, ethics and spiritual territory. To know good and evil is to define it, in the sense of this Hebrew idiom – something only *Yahweh Elohim* can do. Adam and Eve are called to judge between good and evil, but based on *Yahweh*'s true definitions. People who seek to define good and evil differently than does *Yahweh*, have become their own gods, and only have themselves, as a resource, in order to escape evil in the final consequence.

Accordingly, as a creature made in God's image, there is nothing "good" withheld from Adam, as the *akol tokel* idiom of positive freedom already establishes. He is given the "tree of life" to eat from, a tree which is the source for life, for eternal life. A good assumption is that, metabolically, it contributes to the eternal renewal of all the cells in our bodies. Alongside that tree is the forbidden fruit – forbidden if we wish to live. Metabolically, it assaults the renewal of our bodily cells. Then morally, relationally, to eat of the tree of the knowledge of good and evil equals an attempt to digest what we cannot, as if we who are limited by space, time and number, can grasp or wrap ourselves around eternity. We will explode first.

The choice between good and evil is powerfully portrayed by a parallelism in vv. 16 and 17. The phrase in most translations, "you will surely die," is likewise better grasped by the power of the idiom in place. The Hebrew here reads *moth tamuth*, which literally means, "in dying you shall continually die." It is the exact parallel of *akol tokel* in terms of grammatical construct, but with opposite moral nature, with the sequential use of the infinitive absolute and imperfect tenses for "die," carrying with it a force greater than that of an active participle – always dying, yet to die.

Thus, if we partake in the eternal quality of death, which the forbidden fruit introduces, we will continually experience the taste of death. This is the biblical root for the language and metaphors of hell – a chosen death that never stops dying (C.S. Lewis plays with this theme dynamically in his story, *The Great Divorce*). What this also means is that the definition of death is principally theological in nature, and not just in reference to the physical termination of life. Theological death is the brokenness of relationship with *Yahweh Elohim* and one another. It is alienation from his presence.

Adam thus "dies," only to continue "dying." Adam and Eve have been given the tree of life to eat from continually, so as to live forever. Once they partake of the fruit of death, this alienation from *Yahweh Elohim*'s full presence removes from their bodies the regenerative qualities of the tree of life, so they begin to die physically. Adam's life span is shortened from forever to 930 years, and the increase in sin's impact upon the body over the subsequent millennia brings the average life span to well under 100 years.

This contrast of choices in Genesis 2:16-17 is marked, and the reader who knows the Hebrew picks it up immediately:

> in feasting you shall continually feast (*akol tokel*), or
> in dying you shall continually die (*moth tamuth*).

Another way of putting it is:

> an unlimited menu of good choices, or
> a limited menu of only death.

With parallel idioms in place, signaling opposite choices, the power of informed choice is defined:

> feast or die.

The command to feast is *Yahweh Elohim*'s will, but the warning against dying carries with it a power to disobey that will. The very language of "will," or "willpower," connotes the exercise of choice. *Yahweh Elohim*'s choice is that we live forever (e.g. 1 Timothy 2:4; 2 Peter 3:9), but he does not force it on us.

The Origin of Evil

But why would a loving God permit evil to happen? Outside the biblical worldview, the best attempts to understand the origin of evil are to assume it has always been there, in a dualistic tension and co-dependency with the good. And therefore the highest aspirations of dualistic religions cannot see past a negative view of freedom – freedom from violation – which ultimately is an escape from suffering into a forfeiture of individual identity, and thus, into an anesthetized sea of collective loss of memory. The Hindu doctrine of *maya* means suffering is an illusion, and thus the highest goal known is its mere escape. The concept of *nephesh*, resurrection and continued individual identity in shared community, are thus not conceivable.

Such a negative view of freedom is the highest concept of freedom imaginable to cultures that know nothing of creation, sin and redemption. And it is in knowing these biblical doctrines that we find the key to knowing the origin of evil, for evil is a "reversal" of the order of creation. The simplicity of evil's origin may appear to some as a scandal; namely, the origin of evil lies in the goodness of *Yahweh Elohim*. Evil is a parasite, just as darkness is to light.

Therefore, true goodness involves the permission, the freedom to choose evil, as given by *Yahweh*. Evil does not allow the permission, it does not allow the freedom to choose the good.

Evil is a choice, and *Yahweh Elohim*'s goodness necessarily allows this choice because goodness is not forced. *Yahweh Elohim*'s perfect will, and his loving, giving and good nature, is never diminished by this freedom given. The power of informed choice stands above reproach in every measure, and any human attempt to equal or surpass this definition of justice only adds further suffering. *akol tokel* or *moth tamuth*. Feast or die – the choice is ours as the gift of the good and sovereign *Yahweh Elohim*.

Is this a scandal to say that the origin of evil comes as a direct result of the goodness of *Yahweh Elohim*? Only to those who have compromised the sovereignty and goodness of *Yahweh Elohim*.

In Genesis 2:9, the text defines the two trees in the middle of the Garden – one leads to life and the other leads to death. *Yahweh* therefore lays the basis for Adam and Eve to make their choice. This sets up a contrast of opposing ethical systems which highlight the power of informed choice:

56

Yahweh's good ethics = true definition of terms = human freedom = life;

Satan's evil ethics = false definition of terms = human slavery = death.

In Genesis 2:17, *Yahweh* tells Adam that if he disobeys and eats of the forbidden fruit, then *moth tamuth*, "in dying you shall continually die." In Genesis 3:1-5, we see how *Satan*, incarnate as the serpent, reverses the order of creation with false definition of terms, which leads to misinformed choice, which leads to death. In v. 4, the serpent says *lo moth t'muthon*, "In dying you shall not continually die" (or most literally: "Not in dying you shall continually die").

We can note how:

Yahweh's true definition of terms leads to the power of informed choice and life;

Satan's false definition of terms leads to misinformed choice and death.

When *Yahweh* says there is a tree of life, and a tree of death, he speaks accurately. On this basis, people can choose life.

Here is an applied sequence:

1. If man and woman are free, and made in the image of *Yahweh Elohim*, must not *Yahweh Elohim* first be free?
2. If so, is *Yahweh Elohim* free do evil?
3. No, for freedom is the power to do the good; and to do evil is to be a slave to it.
4. And *Yahweh Elohim* is a slave to nothing.
5. Informed choice is predicated on a true definitions of terms, as we see in Genesis 2:9-17: good versus evil, freedom versus slavery, life versus death.

6. Therefore, to be free, we must have a level playing field between these opposites to exercise the power of informed choice; *Satan* fiercely oppose the genuine level playing field.
7. Thus, what is the true definition of terms concerning biological human life, male chauvinism, and the exercise of informed choice in such a context?

Only *Yahweh Elohim* can get away with giving us this radical human freedom. Only *Yahweh* loves us enough to let us choose whether or not to accept his love. This is *Yahweh Elohim*'s nature, which uniquely provides a level playing field to choose between good and evil.

Yahweh Elohim does not force his love on us, for that would deny his very goodness. Goodness is the power to give, and to be forced into accepting his love is an oxymoron. Love is a gift, and human nature as given by *Yahweh* is predicated on the power to give. To be "forced to do the good" would be by definition evil, and thus not possible for goodness to remain good. Or to be more graphic, forced love equals rape. For *Yahweh* to force his love on us would be evil, it would be pagan – it would be the surrender of his sovereignty, it would be a dualistic condescension to the devil's ethics. Here is another sequence:

1. Goodness equals the power to give;
2. Evil equals the power to take; thus
3. Goodness cannot be forced – it can only be a gift received by informed choice.

This contrast jumped out at me in 1994, at Smith College in Northampton, Massachusetts, where I addressed one in my series of Mars Hill Forums. My guest was Patricia Ireland, then president of the National Organization for Women (NOW).

At one juncture when speaking about marriage, I spontaneously said: "There are two choices in life: Give and it will be given, or take before you are taken." Patricia and the mostly skeptical audience responded well. We were addressing controversial issues surrounding feminism and abortion, where women wrestle with painful reactions to male chauvinistic ugliness.

Thus, goodness can never be forced, and when attempted, the good that is envisioned turns into evil. By the same token, evil can never act like a gift – it is always something that is deceptive and/or impositional. Another way of putting it is in this couplet:

> Love is a choice that cannot be faked; and
> Hatred is a choice than cannot be hidden.

As image-bearers of *Yahweh Elohim*, if we were forced to accept his will, the qualities of responsibility ("ability to respond") and creativity would be moot – we would be no more than animals or puppets. And this is precisely how women forced through abortions are treated. Only informed choice can rescue them from the idolatry of a false choice.

The Testimonies of Moses, Joshua and Elijah

The gift of human freedom and therefore, its interpretive importance in defining human nature, is strategically restated as the Bible unfolds. We have it first in the words of *Yahweh* to Adam, then restated in the final public words of Moses, the final public words of Joshua, in the shortest sermon in the Bible, delivered by Elijah at the apex of prophetic witness against Israel's apostasy, and all assumed in the nature and content of the Gospel.

Moses

In Deuteronomy 30:11-20, Moses brings to a conclusion his series of final sermons, the final public words of his life before the Israelites enter the Promised Land. He declares the accessibility of the power of informed choice, setting before all of us "life and good, death and evil" (v. 15). This is the exact choice given Adam and Eve in the Garden, even now in the face of human sin – *akol tokel* or *moth tamuth*.

We do have the power to choose life, but to have such power does not mean our sinful nature has the ability to achieve salvation, to "ascend into the heavens" (v. 12) as it were; rather, there is within our fallen humanity the remains of *Yahweh Elohim*'s image sufficient enough to say "help" (to acknowledge *nephesh*), and whether we say "help" is a matter of the human will.

Our human spirit as touched by the Holy Spirit can respond to God. In fact, this power of informed choice is fully in place for Cain before he murders Abel, one generation after the exile of his parents from the Garden. He could have overcome the sin "crouching at (his) door," but instead chooses to let it come in and rule him (Genesis 4:6-7). The Hebrew verb at play refers to a leopard preparing to spring on its prey, yet man and woman are originally given authority over the animal kingdom. Cain chooses to be ruled by *Satan*.

We can choose life in the face of the destruction and evil of human abortion.

Joshua

When the Israelites complete the conquest of Canaan, as much as they do, Joshua gives his final public address at Shechem. In 24:14-15, we read:

> Now fear *Yahweh* and serve him in soundness and faithfulness. Turn from the gods your fathers served beyond the River and in Egypt, and serve *Yahweh*. If it seems evil in your eyes to serve *Yahweh*, then choose for yourselves this day whom you will serve, whether the gods your fathers served beyond the River, or the gods of the Amorites in whose land you are dwelling. But as for me and my household, we will serve *Yahweh*.

This covenant on the plains of Shechem is the final gathering of the exodus community, and as this passage continues in vv. 16-24, Joshua uses a powerful form of dissuasion, requiring the Israelites to count the cost of discipleship before they say yes. Joshua presses them toward the freedom to choose "no" in order to ensure the integrity of their "yes." No games, no manipulations, no trickery. Joshua is basing his appeal on the power of informed choice.

Theocracy as a Community of Choice

The informed choice Joshua presents is simple. If serving *Yahweh* seems evil, choose to serve a) the Babylonian deities across the River (referring to the Euphrates), b) the Amorite deities of Canaan, or c) the gods of Egypt (where the chief deity, the sun god, can be transliterated as *ra* or *re*, likely a word play on the Hebrew word for evil, *ra*). Who is good and who is evil? *Yahweh Elohim* on the one hand, or *Marduk* and *Ra* on the other?

With this predicate of informed choice, theocratic Israel is a "community of choice." ("Theocracy," a word coined by the first century Jewish historian Josephus, refers to the rule or laws of God.) *Yahweh* commands blessings for those who will obey. His theocratic rule is not a forcing of unwanted legislation down their throats. Rather, *Yahweh* tells the Israelites the exact boundaries of freedom, the power of informed choice. If they do not like or agree with these ethics, they are free to go to Babylonia, Egypt, among the Canaanites, or elsewhere.

They are free to leave anytime if they think anything *Yahweh* says or does is evil. But if they choose to stay in theocratic Israel, it is because they know and trust the goodness, justice and provisions of *Yahweh Elohim*, as demonstrated by the signs and wonders of the Exodus. *Yahweh* has earned their trust. They know *Yahweh*'s goodness (e.g., Deuteronomy 29:2-6). They are free to choose to become part of the "chosen people."

There is also an interesting balance between the words of Moses and Joshua. Moses emphasizes the accessibility of making the right choice, and Joshua emphasizes its difficulty. This is part of the *merismus* of Scripture, "a little part here, a little part there" – when different elements are emphasized in different contexts, in a cooperative tension in the balance of the whole, in the very nature of a storyline. This reflects the balance between *Yahweh Elohim*'s sovereignty and human choice. The right choice is accessible if we accept *Yahweh Elohim*'s grace and admit our needs in his sight; it is

61

inaccessible if we depend on the sinful nature. Joshua is pressing the Israelites to discern the difference.

Elijah

When Israel is led by Ahab and Jezebel (ninth century B.C.), the prophet Elijah challenges the 450 prophets of *Ba'al* and the 400 prophetesses of *Asherah* to a contest on Mount Carmel (see 1 Kings 18:16-40). The devotees of *Ba'al* call on their god to answer with fire from heaven, but in spite of daylong prayer and self-flagellation, there is no response. But *Yahweh* answers Elijah dramatically the moment he prays. In his public address to the apostate Israelites beforehand, Elijah is succinct in assuming the power of informed choice:

> And Elijah drew near to all the people of Israel and said, "How long will you limp upon a divided opinion? If *Yahweh* is the *Elohim*, walk after him; if *Ba'al*, walk after him.' But the people answered not a word" (1 Kings 18:21).

The power of informed choice, the third of the six pillars, and as defined at these interpretively key junctures, continues through the balance of Scripture. Jeremiah says to Israel that if they want to go ahead and sin, they are free to do so (see 15:1-2). He knows they know the power of informed choice, and have chosen disobedience. The power of informed choice is the invitation to believe, reiterated and fulfilled in the gospels (see Matthew 11:28-30), all the way to the final invitation in the Book of Revelation (see 22:17).

Human Abortion

Human abortion is evil not good, slavery not freedom, death not life. It opposes the power of informed choice with its false definition of terms, in making an idol out of such false choice, thus yielding to the enslavement of the soul. This is the nexus of the whole debate, as driven by the evil of male chauvinism, which yields in turn, as we will see, the *Roe* v. *Wade* pretension of ignorance rooted in the lineage of Cain and the enemies of Jesus.

62

Sixth: Hard Questions

The level playing field provides space for the toughest questions to be posed of *Yahweh Elohim*, one another, and especially, of political leaders. This is the fourth of the six pillars of biblical power – the power to love hard questions. It is a cognate to the power of informed choice, namely the freedom to ask questions of *Yahweh* in governing the good creation. The Hebrew Bible and New Testament are unique in that no questions are ever prohibited of *Yahweh Elohim*, the prophets, Jesus and one another. We can note some examples across the biblical text.

Job's friends have an unrestricted freedom to question him about the source of his sufferings. Job poses questions in response, also to *Yahweh*, and then *Yahweh* answers with questions Job cannot answer. And Job is vindicated as a result.

In Genesis 18, Abraham is free to question *Yahweh*'s plan of judgment on Sodom and Gomorrah, as he intercedes on their behalf. Jesus also says "if" Sodom and Gomorrah had seen the miracles he performed in Galilee, they would have been spared. The dynamics of the open-ended "what if" question.

In 1 Kings 10 (cf. 2 Chronicles 9) the Queen of Sheba travels 1,000 miles north to "test" King Solomon with "perplexing questions." He gives her the freedom to literally talk with him about "everything she had on her mind." Solomon answers her questions to the queen's satisfaction, and in conclusion, she praises *Yahweh Elohim*, and his anointing of Solomon to "maintain judgment and righteousness." And Jesus praises the Queen of Sheba for seeking out Solomon (Matthew 12).

The Book of Psalms highlights the power to love hard questions. One scholar has titled it *Out of the Depths* because of its focus on the reality of broken relationships, and the emotional, physical, spiritual and intellectual questions that result. The Psalms are widely loved, and especially Psalm 23 – they minister to the souls of all of us, for we all know heartache. In his painful depths, David is free to cry out to *Elohim* in Psalm 22, "My *Eli*, my

Eli, why have you deserted me?" And Jesus presses these very words to his lips on the cross (Matthew 27 and Mark 15).

The Book of Ecclesiastes reflects the literary device of a man who knew better to begin with, who nonetheless indulges in folly, and emerges afterward knowing better what he knew better to begin with. The purpose of Ecclesiastes is to think aloud in retrospect, and to embrace hard questions in a conversational style. The reader, any reader, is invited to experience the process with the writer.

The prophet Jeremiah pours out his complaint to *Yahweh* following some unexpected suffering (chapter 20). He is free to complain to Yahweh for "opening" (Hebrew *patah*) him up to the mockery of his enemies, as it were. Then he praises *Yahweh,* and yet again, reverts and curses the day of his birth. He is free to lay open his emotions in suffering.

In the Book of Jonah, it concludes with a question of the prophet by *Yahweh* relative to justice and mercy. In the Book of Habakkuk, the prophet poses his toughest questions of *Yahweh* concerning justice, he is given answer, and then rejoices while still facing further suffering.

As the quintessential rabbi, Jesus's teaching style is such that he poses far more questions (188 separate examples in the four gospels) than he gives answers. He proactively goes into the wilderness to face the devil's false questions, gives true answers, and thus the devil is silenced. Jesus teaches in parables that leave open-ended freedom for his hearers to do more thinking, and to embrace further questions. And he celebrates the freedom of his enemies to question him during Passover week, gives answer, and in the end they choose to silence themselves.

When the apostle Paul addresses the Stoic and Epicurean philosophers in Athens (Acts 17), on their turf, he does so in openness to their questions. And when addressing two deeply divisive debates in the early church, Paul insists that "each one in his own mind should be fully convinced" (Romans 14:5).

And with no restrictions on freedom of speech and questions, this also means the freedom to speak to and question political power. This the prophets do across Scripture, for example, with Moses to Pharaoh, Elijah to Ahab, Samuel to Saul, Nathan to David, Jeremiah to Zedekiah, and John the Baptist to Herod. Sometimes these questions yield changes in the political potentate, sometimes the prophet suffers or is killed. And Jesus does it in his own powerful and unique way as the Son of God, as we will see.

Jeremiah and Jesus

The whole Bible is rooted in the assumptions of Genesis 1-2, and this includes its deep pro-life realities. For example, we can note Jeremiah 1:5, where the prophet receives his call in language that employs sequence and parallelism given by the One who is greater than space, time and number. Theologically and anthropologically, Jeremiah's identity suffers no abortion between eternity, the womb, birth and adult life. *Yahweh* says to him:

> Before I formed you in the womb I knew you,
> Before you were brought out of the womb I set you apart,
> And I appointed you as a prophet to the nations.

The gospels of Matthew and Luke also make the same assumptions in how they speak of Jesus before his conception, his time in the womb, and his anointing as the Messiah (Matthew 1:18-25; Luke 1:26-80). The assumption of the goodness of procreation, for its entire natural period, is everywhere assumed in the Bible.

Two Disputed Biblical Texts

There are two major texts that radically affirm the humanity of the unborn, both of which have come under assault by pro-abortion advocates. What are the questions involved, and how do we address them?

1. *"Lex Talionis"*

First, in the Law of Moses we find a passage where people have argued both sides of the abortion debate (Exodus 21:22-25). It is often called *lex talionis*, Latin for the law of retribution, not rooted in human retribution, but in justice for the oppressed, always aiming at redemption. The text reads:

> If (two) men who are struggling fatally strike a pregnant woman and a child is brought forth, but there is no harm, the offender must be fined whatever the woman's husband sets and the court allows. But if there is harm, you are to give soul for soul, eye for eye, tooth for tooth, hand or hand, foot for foot, burn for burn, bruise for bruise, stripe for stripe.

My translation of "fatally strike" is the gravamen of the text. But the "fatal" reality is not the normal English translation (if ever), thus leading to this debate. Thus, on the assumption that the word in question means simply "strike" in a generic capacity, the debate occurs.

Here it is, and it will lead us back to the proper translation. There are two arguments. The first assumes the subject of the text is that the woman is the one "harmed," and the second argues, grammatically, that the subject is the prematurely born child who suffers the "harm." We will walk through the tight territory of these arguments, then arrive at a very simple summation.

First Argument

Abortion advocates argue this passage actually demonstrates that the unborn child is not viewed as a full person, morally or legally. Their argument is that the fetus is treated like a piece of property. There are two scenarios identified for what happens here: a) when there is no harm to the woman, and b) when there is harm to her.

In the first scenario, "A," where there is "no harm," this refers to the woman's estate after having been "struck." A miscarriage has happened but she is okay. Thus a fine is levied as a payment for the loss of the fetus as with a property loss.

In the second scenario, "B," this is taken to mean a "harm" is caused to the woman following the supposed miscarriage, thus the *"lex talionis"* is invoked to cover all possibilities. In this case the "soul for soul" clause is applied to the woman, whereas the fetus in scenario "A" is explicitly treated as property, then in scenario "B," subsequently so. On this rationale, certain religious advocates for abortion say that the woman's life should take precedence, and that abortion is not a moral issue.

Yes, the woman's life should take precedence, for it is with her that the power to give ultimately resides toward the child; but no, even this interpretation cannot reduce the humanity of the unborn. To do so would be for this passage to be used to deny every other witness in the Scripture that undergirds the image of God status, to deny the *nephesh* of the unborn. Neither the unborn, nor any image-bearer of *Yahweh Elohim*, is ever treated as property in Scripture. To do so is classic eisegesis (inserting into the text what is not there). To reify (treat as property) the unborn is a reactionary take before you are taken ethos, not the power to give.

Second Argument

But as Meredith Kline points out in an article "Lex Talionis and the Human Fetus" (*Journal of the Evangelical Theological Society*, September, 1977), this is not what the text says. In fact, he leads off his article with an opposite view:

> The most significant thing about abortion legislation in Biblical law is that there is none. It was so unthinkable that an Israelite woman should desire an abortion that there was no need to mention this offense in the criminal code ...

> This law, found in Exodus 21:22-25, turns out to be perhaps the most decisive positive evidence in Scripture that the fetus is to be regarded as a living person.

A "living person" is *nephesh hayyah*, pace the Hebrew of Genesis 2:7. Kline designates the two scenarios as "A" and "B," as I reflected above. He points out that the hinge words are "strike" and "harm." When it says that the struggling men "strike" the woman, the Hebrew verb is *nagap*. It is not the ordinary term for hitting or striking someone, but its usual reference means "to strike with death" or "to cause fatal divine judgments." Context determines the appropriate translation in Hebrew, and the subject of scenario "A" is the miscarried or prematurely born child – the one to whom the question of "harm" is considered. For indeed, the *nagap* usage already determines that the scenario starts with the woman having been fatally struck – she is dead – and in the process she delivers a premature child due to the trauma. Thus the focus of this law is on the well-being of the untimely born child – one who should have still been unborn, awaiting the completion of the pregnancy. Thus, "soul for soul," that is, *nephesh* for *nephesh* here, ratifies the full humanity of the needful, dependent unborn human child, as per the exegesis of Genesis 2:7.

In scenario "A" there is "no serious injury" (to the unborn), and also the most natural grammar of modification. Kline notes that the Hebrew term here is *ason*. It is a rare term, only used in three other instances, located in Genesis 42 and 44 in reference to Jacob's fear for the "injury" or "harm" that might have befallen his son Benjamin. Jacob fears a calamitous accident, not some normal occurrence. In this sense, it is parallel to the calamity of miscarriage, and as well, to the potential loss of a child.

Thus, both the terms *nagap* and *ason* are unusual terms, and Moses uses them to describe with precision the subject of his concern – the prematurely born child. This is consistent with the Bible's whole treatment of the unborn, and the parallel between the unborn and the prematurely born is as natural as the parallel language of conception and birth (as referenced earlier).

Some abortion advocates then say this reduces the woman to property, because in scenario "A" the woman is dead, the child is fine, and the husband receives a payment for the loss of his wife. However, this misreads the very nature of redemption. What is happening is that the husband is provided by law, in the case of unintentional manslaughter, for financial compensation due to the loss of his wife. Her life cannot be restored, and it is not premeditated murder, so the *"lex talionis"* is referred to specifically in view of this known outcome. Had the husband wanted to demand the life of the men who were fighting, and had the court allowed, the two guilty men nonetheless would have had the option to flee to a city of refuge. There is compensation for the victims, a modicum of payment required of the offender to ease the suffering of the living victims, and to serve as a means of deterrence for future folly. And such a law also benefits a woman who loses her husband to an act of manslaughter.

In scenario "B," the reference is thus to possible outcomes of various forms of serious *ason* to the child, and the *"lex talionis"* is invoked to cover all contingencies. The purpose is to establish the ransom price of the offender's life – what economic levy they have to endure to make up for the loss to the victim, the unborn in this case – since scenario "A" already addresses the husband's wife.

Exodus 21:22-25 is one of those very specific passages in the Mosaic law, and its use of terms is unusual (due to the unique subject matter), and thus the casual reader does not have easy reference to immediately know its exact nuances. But the exegesis of the text shows overwhelming protection for the humanity of the prematurely born child. It is consistent with everything we have seen in Scripture so far, and inconsistent with none of it.

In Sum

Thus, to simplify the warranted exegesis and interpretation of Exodus 21:22-25:

A pregnant woman is struck dead accidentally by two men struggling with each other.

If there is "no harm" to the prematurely born child, a fine is levied against the offender for the loss of the woman's life.

But if the prematurely born child also suffers "harm," the offender is fined according to the nature of the injury caused to the child.

In both cases, *nephesh* for *nephesh* is applied, both mother and unborn child are full image-bearers of God, with equal protection under the law for an equal humanity. The Bible countenances no war between mother and child in competing definitions of the worth of human life based on a pagan achievement ethic.

Psalm 139 and the Presence of *Yahweh*

Psalm 139 is also dynamic in its specific reference to the unborn, and a fine example of parallelism in Hebrew poetry. Exodus 21 is dynamic in affirming the personhood of the unborn in a remedial capacity, and accordingly, its use of language in the context of law. And Psalm 139 is dynamic in its proactive theological construction.

Yet, as we have noted in the case of the Methodist minister with the Religious Coalition for Abortion Rights, at the University of New Hampshire, anyone can twist the biblical text, especially idolaters. Thus, a fuller answer to such a question is edifying.

In the psalm, the second line of each couplet (and the occasional third line of a triplet) reflects the first line, either by repetition of thought in different words, or by expanding on the same train of thought. In addition, each major section of the psalm focuses around one idea, then builds on it through the entire section. The psalm employs all these elements in service to its overall and defining theme – the presence of *Yahweh*.

David begins the psalm by saying that *Yahweh* has searched him and knows him. He concludes it with a prayer to continue this process – for *Yahweh* to search him, know him and deliver him from any sinful ways. After he introduces this idea in the first verse, he immediately embraces the theme of *Yahweh Elohim*'s presence. When he sits and when he rises, when he goes out and lies down, *Yahweh* is with him.

He is hemmed in and protected by the presence of *Yahweh*, and thus David worships him, and then muses on the impossibilities of fleeing from his presence. Whether he flees to the heights of the heavens or to *sheol* ("the

70

depths"); whether he flees to the farthest reaches of the eastern sky ("the wings of the dawn") or to the farthest reaches of the western sky ("the far side of the sea"); all to which David cannot conceptually grasp traveling – he knows *Yahweh* is present with him. He is a member of *Yahweh*'s covenant community, and *Yahweh* keeps his covenant promise to be with him.

This is all "too wonderful" for David to fully grasp (e.g., the "beginning to end," or even "head to tail," in Ecclesiastes 3:11), since it is rooted in *Yahweh*'s eternal nature and perspective. Then David considers the contrast of dark and light. Can he flee *Yahweh*'s presence if he surrounds himself in darkness? No, for he is a member of the covenant community, and he cannot actually embrace ultimate darkness. And even if he could, *Yahweh* is still Lord over the devil's domain. Where light is, darkness cannot abide.

Thus, in beautiful poetic structure, David is examining the possible places to which he can flee and evade *Yahweh*'s presence. He chooses three possibilities, none to which he has or can reasonably conceive of traveling. Finally, in this meditation, David ups the ante and considers the womb from which he comes. Like Nicodemus (John 3:1-4), he knows it is a place to which he cannot return, and when he was there, he was too young to cogently understand his surroundings. He turns to the womb as the final example, in parallelistic structure, of a remote location of which David conceives – indeed, the most remote yet. Is *Yahweh* present there too?

> For you created my inner being;
>> you weaved me together in my mother's womb.
> I praise you above all because I am fearfully set apart;
>> your works are wonderful,
>> My soul knows that full well.
> My bones were not hidden from you
>> when I was made in the hidden place.
> When I was woven together in the depths of the earth,
>> you saw my embryo.
> All the days ordained for me
>> were written in your book
>> before one of them was created (vv. 13-16).

As David considers this scenario, he naturally returns to the context of the order of creation, sharing all its assumptions. David's instincts are the same as he considers the status of the unborn. *Yahweh* is intimately involved in David's creation through the procreation process. To refuse the goodness of procreation is to refuse the goodness of the order of creation itself. It is to mock the image of God. David affirms that his humanity is full, not only when he is visibly human, but when his body is inchoate, an embryo. Even before conception, his identity is present in the eternal mind of *Yahweh Elohim*. The affirmation is in place for the complete humanity of the unborn throughout the entire biological process of pregnancy. And "my soul" in the Hebrew equals "my *nephesh*."

Following this portion of the psalm, David jumps into imprecatory mode, calling down *Yahweh*'s judgment upon the evil (vv. 19-22). This itself is a tough question many pose, indeed, against the whole imprecatory genre in the Hebrew Bible (which I write about elsewhere).

Why such a disjunctive? A reasonable possibility, at least in part if not more so, is that David knows the pagan religions and nations that mock *Yahweh Elohim* and the gift of human life quintessentially in child sacrifice. It is they who are wickedly opposed to the very content of the whole psalm. They recoil from its beautiful affirmation of the unborn, and *Yahweh Elohim*'s eternal presence with them, unlike the finite, petty and destructive gods of their own pagan nations and polities.

Afterward, David completes the psalm in asking *Yahweh* to search his heart and deliver him from any anxious thoughts and offensive ways (vv. 23-24). What a roller coaster, of which the psalms are laden, as human emotions are set free in the presence of *Yahweh Elohim* to pose the most painful of questions.

Human Abortion

In simplicity, and with the full force of biblical theology from its origins, to abort a human being is to abort the chosen and living presence of *Yahweh Elohim*. And to face judgment accordingly.

Biblical Thinking and Theology in the Face of Rape and Incest

We addressed the evil of rape and incest in Chapter One, facing a hard question eyeball-to-eyeball where people suffer. The Bible is the greatest story ever, the only fully true one. And out of true stories comes the formulation of teaching or doctrine. Thus, here, let's take biblical theology and formally look at the question.

The hatred for the evil of rape and incest is best embraced when the humanity of the woman and child are equally and fully embraced.

Since human abortion does not heal the evil and does not unrape the woman, the next question is where healing and justice are to be found. In order to move in this direction, the power to give and the power to forgive must be embraced, and they are rooted in Only Genesis.

Courage is needed to overcome the adversity, but rarely is courage able to be grasped when someone is alone – especially if facing single motherhood with the painful memories of the pregnancy having occurred in such a violent fashion. The power to give trumps the power to destroy, and the raped woman needs love given to her so as to help her overcome such devastation. We love because God first loved us. This is not easy, for evil has occurred. How thus does she overcome?

Thus the church is ordained to be an agent of this love to such a woman, giving her the time, love, counsel, spiritual, psychological and material resources necessary for her to become an overcomer. This is particularly a one-on-one woman-to-woman ministry, though men can be involved in supporting capacities. Here the ministries of Crisis Pregnancy Centers (CPCs) have done yeoman work. Healing is found in the church where Jesus Christ is Lord, where his people are self-giving to such women, where the necessary resources are made available, and where the raped woman chooses to accept such ministry, with her privacy being simultaneously honored.

We need to profile the nature of courage. It is a choice of whether we rise to the challenge or flee from it. In Revelation 2-3, Jesus addresses seven churches in the province of Asia – churches at Ephesus, Smyrna, Pergamum, Thyatira, Sardis, Philadelphia and Laodicea. They are under severe persecution for their faith, from political and cultural opposition orchestrated by the devil, as well as direct assaults from occultic powers. Their lives are threatened, and they suffer many abuses and even death. In history we see the evil of rape in wartime, and for the Christians in these seven cities, it would probably be one of a list of many atrocities they suffer. We all know trials in our lives we need to overcome, whether an actual rape or another evil that strikes at the deepest core of our physical, social, psychological and spiritual well-being.

In the words to each of the seven churches, Jesus specifically calls them to be overcomers. He provides the wherewithal – if only we believe, and that is what he calls us to. The greatest literature in history, and its focus on true heroes and heroines, does not celebrate the cowardly, but the courageous. At the end of Revelation when it diagnoses those who are outside the kingdom of God, the text mentions the "cowardly" (21:8).

To be courageous is not to summon human strength to overcome, and to be cowardly does not refer to the one who cannot summon such strength. The courageous are those, who in acknowledgment of their weaknesses, nonetheless place their trust in the goodness of God, and the cowardly are those who will not embrace such trust and belief. In fact, those with the greatest worldly strength and resources are oftentimes the biggest moral cowards. And the poor and humble are oftentimes the most courageous. The reversal of the reversal. Courage means doing what is right.

When a woman becomes pregnant by rape or incest, she is terribly aware of her weakness and vulnerability. Only a reversal of the reversal can minister to her, and if she embraces it, she is empowered to be an overcomer. Cowardly acts lead to a true loss of humanity, but courageous acts lead to a greater humanity, and it is the courageous whom history fetes. In the face of the destruction and dehumanization of rape and incest, the choice to give life to the unborn is an act of courage. Courage is never easy on the face of it, but it is the right thing to do, and in the long run it produces peace in the soul.

The unborn child is innocent, and if aborted, the child becomes the second victim. It is a question of power – if the child is aborted, the rapist prevails twice. He rapes twice. He has succeeded in having one act of destruction lead to another act of destruction. He has succeeded in prostituting motherhood by causing a mother to forsake her child. This prostitution is his prostitution, not hers, but she is the one in whom the agony is deposited alongside his seed. He is the coward to begin with, and he poisons her with that same cowardice if she yields to an abortion. He has succeeded in having the power to take trump the power to give, he has served the reversal, he has advanced the agenda of the ancient serpent.

What about the woman's emotions? Oftentimes, in pregnancy due to rape, the very thought of giving birth to a rapist's child is repulsive, and even if she overcomes that initial repulsion, the memory of a rapist father will always be there. She cannot but view the child as the offspring of such a "father," and cannot imagine loving such a child. This is why the love of God the Father is indispensable – he who has loved us, when through our sins we have become as unlovely as can the appearance of a rapist's child to the mother, and as obviously hated by the rapist father. Only the love of God the true Father can reverse the reversal in this case, and with a grasp of the power of the cross of Jesus Christ.

Also, in Isaiah 43:25, *Yahweh* declares he is the one who "blots out" our transgressions, he "remembers" our sins no more. The Hebrew terms here are *mahah* and *zakar*, and here in parallel construct. It does not mean that *Yahweh* suffers a loss of divine memory per se, but he cancels our debts as in an accounting book (ergo, "debts" in the Lord's Prayer). Thus, there is no functioning existence of such debts anymore in his presence, and the person is completely free. For the woman who suffers aggravated rape, the sin against her can be wiped out of her spiritual and psychological identity. This is the Good News made possible by the work of the Holy Spirit.

Who has more power – the rapist or the woman? In 1 Corinthians 7, Paul is addressing the question of marriage and divorce, and in this context he says:

75

If a certain brother has a wife who is not a believer and she consents to dwell with him, he must not let her go. And if a woman has a husband who is not a believer and he consents to dwell with her, she must not let her husband go. For the unbelieving husband has been sanctified through his wife, and the unbelieving wife has been sanctified through her believing husband. Otherwise your children would be unclean, but as it is, they are sanctified (vv. 12b-14).

Here Paul says that the believer has more power than the unbeliever, especially in terms of influencing the children. Do we encourage victims of rape to believe this? Are they empowered in the face of the hell they are going through, to overcome the temptation to look at the child as a "rape child," and instead to see him or her as an image-bearer of God in whose life the love of Jesus Christ can triumph? Does a rape victim view the child as her child, the one whom she will influence, or does she buy the devil's lie that the rapist, and the painful memory of him *in absentia*, will be the determining influence?

Thus, biblically, the "rape child" is sanctified by the believing mother. This is true power – to give and to forgive, the bookends of the Bible. The unrepentant rapist chooses the abyss, alongside unrepentant murderers. In Genesis 1:1, creation comes into what is otherwise non-creation, non-existence, non-*nephesh*, the "abyss." In the Revelation, those who refuse *nephesh* join the original Refuser in a chosen return to the "abyss" (chapters 9 and 20). An abyss has no foundation, no embodiment, no relationships.

The percentage of abortions due to rape is very small, and women who abort due to rape, abort at about the same rate as all women who abort their pregnancies. So the emotions and the trauma associated with rape do not produce a higher choice for abortion than women who get pregnant out of a chosen relationship. But because of the huge hormonal changes in a woman's body during the first weeks of pregnancy, a woman is emotionally vulnerable to being pressured into an abortion in the eight to twelve-week range, while her emotions can be reacting to that state of pregnancy, before her hormone shift is complete and she begins to identify with the growing child within her.

This is why CPC ministries are crucial in how they stand in the gap, especially in cases of rape and incest.

Whereas pro-abortion ideologues say that an abortion is necessary to rid the evil of rape and incest, in truth, they take the pain of women so victimized, and employ it to their own ends.

In the early 1970s, an abortionist in California, Dr. Irvin Cushner, said that 98 percent of women who get an abortion do so simply because they do not wish to be pregnant at that particular time, as he testified before the U.S. Congress. They have college or career plans or other priorities. Now, it is my conviction that male abortionists are the most chauvinistic men there are, so we need to be careful with Dr. Cushner's diagnosis. Medically speaking, he understates the case. But he does not note the 93 percent reality, as we have itemized elsewhere, of all abortions being outside of marriage – where male chauvinism reigns (not to mention the fact that nearly the rest of abortions happen because the husband is on the way out the door). So the choice is never a planned choice or a satisfactory one – there are mediating factors. Women are most often pressured into this "choice" by male chauvinists.

This is why the pro-abortion activists, in their ideological zeal, can actually hate women, despite their protestations to such a diagnosis. In the mid-eighties, I traced the data, as far as possible, to arrive at an estimate of the percentage of abortions due to rape and incest, and the figure came out to 1/10 of 1 percent, or about 1600 cases per year (out of 1.6 million total annual abortions at that time). Thus, small in number, huge in imposed hell.

My point here is that upon the backs of raped women do the pro-abortion ideologues market an ideology of sexual promiscuity and abortion-on-demand.

Whereas some of them do genuinely care for women thus victimized, in large part it is the pain of the raped woman that is used to market the justification for abortion in all instances. This is why I started with this issue in Chapter One – to take down a false idol, one that is so blithely used by the "abortion establishment" to try and silence debate on the far larger reality of who gets abortions. The pain of raped women is employed as public rhetoric in service to Planned Parenthood and other abortion marketers. Whenever such pro-abortion ideologues have need for political persuasion to keep abortion legal, they prostitute the emotional identification we all have for compassion upon a rape victim. They try to say that pro-life advocates hate women, and thus the pro-life argument must be rejected in total.

But the pro-abortion ideologues rape these very women all over again, using their pain as chattel.

When we grasp this reality, we can see clearly how the abortion-rights language is in service to the reversal, and we as Christians are called to reverse the reversal. We do this by empowering rape victims to choose life equally for themselves and their unborn children, to embrace overcoming courage and to reject the male chauvinistic cowardice that only knows destruction. We do this by reversing the reversal of public language, and say "no" equally to the physical rapist of the women, and "no" to the spiritual and political rape of these same women by those who are the pro-abortion ideologues.

Another way we can look at this issue is pointing out that we are all children of rape, whether physically or metaphorically. In other words, if we were able to trace every act of sexual union that produced us, from our parents back to the Garden of Eden – how many of these acts were in true marital love with the planned embrace of children so conceived? How many of these sexual unions were in various states of turmoil, and how many were adulterous unions, acts of fornication, acts of rape or acts of incest? For all I know, and I do not know, a drunk fifty-year old man in the highlands of Scotland in the ninth century A.D. raped his thirteen-year old niece, apart from which I would not be here today.

We do know that William I of Normandy was an illegitimate child, known also as "William the Bastard." He shaped history with the crossing of the English Channel in 1066, apart from which not only would I not be here today, but many tens of millions of others as well, including British royalty and most if not all of the signers of the Declaration of Independence.

This returns us to my earlier observations about Genesis 5:1-3, the image of God and the power to pass it on as given to Adam and Seth, even in spite of their sins. Of course too, we know that such sexual sins have also produced evil people like Adolf Hitler. The point is this – none of us come from a lineage that is sexually pure. Thus, if we judge the child of the raped woman to be less than human, then we judge ourselves and our loved ones likewise. As we dehumanize others, we dehumanize ourselves. I would not be surprised to learn that the majority of or all of the human race has literal rape or tabooed incest in their lineages at some point.

If we can answer the question of rape and incest, the toughest in the abortion debate, we can address all cognate questions, and win the largest portion of public sentiment possible. The tragedy of pro-life politicians who carve out an exception for the rare reality of pregnancy due to rape and incest, is that by side-stepping the question, they reduce their ability to tackle the real question of human abortion head-on – the willful destruction of unborn children, which simultaneously assaults the humanity, psychological and physical health of their mothers, and all society. We can only succeed in the overall concerns if first we embrace the power to love hard questions in this regard.

In summary, human abortion is not an answer to the hell of rape or incest:

1. Human abortion does not unrape the woman – it redeems nothing and thus it is in service only to the reversal.
2. Human abortion does not restore the fractured qualities of the POSH Ls of the image of God (peace, order, stability and hope; to live, to love, to laugh, to learn).
3. Human abortion only adds further brokenness, since it equals the intrinsic power to destroy.
4. Human abortion is not compassionate to the woman or her child.
5. Human abortion mocks the power of the woman to overcome the evil she has suffered; it excludes the power and redemptive effect of courage, the powers to give and forgive.
6. Human abortion mocks the *nephesh* of the unborn by killing the child – the other innocent party.

7. Human abortion allows the rapist to triumph twice – to assault both woman and child – to get away with "double murder."
8. Human abortion allows the power to take and destroy of the rapist to vitiate the power to give of the woman.
9. Human abortion allows the pro-abortion ideologues to market "abortion-rights" on the backs of rape victims – it rapes the woman all over again.
10. Human abortion is a tool of the ancient serpent, who would abort us all, since all of us are actually or metaphorically "children of rape."

Human Abortion

No subject matter in the sight of *Yahweh Elohim* and Jesus is exempt from tough questions. Do abortion advocates embrace the toughest questions, or flee from them?

Seventh: Human Sexuality

Genesis 1-2 is the only text in human history that assumes the definition of healthy human sexuality to be one man and one woman in mutual fidelity, as the basis for trust in human relationships, and thus for the building of a healthy social order. And it is a proactive assumption. After *Yahweh* makes the man, gives him the gift of freedom and shows him that he is lonely, he makes the woman to complete the image of *Yahweh Elohim*.

All pagan texts and secular constructs move beyond this boundary of freedom, as broken trust emerges and the reactive posture is assumed. The assumption of healthy human sexuality is thus relentlessly assaulted, and we witness this contest introduced in Genesis 1-19, then across the biblical text until final redemption.

In Genesis 1, the social order is created for male and female together as the image of God to govern his good creation.

In Genesis 2, man and woman become one in marriage as the foundation for the social order.

In Genesis 3, the ancient serpent divorces the decision making between the woman and man in order to destroy marriage and the social order.

In Genesis 4, this brokenness leads to murder and bigamy.

In Genesis 5, the equality and complementarity of male and female, and the goodness marriage and parenthood, are reiterated.

In Genesis 6, the judgment of the Flood is due to the reification (reduction to the status of property) of women in the building of harems – the very mockery of marriage.

In Genesis 9-11, the stage is set for the Canaanites and Babylonians to advance the triad of sorcery, sacred prostitution and child sacrifice, further degrading faithful marriage.

In Genesis 16, Abraham yields to taking a concubine, and this broken marriage yields endless wars between the nations.

In Genesis 19, the judgment on Sodom and Gomorrah is due to a sexual anarchy that morphs into social anarchy and the trampling of the poor and needy, as the biblical concept of marriage is but a distant memory.

One consequence of all this becomes the pagan practice of child sacrifice (e.g., Leviticus 20:1-5), which indeed leads to the metaphor for hell in Jeremiah 19:1ff (where in the Valley of Ben Hinnom, child sacrifice takes place within the ever burning city trash dump; where the Hebrew *g'hinnom* is transliterated into Greek *gehenna* in the Septuagint, and is the New Testament word used for "hell" by Jesus). It is all male chauvinism.

The Feminist Challenge

This assumption of biblical sexuality has been challenged afresh by the rise of pagan and secular feminism in the past half century.

81

Christine Overall, in her Introduction to *Ethics and Human Reproduction*, gives a succinct definition of feminism rooted in five essential components:

1. women's experience;
2. women's victimization by male dominance;
3. understanding the origins of male dominance;
4. rebellion against male dominance; and
5. the creation of structures to teach and reproduce a worldview that succeeds in such a rebellion.

Thus, *sex* → *Choice* → *Life* →/ *God*. This agenda has had great success, to the detriment of society, but also in reaction to the prior evil of male chauvinisms that drive the abortion ethos. Overall's critique is rooted in a reaction to the broken trust between men and women, yet the only remedy is to become rooted in the prior and proactive biblical assumptions of trust.

Male and Female

In Genesis 1:26-28, we read:

> Then *Elohim* said, "Let us make man in our image and likeness, and let them rule among the fish of the sea and the creatures of the heavens, and the livestock, and all the earth, and all the ground creatures."

> So *Elohim* created man in his image,
> in the image of *Elohim* he created him;
> male and female he created them.

> *Elohim* blessed them and said to them, "Be fruitful and multiply; fill the earth and subdue it. Rule among the fish of the sea and the creatures of the heavens and over all the ground creatures."

The exact parallel vertical grammar in the Hebrew equals:

man = the image of God = male and female;
his own image = him = them.

When *Elohim* creates "man," the Hebrew word is *adam*, from whence Adam derives his name. The word *adam* does not mean "male" (like *ish* or *zakar*), but it is the principal word for "mankind" or "humankind" – specifically including both male and female, and/or in plural reference.

Thus, *adam* is gender inclusive, and its use throughout the Hebrew Bible in the generic sense means that mankind includes both male and female. Adam takes on the name of *adam* as a personal name representative of humanity, representative of the unity *Elohim* designs for male and female as his equal image-bearers.

In the restoration of the image of *Yahweh Elohim* in Genesis 5:1-2, this is explicit: "In the day *Elohim* created man, he made him in the likeness of *Elohim*. He created them male and female and blessed them. And when they were created, he named them man."

He calls them *adam*. Thus, the biblical language is poignantly specific from the outset in a) demonstrating the equality of man and woman, that together they equal "man," and b) that the use of the male pronoun when referring to "man" or "mankind" is inclusive of both male and female. Male and female both come from *Yahweh Elohim*, and the use of the "he" refers to his power to give.

The "He" of *Yahweh Elohim*

This leads us to consider the use of the male pronoun, the "he" of Adam, or better yet, the "he" of *Yahweh Elohim*. In Genesis 1:27 we see the use of three sets of nouns in parallel equality at the beginning of each line, and three corresponding pronouns at the end, as cited above.

Thus, the parallels in Genesis 1:27 above are obvious to the Hebrew hearer and reader, and Genesis 5:2 reiterates the same prosaic clarity – male and female are "man."

God the Father is above male and female, for both male and female equally derive from his character, and he is at peace within himself in triune community. He is neither male nor female in the human sexual sense, in terms of a singular sexual identity. Jesus applies a female metaphor to himself (see Luke 13:34), but God is called "Father" (see the language of Deuteronomy 32:6; and especially of Jesus's use of "Father" for God), always uses the masculine pronoun, is never given the title "Mother," and never is described with female pronouns. *Elohim* is "he" and not "she."

So, whereas the Hebrew Bible is unique in describing men and women as equally sharing the image of *Elohim*, the description of *Yahweh Elohim* is in masculine terms. The masculine "man" is the designated term to include man and woman, as opposed to the feminine "woman" being the designated term. This is due to the simplicity of the power to give, and accordingly, the important question to ask is not why *Yahweh Elohim* is called "he," but why Adam is called "he." Or in other words, the "he" of *Yahweh Elohim* is not a designation of being male; and the "he" of Adam is a designation of the power to give as initially received from *Yahweh Elohim*.

Human sexuality, at its deepest core, is designed to be the epitome of where the power to give is expressed in human community, and is designed for the covenant of one man and one woman in marriage. If we make the mistake of looking at *Yahweh Elohim* through the prism of broken human sexuality, then we can end up making him a "male." This is what pagan religions do with male gods and female goddesses.

Adam as male derives the nature of his "he" from *Yahweh Elohim*, and not vice versa. God the Father employs all his power in the power to give, to bless and benefit we who are made in his image. And within the Trinity, we see the dynamics of this relationship as based on giving and receiving. God the Father, Son and Holy Spirit are consistently giving honor to each other (e.g., John 14:25; 17:1), and receiving it from each other, in his unified nature.

This is why Genesis 2:24 says a man will leave his father and mother, cleave to his wife and the two of them become one flesh. The two – male and female – became one because of the prior reality of *Yahweh Elohim*, in whom the three are one; and because the image of *Yahweh Elohim* requires both male and female in order to reflect the nature of the triune God, where unity and diversity exist together in unity, where diversity is in service to unity. This unity and diversity represented in the two becoming one in marriage reflects the unity and diversity within the triune God, the three who are One. True diversity in service to unity is rooted in man and woman in marriage as the purpose for the image of *Yahweh Elohim*.

In the biblical creation, God the Father initiates the power to give as he makes man and woman to receive such giving, and this reflects the dependent and needful nature of the human soul (*nephesh*). Receiving cannot happen without the prior reality of giving; thus *Yahweh Elohim* is the Initiator of all giving. The "he" of *Yahweh Elohim* is best understood as reflecting this ethical dimension, and not to be seen as restricted to a human limitation of the male pronoun.

Adam takes on the designation of "he" because he is the first human to receive from *Yahweh Elohim* in Genesis 2, and thus empowered to be the first human to pass on the power to give. In the finitude of human nature, in order to catalyze the cycle of giving and receiving, *Yahweh* first demonstrates his giving to the one who receives the gift and that such a one naturally gives to another. The "he" of Adam. Giving and receiving is the true nature of all relationships as ordained by *Yahweh*; and in the sexual intimacy of marriage, it reaches the zenith, the most beautiful and complete nature.

All this equals the opposite of male chauvinism.

Three Different Equations for Marriage

Just prior to my 1994 "give and it will be given, or take before you are taken" observation at Smith College, I had observed the three possibilities in human relationships, symbolized in three different types of marriage:

100-0;
50-50; or
100-100.

In the 100-0 option, male chauvinism is operative. Here the man demands 100 percent and gives nothing. This can also be described as "take before you are taken."

The 50-50 option can be described as "egalitarian," and is distinguished philosophically from "equality." In the philosophy of an egalitarian view, the equality of the sexes is defined by an appeal to "sameness." A woman can do anything a man can do, it is said. Accordingly, male and female roles in marriage are said to be interchangeable (apart from the inescapable reality of pregnancy, giving birth and natural succor).

In the "ideal" egalitarian marriage, each partner pursues career goals, defined not by service to the home as with a healthy marriage, but careers, which if push comes to shove, take precedence over the home. Thus, cooking and housework are split evenly if they cannot afford a cook or a maid. If and when they have children, maternity leave applies to the man as well as the woman, and they share 50-50 the work of child rearing. With or without daycare or a nanny, the husband is expected to make the same "sacrifice" of time away from his career, as does his wife. Such "sameness," as a definition for equality, is thus supposed to remove culturally imposed role distinctions between male and female – and lead to true equality.

Yet why is it that the language is one of "sacrificing" a career, and not that of "sacrificing" family? A boomerang against male chauvinisms – namely, where "career" is often the male idol to begin with. For a married man, unless his identify is first in the Gospel, then in his wife and family, it is his error that opens the Pandora's Box of human suffering. Which is the more enduring reality, for the individual and the social order? How many people on their deathbeds regret not having spent more time at their careers, or not having spent more time with their family members, especially children?

As the research makes clear, the upper middle-class ideal of egalitarianism is not only a myth, it is also a destroyer of families and children. As many feminists complain, when they enter such a 50-50 bargain, they discover that their workloads greatly increase, and their husband's workload remains roughly constant. As women, they are desirous or willing to pursue a career

86

outside the home, but men are, as a rule, unwilling to share the domestic work anymore than was otherwise the case (though increasingly with a more "feminized" culture, things are more complex).

This leads to a warfare between one 50 and the other 50. Namely, 50-50 by definition is a taking proposition, with each party making an idol of career or identity outside of God and family. By putting such an idol ahead of relationship, each party clamors to protect his or her 50 percent. In other words, the arrangement is based on the "right to take" the 50 percent that belongs to him or her, and if one spouse takes 51 percent, there is war – the opposite of the power to give.

There is great freedom in a healthy marriage in terms of how income producing work and management of the home are shared, but only when the complementary nature of men and women is affirmed, not when distinctions are blurred. The irony is that the 50-50 proposition is no different than the 100-0 proposition. It too is "take before you are taken."

The Hebrew word for peace is *shalom*, as noted earlier, which primarily refers to integrity and wholeness. The only prescription for social peace is the original one of 100-100 in the Garden of Eden. This is the power to "give and it will be given," where *Yahweh Elohim* gives 100 percent of his divine best to the human Adam, Adam receives the 100 percent and gives 100 percent of his human best to Eve, she receives his 100 percent and returns 100 percent of her human best to Adam; then they together, in the integrity and wholeness as husband and wife, give their 100 percent of their human best in worship to *Yahweh Elohim*.

At Smith, both Patricia Ireland and the audience rejected the 100-0 and 50-50 as I defined them. As I presented the 100-100 option, there was real interest, even hope, but still some apprehension. Who gives the first 100? The only Source is God the Father in how he gives to Adam and Eve.

Hence, two choices – give and it will be given, or take before you are taken. I asked Patricia if she knew of any better arrangement for marriage or the human community. Neither of us could.

We see that Adam receives the "he" in his maleness because *Yahweh* designs him to also give to his wife. Or to put it another way, whoever is made first is by definition male, when male is understood in terms of the "he" of *Yahweh*'s initiation of the power to give in the order of creation, and not in terms of the "he" of male chauvinisms, which does not happen until the reversal.

Having already noted the creation of Adam in Genesis 2:7, we can now note Genesis 2:18-25, where we are introduced to the specifics of the creation of Eve:

> *Yahweh Elohim* said, "It is not good for the man to be alone. I will separate out a helper facing him."

> Now *Yahweh Elohim* had formed out of the ground all the land creatures and all the creatures of the heavens. He brought them to the man to see what he would name them; and whatever the man called each living creature, that was its name. So the man gave names to all the livestock, the creatures of the heavens and all the beasts of the field. But for Adam no suitable helper was found.

> So *Yahweh Elohim* caused the man to fall into a deep sleep; and while he was sleeping, he took one part out of the man's side and closed up the flesh underneath.

> Then *Yahweh Elohim* built a woman from what he had taken from the side of the man, and brought the woman to the man.

> And the man said,

> "This is now substance of my substance
>   and flesh of my flesh;
> she shall be called 'woman,'
>   for she was taken out of man."

Accordingly, a man will leave his father and mother and cling to his wife, and the two will become one flesh.

And the man and his wife were both naked, and felt no shame.

As *Yahweh Elohim* completes the stages of the creative progress defined in the days of creation, we see the idea repeated: "And *Elohim* saw it was good." Then on the sixth day, when man and woman are created, they are his goal, the crown of creation, and then the text says, "*Elohim* saw all he made, and it was very good." Thus, as *Yahweh Elohim* declares something "not good," we face a powerful disjunctive. How can something be "not good" in the order of creation? The answer is straightforward: Something is not yet complete, only "haploid" as it were.

In Genesis 2:18-25, we have the specifics of how and why the woman is made. *Yahweh* has already made Adam out of the dust, breathed the breath of life into him, and gives him the commandment of freedom. The *adam* of Genesis 2:7 is not referring to an androgynous creature, in the sense that *adam* here could be seen as being male and female in one nature and body. We know this because of the subsequent text that treats *adam* as the proper name for the first male, Adam, one in need of his female complement.

Part of Adam's freedom is his authority over and for the created order as *Yahweh*'s vassal – the "why" of Adam's existence. So there Adam stands – naked, innocent and free in the presence of his Creator. Yet something is missing. Adam needs a "helper facing him." The Hebrew term for "helper" is *ezer*, and it has no sense of subordination. Indeed, the verb employed here (*neged*) says the "helper" is "facing" him, giving a visual of them both standing eyeball-to-eyeball as equals and complements. As well, whereas it refers to the act of giving assistance, it is more often used to specify the one who gives the help – to the power to give, which equals *Yahweh Elohim*'s nature, and human nature in his image.

The most frequent use of *ezer* in the Hebrew Scriptures is in reference to *Yahweh* himself as the divine helper, and Eve reflects the image of *Yahweh Elohim* as she comes to help Adam. Here, *ezer* is a word for moral and relational equality, based on a mutual power to give and receive. Also, in the New Testament, the Holy Spirit is also called the "helper" or "advocate" (*parakletos* in John 14:16; 26; 15:26; 16:7).

In other words, Adam by himself does not fully bear the image of *Yahweh Elohim*. We already know this by the text in Genesis 1:27, where the language of mankind, and the inclusiveness of male and female, is descriptive of the image of *Elohim*. Here in Genesis 2, we see *Yahweh Elohim* demonstrating to Adam his need for a helper. *Yahweh* declares it is "not good" for the man to be alone, and then brings him various creatures in order for Adam to give them names.

What does the naming of the animals have to do with addressing Adam's loneliness? *Yahweh* is demonstrating to Adam the power to give, where the act of giving is intrinsically satisfying. In other words, we need to give – we need someone to whom to give, otherwise giving is not possible, and receiving is out of the question. The need to give and receive is provided for within the Trinity, and here *Yahweh* walks Adam through the steps of recognizing that as an image-bearer, he, too, is designed to give and receive.

Now that Adam has received, he is equipped to give, and at the same time is not complete without someone to whom to give, someone who is his equal. He can give back to God, but as a creature, not an equal. He cannot give to an animal and receive back with reciprocity, for he is not an animal. He needs a helper so that he can exercise the power to give, so that reciprocity in giving returns to him. His helper cannot be his mirror image – another man. He needs an equal who is also a complement, facing him as such, where between the two they complete each other, where they add unique dimensions the other does not possess.

He needs a woman. Adam needs Eve to give to and receive from in order for the image of *Yahweh Elohim* to be complete. He is made for communication, to share with an equal, not to be lonely. And giving must be initiated. Giving begets giving; but if taking is the initiative, then taking begets taking. The former is the prescription for peace. The latter is the prescription for war.

In the Garden, *Yahweh* initiates the power to give, and Adam needs to do the same in order to reflect his image as a male, to reflect the "he." Then Eve, as a female, receives, and is thus empowered to give and receive as "she." The cycle of giving and receiving is catalyzed, and either party can initiate the act of giving any time henceforth.

The Garden of Eden and all creation are before Adam, and he is given the power to name the creatures – the power to affirm the goodness of *Yahweh Elohim*'s created order. This naming process is an initial exercise of his status as *Yahweh Elohim*'s image-bearer. As *Yahweh* creates, now Adam is given the privilege to be procreative in the fullest sense of the term (to procreate is not only to have children; it is to be creative in all contexts with the resources *Yahweh Elohim* gives us in creation). *Yahweh Elohim* is the Creator, and Adam is now called to be the procreator. But his procreation is limited when his only relationship here is with the animals. Procreation comes as the gift of the Creator, the Father of us all.

Adam is alone, the giving of names is creative, and he also discovers firsthand the difference between man and animal. He does not smell like them or look like them; he notices the animals are in twos and he is in ones; he is lonely and does not want to (indeed, cannot) mate with any of them.

Yahweh Elohim teaches Adam in this exercise that:

1. he is made in *Yahweh Elohim*'s image;
2. animals are not;
3. he is not an animal; and
4. his image-bearing status is not complete without "a helper facing him."

Most powerfully, *Yahweh* demonstrates to Adam, "You are not it." Adam alone is not the complete bearer of *Yahweh Elohim*'s image, and he is in need of his equal who completes him, and whom he completes. Therefore, all power Adam exercises toward Eve is designed to be the power to give, not the power to take. And apart from woman, he is unable to give in a way that completely fulfills the image of *Yahweh Elohim*.

Among pagan feminists and other skeptics of the biblical worldview, rooted in real pain, their instinct is that the Bible is the source for male chauvinism, whereas it is quite otherwise. Such feminists often argue that Genesis 2:18-25 treats women as second-class, or even as an afterthought. But this is because post-biblical and current assumptions are brought to bear on the story. For example, the idea of "helper" can be wrongly viewed as subordinate and not equal.

Such pagan feminists challenge the Genesis text, saying that since Eve is created last, she is therefore an inferior afterthought in the minds of the male chauvinists who are said to have written the story that assumes a male god. But this reading of the text has a foreign concept of chronology and moral order – that somehow the first is best, and the last is least.

In contrast, the whole thrust of Genesis 1 is that *Elohim* starts with the most remote and inanimate portions of the universe, then systematically orders everything as he moves up to more and more complex life forms, and when all is done, when the habitat is prepared for the crown of his creation, *Elohim* makes man and woman to govern and steward it all. But man is not fully male without woman, nor is woman fully female without man.

Paul says that man is "the image and glory of God; but the woman is the glory of man" (1 Corinthians 11:7). There is a symbiosis in place here. Man and woman together equal the image of God; yet in the making of man first, and showing his need for woman, she is his glory. And this is powerful language, since man is God's glory, the one in whom he delights, and woman's glory is that in which man delights. The power to give accrues and gives honor to the woman as the completion of the glory of the image of God.

As well, in the order of creation, *Yahweh* is always aiming at completion; thus, with the passing days of creation, he repeatedly states it is "good" as completion is achieved. With Adam in Genesis 2, *Yahweh* says it is "not good" for him to be alone – goodness is not achieved until the image of *Yahweh Elohim* is complete, until woman is made. Woman completes what lacks in man, so that together they equal mankind. When man and woman are finally standing side-by-side, as creation is complete, it is "very good."

Another concern raised by pagan feminists is the idea that the woman is made from one of Adam's "ribs." Thus, since woman is made from man, it is argued that she must be subordinate and of less worth in the eyes of the biblical writer. However, the language is otherwise. It can be looked at this way: If we had the choice, which would we prefer – to be made from human flesh and bone, or to be made from a pile of dry earth? After all, Eve is made from human tissue, and Adam comes directly from the dust.

In most translations, the word "rib" is used for what *Yahweh* takes out of Adam to make Eve. The Hebrew word is *tselah*, which means "an aspect of the personality." "Rib" is an accurate word for "an aspect" or "part" of Adam's person in physical terms, but I have chosen a more literal translation, "part." Eve is made from Adam to indicate her union with him, her complementary equality, with no view toward a divisive understanding of woman at war with man that later comes with the fallout of human sin. Whether, in the case of *Yahweh* forming Adam out of the dust, or of *Yahweh* forming Eve out of her husband's body, in both cases it involves *Yahweh*'s direct creative action.

Genesis 1:27 identifies their theological union as joint image-bearers, and Genesis 2 identifies their physical union as it shows us the order in which they are created to serve the initiative and reciprocity of the power to give. Genesis 2:7 gives us the explicit language of *Yahweh Elohim* breathing the breath of life into Adam; and though 2:21-22 does not explicitly say that of Eve, it is implicitly required by the structure of the text. And given the unity of man and woman in their creation in 1:26-28, this is further ratified.

Eve is an image-bearer, a needed helper for her otherwise incomplete husband, formed by *Yahweh*'s direct work, and presented to Adam as a living breathing person. *Yahweh Elohim* breathes of his Spirit directly into Eve as he does with Adam. Also, the only difference between the dust of the ground and one of Adam's "ribs" or "parts" is that of molecular organization. Man and woman are both made from the same stuff of the universe, and we are distinguished from the rest of creation by the image of *Elohim* breathed into us.

When Adam awakes from his sleep and views Eve, we have the first poem in human history. Adam sees his helper, his complement, his equal. And as some like to say, a rough paraphrase of this poem is "Wow!" Adam has just named the animals, and in the process, realizes he is uniquely an image-bearer of *Yahweh Elohim*, and that all other creatures are not. The image of *Yahweh Elohim* within him – with the gifts of creativity, intelligence, choice, aesthetics and dexterity – need an equal and complementary partner with whom he also shares these gifts.

Inclusive Spheres of Rule

In the Genesis 1:26-28 passage, Adam and Eve are called to "rule" the work of creation together, under *Elohim* and for their joy. In the words "fill and subdue," we see a phrase that defines the inclusive spheres of rule for Adam and Eve. "Inclusive" means that *Elohim* gives to Adam and Eve unique dimensions not replicated in each other, so that true complementarity is possible.

By the same token, there is much overlap in gifts and nature between the man and woman, so that the spheres of rule are not "exclusive" domains. Men and women are equally human, men and women are different, and men and women need each other for a shared humanity. This balance is uniquely provided for in the biblical language.

"Filling and subduing" the earth refers to the dimensions of procreation and to the cultivating of the Garden of Eden to enjoy its fruit, and hence, to cultivate the planet, to build civilization. An inclusive and mutually submissive reality can be seen by the comparison of the muscular strengths between man and woman. The woman's greatest exertion of strength is in her uterine and thigh muscles, and this strength is taxed most in pregnancy and childbirth, in need for the critical moments. The man's greatest exertion of strength is in his shoulders and biceps, this strength is taxed most in heavy labor such as moving boulders, and built for endurance. A man cannot give birth or natural succor to a child; and a woman qua woman cannot lift nearly as much weight as can a man. But a man can hold an infant close in comfort – as a man. And a woman can do hard and diligent physical labor – as a woman. The distinctives remain.

This complementarity is seen in Genesis 2:7 and 2:22. In 2:7, when *Yahweh Elohim* "formed" the man from the dust, the verb employed is *yetzer*. The idea reflects *Yahweh* as the divine Potter, forming Adam literally from the clay, the red earth, or from the raw materials as it were. In 2:22, when *Yahweh* builds the woman from the man's substance, the verb employed is *banah*. It does not begin with the raw materials, but begins with the formed substance already in place. A suitable analogy is to compare the outward building of a house, beginning with the hewing of the lumber from the trees, in the forming of Adam, on the one hand; with the inner finishing of the house, as with beautification details such as furnishings and artwork, in the forming of Eve, on the other.

As we have already seen in *nephesh*, the human soul is by definition needful of *Yahweh Elohim*'s original and continued provisions. His breath provides Adam with his original breath. Also, it means that the human body is a good gift, meant to live forever. Thus, human strength starts with the power to receive and be needful of *Yahweh Elohim*'s power to give.

In reflecting on *nephesh*, we see the mutual dependency as designed by *Yahweh Elohim*. In the order of creation, it is the strength of the man to do the heavy labor, to work as the provider who builds the house and shelters his family from climatic extremes. In the order of creation, it is the strength of the woman in pregnancy, childbirth and succor to build the family that lives in the house. These are inclusive spheres of rule – to "fill and subdue" is a whole unit that requires a whole marriage unit to accomplish it. And when these spheres are honored, all subsequent blessings come. Men work inside the home and women work outside the home in many overlapping functions, but according to their God-given natures, not in contrast to them, and always in service to the home. No atomistic exclusivity.

95

In the Greek, the word for "household" is *oikos*, and the "rule of the household" is *oikonomos*, from whence we derive the word "economics." The married household with children is the original economic engine, where both husband and wife are joint partners in the true economy. Before the Industrial Revolution, more proximity and interface was possible; since then, it is a different and ever complicating matter as the nuclear and extended family units are increasingly fractured.

Important Territory

This is important to understand, if we want to change the language of the abortion debate. When I was studying for my Th.M. in Ethics and Public Policy at Harvard Divinity School, I interacted with many feminists who believed in abortion rights. And they thought that the God of the Bible was a male chauvinist, and such a wrong view of the text needs to be remedied.

Harvard psychologist Carol Gilligan published her influential book in 1982, *In a Different Voice*. It changed the feminist movement with her clinical observations that women think differently than men, and accordingly, models for healthy psychologies cannot be made to apply to girls if the only studies were done on boys – as the reigning psychological paradigm of Lawrence Kohlberg then assumed. She thus addresses the abortion question from the woman's relational priority, opposite male insensitivity.

But Gilligan, despite some good analysis, and in view of Kohlberg's imbalance, says that the problem "all goes back, of course, to Adam and Eve – a story which shows, among other things, that if you make a woman out of a man, you are bound to get into trouble. In the life cycle, as in the Garden of Eden, the woman has become the deviant" (p. 6).

Gilligan's comment about the nature of Adam and Eve and the Garden of Eden is unfortunately the norm among many scholars. Such an assumption then influences those who read these scholars, which translates into the influencing of the cultural elite who determine so much of what assumptions are filtered for the rest of society to hear. Thus, public perception and public policy are affected – many times against the better instincts and common sense of the population at large.

Somewhere in her training, Gilligan accepted an item of biblical "eisegesis" (a word that refers to placing something into the source, pretending it was there all along, then discovering it later; it is the opposite of "exegesis," which refers to discovering what is truly in the source to begin with). That is, this reflects some woman's interpretation of the text that comes not from an understanding of the Bible on its own terms, but from refracting the Bible through the myopia of sin and brokenness. And the chief sin here is that of male chauvinism, where too many girls grow up not seeing the power to give in their father (or father-figure when need be), and thus they cannot see the power to give in God the Father in the biblical witness.

Another way to sum up this balance is to say that the man naturally leads in task-orientation, and the woman naturally leads in relationship-building. A mutual submission to this reality leads to healthy marriages and a healthy society. A mutual submission to the power to give.

Broken Human Sexuality

Earlier we noted the four definitive subjects in Genesis 1-2:

> The order of creation = God → life → choice → sex;
> The reversal = sex → choice → life →/God.

And as *Satan*, the ancient serpent, seeks to reverse the order of creation, we see his agenda. There is also another order and reversal in place:

> The order of creation = *Yahweh* → (Adam & Eve) → serpent;
> The reversal = serpent → (Eve → Adam) →/*Yahweh*.

Genesis 3:1-7 reads:

> Now the serpent was craftier than any of the living land creatures *Yahweh Elohim* had made. And he said angrily to the woman, "Did

97

Elohim really say, 'You must not eat from any tree in the garden'?"

The woman said to the serpent, "We may eat fruit from the trees in the garden, but *Elohim* did say, 'You must not eat fruit from the tree that is in the middle of the garden, and you must not touch it, or you shall die.' "

So the serpent said to the woman, "In dying you shall not continually die, for *Elohim* knows that in the day you eat of it your eyes will be opened, and you will be like *Elohim*, knowing good and evil."

When the woman saw the fruit of the tree was good for food and desirable to the eye, and desirable for gaining wisdom, she took some some and ate it. She also gave some to her husband, who was with her, and he ate it. Then the eyes of the two of them were opened, and they knew they were naked; so they sewed leaves of a fig tree together and made loin coverings for themselves.

The ancient serpent approaches Eve alone, a deliberate strategy to divorce her unity with Adam in making decisions. In other words, it is a calculated assault on marriage. The devil is also masquerading as a member of the animal kingdom, thus assaulting the governing authority of the image of *Yahweh Elohim*.

His question is perverse and angry. Anger always has a history, but that begs a deeper discussion on the origins of the devil, about which I write elsewhere. In the literal Hebrew, the word for nose (*nagap*) is also the word for anger. The serpent "gets in Eve's face" as it were. He is challenging *Yahweh Elohim* with a false question ("Did *Elohim* really say ...?"), followed by a deliberate misquote of what *Yahweh Elohim* actually did say. The devil is marking out a false prohibition, trying to get the woman to agree with the prohibition of the good (!) and its freedom, thus agreeing with the evil (the earliest form of syncretism and dualism in history), in saying that *Elohim* is prohibiting Eve from eating from "any tree in the garden." No, it is only the one tree that is prohibited, the poisonous one, in order that Adam and Eve can live free.

In the gospels, many religious elitists who oppose Jesus are said by him to have as their "father, the devil," with the devil also being called "the father of lies" (John 8:44). So the devil is a liar in the Garden, and in Matthew 19:1-9, a group of Pharisees does the same. They seek to trap Jesus on the matter of divorce, asking: "Is it lawful for a man to release his wife for any reason?" They know this is a false question, just as the ancient serpent uses the word "any" for the purpose of distortion:

> He answered them, "Haven't you read that at the beginning the Creator made them male and female? And for this reason a man will leave his father and mother and cleave to his wife, and the two will become one flesh? So they are no longer two, but one. Therefore, what God has joined together, let man not separate."

In his answer, Jesus unites the language of the grand design of male and female in Genesis 1, with the specific covenant of marriage in Genesis 2. The devil and this group of Pharisees use the same tactics to avoid a proper definition of terms, and Jesus says no to any attempt to divide a married couple, whether by the ancient serpent or by the Pharisees.

Yet the Pharisees persist:

> They said to him, "Why then did Moses command that a man give his wife a certificate of divorce and release her?"

> Jesus replied, "Moses permitted you, in the hardness of your hearts, to release your wives. But from the beginning it was not so. I tell you that anyone who releases his wife, except for fornication, and marries another woman, commits adultery."

Again, they lie in a slippery way. Moses makes no such command, but only allows divorce in the case of fornication (*porneia* in the Greek, any sexual encounter outside of marriage, or broken trust relating to emotional or physical violence). In the Sermon on the Mount, Jesus intensifies this reality of *porneia* with stronger language yet: "But I tell you that anyone who looks at a woman lustfully has already committed adultery with her in his heart"

(Matthew 5:28). As we return momentarily to the reversal in Genesis 3, we will see how the original definition of sin is that of broken trust. The word in Matthew for lust is *epithumeo*, "to sexually desire" a woman, thus broken trust, broken union in marriage is the essence. The English word for "pornography" comes from the Greek roots of *porneia* and *graphe* (writing), namely, words or pictures that incite lust. Porn destroys marriage, and dehumanizes and reifies people at the same time, no matter what form it takes. It causes immense suffering for the innocent as well as the guilty parties.

And before the Pharisees persist in their deceit with Jesus, so had the ancient serpent beforehand – their very model. The woman gives an honest answer about her freedom to eat the good fruit, alongside the prohibition of the poisonous fruit, even intensifying the prohibition, "and you must not touch it." Eve learns the original words of the prohibition, in communication with Adam, since they were spoken before she was created, and also in communication with *Yahweh* thereafter.

There is a season when they are one flesh, thus being mature enough to give answer and rule over the ancient serpent when he comes calling. Eve is free to add her own words faithfully reflecting the truth, or the intensifier was spoken by *Yahweh* to them at another time. This is an assumption the text virtually requires, and as we read the Bible, we will see this often, where *Yahweh Elohim* invests in us as his image-bearers the ability to read the storyline and understand deeper assumptions and connections.

So the ancient serpent again lies, and here is the reversal:

> In Genesis 2:17, *Yahweh* says *moth tamuth*, "in dying you shall continually die."

> In Genesis 3:4, the ancient serpent says *lo moth t'muthon*, "in dying' you shall not continually die."

The ancient serpent calls the words of *Yahweh Elohim* a lie, and quite transparently and brashly so (the nature of anger). He simply places a negative in front of *Yahweh*'s words (*lo*). Thus, the grammatical power of the infinitive absolute imperfect tense rendered "in dying you shall continually die" is literalistically "not in dying you shall continually die"! Quite the oxymoron.

How then does Eve succumb? The ancient serpent strategically succeeds in getting her to respond to him without consulting *Yahweh* or her husband. She is somehow isolated in her attention, and thus without the wisdom that communication within God-given unity and checks and balances of a healthy marriage brings. Then an unchecked desire enters her soul and she eats of the forbidden fruit.

Where is Adam? He is "with her." So how does it happen? In consideration of the "in your face" anger (*nagap*) reality in the serpent's original approach to Eve (verse 1), my best plausibility is to imagine a hushed anger of the devil, trying not to be overheard, and perhaps using natural noise distraction as well, timing it just right in the presence of rushing water or a rushing wind, or maybe something in the Garden is positively distracting Adam's attention. Or perhaps Adam does hear something, is uncurious, or in some fashion proactively fails simultaneously in not guarding (*shamar*) the garden and his wife.

Regardless, what should Eve have done? She could have, consciously in the presence of the living *Yahweh Elohim*, and in the strength of union with her husband, given Adam a pre-lapsarian nudge, and said: "Honey, there is something fishy going on here [pardon an import of a later metaphor]. There is a talking snake calling *Yahweh Elohim* a liar, and telling me to disobey him and eat the forbidden fruit."

If we grasp the power to give as the nature of true authority, and what it means to "rule" the animal kingdom, Adam's response would have been simple. He should have interrogated the serpent, and then judged it by crushing its head, his heel coming down in force, for rebelling against *Yahweh* and man. And since Adam would not have eaten the fruit, the sin could be atoned for by simple repentance on Eve's part, and the unity of man and woman would have remained unbroken. But instead, Adam acts

101

independently of *Yahweh* and his wife by not asking him or her about the source of the fruit. And given the proximity they have to the tree of the knowledge of good and evil, and their experience in eating other fruit, Adam knows better. The fault is fully mutual.

The net result is this:

> The woman acts independently of *Yahweh* and of Adam;
> The man acts independently of *Yahweh* and Eve.

Trust is broken vertically between both of them and their Creator, and horizontally between themselves as husband and wife, fellow image-bearers of *Yahweh Elohim*. Jesus, in summing up as the Law of Moses, heals the broken trust by empowering us to love God and one another, reversing the reversal both vertically and laterally as cause and effect necessitate.

Thus we see the original definition of "sin" (a word not used here but later): namely, broken trust.

The Thunder of *Yahweh*'s Judgment

The seriousness of this broken trust is seen in understanding the Hebrew language in vv. 8-10.

> And they heard the thunder of *Yahweh Elohim* marching into the garden in the Spirit-driven storm of the moment, and the man and the woman hid from *Yahweh Elohim* in the trees of the garden.

> But *Yahweh Elohim* called to the man and said, "Where do you belong?" He answered, "I heard your thunder in the garden, and I was afraid because I was naked; so I hid."

In so many translations, verse 8 is rendered something like: "The man and his wife heard the sound of the LORD God as walking in the garden in the cool of the day." This leads to all sorts of silliness. As though the Creator of

102

the universe were out for his morning or evening stroll, and just happens to casually call out to the man to see where he is.

The Hebrew text tells a very different story. The word for "sound" is *qol*, and it can mean anything from a whisper to a thunderclap, depending on context, and often translated as "voice."

The word for "walking" is from *halak*, an act of going that can mean anything from a tiptoe to a military march, depending on context.

There is no word "cool" in the Hebrew text, and much speculation as to how it got there. The word for "breeze" is *ruach*, it is the term for wind or spirit (including the Holy Spirit), and can range in meaning from a breeze to a hurricane or tornado. Perhaps some translator, many centuries past, first had in mind a pristine Garden of Eden, and took the *ruach* as a "cool breeze."

Finally, the word for "day" is *yom*, a word marking time that can range in meaning from a moment to eons, but most commonly as a "day."

Thus, a wooden and sterile translation could be, "And they heard the sound of *Yahweh Elohim* as he was going in the garden in the wind of the time." In Hebrew, context determines how best to translate a given word.

So what is the context here? *Yahweh* promises in Genesis 2:17 that in the *yom* (the day, even the very moment) Adam eats of the forbidden fruit, death will enter the creation. This is the largest possible disruption, as the ancient serpent lies about the very language. So *Yahweh* is not caught off guard, rather he is completely aware of what has just happened. Nor is Adam caught off guard – he and Eve are hiding from the thunderous approach of *Yahweh* who promised immediate judgment on what they know they have just done. And as evidenced in how they are now ashamed of their prior naked freedom, and seek to cover it up. Yet still, *Yahweh* uses the power to ask a hard question of Adam, as questions produce ownership of the answers.

Thus I have translated it: "And the man and his wife heard the thunder of *Yahweh Elohim* marching into the garden in the Spirit-driven storm of the moment." Translation matters, and thus we grasp why Adam and Eve are hiding, why Adam is afraid. The wrath of *Yahweh Elohim* is upon them like a freight train of enormous proportion, a category 5 tornado. They are no longer free in their nakedness in the sight of *Yahweh Elohim* and one another. The ancient serpent succeeds in causing the great rift, the great divorce. And he gains the driver's seat through dishonest language, just as does the pro-abortion advocacy today.

Blame and Prophecy of Rescue

This rift is immediately seen in the subsequent text as Adam answers *Yahweh* by dishonestly blaming Eve (he knew the fruit he was eating), and then Eve honestly answers the Lord by confessing that she was deceived by the serpent. Then the devil, in his serpent masquerade, is cursed by *Yahweh* to live like such an animal, and the prophecy of the devil's demise follows:

> And I will put an imposition between you and the woman,
>> and between your seed and hers;
>> he will crush your head, and you will bruise his heel (3:15).

This is the first Messianic prophecy, and is fulfilled on the cross as Jesus brings his heel down on the devil's head, his very authority (see Colossians 2:15) while also, just before the crushing, the ancient serpent strikes poison into the heel. Jesus comes as the "second Adam" to pronounce judgment on the devil as Adam failed to do. The focus is on how, at every level, the devil's agenda was, and still is, to crush the union of marriage between man and woman in striking against, seeking to bruise, *Yahweh*.

Immediately thereafter, *Yahweh* pronounces the curses on the woman and man, and it is in the curse on the woman where we see the burden of a broken marriage:

> I will greatly increase your pains in pregnancy;
>> with pain you will give birth to sons.
> Your desire will be for your husband,
>> and he will govern you (3:16).

104

The word for "desire" is *shuq*, and can also be translated as "longing." and the verb for "govern" is *mashal*, the first verb given for "governing" in Genesis (1:16), where stewardship of the good creation is in order, and where the Garden is to be guarded from the intrusion of the ancient serpent. *shuq* and *mashal* are likewise used in Genesis 4:7, where *Yahweh* says to an angry Cain, "Sin is crouching at your door; it desires to have you, but you must govern it." But context determines usage in Hebrew. The language for Cain is that of a leopard ready to pounce, "desiring" and "longing" to devour Cain, just as the devil is profiled as a lion on the prowl (see 1 Peter 5:8).

But in Genesis 3:16, the contextual usage is very different ahead of 4:7, with opposite purpose. Adam and Eve, with the broken trust now sown into their souls, are nonetheless image-bearers of *Yahweh Elohim* looking forward to the coming Redeemer. They have yet to hear of their exile from the Garden, their souls are trembling in the face of the judgment, sensing they have polluted the good Garden, and will thus lose its blessings in some capacity. They have broken trust with *Yahweh*.

Thus, they naturally cling to each other, and too, use human reasoning to plot how they might now build a life together. So given their complementary but now broken strengths, and in balance of the right and left half sides of the brain, Eve desires and longs for unity with her husband, saying, as it were, "Just hold me tight, and we will be one." Her leading desire is relational. Adam responds, as it were, "Just do as I say and all will be well." His leading desire is task oriented.

They each think in terms of how they can resolve the fracture in a "power to take" mode, not in the power to give to the other first. The woman does not want to rule over the man, rather, she wants to be one with him. But she will do it her way. The man does not want to rule over her, he wants to protect her. But he will do it his way. However, neither will work, as the rest of biblical history painfully demonstrates.

Bigamy and Violence

With Adam's failure to cherish his wife and guard the Garden from the intrusion of the ancient serpent, the door is opened for inchoate then full-blown male chauvinism. Violence first erupts as Cain murders Abel in the first generation from Adam. Cain becomes a wanderer from his parents as a result, builds a city, and as the seventh generation reaches Lamech, marriage suffers another assault as violence is combined with bigamy:

> Lamech took two women, one named Adah and the other Zillah.
> Adah gave birth to Jabal; he was the father of those who dwell in tents
> and raise livestock. The name of his brother was Tubal; he was the
> father of all who play the harp and flute. Zillah also had a son, Tubal-
> Cain, who hammered tools out of copper, bronze and iron. Tubal-
> Cain's sister was Naamah.

> Lamech said to his women:

> "Adah and Zillah, listen to me;
>   wives of Lamech, weigh my speech.
> For I have killed a man for bruising me,
>   a youth for striking me.
> If Cain is avenged seven times,
>   then Lamech seventy-seven times" (4:19-24).

The biblical text is carefully written, all building on prior assumptions and storyline. Here we have the first example of bigamy, and the paving of the way toward full blown polygamy. It happens in the context of building civilization, but on a broken foundation. Thus, male chauvinism rears its ugly head, and women are treated as property. Along with the technicalities in grammar and syntax, all languages have their moods and tonalities, and to grasp them, it requires a depth of swimming within the given language and its cultural context.

Here, Lamech "takes" (the verb is *laqah*) two "women" (*nashim*) which can also be translated "wives," for in antiquity, when a man sleeps with a woman, they are considered married. We see Lamech leering over Adah and Zillah, as it were: "Listen up, you who belong to me." The ancient serpent shows self-righteous anger as he seeks destroys the marriage of Adam and Eve, Cain is downcast with anger and thus kills his brother, and here we can sense Lamech's tone rooted in the self-righteous anger of misogyny. Now the word choices, grammar and mood make this evident. But as well, this is seen as a continued repudiation of the order of creation. The man and woman are to be one in marriage. To "marry" two women simultaneously pollutes such unity, introduces conflict, and per force, treats women as property. It is literally the action of *laqah*, the power to take.

This violates women, and to protect his "estate," Lamech is willing to kill those who bruise him, regardless of age. Lamech will make sure anyone who kills or injures him will be avenged 77 times, making himself that much greater than *Yahweh* in his own pretense, as *Yahweh* promises to avenge Cain seven times in Genesis 4:15. Lamech also destroys the lives and properties of any and all associated with such a person, claiming divine prerogative for vengeance, and rooted in the chauvinism of bigamy and the murder of young men. He is his own god, choosing to yearn after the forbidden fruit.

The ancient serpent assaults marriage in the Garden, the second generation instigates murder, the seventh generation reifies women in further assault on marriage, and in the same breath, intensifies murder and revenge. The assumptions in the storyline are clear: immediate and huge consequence to sin. Namely, the destruction of the social order follows, that which was originally rooted in the mutual trust of one man and one woman married in mutual fidelity.

Contrasting Lineages

In the subsequent verses in Genesis 4, we read:

> Adam knew his wife again, and she gave birth to a son and named him Seth, saying, "because *Elohim* has given me another seed in place of Abel, because Cain killed him." And Seth himself had a son, and he named him Enosh. At that time men began to call on the name of

107

Yahweh (vv. 25-26).

In Eve's voice we can sense the pain and hope. The pain of losing the second son from her womb (the greater pain of the curse on childbirth made ten thousand times worse), and now the hope placed in another son in his stead.

Thus, from Cain to Lamech we see the outworking of sin, the unfaithful lineage governed by the ancient serpent. Then, with the birth of Seth we see the contrasting lineage, the faithful line that leads to the Messiah from the offspring of Eve. This is marked by the note that, with the arrival of Seth and Enosh, men begin (again) to call on the name of *Yahweh*. That is, moving from just a Gentile acknowledgement of the *Elohim* of creation, to the covenant-keeping Name of *Yahweh*.

These are the "unfaithful" and "faithful" lineages. Cain's line shows what happens when unfaithfulness to *Yahweh* governs the social order, where men set themselves up as their own gods, defining good and evil in their own self-aggrandizing terms. Seth's line, in contrast, is rooted in an acknowledgement of *nephesh* and thus his lineage calls on *Yahweh* in faith, trusting in his goodness. All that follows in the Hebrew Bible is rooted in this assumption of contrasting lineages, with the emphasis on that which leads to the Messiah.

Male and Female Affirmed in the Face of Social Disintegration

We earlier referenced Genesis 5:1-5. In vv. 3-5, we read:

> When Adam had lived 130 years, he had a son in his own likeness and image; and he named him Seth. After Seth was born, Adam lived 800 years and bore other sons and daughters. In all, Adam lived 930 years, and then he died.

Now that the Messianic lineage is introduced for the redemption of mankind, the very language of the order of creation is restated. It involves the centrality of male and female, and then most powerfully, the explicit passing

108

on of the image of *Yahweh Elohim* through Adam, even in spite of human sin. The broken remains of this image is the platform for *Yahweh*'s redemptive work. And redemption is thus hugely concerned with male and female in marriage. No matter how deeply sin has broken mankind, the love and redemptive power of *Yahweh Elohim* is deeper yet. From this point, the rest of Genesis 5 traces the faithful lineage all the way to Noah (nine generations from Adam) – in contrast to the seven generations through Cain to Lamech.

The Flood as Judgment on Polygamy in Genesis 6

Genesis 6:1-12 reads:

> When man began to multiply on the face of the earth, and daughters were born to them, the sons of the gods saw that the daughters of men were a good thing, and they took any woman they chose. So *Yahweh* said, "My Spirit will not be with mankind for a long duration, for he is flesh, and his days will be a hundred and twenty years."

> The Nephilim were on the earth in those days, and afterward, when the sons of the gods went to the daughters of men and bore children. They were the mighty men of antiquity, men of renowned name.

> *Yahweh* saw how great mankind's evil on the earth had become, and that all the thoughts of his mind and will were altogether evil all the day long. *Yahweh* was sorry that he had made the man in the earth, and his heart was pained. So *Yahweh* said, "I will blot out the man whom I have created, from the face of the ground – man and animal, and ground creatures, and creatures of the heavens – for I am sorry that I have made them." But Noah found favor in the eyes of *Yahweh*.

> These are the generations of Noah.

> Noah was a just man, of sound judgment among the people of his time, and Noah walked with *Elohim*. Noah had three sons: Shem, Ham and Japheth.

Now the earth was marred in face of *Elohim*, and the ground was full of violence. *Elohim* saw, behold, how corrupt the earth had become, for all flesh on earth had corrupted their ways.

The trajectory of Genesis 1-5 hits a painful apex here in the destruction of marriage and human civilization. The "sons of the gods" in v. 2 is an ancient near eastern term, here designating self-aggrandizing sons of human kings who claim to be gods (cf. Psalm 82). Adam and Seth are sons of *Elohim* literally (see Genesis 5:1-3; Luke 3:38), but submit to his power to give.

As human population becomes quite substantial, such "god-men" use their positions of top-down power to build harems – they "take" as many women as they choose, women who are "daughters of men," including women from the "non-royal" social order. In the Hebrew, a man having sex with a woman means literally "to marry" her. The union of man and woman, once consummated, forever changes the dynamics between them. If marriage is rooted in the mutual fidelity of one man and one woman for one lifetime, it is "very good." Breaking this life-giving boundary of freedom portends great evil.

So here, we see male chauvinism at a new threshold of polygamy – wholesale reification of women, property to be hoarded and walled off. The marriage of one man and one woman in mutual fidelity is mocked, and thus, women and their children suffer the most. *Yahweh* thus declares a one-hundred and twenty-year timeline until the judgment of the Flood, during which Noah preaches the coming judgment on mankind (cf. 2 Peter 2:5), but still, no one listens outside his immediate family.

The text then notes the Nephilim (proper Hebrew name for the "fallen ones"). They are the descendants of these harem building kings, with wealth, power and exploits, whose family line and reputations span the generations, and whose lineage survives the Flood through Noah's daughters-in-law. The earth is full of non-stop evil thoughts, and all forms of evil, corruption and violence – the exact lineage of Cain through Lamech. The building of harems is the epitome of it all.

With sin having become the cultural norm, *Yahweh Elohim* is determined to work with the most faithful, with the "remnant." This is his purpose for Seth's line, which leads to Noah, a just man with sound wisdom, so easily distinguishable in that day. Also, he is a) a true son of *Yahweh Elohim* who walks with his heavenly Father, b) clearly a leader, and c) maintains fidelity in his marriage.

The Canaanites and the Babylonian Genesis in Genesis 9-11

In Genesis 9, following the Flood, conflict emerges between Noah's sons as Ham (the father of Canaan) mocks his father Noah who lay in his tent naked after having become drunk. A curse lands on Canaan, and it is the Canaanites who later excel in sorcery (treating the sun, moon and stars as sexually promiscuous gods and goddesses, in a fatalistic dependency on them); followed by sacred prostitution and child sacrifice (pre-parallel to human abortion), all in a deeper affront to marriage and life.

In Genesis 10, the table of nations is detailed, where pagan nations trace their origins from Japheth and Ham. Those who come from Shem are the Semites, out of whom Abraham and the Hebrews come, the line of the Messiah. A new round of the unfaithful and faithful lineages emerges.

In Genesis 11, the Tower of Babel, an astrological ziggurat, is built at the center of a city in a human attempt to reach "the heavens," that is, for man to build civilization on his own terms, as self-appointed "gods," in the line of Cain and Lamech (now through the Nephilim), over and against *Yahweh*. The Babylonian genesis is rooted here, and its assumptions of sexually promiscuous, violent and murderous gods and goddesses. The history and subsequent metaphor of Babylon is a major theme across the Bible, and concludes as emblematic for all rebellion against God in Revelation 18, the great demonic prostitute. The assault on marriage continues relentlessly.

Excursus: Babylonian Genesis: Creation or Destruction?

The proactive of Genesis 1-2 is the Creator, *Yahweh Elohim*.

111

The reactive is originally expressed in what is known as the Babylonian Genesis (aka *Enuma Elish*), written about the tenth century B.C. (the time of King David), but in oral tradition goes back centuries before that. The opening chapters of Genesis trace in written form to Moses in the middle of the fifteenth century B.C. as part of the Pentateuch, but trace back in written and oral forms to Adam in the early fourth millennium B.C.

Now for some logic.

Can something be destroyed that is not first created? This is the dilemma of pagan religion. There are two ways to define the existence of the universe and human life – through creation or destruction.

On the one hand is creation in the biblical Genesis, in which the eternal *Yahweh Elohim* is good, creation is good and human life is good. On the other hand, the oldest and most influential of ancient pagan origin stories, the Babylonian Genesis, starts with destruction, with no concept of original or final goodness. It assumes, but does not explain, the existence of finite, petty, jealous and sexually promiscuous gods and goddesses who beat up on each other and beat up on us. It assumes that the heavens and earth are created by one god, but out of an act of destruction, and out of prior undefined eternal matter.

This is also known as "dualism" – the most ancient non-biblical concept. Creation and destruction are seen as the opposite sides of the same coin; and likewise with good and evil (contra Genesis 2:9-17). Accordingly, there is no original and greater goodness that will triumph over evil in the end.

But how can Babylonian religion and paganism make any sense? Does not the power to destroy require a prior power to create what is then destroyed? Unless the gods, goddesses and their undefined habitat are first created, where does it all begin? All pagan origin stories cannot resolve this dilemma, and thus they ratify the uniqueness of the biblical Genesis. Secular humanism and atheism, both philosophical and ethical cognates of the older pagan religions, cannot resolve this dilemma either. And neither can Islam, which is outside of the creation → sin → redemption motif.

Which satisfies the human soul – creation or destruction?

In the Babylonian Genesis, the power to take before being taken is assumed from the outset, and it precedes and defines all. It cannot compare with three key assumptions in the biblical order of creation:

1. *Yahweh Elohim* is the eternal and good Creator.
2. The creation is ordered and good.
3. Man and woman are the crown of *Yahweh Elohim*'s good creation and made free.

In contrast, three key assumptions of the Babylonian Genesis are these:

1. *Marduk* (the key chief Babylonian deity) is finite and destructive.
2. The creation is rootless, chaotic and evil.
3. Man and woman are a by-product intended for slavery.

The Babylonian Genesis starts with the assumption of a pantheon of time-bound, sexually promiscuous and pre-existent gods and goddesses, engaging in an intramural and internecine warfare. A second-level deity at the outset, *Marduk*, creates the universe by killing the chief goddess *Tiamat*, and dissecting her body – splitting it open like a mussel shell, making the heavens with one half of her carcass, and the earth with the other half. He then makes the defeated gods of *Tiamat's* army into slaves, but they complain about this status. In response, *Marduk* kills his chief remaining opponent, *Kingu*, severs his arteries, and from his blood *Marduk* creates mankind to serve as slaves to the defeated pantheonic remnant of *Tiamat* and *Kingu's* army.

Here we see the assumption of destruction. Mankind has to serve as slaves to the whims and caprice of defeated gods and goddesses, revealing a remarkably low view of man and woman. The Babylonians think they are bound by the positions of the sun, moon, planets and stars as gods (idolatry and astrology) in mundane and important decisions. They are bound to try and wrest favors from their fatalisms (sorcery). At the extreme in many related religions, they feel compelled to make human sacrifice to placate the gods – to gain fertility, good crops and peace, all in an attempt to survive in a hostile universe as they understand it.

But they also choose this worldview. Is our worth as human beings elevated or trashed by such a view? Do we take joy in a myth that the heavens and earth are made out of the dissected and bleeding carcass of a slaughtered goddess, and that we are made out of the blood of another dead god to be slaves to the defeated gods? Slaves to slaves? This is Babylon's height.

Babylonian religion starts with the assumption of destruction, then interjects a hope (of carving out survival) that is destined to disappoint, and it concludes with destruction remaining in its dualistic continuity. In other words, the reversal of Genesis 1-3:

> destruction → disappointing hope → return to destruction, versus
> creation → sin → redemption.

But again, by definition, how can destruction precede creation? Destruction can only destroy what is already created. The Babylonian "genesis" is a reversal of reality.

Now, for a remarkable observation per our subject matter. In this myth, as *Marduk* dissects *Tiamat's* body, the text reads:

> The lord rested, examining her dead body,
> To divide the abortion (and) to create ingenious things (therewith).
> He split her open like a mussel (?) into two parts;
> Half of her he set in place and formed the sky (therewith) as a
>   roof...
> (Tablet IV, lines 135-138, translation of Alexander Heidel).

The word "abortion," an act of intrinsic destruction, is used here to describe *Tiamat's* corpse. Her born life is aborted. Abortion is viewed as parallel to the corpse of one killed by an act of aggression, and as a means to create the universe. This is the Babylonian genesis versus Genesis in the Hebrew Bible.

114

In other words, pagan religion in its archetypical form, in opposition to *Yahweh* and *Yahweh* incarnate, Jesus, and seen from Genesis to Revelation, believes that destruction creates creation. And a chosen metaphor to illustrate this is that of deicide as abortion. This is to believe that abortion = creation. Just like the idolatry of making abortion into a modern "sacrament," a "blessing," something intrinsically good. No, it is intrinsically pagan with no biblical truck.

Or to put it another way, the debate over human abortion pits *Yahweh* versus *Marduk*, Jesus versus *Satan*, the kingdom of the heavens versus the sucking hole of the abyss, and the new Jerusalem against Babylon the harlot city doomed to destruction.

All cultures eventually trace back to Genesis, to Adam's lineage at the first, then through Noah's lineage. As peoples migrate away from Eden, then away from earliest Mesopotamia – into an unpopulated, wild and wonderful world – and likewise later following Noah's flood, they gradually mix mythologies in with dimming recollections of *Yahweh Elohim*'s revelation to Adam about creation.

Their oral traditions and written texts reflect a confusion of creation with destruction, despite their best hopes, since it is the only experience by which they can judge. And in a sinful world, with no faithful record of the order of creation at hand, destruction takes over – the power to take before being taken. Only in such a context and its influence can human abortion be rationalized. Thus, for reality and hope, we root ourselves in the opening good assumptions of Genesis 1-2.

Abraham's Concubine in Genesis 16

Excursus over, we pick back up in Genesis 12, where Abram (later called Abraham) is called by *Yahweh* as just about the one remaining non-idolater. He is promised a son through whom all nations will be blessed en route to the coming Messiah. But in Genesis 16, his wife Sarai (later called Sarah) gets impatient as their ages advance, and gives her maidservant Hagar to Abram to become his concubine, or second "wife" (literally again, "woman"). This

115

is worse than straight bigamy, for Hagar has no marital or inheritance rights in view. Sarai is using her as a slave, and Abram foolishly agrees. This is a human attempt to fulfill *Yahweh*'s promise, and though Abram's character far exceeds that of Cain and Lamech and Babel, he agrees with Sarai in an attempt to build civilization on sinful terms.

Thus Hagar's womb is treated as Sarai's property, with Hagar as a disposable concubine who will not be allowed to rear her own son. Hagar realizes this when she becomes pregnant and thus despises Sarai. A war between the women ensues. When the angel of *Yahweh* comforts Hagar as she flees Sarai's mistreatment, he says of her unborn son Ishmael:

> He will be a wild donkey of a man;
>> his hand will be against all
>> and everyone's hand against him,
>> and in the face of his brothers he will dwell (16:12).

This is the quintessential profile of a fatherless boy. (And an aborted child is quintessentially fatherless [cf. Isaiah 1:17, representative of a consistent biblical concern]). Sarai opposes Hagar when she returns after the angel speaks to her, and does not want Hagar's son in her life, or in Abram's life. So she clearly opposes the present and loving fatherhood Abram is eager to give. Isaac is born thirteen years later to Sarah, this time not by human manipulation and surrogacy, but by the intervention of the Holy Spirit. However, when Ishmael mocks the boy Isaac, he is driven away by Sarah. The war between the women becomes a war between the sons, and thus a war between the nations that come from both sons.

As the Arab peoples are descendants of Ishmael, and as Muhammad traces his lineage to Ishmael 2400 years later, and as we see the conflict of Islam versus the Jewish and Christian peoples to this day, we see it all rooted in the breaking of the marriage covenant.

Sodom and Gomorrah's Nadir of Depravity in Genesis 19

The reputation of the evil of Sodom and Gomorrah is well known in its day (thus, a return to that which causes the Flood, a return to Cain's lineage). Abraham is apprised by *Yahweh* of its coming judgment, is able to intercede on their behalf, but in the end also sees their great evil. Sodom and Gomorrah is summed up across the whole biblical witness, from Genesis to Revelation, as sexual anarchy leading to social anarchy and the trampling of the poor and needy.

The sins of Sodom and Gomorrah are anteceded in Genesis 13:13, "Now the men of Sodom were evil and great sinners against *Yahweh*," and 18:20 speaks of the "outcry" against the city, a deeply pained anguish seeking help.

This sexual anarchy, this being the most damning assault on marriage, is at play. In Genesis 19:1-5, two angels of *Yahweh*, appearing as men, come to Lot's house (nephew of Abraham) to evacuate him and his family from the coming destruction. Lot, sitting at the city gates, thus being an elder of sorts, invites them to lodge with him for the night:

"No," they said, "we will lodge in the city square."

But he pushed so forcefully that they came into his house. He made a feast for them, baking unleavened bread, and they ate. Before they laid down, men from the city of Sodom surrounded the house, young and old with all their relatives, near and distant. They called to Lot, "Where are the men who came to you tonight? Bring them out to us so that we can know them" (vv. 2b-5)

The Hebrew verb *yadha*, "to know," in some thirty out of about 830 usages in the Hebrew, refers to "sexual knowledge" (as in Genesis 4:1, 25). (vv. 2b-5). Lot knows how dangerous it is in the public square at night, but too, he is a compromised man who loves the city and its "culture" (despite knowing better, cf. 2 Peter 2:7). His thus foolishly seeks to avert the evil of a gang rape by at least hundreds, likely thousands of pansexual men. He offers, wickedly himself, to barter his two virgin (and engaged!) daughters to the

Sodomites instead. His wife is so at home in the culture, that she then proves not to want to leave, and his sons-in-law think he is joking about the coming judgment, being unfazed by the attempted gang pansexual rape.

This same attempted pansexual gang rape of men is found, rooted in a lawless culture (Judges 19 at Gibeah), with evil results visited on innocent people, in an explosion of social and violent anarchy.

"Pansexuality" is a term that describes sexual relations with "any and all" possible partners, human or otherwise. Homosexuality is a subcategory, and here in Sodom it is not "homosexuals qua homosexuals" that seek the gang rape, but bisexuals or pansexuals who do so.

The reason why Sodom (and Gomorrah) becomes such a leading metaphor for wickedness, from Genesis to Revelation, is seen here. From the ancient serpent to Cain to Lamech to the "sons of the gods" to Babel and now Sodom, the assault on marriage and the cognates of violence and murder are the result. Thus, the assumptions of creation → sin → redemption in Genesis 1-3, and the assumption of the goodness of the marriage of one man and one woman for one lifetime as the basis for a healthy social order, is seen to be continually under assault. After Genesis 19, across the whole biblical text, this reality is profiled a thousand different ways.

In the midst of it all, *Yahweh* calls Israel to be faithful to him alone, as her husband (cf. Isaiah 54:5; Jeremiah 3:20), and not prostitute themselves to pagan deities. And the church is the bride of Jesus, called to be pure in her fidelity to him (Revelation 21:2, 9). This divine metaphor of marital fidelity points to something much deeper than sex itself. Namely, unbroken trust as present in the triune God leads to the gift of unbroken trust in the marriage of Adam and Eve, and thus, as the basis for a healthy social order.

Assumptions Compared

We have noted the proactive biblical assumptions in Genesis 1-2 about male and female as equals and complements in marriage, and as the source for trust and a healthy social order. Then we have noted how in Genesis 3, 4,

118

5, 6, 9-11, 16 and 19 it is a relentless downgrade. This sets up all that follows in the Bible, and child sacrifice and human abortion are cognates.

In my quote from Christine Overall earlier, I sought to identify core assumptions in the larger pagan and secular feminist construct that ratify it as a reaction to male chauvinism. Thus, as we grasp the good biblical assumptions, and the diagnosis of male chauvinism in its assault on marriage, is there any finer basis from which to answer such a human cry?

Human Abortion

Human sexuality in Genesis 1-2 is remarkable, profiled in great depth, and utterly unique in all history – the given equality and complementary of man and woman in marriage. In the outflow of broken trust in Genesis 3, and the agenda of the ancient serpent to divorce decision making between the man and woman, human abortion exacerbates broken trust as it divorces child from the father and mother alike, increasing the further brokenness of the marriage covenant, and thus more deeply yet assaults the social order. As Adam is called to "guard" (*shamar*) the Garden from Satan's intrusion, so too is he called to guard Eve's integrity in her natural guarding of the womb. As male passivity morphs into raging male chauvinism, the very engine for sorcery, sacred prostitution and child sacrifice in antiquity, it sets the foundation for the modern abortion ethos and industry.

Eighth: Science and the Scientific Method

Beginning with the assumption in Genesis 1:1, "In the beginning *Elohim* created the heavens and the earth," all else follows in human history and reality. Certainly so with scientific inquiry.

The debate over the days of creation rages within the church and in the face of the scientific community. As I write about elsewhere, the best exegetical grasp of Genesis 1 and the days of creation is that they are a literary and parallelistic framework to give eternal purpose to our literal weeks – the teleology of the Sabbath and eternal life. There is no chronological timetable per se (but certainly an order), nor are the days used in the Hebrew structure as 24-hour periods. Just as the metaphor of the human body describes the church in 1 Corinthians 12:12ff, so the literary device of the days of the week teaches us about the nature being created in the image of God, and how to order our literal weeks.

Genesis 1 is also structured where the universe is ordered from the most remote to the most immediate, from the lowest forms of life to the highest, then with man and woman set to govern it all in stewardship of *Elohim*'s goodness. Every form of life reproduces after its own kind, man and woman are made after *Elohim*'s own kind, and there is no place for macroevolution. All of which merits the closet scientific inquiry and tough questions.

But where does science and the scientific method originate? "Observed reality" is what the discipline of "science" is all about. The Latin term *scientia* simply means knowledge. In every dimension, the Bible profiles knowledge and reality, things as they are, and all is rooted in the deeper reality of *Yahweh Elohim*'s nature and human nature in his image. As well, these eleven major assumptions from Only Genesis equal the basis for "the liberal arts and sciences." All the disciplines are intertwined, where for example, music is completely mathematical in its structure and ability for giving aesthetic pleasures as manipulated sound waves massage somatic reality, able to produce great joy.

Celestial Objects

We read in Genesis 1:14-19:

> And *Elohim* said, "Let there be light in the expanse of the heavens to separate the day from the night, to be signs for seasons and days and years. And let them be luminaries in the heavens to give light above the earth. And it was so. *Elohim* made two great luminaries – the greater luminary to govern the day and the smaller luminary to govern the night, and he also made the stars. *Elohim* set them in the expanse of the heavens to give light on the earth, to govern the day and night, and to separate the light from the darkness. And *Elohim* saw that it was good. And there evening and there was morning – the fourth day.

120

Rooted in the assumption of sound and light in Genesis 1:3, we see an example in Genesis 1:14-19. There, *Elohim* makes the sun, moon and stars to mark out seasons and give light to the earth. And too, sound and light are scientifically the most basic properties in the universe.

Moses knows the Israelites are coming out of 400 years in a pagan nation. Thus, and as led by the Spirit, he knows well their need to be completely separate from the pagan deities they and their forefathers had encountered back to Abraham's father and prior. Separate from lurking Egyptian, Canaanite and Babylonian mythologies.

These paganisms assume the sun, moon and stars are gods and goddesses, with the astrological calendars and fatalisms that follow. In Egypt, the sun and moon are capricious deities, and given how the languages of proximate nations are cognates of proto-Semitic languages, Moses knows that the Israelites need to be freed from such idolatry.

Thus, Moses does not use the words for the "sun" or "moon" or any specifically identified star that carries with it a pagan identity. Rather he is descriptive in speaking of the greater and smaller luminaries, and in making such a simple physical observation, along with the generic stars in describing them for what they are, Moses is being scientific before modern "science" has such an identity. Moses defines the sun, moon and stars as inanimate material objects, not as animated deities as in pagan religion. Reality. Science is the ability to look at things as they are. Biblical revelation shows things for what they are.

In fact, honest science traces to the biblical worldview, all because creation is a gift of *Yahweh Elohim*, and not animate forces to be worshiped. There is no basis for science in pagan religion. At a simple level, it is the difference between astronomy and astrology.

Stewardship of the Good Earth

In view of environmental sciences, we can make another observation. In Genesis 1:26-28, when the man and woman are made, they are called to

121

"rule" (*radah* in the sense of human vis-à-vis the non-human) the created order. And in Genesis 2:15, Adam is commissioned to work and guard the garden. The Garden of Eden includes a vast area, but too, this is the starting point for Adam and Eve caring for the whole earth and its ecosphere that sustains their lives. They are stewards. No possible toxic pollutions are in view that only intrude with sin.

Since the Bible defines the human body, the planet and ecosphere as good, such environment stewardship, and its work including necessary scientific study, is also good. It is a general truth that nations and states rooted in biblical ethics take care of the environment; those rooted in paganism do not.

Yet, there is a caveat. Within environmental science today, and as it grows increasingly secular and pagan, human beings become increasingly enslaved to the worship of the creation instead of worshiping the Creator. Thus, for example, much money and political energy is spent on theories concerning climate change as a (largely) future concern based mostly on computer models that cannot predict warming or cooling, and their respective seasons, across the decades and centuries. Yet at the same time, the priority for addressing dirty water and air, in second and third world countries, is thus mitigated, even though large numbers of people die daily.

Human Abortion

The womb is the first ecosphere we all enter, with the amniotic sac of protection. We should not puncture or pollute it. Likewise, we have all graduated to the corporate ecosphere of the planet's womb, protected by the atmosphere, and we should likewise neither puncture nor pollute it. Both wombs are given for the protection and nourishment of human life, and we are to guard the Garden outward to the whole planet.

The Principle of Falsification

In the Law of Moses, we find the ethical basis for the scientific method based on "the principle of falsification." In scientific research and discovery, if a theory is proposed to explain something, standards for testing that theory are set in place where all the variables are controlled as tightly as possible. If a theory has to do with the amount of electromagnetic energy in a certain substance, then a test is devised to measure that energy. For the theory to be "proven" true, it must produce the same results under the same conditions every time. If one measurement is evidenced 1,000 times in a row, then that measurement can be said to have a scientific basis, of a theory established.

But also, a theory "proven" is always open to being disproven. If the measurement is consistent 10,000 times, then different a subsequent time, the theory is disproved, falsified, if all the variables are certifiably the same. A new theory is proposed to take into consideration this variation, and a process pursued until no variations occur again.

At the ethical level, I have confidence equal to any measurement of scientific fact, that the storyline and doctrines of creation → sin → redemption, and their assumptions, interpret all Scripture and life accurately. I have confidence likewise in the God → life → choice → sex paradigm, the eleven positive assumptions of Only Genesis, and the six pillars of biblical power. In fact, the power to love hard questions undergirds all honest science and all academic studies.

Do I expect evidence ever to be presented facts that would alter these relentlessly tested convictions? Do I ever expect that $1 + 1 = 2$ will be disproved mathematically? No on both counts. But too, the more secure I am in both questions, the freer I am to entertain skeptical perspectives that might seek to dislodge these convictions.

We see the principle of falsification in Deuteronomy 18:9-22 as Moses defines opposition to the demonic non-science of sorcery and witchcraft (intertwined ethically with child sacrifice). Namely, if a "prophet" speaks a word in the name of *Yahweh*, and it fails to come to pass, he is falsified, and liable to the death penalty.

Thus, the standard for a true prophet in the Law of Moses is 100 percent accuracy, a 1.000 batting average. This is the most severe scrutiny possible, paving the way uniquely for the same ethical standard for honest science.

Has any other religion or nation ever subjected is prophets or counselors or wise men or sorcerers to such a high standard?

Theocratic Israel is a community of choice, and those who wish to disobey *Yahweh*'s laws, or to believe in other gods, are free to go to other nations where such is acceptable. But to remain in theocratic Israel and to prophesy falsely is an act of treason, aims to upend the goodness of *Yahweh*'s laws, the well-being and survival of the nation, and the lineage of the Messiah.

Jesus and the "If" Clause

In the Deuteronomy 18 text, *Yahweh* says he will raise up a prophet, like Moses, one who will speak the truth to them. This Prophet is the measure of the truth and ethics necessary for the principle of falsification. This is a Messianic prophecy that refers to Jesus as the ultimate Prophet, as Peter explicitly teaches in Acts 3:19-23. Jesus is the standard. In John's gospel, we see Jesus submitting himself to the principle of falsification as he challenges his religious elitist enemies in John 8:42-47. He uses the "if" clause ("If I am telling you the truth …"), which Moses uses often as well, in questioning whether his enemies are truly serving God as their Father, on the one hand, and whether he is telling the truth, on the other. Later, in John 10:36-37, he reiterates the challenge of his own trustworthiness. The principle of falsification is the measure Jesus chooses to use.

1 + 1 = 2

Returning to a prior allusion concerning mathematical certainty, we can note how we all make assumptions, from the macro to the micro, and they affect our lives profoundly. The question is to what extent these assumptions are true or false. And, how well do we test our assumptions?

Kurt Gödel is the most eminent mathematician in the twentieth century, colleague of Albert Einstein. In mathematics, Gödel (in his *Incompleteness Theorems*) demonstrates that within its closed system it cannot be proven that $1 + 1 = 2$ (e.g., decimally). It must first be assumed (from outside and prior to the system), and then all mathematics works beautifully.

Namely, unless this simplicity is first assumed, then mathematical equations, by definition, are not possible. When the assumption of $1 + 1 = 2$ is in place, physics, engineering, architecture, music, art and other cognate sciences become possible. Mathematics is thus objective and utterly consistent in all means of human measurement.

In the expanding cosmos, the existence and properties of gravity have to be assumed, and accordingly all astrophysics work beautifully. In cultural anthropology, unwritten assumptions are the key to the core of the given (and usually ancient and extinct) social order.

And the greatest governing assumption is Genesis 1:1, including its unique provision for science and the scientific method.

Human Abortion

The science of conception and the biological humanity of the unborn is clear. It is abortion advocates who seek to mute or discard any scientific knowledge incongruent with their politics, and for whom the idea of testing competing ideas, per the scientific method, is foreign.

Ninth: Verifiable History

Genesis 1 is the theological grand design, and in Genesis 2:4-7 we have segue to the specificity of Genesis 2:8-14. This is just prior to the gift of human freedom:

> Now *Yahweh Elohim* had planted a garden in the east, in Eden; and there he put the man he had formed. And *Yahweh Elohim* made all kinds of trees grow out of the ground – trees that were desirable in appearance and good for food. The tree of life was in the middle of the garden, along with the tree of the knowledge of good and evil.
>
> A river coming out of Eden watered the garden; from there it was separated into four headwaters. The name of the one is the Pishon; it winds through the entire land of Havilah, where there is gold. The gold

of that land is good; bdellium and onyx are there. And the name of the second river is the Gihon; it winds through the entire land of Cush. The name of the third river is the Tigris; it runs along the east of the Asshur. And the fourth river is the Euphrates.

The assumption in place is verifiable eye-witness history. The Bible is unique in this regard.

In Contrast to Pagan Stories

Regardless of pagan origin understandings we can grasp in various texts – the Babylonian *Enuma elish*, the Egyptian story of *Isis* and *Osirus*, Greek and Roman mythologies, the Vedas, the Mayan *Popul Vuh*, Celtic or Native American stories, or any number of others – we can note one similarity. They each begin with a mythological past that has no historical verifiability, nor do they have concern to rely on such an origin in historical terms. They merge the mythological past, at some point, with dim recollections of a historical one, each in their own way, until they come into more recent history and some verifiability grows in strength.

Islam, beginning in 622 A.D., is a different matter, since it says it affirms Jewish and Christian history. But this is only selective, and through its own prism. The Qur'an does not quote the Bible at all, but cites many of its stories, recasting them all according to Islamic purpose, thus vitiating biblical history. It deviates consistently from the verifiable historical witness of the Bible. The ancient and authoritative biography of Muhammad by Ibn Ishaq attempts to be very historical, but is not considered apart of sacred scripture. And too, unlike the certainty of the Bible's historical statements, Ibn Ishaq often states that the verifiability of certain stories is uncertain.

In Contrast to "Higher Criticism"

With the advent of "higher criticism" (the Graf-Wellhausen hypothesis) in the mid-nineteenth century, beginning in Germany, particular aim is taken against the historicity of Genesis 1-3. There are many means by which this is sought, and central to this thinking is the hypothesis that Hebrew

126

monotheism evolved from a background of pagan polytheisms. Accordingly, the ethos of pagan mythology is then applied to an understanding of the origins of Genesis. There is much academic territory here, where I see no sustainable warrant for the hypothesis, but for here, let's pose a simple question: Where, in human history has unity ever emerged from the disunity of competing diversities?

Historical Details

Moses writes Genesis for his Hebrew audience during the exodus, ca. 1446 B.C. ff. He has, as his source, the written and oral traditions tracing back to Adam, a common possession of the covenant community. As Moses writes, he gives the exact location of the Garden of Eden, where Adam is presented the choice between the tree of life and the tree of the knowledge of good and evil. Nothing in the text allows these trees to be seen as allegorical, or the story to be seen as a myth. They are actual trees in a known location, at a certain time when Adam and Eve eat real fruit from them.

Some 2300 years later Moses verifies such a historical claim for his readers. He names the four headwaters that come out of the river that begins in Eden. The Flood has not marred their identities. This is to say that Moses is speaking about references that are common knowledge to his readers. His assumption of its historical reality is seen in the ease by which he expects his readers to immediately know what he is talking about.

The geographical scenario is that the Pishon and the Gihon are streams that feed the well-known Tigris and Euphrates. The Hebrew word for the Pishon likely means "gusher," and for the Gihon, the word likely means "spurter." This could describe streams fed by springs or an underground river, beginning in the mountains of Eden, and feeding the Tigris and the Euphrates.

The Garden of Eden, thus described biblically, traces to the current borders of Iran, Iraq and Turkey. A fertile plain surrounded by large mountains fits the description of the Garden, writ large, as its Hebrew word, *gan*, means "walled garden." From this "garden" region, the Tigris and Euphrates originate, separate and re-converge before arriving in the Persian Gulf.

So too, the Araxes and Uizhun rivers originate here, and flow from there into the Caspian Sea. The Araxes is likened to the Gihon in its winding and twisting characteristics through the land of Cush. And the Uizhun is like the Pishon, where in the land of Havilah, it weaves its way through ancient gold mines and areas of lapis lazuli. To this day it is called the "Golden River," and local people maintain that their area traces to the Garden of Eden. To the east of this region, where two salt lakes, Urmia and Van, are located, is an area called Noqdi, perhaps the original land of Nod to which Adam and Eve depart when exiled from Eden by *Yahweh*. As well, north of this area is a place called the "Kusheh Dagh," or the Mountain of Kush. Sounds like the Cush the eldest son of Ham (Genesis 10:6).

Regardless of our present understanding, from the vantage-point of Moses, it is an assumed and known reality to a people familiar with the geography and its names. There is far more cultural continuity between Adam and Moses, in the ancient near east, than between Moses and the modern world. Moses tells his readers that the Pishon winds through the land of Havilah, and he even takes a parenthetical aside to describe Havilah's reputation for good gold, bdellium and onyx. He also tells his readers that the Gihon winds through Kush, a local name at the time that could have preceded its later use as a description of Egypt. Thus, we have an ancient historical witness by which to compare our perspectives and research today.

In the assumptions of Moses based on the historical nature of *Yahweh*'s revelation to Adam and Eve, he knows how important it is to give his readers geographical and historical markers known to them, so they can locate the reality of the Garden of Eden in space and time.

In fact, the entire Bible is constantly including even minor details as its stories unfold. The God of the biblical authors is the God of history. As one of a thousand examples of this detailed orientation to history, we can consider a verse proximate to what we already looked at when Hagar flees

Sarai. Genesis 16:14 identifies the well named by Hagar, called Beer Lahai Roi.

Some four hundred years later, Moses inserts a marker for his readers to know exactly where the well is, where God meets Hagar's need – it still remains between Kadesh and Bered – known territory to his readers. This is why Jerusalem and Israel are so important today. So many historical markers are still known despite the ravages of war, erosion and exile which the land has seen over the millennia. Pagan cultures also have their historical markers, but they cannot trace them back to the mythological origins. Their cultures are only traceable to remaining undimmed elements of their known history as a people.

Historicity of the Genealogies

The Messianic lineage is comprehensive from Adam to Jesus, from the first Adam to the second Adam. Where else in all human history can anything compare with such a testimony to verifiable eye-witness history?

As Jesus comes to fulfill the Law of Moses, he does so being rooted in the assumption of the historical verifiability of the *Tanakh* (a translated acronym for the Law [*torah*], the Prophets [*nava'im*] and the Writings [*ketuvim*]). He repeatedly cites the Law, the Prophets and the Writings, and at a critical juncture, assumes and cites the historicity of Adam and Eve (see Matthew 19:2-6), coming also as the second Adam.

This reliance on the same, for example, is central to both Luke, in his gospel and the Book of Acts, and of John in his gospel and first letter.

Luke states:

> Inasmuch as many have endeavored to compile an account of the things that have been accomplished among us, just as they were handed over to us by those who from the first were witnesses and servants of the word, I have followed closely from above and carefully, and written a successive account for you, excellent Theophilus, in order that you

may know the certainty of what you have been taught orally (1:1-4).

And then, in the Book of Acts:

> In the former book I made, O Theophilus, concerning all that Jesus began to do and to teach until the day he was taken up, after giving commands through the Holy Spirit to the apostles he had chosen, he presented himself to them after his suffering, giving many proofs that he was alive, and appeared to them for forty days and spoke about the kingdom of God (1:1-3).

Luke, both a physician and historian, and rooted in the biblical assumption of verifiable history, does his careful fact-checking work within the covenant community that requires it. He thus gives to Theophilus a historically accurate account of the life, death, resurrection and ascension of Jesus, and of the early church, so that Theophilus might have historical certainty concerning what he has been taught.

The apostle John makes the same reliance on verifiable history with reference to Jesus, as seen in his gospel (20:30-31 and 21:25). He knows that he can only give a brief profile of his witness – the world could be filled beyond the brim with books giving testimony to the details of what Jesus said and did.

Then in his first letter, John is combating the rise of early Gnosticism and its ahistorical and dualistic presuppositions that sought to deny that Jesus came in a physical body. He counters with verifiable eye and touch-witness history:

> That which was from the beginning, which we have heard, which we have seen with our eyes, which we have beheld, and our hands have touched – we proclaim concerning the Word of life. And the life was made manifest; we have seen it and bear witness to it, and we announce eternal life, which was with the Father and has been made manifest to us. What we have seen and heard we announce to you, so that you also may have fellowship with us, and our fellowship is with the Father and

with his Son, Jesus Christ. We write this in order to make our joy full (1:1-4).

The Book of Esther

Among adherents to "higher criticism," the Book of Esther comes under particular scrutiny. The critique is that it does not mention *Yahweh Elohim* once, and only makes one subtle reference to his activity in 4:14-15 (though some might not even grant this). Thus, they view it as a "secular" book, being only concerned with "history."

So, the concern with verifiable history is affirmed, even by skeptics, as the book details how a Jewess is enabled to become queen in pagan Persia during the post-exilic era (ca. 460 B.C.), and from that position to intercede for and save the Jews from a plot to wipe them out. And since Esther is written in pagan Persia, the author is likely content to simply write down the historical facts that could simultaneously be entered into the royal court records, with his Jewish readers readily grasping the larger picture.

Also, there is extraordinary theology in place concerning Haman as a descendent of the Amalekites (see Chapter Nine vis-à-vis spiritual warfare), who seeks to destroy the Messianic lineage just after they flee Egypt. Which is to say: there is a unity between theological and historical purpose in the Bible, and not a divorce as "higher criticism" is wont to assume. And in modern secular thought, why is it concerned with historical verifiability to begin with, apart from prior biblical influences?

History Matters

The Bible, in an assumption from the beginning, submits itself to the most stringent requirements for verifiable eye-witness history, as it does in terms of science and the scientific method. Integrity, of truth-telling, in all matters.

Human Abortion

To what extent do abortion advocates submit themselves to the true history of abortion, its effects on women and culture, its historical alignment with child sacrifice and repudiation by the early church?

Tenth: Covenantal Law

In the biblical series of covenantal law, *Yahweh* enters into mutual promises with us, in first giving freedom in the Garden, then in protecting it in the face of sin as we look forward to the coming Redeemer. There are six major covenants in the Bible – the Adamic, Noahic, Abrahamic, Mosaic, Davidic, and Messianic.

In the order of creation, *Yahweh* makes the original covenant of freedom with Adam. When, following the reversal, and as Noah becomes the sole remaining remnant of the faithful lineage, the next covenant is given. Sin rushes in again, later leaving Abram as the sole remaining remnant of the faithful lineage, and he is given a covenant. When his line is enslaved in Egypt, *Yahweh* raises Moses up and he is given a covenant for the nation of Israel. His successor Joshua ratifies it, and sees its effective implementation so long as he is alive. Later, after the days of Samuel, this covenant is rejected by Israel in favor of a pagan kingship, and *Yahweh* raises David up afterward, and gives him a covenant. And finally, this covenant is broken, the nation and city are destroyed, and the prophecy of the New Covenant of the Messiah is given.

Specific Nature of Covenant

The word for "covenant" is the Hebrew term *b'rith*. It involves the elements of establishing a legal relationship "between" parties, ritualized in a sacrificial meal where the food offering is "cut up" for that purpose. A crucial part involves each party, referring to the cut animal parts, giving a self-maledictory oath: "May this happen to me if I ever break this covenant." Thus, to "make a covenant" is translated by the idiom, "to cut a covenant." In ancient near eastern societies, the closest allegiance known between two parties is that which involves blood relationships, and next to that is the loyalty derived from the oaths involved in "cutting a covenant."

And uniquely, in biblical covenants, the first covenant in Genesis 2, before the advent of human sin, needs no cutting, no self-maledictory oaths. In all biblical covenants, *Yahweh Elohim* first holds himself accountable to the promises he makes to his image-bearers. Pagan kings (and deities) do not do so. In other words, the difference between the power to give and it will be given, versus take before you are taken.

In law, which do we have? Fidelity from the ruler for the well-being of all people equally, or totalitarian imposition and favoritism used to curry enough favor among the elites to stay in power? Jewish political theologian, Daniel J. Elazar, does yeoman work in linking Hebrew covenant with federalism (from the Latin *foedus* for covenant). And as the foundation for the United States Constitution.

Human Abortion

Does the killing of the unborn find source in covenant and constitutional law, or in the forsaking and evisceration of both? In the next chapter, as we look at the 1973 *Roe* v. *Wade* decision legalizing human abortion, this will become clear.

Eleventh: Unalienable Rights

In our review of biblical theology, we can note again a reprise of the God → life → choice → sex paradigm. It is located in Genesis 1-2, describing the four all-defining subjects of the universe. Every issue we confront finds its basis in how these four subjects are defined and how they relate to each other, and also fully defines the abortion debate.

These subjects equal the content of Genesis 1-2:

> *Yahweh Elohim* is sovereign, and his purpose in creation is to give
> the gift of life, especially human life – to man and woman as made in

133

his image to rule over his handiwork. Then comes the gift of moral and aesthetic choice that serves the prior gift of human life. Finally, in the order of creation, is the gift of sex within marriage: here is the power to pass on the gifts of life, choice and sex through procreation to our offspring, to celebrate the height of what it means to be made in *Yahweh Elohim*'s image.

Or to put it another way, true sexuality is an expression of godly choice that serves the gift of human life that comes from *Yahweh Elohim*.

And too, we find a remarkable parallel in the 1776 Declaration of Independence, where based on the antecedents of John Locke, John Adams and Thomas Jefferson, we encounter the language of "life, liberty and property/pursuit of happiness." We read:

> WE hold these truths to be self-evident, that all Men are created equal, that they are endowed by their Creator with certain unalienable Rights, that among these are Life, Liberty, and the Pursuit of Happiness – That to secure these Rights, Governments are instituted among Men, deriving there just Powers from the Consent of the Governed …

These rights, these gifts of life, liberty and property/pursuit of happiness, are necessary assumptions for a healthy social order, rooted in the Creator under the rubric of "unalienable rights." (Note: "the pursuit of happiness" is Jefferson's philosophic clause in the declaration, made possible by property rights, as the Fifth and Fourteenth Amendments legally codify it.) The language of unalienable rights is of course a double negative – that which cannot be alienated or taken away. It is articulated in the face of broken trust, but rooted in that which precedes such brokenness, the positive reality of Genesis 1-2.

The parallels stand out:

God = the Creator.
Life = Life.
Choice = Liberty.

Sex = Property/Pursuit of Happiness.

The first three parallels are obvious. But the fourth? A closer look at the language is helpful.

In Genesis 2:24, a man leaves his parent's household to join with his wife and form a new household. The Hebrew term for household or family is *bayith*, and in the Greek of the Septuagint, it is translated *oikos*. The rule of the household *is oikonomos*, as noted earlier, from whence we derive the English word "economics."

Across the history of human civilizations, when a man is faithful to his wife and the raising of their children, the strongest possible economic unit follows. And the biblical assumption of fidelity in marriage and parenthood is the only foundation for the economic activity in creating, producing, selling, buying and trading property or goods.

Adam and Eve are created to be stewards of the good earth. This defines the nature and purpose of owning property, namely, for that which strengthens the family and social order. Thus, the idea of happiness is rooted in social health, not in a self-centered individualism.

The parallel with the subject matters of Genesis 1-2 is complete, but at a deeper level, what we witness here is the power of assumptions in the Declaration itself. Namely, these realities are viewed as "self-evident" to the signatories, the majority of whom were orthodox Protestants, along with the one Roman Catholic and the various heterodox in their midst. Self-evident as rooted in the Creator.

Despite the heterodoxies, the Declaration is written by a deeply covenantal people who are ethically orthodox, loath to break with England, but are finally pushed into it as King George III breaks covenant after covenant with the Colonies. Thus, since he is head of the church as well as head of the state, they have to go over his head – to the commonly acknowledged Creator. Back to the opening assumptions in Genesis.

There is no other source for unalienable rights, certainly not among pagan religions, not in secular constructs, and not in the Enlightenment where an ahistorical and amorphously distant deity is not, as such, concerned with human affairs.

The one true Creator gives the rights to life, liberty and property, and in the second category, religious, political and economic liberty. They are not defined by human government, cannot be given or taken away, only honored as an inviolable assumption.

Unalienable rights are protected in the Fifth and Fourteenth Amendments to the U.S. Constitution, where no person shall be deprived of "life, liberty, or property, without due process of law." Namely, people are fully free in their personal matters, so long as they do not violate the lives, liberties and properties of others.

Thus, there is a continuum between biblically legitimate and illegitimate governments – those which honor unalienable rights from the Creator on the one hand, and as ratified by the consent of the governed; and those who do not, those that are ultimately totalitarian.

Human Abortion

Human abortion assaults the unalienable rights of life, liberty and property of the unborn, and is grounded in ever metastasizing lawlessness. This we will also see in the next chapter.

The Six Pillars of Biblical Power

The six pillars of biblical power, as well as their cognate six pillars of honest politics, are each addressed in depth elsewhere, as are the eleven positive assumptions in Genesis 1-2. The six pillars equal biblical ethics (how we treat each other) that flow out of the eleven positives which equal biblical theology (what we believe).

For our purposes in these pages, in Biblical Theology 101, it is honed in its proper address concerning human abortion. And thus it is easy to then note the first four pillars therein. The remaining two pillars are addressed by Jesus in the Sermon on the Mount, where he redeems the broken four pillars.

The Power to Love Enemies

In Matthew 5:44, Jesus says: "Love those who hate you, and pray for those who persecute you." He then speaks of how the sun rises on the "evil and the good" alike. This is a dynamic appeal to the image of God in Genesis 1-2, prior to the history of sin as seen in 3-19. In that process, *Yahweh Elohim* shows great patience prior to the Flood (120 years of warning), prior to Sodom and Gomorrah (the power of Abraham's invitation to intercede, even after years of pending judgment), and later, prior to the Exodus (400 years in which the Canaanites refuse to repent). The whole book of Revelation ratchets up to pending judgment, with great patience given, but finally, we all own our own informed choices – the heavens or the abyss.

This is all *Yahweh Elohim*'s love for his enemies – the power of informed choice. His covenant community of Israel is called on to live it even as surrounded by the opposite. In Exodus 22:21, *Yahweh* tells them not to oppress the sojourner, for they were once sojourners in Egypt. The Sabbath rest, invitation to join the Passover meal (beginning in Egypt) and all measures of justice equally apply to sojourners in the midst of Israel (e.g., Exodus 12:49; Leviticus 24:22), but there is no such reciprocal reality in the pagan nations (and in contrast, see how Elisha treats the enemies of Israel in 2 Kings 6:21-23). In Romans 5:6-11, Paul encapsulates the love for enemies found in Jesus. And to reiterate, all of this is congruent with the power of informed choice, thus, in advancing the same, we love those who may be living as enemies of the Gospel.

In these pages, I seek to note in the course of various lived anecdotes, the power of loving those who consider themselves our enemies. Such love is a necessary engine that undergirds faithful pro-life advocacy, and as rooted in the prior pillars.

The Power to Forgive

And likewise in terms of forgiving those who hate and plot against us. The bookends of the Bible, in the storyline of creation, sin and redemption, are the powers to give and forgive. Or to sum up all the Bible this way:

Yahweh Elohim gives, we blow it, and he forgives.

If we are willing to receive it. In the prophecy of the new covenant in Jeremiah 31:31-34 the capstone is *Yahweh*'s forgiveness of our evil, where he "remembers (*zakar*) our sins no more" (note also in the prior v. 30, re: reaping what we sow pace the power of informed choice). In the Sermon on the Mount, the Lord's prayer concludes with the need to forgive as we are forgiven, otherwise there is none for us remaining (Matthew 6:12; 14-15). Again, this is the power of informed choice in action. Jesus, in dying on the cross, utters: "Father, forgive them ..." (Luke 23:24).

As I note elsewhere in these pages, in interacting with Kate Michelman, president of the National Abortion Rights Action League (NARAL), and Patricia Ireland, president of the National Organization for Women (NOW), the need for knowing the forgiveness in the name of Jesus irresistibly percolates. And indeed, as the Crisis Pregnancy Centers know so well, this is what women need for themselves, and toward the chauvinists who have abused them. We are forgiven by Jesus as we forgive others, we all need it, and only a forgiven people can change the language of the abortion debate.

Human Abortion

The very nature of political pro-abortion advocates is the preponderance of hatred toward those who disagree with them, e.g., the rhetoric of "anti-choice," out of their own deep pains, then chosen rebellions.

The very nature of the abortion industry mocks the need for forgiveness, whether in dealing with the trauma of male chauvinism or that of human abortion itself. The Crisis Pregnancy Center ministries are rooted in the ministry of forgiveness, in helping women – and men – work through post-abortion trauma. This is a reality fiercely opposed by pro-abortion advocates, and they do much work trying to slander and shut down such ministries.

In Sum

In this review of Biblical Theology 101, we see how human abortion is quintessentially unbiblical in nature – at every turn, in grand themes, minor themes, necessary nuance and in the smallest details. No person who supports human abortion, save when the mother's life is in genuine jeopardy, can claim a whit of biblical support. The question is thus how to bring biblical literacy into the church, and too, grasping and implementing a biblical strategy for winning the full legal protection for women and their unborn equally.

◆ ◆ ◆

Chapter Four

Biblical Critique of *Roe* v. *Wade*

With a Biblical Theology 101 in place, let's review the 1973 *Roe* v. *Wade* U.S. Supreme Court decision that overturned all fifty States and imposed legalized human abortion, virtually on demand.

The Declaration of Independence defines "life" as the first unalienable right, but do the unborn qualify legally as well as biologically?

In *Roe* the Court seeks to distinguish between biological and legal humanity or personhood. The 7-2 majority opinion makes an appeal to the Fourteenth Amendment, Section 1, of the Constitution, which reads:

> All persons born or naturalized in the United States, and subject to the jurisdiction thereof, are citizens of the United States and of the State wherein they reside. No State shall make or enforce any law which shall abridge the privileges or immunities of citizens of the United States, nor shall any State deprive any person of life, liberty, or property, without due process of law; nor deny to any person within its jurisdiction the equal protection of the laws.

The first section of the Fourteenth Amendment is in concert with the Thirteenth and Fifteenth Amendments. These three Amendments are enacted following the Civil War as the Constitutional means to redress the evil of slavery, ratified respectively in 1865, 1868 and 1870. First, slavery is abolished; second, legal personhood is granted to the former slaves with the accompanying unalienable rights, referring to the Declaration of Independence; and third, the specific right to vote is given to the former slaves. The *Roe* Court argues:

> The appellee and certain amici argue that the fetus is a "person" within the language and meaning of the Fourteenth Amendment. In support of this, they outline at length and in detail the well known facts of fetal development. If this suggestion of personhood is established,

the appellant's case, of course, collapses for the fetus' right to life is then guaranteed specifically by the Amendment. The appellant conceded as much on reargument. On the other hand, the appellee conceded on reargument that no case could be cited that holds that a fetus is a person within the meaning of the Fourteenth Amendment ...

The Constitution does not define "person" in so many words ...

The background for this logic is the language of "born or naturalized," where the *Roe* Court insinuates that such language excludes the unborn. But in truth, this language is a positive definition to include Black Americans without singling out their race – all persons have unalienable rights, period. The difficulty for the appellee (those defending the Texas laws which protected the unborn) is that the Constitution never addresses the subject of the unborn (nor does it explicitly mention marriage – but it everywhere assumes the marriage of one man and one woman as the bedrock for civil society, and part of this includes the well-being of unborn children).

This proves a huge lacuna missed by Texas, in the legal argument for the unborn, allowing such a silence to be controverted by *Roe* into a pretense to dismiss their legal personhood, and remarkably, such pretense remained unchallenged. The Court has to concede the "well known facts of fetal development," but then it separates out its relevance. The Court also has to concede that the Constitution does not define "person" in so many words, which is to say that it has no basis to say it does not include the unborn. But the ulterior non-legal agenda is in place – a true act of eisegesis.

[**Biblical critique**: *Roe* opposes the fifth assumption in Genesis 1-2, and thus the second pillar, the power of informed choice, where true definition of terms is prerequisite. This presupposition governs all of *Roe*, for indeed, *Roe* is truly "anti-choice."]

The history of U.S. Constitutional Law traces through English Common Law back to the Bible.

[**Biblical critique**: *Roe* opposes the fourth positive assumption in Genesis 1-2, human nature created in the image of God. We have already seen the complete biblical affirmation of the image of God for the unborn, their personhood as defined by *nephesh*, and therefore the basis for legal protection. As well, *Roe* necessarily opposes the eleventh positive assumption in Genesis 1-2, unalienable rights. *Roe* is truly "anti-life," a presupposition governing the entire decision.]

In English Common Law, the concept of personhood and its legal protection begins with the moment of "quickening," viz., when the mother first feels movement of the child within her. And thus, some abortion-rights supporters say this is the point when legal personhood begins, and certainly no sooner.

However, this ignores the reason why quickening is chosen. In the medieval period, with no diagnostic ability to prove that conception has taken place, and prior to the knowledge of the sperm and egg as haploid cells becoming a diploid cell, quickening is the first legally verifiable sign they can rely on to certify that there is a pregnancy (the woman herself knows much earlier). Today, we can verify it very shortly after conception, and with the knowledge that conception is the exact moment when individual and discrete biological human life begins. We are grateful today for so many advances in scientific and medical diagnostics, but pro-abortion ideologues choose to ignore the science of conception.

[**Biblical critique**: *Roe* opposes the eighth positive assumption in Genesis 1-2 – honest science and the scientific method – a presupposition governing its entire decision.]

We can ratify this interpretation, in that English Common Law does protect humans from the point of conception onward, with a retrospective diagnosis in the context of inheritance laws. Namely, if a man dies, and it is later discovered (i.e., by means of the onset of quickening) that his wife is pregnant by him before he died, then his son or daughter is given full inheritance rights according to the laws of the time. These laws do not come in force until birth, but this is not due to a view that personhood does not begin until birth. Rather, it is a view that birth is the time when a child can be determined to be male or female, named, baptized (as was the consistent custom then) and thus registered as a specific individual in the sight of the family, church and state. There are many stillbirths in those days, and infant mortality is high as well. But according to their ability to measure the existence of individual biological humanity, legal personhood is affirmed.

As well, as we have noted earlier, the *Roe* opinion ignores an established consensus on the humanity of the unborn child which exists at the time of the Fourteenth Amendment. This Chief Justice William Rehnquist itemizes:

> To reach its result the Court necessarily has had to find within the scope of the Fourteenth Amendment a right that was apparently completely unknown to the drafters of the Amendment. As early as 1821, the first state law dealing directly with abortion was enacted by the Connecticut Legislature. Conn. Stat. Tit. 20, §§ 14, 16 (1821). By the time of the Fourteenth [410 U.S. 175] Amendment in 1868, there were at least 36 laws enacted by state or territorial legislatures limiting abortion. While many States have amended or updated [410 U.S. 176] their laws, 21 of the laws on the books in 1868 remain in effect today. Indeed, the Texas statute struck down today was, as the majority notes, first enacted in 1857 [410 U.S.177] and "has remained substantially unchanged to the present time." *Ante* at 119, 35 L. Ed.2d at 158.

> There apparently was no question concerning the validity of this provision or of any other statutes when the Fourteenth Amendment was adopted. The only conclusion is that the drafters did not intend to have the Fourteenth Amendment withdraw from the States the power to legislate with respect to this matter [410 U.S. at 174-177].

Justice Rehnquist is pointing out that the *Roe* majority is bastardizing the Fourteenth Amendment, making it apply in 1973 to something it never applied to in 1868. The *Roe* Court wants to discover a rationalization to deny the legal personhood of the unborn, and they are as creative as possible, ignoring historical context. In 1967, every state and territory in the United States has laws on the books which severely or substantially restricted human abortion, and like the early church, they assume the humanity of the unborn as the premise for their legal concerns.

[**Biblical critique**: The *Roe* Court opposes the ninth positive assumption in Genesis 1-2, verifiable history, as it begins to establish its own deliberate pattern of selective, atomistic and myopic historicism.]

In making mention of the early church, we can note that it is a natural conclusion for them to be unified in opposition to the practice of human abortion in the Greco-Roman culture, rooted in biblical assumptions. The church is likewise united in opposition to infanticide, the practice of infant exposure, as they rescued as many of these abandoned children as possible.

In the early church writings that oppose abortion, the consistent appeal is for the sake of the humanity of the unborn, consistent with the order of creation. This witness is maintained with integrity even by some church fathers who were de facto misogynist in their writings, due to gnostic influences, where on the one hand they served, but on the other hand they forsook the order of creation.

The earliest post-biblical documents of the church are the Epistle of Barnabas and the Didache, both of which say an explicit no to human abortion. The Didache divides itself into two parts. The first deals with the "two ways" (one to life and one to death) as a catechism to young converts, and the second with church organization. In the first part it says "no" to the practice of human abortion, which at that time is usually attempted by drugs meant to expel the fetus. The success rate of these drugs is poor, and many women die in the process. The word used for such an abortifacient drug in the Didache comes from the Greek term *pharmakeia*, from which we get the English word "pharmaceutical." Its primary meaning refers to "sorcery" and "magic arts" in its six New Testament uses.

The idea of drugs interfacing with sorcery is the common assumption in many pagan societies, where the witch doctor or sorcerer is also the medicine man. The mystery Greek cults go into drug induced trances in their orgies, de facto inviting a demonic presence – the opposite of self-control, a fruit of the

Holy Spirit (Galatians 5:23). Thus, the word for abortifacient drugs is *pharmakeia* in the pagan Greek culture, which the Didache then prohibits. In the Bible's opposition to the triad of sorcery, sacred prostitution and child sacrifice, anything related to *pharmakeia* is opposed – and human abortion is in the middle of this context.

Early church fathers such as Clement of Alexandria and Tertullian explicitly oppose human abortion, and Athenagoras, in his opposition to human abortion, describe the fetus as a "living being," which in the Greek is equivalent to the Hebrew *nephesh hayyah* from Genesis 2:7 (as already noted, the biblical definition of human personhood). Once again, this affirms the order of creation, that the nature of *nephesh* and the image of God belong to the unborn.

The witness of the church continues in explicit statements for the humanity of the unborn and against human abortion by such well known leaders as Martin Luther, John Calvin, John Donne, Karl Barth and Dietrich Bonhoeffer – as well as in denominational structures such as the Presbyterian convention of 1869. The witness of the church before the mid-twentieth century is virtually uninterrupted in its affirmation of the humanity of the unborn and thus in its opposition to human abortion. It has only changed in the more recently, among those who have simultaneously forfeited belief in the biblical foundation of the order of creation, and hence we again see the conflict of *God* → *life* → *choice* → *sex* versus *sex* → *choice* → *life* →/*God*.

Between 1967 and 1973 several states compromise their positions as the organized pro-abortion movement works state-by-state to secure their aims. They run into growing resistance, even in New York state, where they have early success. New York City becomes the abortion capital of the world, then later the legislature overturns the recently liberalized abortion law, but Governor Nelson Rockefeller keeps abortion legal with a veto. Thus, the pro-abortion ideologues concoct a strategy to have the U.S. Supreme Court overturn all state laws restricting human abortion.

The Fourteenth Amendment is also bastardized by the *Roe* Court in that its original purpose is to grant legal personhood to a class of people who have been denied it – Black Americans in particular. *Roe* is thus a classic legal example of the reversal. As the agitation grows for the abolition of slavery, the 1857 U.S. Supreme Court in its *Dred Scott* decision claims that the American Negro is not a legal person under federal law, and therefore not entitled to unalienable rights. The Fourteenth Amendment reverses this reversal along with the Thirteenth and Fifteenth.

But the *Roe* Court takes an Amendment that gives legal personhood to a class of people (the blacks) who have been denied it, and then applies it non-historically so as to deny legal personhood to a class of people (the unborn) for whom every state at one time had recognized. This is the height of dishonest lawmaking (by the Court, which is not constituted to make new law, but to interpret existing law – thus increasing the scandal).

The dishonesty is compounded by the drafting of the "born or naturalized" phrase against the unborn. In other words, this phrase in its context has nothing to do with saying no to the unborn, or even to the "pre-naturalized." In the context of the existing state laws and English Common Law, it is understood that rights are conferred when an individual is born and named, but in the positive sense where there is no dehumanization of the unborn.

(Here the word "unborn" is specific in its usage in contrast with the word "pre-born" which many pro-lifers employ today. "Pre-born" is not a description; it is a hopeful prophecy, and one that is, tragically, not always fulfilled. If an unborn child dies in utero, then he or she is never pre-born, because birth is never reached. "Unborn" is descriptively accurate because it describes a full humanity at any stage regardless of actual destiny. Thus I find "unborn" a more accurate, and a more powerful term than "pre-born.")

This implicit distinction is in place in the language of the Fourteenth Amendment. Namely, no "pre" language is in place, because it is not needed, since citizenship is assumed for the sake of all those who are actually born. All those who are "born" are once "pre-born," and existent in that state, and all who are "naturalized" are assumed to have once been "pre-naturalized," and existent in that state. The description of an "unborn" or "unnaturalized" status has no purpose in this context. Because it is the American Negro in

146

focus here, and not the unborn, the power of assumption is natural in the language. The *Roe* Court prostitutes this language in service to the Destroyer.

Also, the *Roe* Court ignores another overwhelming reality. Namely, though Connecticut leads the way in protecting the unborn in 1821, most of the other 35 states and territories write their pro-life laws in the 1840s on forward, with other states doing so after 1868. Specifically, the very state legislatures that ratify the Fourteenth Amendment are composed of various of the same people who write the original anti-abortion laws in their respective states, or people who know and agree with the pro-life drafters. Thus, at every turn, we see how the *Roe* Court's denial of legal personhood to the unborn based on the Fourteenth Amendment is a reversal of historical and legal reality. It is also ironic that my native Connecticut, being the first state to give legal protection to the unborn, also leads the way in the 1965 U.S. Supreme Court *Griswold v. Connecticut* decision on birth-control that then opens the way for legalized human abortion based on a cognate logic in *Roe*, and has to this day the toughest pro-abortion laws of virtually any state.

In 1847, in this historical period preceding the Fourteenth Amendment, the American Medical Association (AMA) is founded, and it takes a strong stand against human abortion. In 1857, Dr. Horatio R. Storer of Boston is appointed head of the AMA's Committee on Criminal Abortion, and in 1859 the fertilization of an ovum by a spermatazoon is first observed in a petri dish. That same year, the Committee makes the following recommendations:

> Resolved, That while physicians have long been united in condemning the act of producing abortion, at every period of gestation, except as necessary for preserving the life of either mother or child, it as become the duty of this Association, in view of the prevalence and increasing frequency of this crime, publicly to enter an earnest and solemn protest against such unwarrantable destruction of human life ...

> Resolved, That the Association request the zealous co-operation of the various State Medical Societies in pressing this subject upon the legislatures of their respective states ..." (*The Human Life Review*, Vol. XIII, Winter 1982, pp. 95-96).

Thus we see again how the era of the Fourteenth Amendment, in medical science and in the contemporaneous legal construction of the States, is arguing for the protection of unborn human life. In fact, the focus of the States is on defining "human life" as protected by law, prior to any legal definitions of "personhood." *Roe* reverses this reality, imposing a false definition of personhood over and against discrete human life.

In 1959, exactly 100 years later, the AMA reverses its position, and states that "conception" is not such a precise term after all, but they give no new scientific data to dispute the certainty they had in 1859 that conception (parallel to the more technical "fertilization") is the moment when a discrete biological human life begins. The AMA reverses themselves in 1959 because of a growing lobby, within their midst and society at large, to legalize human abortion. It is a manufactured pretension of ignorance (an antecedent to *Roe* fifteen years later), opposite to an honest definition of terms requisite for informed choice. As 1859 precedes 1868 where both the unborn and the American Negro are affirmed in their legal personhood, so 1959 precedes 1965 and 1973 in a reversal where the unborn lose their legal protection. The *Roe* Court prostitutes the reality of 1868 in service to the destructive agenda of 1973.

The *Roe* Court tacitly recognizes that if legal personhood for the unborn can be reconciled with the Fourteenth Amendment, then there is no legal basis for human abortion. We have seen how it is reconciled, and how perverted the abortion-rights argument is in its misuse of this Amendment. So whereas we can win this argument legally with constitutionally honest people, the cultural elitists will resist a level playing field for this debate as much as possible. A more radical and grass-roots strategy is needed to undergird this argument.

Theological, Philosophical and Political Nature of *Roe* v. *Wade*

The nature of the 1973 *Roe v. Wade* decision that overturns state laws prohibiting human abortion is rooted in deeply philosophical and religious assumptions. Not the law.

148

[**Biblical critique**: Indeed, *Roe* opposes the tenth positive assumption in Genesis 1-2 – that of covenantal law – for its pagan and secular ethics put constitutional law (read *b'rith* and *foedus*) aside.

In *Roe* and its companion decision, *Doe v. Bolton*, for literary purposes, I always subsume *Doe* under *Roe* in my references, apart from otherwise needed specificity. In *Roe*, the U.S. Supreme Court discovers a "penumbra" of the Constitution that equals a broad "right to privacy," as rooted in the 1965 *Griswold v. Connecticut* ruling regarding birth control. Then they declare there is a "right to privacy" broad enough to encompass a woman's "fundamental right" to an abortion. (A question, however, that abortion-rights partisans cannot answer is this: Can you show any philosophical or historical linkage between unalienable rights and the putative "fundamental right to abortion?").

Roe establishes an artificial three-trimester paradigm for legalized abortion, making some theoretical restrictions during the third such; but *Doe* gives a "health" of the mother exception for the third trimester, a huge loophole that virtually assures "abortion on demand," that which Chief Justice Warren Burger said would not be the case, only to deeply rue his opinion some years later.

The "logic" *Roe* follows is a classic example of the reversal – theologically and politically. There are eight major points to analyze.

1. The Pretension of Objectivity

First, *Roe* begins by citing the "emotional nature of the abortion controversy" that involves people's philosophy, experiences, their "exposure to the raw edges of human experience," their religious training and attitude toward "life and family."

[**Biblical critique**: From this point forward, with the reference to religious training, the Court is laden with pagan and secular assumptions about God's nature, contrary to the first positive assumption in Genesis 1-2 where God is good and, per the first pillar, his power is the power to give.]

149

Then it throws in issues of "population growth, pollution, poverty and racial overtones [which] tend to complicate." But *Roe* never addresses these issues (other than a secondary reference to poverty in the *Doe* ruling), and never prescribes their successful redress and/or how liberalized abortion laws would contribute to such a redress. Having diagnosed this territory, it then pretends to be objective and rise above its pedestrian folly:

> Our task, of course, is to resolve the issue by constitutional measurement, free of emotion and predilection (410 U.S. 113 at 116)."

What we discover instead is that a) there is no honest constitutional measurement employed in *Roe*, and b) the Court's ruling is based entirely on its predilections in favor of human abortion. It is an elitist posture seen often in the mainstream media's reporting ethics – whether on television news, radio news or in newspapers. Namely, there is a facade presented that the "news" is being reported by "objective" reporters, when indeed, so often there is bias in what "news" is covered, and how it is "slanted" to serve a certain predilection.

Honesty in the media would be far better served if the reporters were up front about their biases or worldviews, thus giving to the viewers, listeners and readers, the power of informed choice to consider such factors. (The internet is freer from the pretense to objectivity, as much as it can also be crazy.) To pretend to be objective rejects the power to live in the light. So too *Roe*.

[**Biblical critique**: Thus, contrary to the second positive assumption in Genesis 1-2 defining honest communication, and the second pillar rooted there, the power to live in the light, the *Roe* Court proceeds and does not turn back.]

2. False Definition of Terms

Second, *Roe* sets the stage for a false definition of terms (which equals misinformed choice), when it draws in the language of the "penumbras" of the Bill of Rights. *The Random House Dictionary of the English Language*,

Second Edition (1987), Unabridged, introduces the definition of the word penumbra:

1. *Astron.* a. the partial or imperfect shadow outside the complete shadow of an opaque body, as a planet, where the light from the source of illumination is only partly cut off. Cf. *umbra* (def. 3a). b. the grayish marginal portion of a sunspot. Cf. *umbra* (def. 3b). 2. a shadow, indefinite, or marginal area.

The most classic example of a penumbra is what forms in a total eclipse of the sun by the moon. Thus, the Court bases its ruling on what it declares to be a "fundamental right," on "indefinite, imperfect or marginal shadows." This shows the deep weakness of its position. It is ethically occultic – it is a ruling from the darkness masquerading as the light.

[**Biblical critique**: *Roe* rejects the second positive assumption in Genesis 1-2 concerning God's heavenly court and the light of *Yahweh Elohim*'s presence, instead siding with *ha'satan*, the accuser's dark abysmal court].

By fabricating a definition from the undefined shadows, it then imports such a definition into the core of the light of the Bill of Rights, and pretends it is there all along. Placing into the text what was not there, and then pretending it was there all along, is the classic definition of eisegesis. Theology is still the queen of the sciences.

3. Anti-Christian Bias Employed as a Pretense to Dismiss Scientific Fact

Third, *Roe* had to get rid of a time-honored definition of medical science which opposes human abortion as the destruction of human life. This it does hand in glove with a bias against biblical faith. Abortion is shown to be acceptable in ancient pagan cultures, specifically in the Greco-Roman period, and we have already noted the witness of the early church on forward. This the *Roe* Court does not address, but they do have a large obstacle in advancing their argument – the Hippocratic Oath, adopted in pre-Christian Greek culture, which becomes the most widely respected ethical guide for physicians in western history. Part of the oath includes a pledge never to give a woman any drugs to produce an abortion. Up until the mid-twentieth century, medical school graduates would recite the Hippocratic Oath upon graduation. Now, however, wherever, if at all it is still recited, the portion that renounces abortion is overwhelmingly removed.

To cast aside the Oath, the Court adopted the "theory" of a notorious abortionist:

> Dr. Edelstein then concludes that the Oath originated in a group representing only a small section of Greek opinion and that it certainly was not accepted by all ancient physicians. He points out that medical writings down to Galen (A.D. 130-200) "give evidence of the violation of almost every one of its injunctions." But with the end of antiquity a decided change took place. Resistance against suicide and against abortion became common. The Oath came to be popular. The emerging teachings of Christianity were in agreement with the Pythagorean ethic.
>
> The Oath "became the nucleus of all medical ethics" and "was applauded as the embodiment of truth." Thus, suggests Dr. Edelstein, it is "a Pythagorean manifesto and not the expression of an absolute standard of medical conduct."
>
> This, it seems to us, is a satisfactory and acceptable explanation of the Hippocratic Oath's apparent rigidity. It enables us to understand, in historical context, a long-accepted and revered statement of medical ethics (410 U.S. 113 at 132).

Roe is a 7-2 majority decision, written by Justice Harry Blackmun, and it selectively chooses sources to suit its biases. Dr. Edelstein's bias is publicly known to be as strong as it gets in favor of legalized abortion, and therefore he is purposed in his agenda to dismiss the Hippocratic Oath. The Oath is of course a minority opinion among the Greeks to start with, as "abortion-rights" is a minority opinion in the AMA until the time of *Roe*. And just because ethics are violated does not mean they are to be thrown aside. Do we get rid of certain laws for human rights, for example, just as the majority of

German culture either acquiesced, or were terrorized into silence, thus allowing Hitler to kill six million Jews? Edelstein's argument is in favor of returning to a period where the rule of law is not honored, which is an intrinsic element of human abortion to begin with.

Thus, based on the diagnosis of a searched out and discovered "minority opinion," *Roe* agrees with Edelstein and then shows its anti-Christian bigotry by stating that it is the Christian embrace of the "Pythagorean ethic" of the Hippocratic school that essentially fuels its social embrace. As *Roe* constructs its report of Edelstein's argument, it then ratifies the dismissal of the Oath as a "manifesto" of a minority upon the majority – which it is not. In other words, as it were, "an intolerant Christianity upon secular society."

To say this is to say that the Greco-Roman culture's gradual openness to Christianity until the early fourth century A.D. is not based on their informed choice, but is dictated from above. (The early church is a martyr church, advancing the Gospel only through suffering and informed choice, but sadly, with the advent of Constantine, Theodosius and Justinian, and to the deepest chagrin of biblical faith, the pollution of the church happens, thus providing the basis for many to oppose Christianity, as now exemplified in the *Roe* Court, in a conflation of many theological and historical cross-currents).

Roe begins as a minority opinion in a biblically tutored culture, and as per any revolutionary changes, gradually then gains acceptance until a turning point is reached. Also, the truth is that the Christian opposition to human abortion is a quintessentially Hebrew position of honoring *nephesh* in the order of creation, now understood through the Messiah, and is not conforming itself to the Hippocratic Oath. Rather, the Oath happens to coincide with Hebrew assumptions, and thus it gains currency as the Gospel is lived, preached and received within the Greco-Roman culture.

Roe thus eisegetes and does not exegete the "historical context." By implicitly assigning the Hippocratic Oath's "apparent rigidity" to its convergence with the Gospel, it becomes for the Court "a satisfactory and acceptable explanation" sufficient for the moment to dispense with "a long revered statement of medical ethics." (But too, the Court cannot be too

153

explicit in its anti-Christian bigotry and get away it, thus it virtually ignores church history, and syntactically cloaks its bias with the Pythagorean ethic – but historians know that it is the Gospel that provides for the enduring success of the Oath.) At every turn, *Roe* operates within this "penumbra" of shadowy edges. *Roe* is not looking for the core truth, but for whatever is passable, as served by willing biases within elitist culture. *Roe* operates in the darkness, and mocks the power to live in the light.

4. The Dismissal of the American Medical Association's Historical Consensus

Fourth, *Roe* has to dismiss the position of the American Medical Association (AMA) in its opposition to abortion beginning with its 1859 report. A Committee on Criminal Abortion is formed in 1857 under the leadership of Boston physician, Dr. Horatio R. Storer, and in 1859 it makes the recommendations we have quoted above. Of central importance are two concerns, a) the definition that "human life" is present "at every period of gestation," and b) the only exception for abortion is to save the life of the mother.

The language here makes clear that the humanity of the unborn is the focus of concern. In James Mohr's book, *Abortion in America* (1978), and appealed to often by abortion-rights advocates, he argues that the reason the AMA opposes abortion, is for the ulterior purpose of establishing the hegemony of its guild against "unlicensed" medical practitioners. And he says that part of this involves an attempt to put abortionists out of business, especially women abortionists. No doubt the AMA sought to do so, but this was not why human abortion is opposed – it is opposed first because of its intrinsic destruction of human life.

In addition, the *Roe* Court argues that the AMA's position is not truly in regard to the well-being of the unborn child, but is out of concern for the woman – since human abortion is so dangerous to women at the time. Here is another eisegetical example – for the AMA's language is clear in its concern for the unborn as fully human. Certainly the concern is equally for the mother and her unborn, and this is why the exception clause for her life is included. But there is no setting of the mother over and against her unborn child as does *Roe*, or vice versa as abortion proponents accuse the pro-life advocates of supporting. The Court does not quote the above section of the AMA's 1859 decision as I have – they choose another section, separated thus from the full context of the AMA's decision, and thus atomistically serving their bias against the unborn.

And in the medical practices of the time, a child's life could be threatened by a continued pregnancy, and in such situations today we have excellent neo-natal care units to follow a Caesarean section, making this concern a non-issue in the developed world. The concern for the mother's life then becomes a matter of when the child is too young for early delivery, and even so, this is the exception.

5. The Dehumanizing of the Unborn

Fifth, the *Roe* Court has to dismiss the AMA's concern for the humanity of the unborn (which the AMA maintained at least until 1967), and to dismiss any "theory" that human life begins at conception. Thus, *Roe* tendentiously embraces Edelstein's "theory" of the Hippocratic Oath with its anti-Christian bigotry, and must now dispense with biological fact, by labeling it instead as a dispensable "theory." *Roe* argues:

> The third reason is the State's interest – some phrase it in terms of duty – in protecting prenatal life. Some of the argument for this justification rests in the theory that a new human life is present from the moment of conception. The State's interest and general obligation to protect life then extends, it is argued, to prenatal life. Only when the life of the pregnant mother herself is at stake, balanced against the life she carries within her, should the interest of the embryo or fetus not prevail.

> Logically, of course, a legitimate state interest in this area need not stand or fall on acceptance of the belief that life begins at conception or at some other point prior to live birth. In assessing the State's interest, recognition may be given less rigid claim that as long as at least

155

potential life is involved, the State may assert interests beyond the protection of pregnant women alone (410 U.S. 113 at 150).

Near the conclusion of the *Roe* decision, it is explicit in the purpose for this language:

> In view of all this, we do not agree that by adopting one theory of life, Texas may override the rights of the pregnant woman that are at stake (e.g., for an abortion) [ibid. 162].

In other words, *Roe* injects a "logic" that has no logic. It dismisses any concern for biological reality to impact the discussion of human life, reducing the question to one of many competing "theories" (read: classic syncretistic dualism in opposition to true definition of terms). It speaks of the biology of conception as a "belief," in a pejorative sense, as though biological fact is religiously impositional and therefore invalid in the public domain. In truth though, *Roe*'s actual "belief" is opposed to scientific fact, and cloaked in legal hubris which mocks accurate definition of terms, and therefore, mocks the power of informed choice. This reasoning serves the reversal.

Then the Court further dehumanizes the unborn by calling for a "less rigid" interpretation of terms (read: amorphous, lacking definition), and thus, an invention of the term "*potential*" life – so central in *Roe*'s thinking that it is placed in italics. How for example, can embryonic human life be "potential" and not "actual"? Potential for what? It is not potentially human, but it is actually human in its essence and existence. And the unborn human has no potential to be other than human. The only potential is for the choices such a "little person" (the meaning of the Latin term *foetus*) will make, and if his or her life is protected to the point where these choices can be made.

6. The Invention of the "Right to Privacy"

Sixth, now that the humanity of the unborn is denigrated based on a manufacture of religious bias, a war is concocted between mother and child, and the woman is made to hold a superior position of "rights" (the power to

156

take and destroy in the reversal of the power to give). Then *Roe* sets about to invent the "right of privacy" that allows a woman to abort the "potential life" of her unborn child, with a logic that starts with a confession:

> The Constitution does not explicitly mention any right of privacy (ibid. at 152).

Then *Roe* makes an eisegetical case that takes specific "zones of privacy" which the Constitution does mention, and extends them to a general "right of privacy" that nowhere exists in the Constitution, and applies it to what it ends up calling a "fundamental" right to abortion.

Whereas the Constitution, in the Bill of Rights (the Fourth and Fifth Amendments), speaks of specific privacy rights – the right not to be forced to quarter soldiers in your home, and the right against search and seizure without a warrant – there is no broad "right to privacy" spelled out. Not to mention a "fundamental right" to destroy unborn human life. There is an assumed right, parallel to a concept of privacy, that the unalienable rights of life, liberty and property cannot be deprived apart from due process of law – of which the rights against quartering soldiers and unwarranted search and seizure are specific examples. This properly assumed right is turned on its head by *Roe* into an unassumed and fictitious "right."

The *Roe* Court invents a broader "right to privacy" out of whole cloth for the sake of securing the "right" to human abortion. This can only be done by denying the humanity of the unborn, and therefore their right to privacy (e.g., the right to the sanctuary of the womb, against the search and seizure of their unborn human lives, would be the only consistent logic here). This is to say that the assumed "privacy rights" of the inviolability of a person's life, liberty and property – for the woman to secure an abortion – comes at the price of destroying the "privacy rights" of the unborn to life, liberty and property. The unborn can thus be searched out and their lives seized, given a virtual *carte blanche* given by the Court.

So, with no broad "right of privacy" located in the Constitution, the Court's "logic" then makes another blind but calculated leap:

157

This right to privacy, whether it be founded in the Fourteenth Amendment's concept of personal liberty and restrictions upon state action, as we feel it is, or as the District Court determined, in the Ninth Amendment's reservation of rights to the people, is broad enough to encompass a woman's decision whether or not to terminate her pregnancy (ibid. at 153).

Thus, though there is no "right of privacy" in the Constitution, *Roe* – with intrepid bias – invents and discovers one. Classic eisegesis. And it is predicated on a bias against the integrity of marriage. The Court's decision not only rends child from mother, but also child from father, husband from wife, and thus man from woman in the larger context, in service to the male chauvinism of the abortion ethos. The husband and/or father never receives any mention in *Roe* relative to the abortion decision. As well, Orwellian doublespeak now changes "abortion" into "termination of pregnancy."

[**Biblical critique**: Here *Roe* arrives at the penultimate gravamen to its argument – a rejection of the seventh positive assumption in Genesis 1-2, viz., a positive view of human sexuality as rooted in the equality and complementarity of marriage, here exorcising the man from the equation, as the male chauvinistic nature of abortion is now being ratified by the Court, in service to men who do not marry the mother of their children.]

In subsequent context, *Roe* defines why this "right of privacy" is needed:

The detriment that the State would impose upon the pregnant woman by denying this choice altogether is apparent. Specific and direct harm medically diagnosable even in early pregnancy may be involved. Maternity, or additional offspring, may force upon the woman a distressful life and future. Psychological harm may be imminent. Mental and physical health may be taxed by child care. There is also the distress, for all concerned, associated with the unwanted child, and there is the problem of bringing a child into a family already unable, psychologically and otherwise, to care for it. In other cases, as in this one, the additional difficulties and continuing stigma of unwed motherhood may be involved. All these are factors the woman and her responsible physician necessarily will consider in consultation (ibid. at 153).

Roe regards the woman as autonomous, and this is not surprising since the Court has already separated the child from her. Now it excludes the man, who makes her pregnant, from the equation, then slides away from the assumption of the context of marriage into unwed motherhood. *Roe* is actively embracing the reversal order of *Sex → Choice → Life →/ God*. In the process, the Court further dehumanizes the unborn child by assigning him or her the status of "unwanted," like disposable garbage. Yet its language cannot avoid the human pregnancy dimension to this dehumanized object. The schizophrenia of the abortion-rights position.

Then, upon the concoction of a laundry list of "potential" distresses, *Roe* invests its trust in those potential distresses. Thus we note two points of intellectual and moral schizophrenia. First, *Roe* trusts a biased "theory" by which to dismiss the Hippocratic Oath, then the Court throws out biological fact by relegating it to the status of "one theory." Accept one "theory" and reject another "theory" according to what serves the desired bias. And second, *Roe* uses the "potentiality" of the positive (human life) to dismiss the actual humanity of the unborn on the one hand, then uses the "potentiality" of the negative (human distress) to dismiss the actual humanity of the unborn on the other hand. This is the reversal in definition of terms, just like the ancient serpent in *moth tamuth* to *lo moth t'muthon*.

The potentials for distress are real. But the question is whether or not we invest our trust in the power to give or in the power to destroy. The first is biblical, but the *Roe* Court chooses the latter in accord with its anti-Christian bias. And the Court chooses the power to destroy by also rejecting the priority of faithful marriage. For *Roe*, the "private" relationship between the woman and her "responsible physician" merits note, but not the truly private relationship with her husband (in those cases where it actually is the husband; and *Roe* does not address the extra-marital preponderance to begin with).

159

Thus the Court invents a false right to privacy to destroy a true right to privacy. And the former "right" turns out to be a mockery, in that the overwhelming number of abortions since 1973 have little to do with a woman's relationship with a "responsible physician," and far more to do with an abortionist, theretofore and subsequently unknown, almost always male, and who is there only to evacuate her womb, make a profit, and send her on her way – all in service to the prevailing male chauvinism of the abortion ethos and industry.

7. Perversion of the Fourteenth Amendment

Seventh, the Fourteenth Amendment is perverted by the *Roe* Court to further dehumanize the unborn. This has been done biologically already, now the need is to remove the constitutional language of "personhood" from the unborn as well. Its decision reasons this way, the first section of which we have already noted:

> The appellee and certain *amici* argue that the fetus is a "person" within the language and meaning of the Fourteenth Amendment. In support of this, they outline at length and in detail the well-known facts of fetal development. If this suggestion of personhood is established, the appellant's case, of course, collapses, for the fetus' right to life would then be guaranteed specifically by the Amendment. The appellant conceded as much on reargument. On the other hand, the appellee conceded on reargument that no case could be cited that holds that a fetus is a person within the meaning of the Fourteenth Amendment.

> The Constitution does not define 'person' in so many words. Section 1 of the Fourteenth Amendment contains three references to 'person.' The first, in defining 'citizens,' speaks of 'persons' born or naturalized in the United States. The word also appears both in the Due Process Clause and in the Equal Protection Clause …

> But in nearly all these instances, the use of the word is such that it has application only postnatally. None indicates, with any assurance, that it

160

has any possible pre-natal application. All this, together with our observation, *supra*, that throughout the major portion of the 19th century prevailing legal abortion practices were far freer than they are today, persuades us that the word "person," as used in the Fourteenth Amendment, does not include the unborn (ibid. at 156-158).

Beyond our prior note that *Roe* invents a lacuna of non-applicability to the non-addressed unborn as subjects in the Fourteenth Amendment, and against the contemporaneous construction of legal personhood in 36 state laws, 1821ff, here *Roe* again dismisses the importance of biological humanity, seeking in its well thought out strategy to separate this question from that of legal personhood.

The goal of *Roe* is to disinclude the humanity of the unborn. The Court is condescending with respect to the "well-known facts of fetal development." Since these facts are well-known and clear, and since they militate against the Court's bias, *Roe* has to define them off the table before dealing with the issue of legal personhood. *Roe* makes this clear as it acknowledges that both sides of the dispute admit that if an unborn child is defined as a "person" under the Fourteenth Amendment, then the unborn has a constitutional "right to life." As well, the Court, in militating against the acknowledged humanity of the unborn, invents a "far freer" diagnosis of abortion's availability in the 19th century (contra state laws and their rationale for honoring human life), but such availability is only due to means of a de facto underground industry. *Roe* supports not law, but lawlessness.

We need to demonstrate the legal personhood of the unborn in order to win their legal protection. However, the argument about the language of the Fourteenth Amendment is off track for a number of reasons. The state of Texas, in arguing for the legal protection of the unborn, appeals to the Fourteenth Amendment. This is ill-advised, since the Fourteenth Amendment addresses former slaves, not the unborn. But as well, this fact shows the dishonesty of *Roe*'s response.

In other words, just as *Roe* admits that the Constitution does not mention any "right of privacy," it also admits that the Constitution does not define "person" in explicit terms. Therefore, the two key terms in the debate lack constitutional definition, but *Roe* stands athwart history, and accordingly defines their non-definition for its own pre-defined purposes, all in hatred of the biblical power of honest definition of terms in service to informed choice. In both cases, the Court then argues from silence, not doing the honest work of examining the biblical assumptions underlying the language of the Declaration of Independence and the Bill of Rights. Rather, it eisegetes its anti-biblical bias into the text. The argument from silence is always convenient for the eisegete, and as well it is convenient to invent a "general" right to call into existence a "specific" right that is not in the Constitution.

The Court's legal and moral schizophrenia is then evident; in the first instance it uses the invented general "right to privacy" to create a specific "right to privacy" entirely foreign to the Constitution and its moral foundations; and in the second instance, it refuses to acknowledge a moral definition of personhood that precedes legal language, and nitpicks among specific uses of "person" in contexts which do not refer to the unborn – in order to say that they do not refer to the unborn, and therefore the unborn are unreferenced, and thus there is no need to explore the issue further.

A false sequence is ramped up, embraced by the absurdity of the Court's logic:

1. *Roe* invents a "right to privacy" that does not exist in the Constitution.
2. *Roe* refuses to acknowledge the true nature of moral and biological "personhood" as per the Constitution.
3. *Roe* eisegetically examines certain legal language of "personhood" in the Fourteenth Amendment, so as to a priori preclude the unborn.
4. *Roe* then says this pre-selected language does not include the unborn, drawn from an Amendment that is not addressing the subject of the unborn.
5. *Roe* thus says the unborn are not referred to therein.
6. *Roe* thus says the issue deserves no further investigation at this point.

As noted earlier, the Fourteenth Amendment, in conjunction with the Thirteenth and Fifteenth, is drafted and ratified in order to give legal personhood to a class of people who have unconstitutionally been denied that right under the 1857 *Dred Scott* U.S. Supreme Court decision – Black Americans. It has nothing specifically to do with the unborn, thus it should not have been referenced, either positively or negatively, on the question that *Roe* faced. Yet ironically, language that is drafted to acknowledge unalienable rights for one dehumanized class – Black Americans – is then reversed by *Roe* to deny the unalienable rights to a formerly humanized class – the unborn – who thus become dehumanized.

(Today, the U.S. social order raises the question on how anyone in the 19th century, and prior, could have permitted the racial discrimination and dehumanization of slavery. When, in the future, will we look back and ask the same question of those "enlightened" people, who today, permit the chronological discrimination and dehumanization of those in utero?)

Nonetheless, even though the Fourteenth Amendment is not the proper place to argue for the humanity of the unborn, once it is brought into the issue, it is helpful to show how the true exegesis in fact serves the humanity of the unborn.

To start with some reiteration, during the nineteenth century, all the states that pass anti-abortion laws do so, based on the humanity, indeed on the assumption of the legal personhood of the unborn (contra Mohr, cited above). These are the same state legislatures, whether including some of the same individual legislators, or subsequent legislators who believe the same way, who also ratify the Fourteenth Amendment. Accordingly, in their ratification of the Fourteenth Amendment which gives legal personhood to the blacks, they also assume the legal personhood of the unborn. For *Roe* to argue that the Fourteenth Amendment does not include the unborn is thus a syntactically eisegetical nitpick designed to negate the larger reality that its context actually assumes the legal personhood of the unborn.

In his dissent to *Roe*, Justice Rehnquist makes this point clear, as we quoted earlier (410 U.S. at 174-177). In testimony before the House

163

Subcommittee on Civil and Constitutional Rights of the House Committee on the Judiciary in 1976, University of Texas Law School professor Joseph Witherspoon sums up a key element here:

> The conjunction of state ratification of these Amendments (the Thirteenth, Fourteenth, and Fifteenth) with state adoption or modification (i.e., to make them more restrictive) of anti-abortion statutes designed to protect unborn children constitutes a contemporaneous legislative construction by states of the meaning of the Amendment they ratified. That construction can only mean that unborn children are human beings and persons under the Constitution. Any other view of their action would be out of line with the history of this period (*Congressional Record*, March 3, 1976, p. 5108).

In other words, there is an unchallenged positive consensus at the time – that human life is fully and legally present "at every period of gestation" (quoting the 1859 AMA report). Gestation begins exactly at the moment of "conception" and this biological fact has never been challenged since the 1859 AMA report. In 1959, the AMA tries to enlarge its concept of conception, helping to prepare the way for the fuzzy thinking of *Roe*. But it does not do so with any new biological facts, and in 1967 it still officially opposes human abortion.

Thus, *Texas* as an appellee, in basing its appeal on the Fourteenth Amendment, plays into the hands of the abortion proponents who know they can manipulate this territory to their advantage. *Roe* not *Texas* is now in the driver's seat. How therefore does truth gain the driver's seat, in this dark and boiling caldron of political and judicial idolatry?

8. The Pretension of Ignorance

Eighth, *Roe* is the first legal interpretation in U.S. history based on the assumption of a "non-consensus" as to the central fact of the case. It is based on a pretension of ignorance.

Texas urges that, apart from the Fourteenth Amendment, life begins at conception and is present throughout pregnancy, and that, therefore, the State has a compelling interest in protecting that life from and after conception. We need not resolve this difficult question of when life begins. When those trained in the respective disciplines of medicine, philosophy and theology are unable to arrive at any consensus, the judiciary, at this point in the development of man's knowledge, is not in a position to speculate as to the answer (410 U.S. 113 at 159).

[**Biblical Critique**: *Roe* now arrives at the ultimate gravamen in its argument, avoiding the central question of the debate in a pretension of ignorance, an intellectual and moral cowardice in saying no to the sixth positive assumption in Genesis 1-2, the power to hard questions. We have now itemized *Roe*'s rejection of all eleven positive assumptions in Genesis 1-2, and the concomitant first four ethical pillars, showing *Roe*'s utterly anti-biblical grounding. It's anti-Christian bias violates the fifth pillar, and the reality of the sixth is not even in the ballpark for their consideration.]

What the 1973 *Roe* Court does to this point is a set-up for this pretension of ignorance, establishing a nine-point argument:

1. *Roe* chides the "emotional" nature of the debate and pretends to rise above it, all the while conforming to its own unstated biases;
2. *Roe* sanctions a war between the mother and unborn child, by first setting up a war between the mother and father of the same unborn child;
3. *Roe* invents a "penumbra" of undefined shadows in which to avoid an accurate definition of terms;
4. *Roe* dispenses with the history of Hippocratic and Christian medical ethics that opposes human abortion;
5. *Roe* dispenses with the AMA's original history of opposing human abortion;
6. *Roe* dispenses with the biological facts of conception which would inform the discussion, claiming their irrelevance;
7. *Roe* invents a broad then narrowly applied "right of privacy" to allow a woman to abort an undefined "potential" life; and

8. *Roe* further wages war on the unborn by denying them their constitutional personhood.

This is *Roe*'s greatest fear and weakness – the Court knows that the unborn child is human, and that abortion destroys a human life. *Roe* constructs a relentless artifice to get around the obvious, to adopt every conceivable angle to deny the humanity and civil rights of the unborn. But the Court has yet to convince itself – that is why it conducts such a remarkable fishing expedition. Thus the Court now reveals its true theological colors, which the biblically literate will recognize. Namely, the *Roe* Court appeals to the weakest form of known moral argument in its final point:

9. *Roe* makes a pretense of ignorance about the humanity of the unborn, and rationalizes their legalized destruction – its tendentious goal from the outset.

After Cain murders his brother Abel, *Yahweh* questions him, and Cain pretends to be ignorant of the reality as he also lies (Genesis 4:1-12). When the disciples of the Pharisees try to entrap Jesus, he questions them, and they pretend to be ignorant (Matthew 21:23-27). For the singular Cain, it is the "I don't know" argument; for the plural yet to be Pharisees, it is the "We don't know" argument. The *Roe* Court follows the logic of Cain and the Pharisees, its spiritual forefathers:

1. When dishonest elitists do not have the courage to admit true definition of terms and then make their case; and
2. When they cannot market a false definition of terms, because they know they cannot fool *Yahweh*, Jesus or the common people with it; then
3. They pretend to be ignorant of reality.

As Cain kills his brother, as the devil always seeks to kill the Messianic lineage, and as the religious elitists seek to kill Jesus, so too does *Roe* serve the agenda of the ancient serpent – to allow the killing of the most vulnerable image-bearers of God in our midst, the very unborn. And as the religious

166

elitists fear the common people who believe in Jesus, so too does the elitist *Roe* Court majority fear the "consent of the governed."

The pretension of ignorance is the weakest form of moral argument in history, and *Roe* lifts it from the enemies of the Messiah. The fact that this law still stands in 2016 is an indictment against the church.

The Court thus makes a pretension of ignorance under the rubric of posing a non-existent "non-consensus." Then to say that there is no "need" to resolve the central question of fact is as legally dishonest as it gets.

But in normal jurisprudence, when a jury renders a verdict (or a judge in cases where there is no jury), their simple duty is to determine what the facts of the case are. The judge is then the one who passes sentence. The jury must decide whether or not the accused man actually pulled the trigger, if the accused woman did actually run the stop sign, or if the blood alcohol truly exceeded the legal limit, and so forth.

Only when such facts are agreed upon, can a verdict of "guilty" or "not guilty" be reached, after which the judge will sentence the "guilty" or excuse the "not guilty." In criminal cases, the jury must be unanimous, or else there is a "hung jury." In civil cases, there usually has to be a 5-1 or 10-2 majority to render a verdict, or else there is a "hung jury." If a "hung jury" does result, the judge must then decide whether to retry the case with a new jury, remand the case to a lower court if applicable, or throw out the case entirely.

The *Roe* Court considers none of this when it states in essence that there is a "hung jury," a "non-consensus" as to when "life begins." The context is biological human life, and *Roe* seeks again to fuzz this central question by introducing issues of unspecified philosophy and theology into the mix. As we have evidenced, the biology of conception is straightforward, and it is the unique foundation in Genesis 1-2 that affirms such biological fact. But the Court is biased against biblical faith, against the ethics and factual substance of Genesis 1-2, saying Christianity is prejudicial against women and their putative "right to privacy." Thus *Roe*'s introduction here of theology is only for the sake of a straw figure helpful to its dismissal of biological fact. *Roe* is also careful not to speak of "individual biological human life," but speaks in terms of "when life begins," again to make it as amorphous as possible – to stay away from the specific fact that a single abortion destroys a single and discrete human life, if not two or more discrete human lives (in the case of twins, et al.).

Moreover, the Court's introduction of the alleged "non-consensus" gives no evidence that such a "non-consensus" actually exists. On the contrary, as already noted, there is the overwhelming consensus regarding the humanity of the unborn and the biological facts of conception. And Professor Witherspoon demonstrates the "contemporaneous legislative construction" to the Fourteenth Amendment that affirms personhood for the unborn, and Justice Rehnquist cites the data that confirm this same view. The *Roe* majority constructs its artifice, and now that it nears the end, the Court appeals to ignorance as its best source of authority.

But even if there were a "non-consensus" on the biological issue within the medical community, or on the application of "personhood" to the unborn in the legal community, we still have a "hung jury" according to *Roe*'s own admission. Thus, the *Roe* Court should not have ruled on the matter at all – it should have a) not heard the case, or b) remanded it back to the appeals court (and for *Doe* likewise). But since it is not interested in interpreting the law as handed down from the U.S. Constitution, but in making new law to suit a predilection to allow legalized human abortion, *Roe* has to invent the most serviceable excuse.

The *Roe* Court is a) unwilling to admit the truth, and it is b) unable to market a lie and define a different point when "life begins" (i.e. some point after conception such as birth that would allow their agenda to be rationalized). Thus, the Court c) pretends to be ignorant as they postulate a non-existent "non-consensus" among a certain cultural elite. As Solomon says, "(T)here is nothing new under the sun" (Ecclesiastes 1:9b), and the *Roe* Court cannot not rise above the unoriginality of mimicking Cain against *Yahweh* and the religious elitists against Jesus. They adopt the weakest form of moral argument there is, in the pretension of ignorance, and the fact that this pretension has stood since 1973 is an indictment against the people of the

168

United States. We have been too biblically illiterate and morally uncourageous to diagnose and overcome such a weak position which comes from the ancient serpent.

The Raw Judicial Power to Invent a New Right: Abortion on Demand

On the basis of *Roe*'s argument, the Court declares a woman has a "fundamental right" to abortion, and it creates an artifice that divides pregnancy into three stages. In the first "trimester," no state laws can regulate abortion. In the second trimester, the states can only regulate the medical conditions under which abortions are performed. And in the third trimester, per *Doe*, states cannot restrict abortion except when the "life or health" of the mother is at stake.

In his concurring opinion following *Doe*, Chief Justice Warren Burger said:

> I do not read the Court's holdings today as having the sweeping consequences attributed to them by the dissenting Justices; the dissenting views discount the reality that the vast majority of physicians observe the standards of their profession, and act only on the basis of carefully deliberated medical judgments relating to life and health.

> Plainly, the Court today rejects any claim that the Constitution requires abortion on demand (410 U.S. 179 at 208).

Before leaving the Supreme Court some years later, Burger regretted these words and called for the Court to review *Roe,* to consider its reversal. He had bought the lie that *Roe* and *Doe* were motivated by compassion for women facing dire straits with the continuation of a pregnancy, and believed that the "restrictions" in place were reasonable because the medical profession had a standard of ethical conduct to safeguard against the possibility of "abortion on demand." These three words haunted Burger because they describe exactly what came to pass.

Whereas most physicians do conduct themselves as Burger believed, it was not they who come to perform the abortions for the most part. The least reputable of physicians become the abortionists, making "blood money" wages, because so few physicians want to be a part of this sordid business in actuality (though many of them defend theoretically the "right" to an abortion, very few want to do the grisly work of performing one – they know abortion destroys a nascent human life).

Thus, in the second trimester, concern for proper medical conditions has been consistently mocked, and many abortion centers operate in unsanitary conditions that are nowhere else tolerated in the medical community. In the third trimester, the "health" of the mother clause has been used as a canopy for any rationalization, including "emotional" health, and has led to a wide availability of third-term abortions, and also, the reality of "partial-birth" abortions, subsequently outlawed by the U.S. Congress (where a late-term unborn child is prematurely forced down the birth canal, in order for the abortionist to crush his or her skull, evacuate the brain, and thus make his work "easier" than in other methods, and to serve the black market for intact fetal body parts). What woman in the U.S. today cannot have an abortion up to nine months if she has the money? And too, Planned Parenthood is relentless in lobbying for taxpayer funded abortions as a "constitutional right" – the very opposite of what Burger envisioned.

In his dissent to *Roe* and *Doe*, Justice Byron White sums up what the Court does on January 22, 1973:

> The Court simply fashions and announces a new constitutional right for pregnant mothers and, with scarcely any reason or authority for its action, invests that right with sufficient substance to override state abortion statutes. The upshot is that the people and the legislatures of the 50 States are constitutionally disentitled to weigh the relative importance of the continued existence and development of the fetus, on the one hand, against a spectrum of possible impacts on the mother, on the other hand. As an exercise of raw judicial power, the Court perhaps has the authority to do what it does today; but in my view its judgment is an improvident and extravagant exercise of the power of judicial review that the Constitution extends to the Court.

The Court apparently values the convenience of the pregnant mother more than the continued existence and development of the life or potential life that she carries. Whether or not I might agree with that marshaling of values, I can in no event join the Court's judgment because I find no constitutional warrant for imposing such an order of priorities on the people and legislatures of the States (ibid. at 221-222).

Justice White is mostly on target. But he does work with the "potential life" language, and he separates his personal considerations from the subject (which if he at all wished to make human abortion legal, is at least intellectually and constitutionally honest on his part). And he still concludes that *Roe* is an exercise of "raw judicial power" which vitiates the "consent of the governed" (he does, however, concede that the Court "perhaps" has the legal if not moral authority to do so, and here I disagree with him – it has neither). Between 1967 and 1972 the abortion-rights movement was seeking to win its legalization through state legislatures – but that process hit a dead end and was beginning to reverse itself. So it bypasses the democratic process of an informed electorate and succeeds in getting the Supreme Court to rule by judicial fiat.

Two Postscripts

Questions That Could Have Been Posed in the Judge Sonia Sotomayor Confirmation Hearing, 2009

On August 1, 2009, a week before Judge Sonia Sotomayor was confirmed to the U.S. Supreme Court, I composed an open letter to the judge, with respect to *Roe* v. *Wade* and *Doe* v. *Bolton*.

---

1. In reference to the 1965 *Griswold v. Connecticut* decision, the Court discovers a "penumbra" of the Constitution that includes a broad "right to privacy," sufficient enough to include a woman's atomistic right to an abortion. Yet, too, the Court also says "The Constitution does not explicitly mention any right of privacy" (410. U.S. 113 at 152).

171

Judge Sotomayor, can you define the nature of that "penumbra," and how prior to 1965, it was used to discover other Constitutional rights? As well, if there is no "right to privacy" explicitly set forth in the Constitution, does the appeal to the shadows of a penumbra have any constitutional substance?

2. The *Roe* decision speaks of the "emotional nature of the abortion controversy" that involves people's philosophy, their "exposure to the raw edges of human experience," along with their religious training and attitude toward "life and family." Then *Roe* mentions the issues of "population growth, pollution, poverty and racial overtones (which) tend to complicate." But *Roe* never addresses these issues, other than a secondary reference in *Doe*, and it also says "Our task, of course, is to resolve the issue by constitutional measurement, free of emotion and predilection" (410 U.S. 113 at 116).

Judge Sotomayor, you have spoken of the need for the Court to be "empathetic" to human need while applying the law. As *Roe* notes the "raw edges of human experience," this seems to be one of these places where law and empathy interface. Can you explain why *Roe* makes specific reference to issues it then did not address, e.g., giving no recommendations as to how legalized abortion would address them lawfully and empathetically, thus improving the human experience? And if empathy and law are to interface, why does the *Roe* Court declare the need to be "free of emotion" in deciding the law?

Judge Sotomayor, the *Roe* decision mentions "racial overtones" as a concern. Since 1973, abortion rates for Black Americans have averaged 23 percent of all abortions, now up to some 38 or 39 percent, yet Black Americans represent only 12 percent of all Americans. Is this high rate of abortions – double to triple the national average – good for addressing "racial overtones," or has it only exacerbated racial suffering?

3. The *Roe* decision distances itself from the 2,400 year-old Hippocratic oath that prohibits physicians from doing abortions. The Court says that the Hippocratic Oath is a minority opinion in its time,

a "Pythagorean manifesto and not the expression of an absolute standard of medical conduct." As well, the Court notes that the emerging teachings of Christianity are in agreement with this Pythagorean manifesto. "This, it seems to us, is a satisfactory and acceptable explanation of the Hippocratic Oath's apparent rigidity. It enables us to understand, in historical context, a long-accepted and revered statement of medical ethics" (410 U.S. 113 at 132).

Judge Sotomayor, it seems that the *Roe* Court regards a 2,400-year-old medical ethic as a minority sectarian manifesto in Greek philosophy, and that it gains long term reputation essentially through its embrace by early Christianity. Do you agree with this, and if so, does the *Roe* decision indicate that it has no empathy with Christian conviction? Further, does it mean that Christianity's historical reasons for moral decisions no longer apply to the United States, since we are, in a sense, a post-Christian nation? Or if you disagree, I am pleased to hear your thoughts.

4. The *Roe* decision speaks of "psychological harm," the taxation of "physical health," various sociological ills and even the "stigma" of unwed motherhood, as reasons for legalized abortion (410 U.S. 113 at 153). Yet, in all these concerns, *Roe* virtually excludes the role of the husband or biological father. The Alan Guttmacher Institute, research arm for Planned Parenthood Federation, shows consistently over the years that some 82 percent of all abortions are performed on unmarried women. Of the remaining 18 percent, the consistent experience of pregnancy resource centers is that three-quarters of these married women are pregnant through adultery; and of the remaining one-quarter of the 18 percent, the man is usually in the process of leaving the marriage. In other words, and in knowing that exceptions prove the rule, the dominant psychological and social force driving the abortion ethos is male abandonment of women and their children.

Judge Sotomayor, in light of this reality, do you believe *Roe* has been empathetic to women in their plight, or has it actually encouraged male chauvinism instead?

173

5. The Fourteenth Amendment, along with the Thirteenth and Fifteenth, redresses the evil of slavery. It applies the language of personhood to all people, yet *Roe* argues that it is postnatal in application, not prenatal. Accordingly, *Roe* says that personhood excludes the unborn in legal terms. Yet too, *Roe* also says "The Constitution does not define 'person' in so many words (410 U.S. 113 at 156). The Fourteenth Amendment is not addressing the subject of the unborn, but it in fact gives personhood to a class of people theretofore denied personhood – Black Americans. The unborn have the legal protection of personhood prior to *Roe*, but then they lose that protection. Thus, what the Fourteenth Amendment acknowledges for black persons, it denies for the unborn, and indeed, Black Americans are now suffering the scourge of abortion at nearly three times the national average.

Judge Sotomayor, what is your understanding of the definition of personhood in the Constitution? As well, and in view of Black Americans and the unborn alike, do you think *Roe* has been consistent here, logically, legally or empathetically?

6. The *Roe* decision says that it cannot adopt "one theory of life" over and against another (410 U.S. 113 at 162). This relates to terms such as conception, nidation, implantation, viability and birth. "Texas urged that, apart from the Fourteenth Amendment, life begins at conception and is present throughout pregnancy, and that, therefore, the State has a compelling interest in protecting that life from and after conception. When those trained in the respective disciplines of medicine, philosophy and theology are unable to arrive at any consensus, the judiciary, at this point in the development of man's knowledge, is not in position to speculate as to the answer" (410 U.S. 113 at 159). Namely, as to the central factual issue at hand, the Court says it is ignorant.

Judge Sotomayor, do you know of any lack of consensus as to the biological humanity of the unborn since the American Medical Association, in 1859, cited the original experiment that showed the fertilization of a human egg? Also, if the central fact of a case under legal review cannot be determined, is it not the Court's responsibility not to rule on the case? And doesn't *Roe*, while nonetheless making a ruling based on stated ignorance (declaring it does not know "when life begins"), also leave the door open for further information? Namely, does not the whole in vitro fertilization industry, and cognate technologies, base themselves on the scientific facts of fertilization/conception? Specifically: When a haploid spermatozoon fertilizes a haploid ovum, the immediate result is a diploid and one-celled human zygote which equals a whole biological life; and such biological human life is now set for the first time to multiply cells with a genetic code that did not exist beforehand and will never again change. Were not all of us once one-celled human zygotes? It seems that the only difference between us then, and now, is a question of whether or not we were nurtured in our vulnerability through pregnancy and childhood. Would you agree? If not, what is your contrary scientific understanding?

7. Finally, we understand that the 1857 Dred Scott decision rationalizes slavery and the dehumanization of Black Americans. It is overturned by the Emancipation Proclamation, and by the Thirteenth, Fourteenth and Fifteenth Amendments. In other words, *stare decisis* is powerful but not absolute.

Judge Sotomayor, in view of questions of law, science and empathy, and even in its own language, is not *Roe* subject to review if a compelling case were to be presented?

A Question I Posed of Supreme Court Justice Antonin Scalia, 2012

On September 18, 2012, I had opportunity to listen to U.S. Supreme Court Justice Antonin Scalia. He was speaking to the Federalist Society in New York City, on a tour for his new book: *Reading Law: The Interpretation of Legal Texts*. Questions were submitted to him on index cards. My question referred to James Madison's concern (Federalist Papers, 62) that if laws becomes too "voluminous that they cannot be read, or so incoherent that they cannot be understood," then our republic is in danger.

I asked how soon we might reach such a point. Justice Scalia, in his answer, mused in diagnosis of the situation that "we cannot afford to devote our best minds" to work "that produces nothing." He then added, "We're probably at that point now" and we "need to simplify the law ... but how, I do not know."

Roe is a key catalyst to this reality – having opened the floodgates to a growing swell of elitist idolatries that demand the sacrifice of human abortion – and in so doing, speeds along the multiplication of broken trust in marriage, the family (*oikonomos*), and thus the whole social order. This yields increasing lawlessness, and a nearly irresistible tide of overwhelming and metastasizing bureaucracy that assaults unalienable rights.

In Sum

How can any biblically rooted Jew or Christian even give an ounce of credence to the 1973 *Roe v. Wade* U.S. Supreme Court decision? It opposes all the Bible is and stands for, and this we have abundantly – and with no exceptions – given evidence.

The *Roe* Court, as it tries to convince itself of the logic of its own position, has to include a phrase in order to maintain an appearance of intellectual respectability when it posits the "non-consensus." The Court says "[a]t this point in the development of man's knowledge ..." This leaves an open door for redress (which exists in the First Amendment to begin with), one where further "knowledge" can be brought to bear.

This was the purpose of a meeting of the U.S. Senate Subcommittee on the Judiciary, on April 23-24, 1981. It convened to see if there were any consensus as to the question of when an individual biological human life begins, in direct response to the language of *Roe*. An internationally distinguished panel of experts testified as to the reality of conception, including U.S. Surgeon General Dr. C. Everett Koop and French geneticist Dr. Jerome LeJeune.

When Senator Max Baucus was invited to produce expert witnesses who would demonstrate a different point of biological origin, he did not produce any in the first round of testimony. In total, there was only one witness to challenge the consensus on conception at the hearings, professor Leon Rosenberg. But he failed to address the biological question of when an individual human life begins, and instead dismissed it as a religious and metaphysical issue outside the purview of scientific inquiry. Thus, the Subcommittee showed the *Roe* Court to be wrong – there is a complete consensus as to conception, and the abortion-rights argument is based on a pretension of ignorance, and on a religious bias against the good science which a biblical worldview underscores.

And the fruit of such a consensus? It is swept under the rug politically. *Roe* cannot be reversed by a fiat in the other direction by a new Supreme Court decision, nor by the U.S. Senate holding a hearing, in a vacuum, to show *Roe*'s error. It can only be reversed by a grass-roots consensus on a) a true definition of human life that includes the humanity of the unborn, b) to simultaneously expose the fiction that abortion is a "woman's right," that it is rather the domain of male chauvinism, and c) likewise exposing the Court's pretension of ignorance. Or to sum up these realities:

Human abortion is inhuman, male chauvinistic and ignorant.

In the meantime, we need to hold all men legally accountable for parenthood, and in demonstrating reality through processes of informed choice, we can confidently aim to win the hearts and minds of the nation in order to win full legal protection for women and their unborn equally.

The trajectory of these pages aims for the strategic starting point to reverse *Roe*.

♦ ♦ ♦

Chapter Five

On the University Campuses and Elsewhere

We started these pages looking at face-to-face encounters I have had addressing the hellish violation of women via rape and incest, and made pregnant accordingly. This serves as an introduction to the need for a Biblical Theology 101, with its embrace of any and all hard questions. And as the necessary foundation for how to change the language of the abortion debate, gain the driver's seat in defining the terms, and thus, to win the equal legal protection for women and their unborn.

Then, in diagnosing the idolatry of choice in the Religious Coalition for Abortion Rights (RCAR), some other encounters in the debate come to the fore. In all, I ran into many aha moments that enrich me deeply in seeking to live and share the Gospel in the face of a broken humanity.

I have also said that a remnant in the church needs a "lived biblical theology" in order for us to succeed, and this I have sought to learn and do. With such a theology now set forth, let me return to a lived reality in the work of pro-life ministry in the presence of dissenters.

This chapter is essentially some select story-telling, where aha moments happen (at least for me), and hopefully this, combined with the theology in place, will help us all to think and act as biblically as possible.

And also, this is to encourage as many of us as possible to a) address our own brokennesses through the power of the Gospel, so as to b) take the risk of love and a sound mind in ministering to a culture torn apart by the "legalized" blood of nearly sixty million little ones since *Roe*. And to the tens of millions of women who have and still suffer such a soul violence. And to all the men who actively or passively lived a male chauvinism in this regard, whose souls have deadened some or very much as a result. And to the men who wanted to be fathers, but were disempowered or denied from one angle or another. And to the millions who explicitly or intuitively know they have lost siblings and thus, shared childhoods.

178

We are a nation wounded to the core, incapable thus to address all the concentric ripples of brokenness that have followed since, and have literally brought us to an existential civilizational crisis. Only in the Name of Jesus, in the power of his cross and resurrection, and the forgiveness that flows, can we be healed.

Bill Baird – Five Interfaces 1985-1991

North Adams State College, 1985

My second debate in pro-life ministry was with Bill Baird at North Adams State College, North Adams, Massachusetts, on March 6, 1985. He was scheduled to address an audience himself, and some local members of the Massachusetts Citizens for Life (MCFL) wanted to find someone to debate him instead. I served on the MCFL statewide board for a season, a delightful group of mostly Roman Catholics, and I was also able to bring many evangelicals into their midst over the years. So the local chapter gained permission from the college, and I was invited to debate Mr. Baird.

Baird owned abortion centers in New York and Boston, and was infamous (to the pro-life movement) for pushing birth control and abortion. He was arrested and jailed on April 6, 1967 for passing out contraceptives to a female student at Boston University, his appeal eventually went to the U.S. Supreme Court in 1972, *Eisenstadt* v. *Baird*, and he won, establishing the "right" of contraceptives for unmarried persons. His won two other Supreme Court victories (*Baird* v. *Bellotti* [1976] and *Baird* v. *Bellotti* [1979]), establishing the "right" for minors to have abortions without parental consent. For all this he was called by some "the father of the abortion-rights movement."

One friend told me of speaking to him face-to-face some years prior, where Baird was telling him to give up the fight. My friend pressed up to his face, and said, "I will die first, with my pro-life convictions like a knife held between my teeth, rather than give up!"

179

In the Sentinel-Enterprise in Fitchburg, MA, Baird was quoted on September 30, 1987, speaking of firebombed abortion centers by "pro-life" activists, raids that destroyed medical equipment and such, saying: "The anti-abortion people are on this crusade that they're so holy, that those of us of another persuasion are lower than human."

Mr. Baird was the visceral street-fighter of many years before and following our debate that evening, he who was on the pro-abortion crusade well before the pro-life movement came into existence. He was also a Unitarian who believes in sexual promiscuity (as he bragged to me years later in Boston). He who believes he was being treated as "lower than human" is the one who, prior, treats the unborn as "lower than human."

So it was a charged evening to start, given Baird's love of controversy. When I arrived, he had arranged a large table next to the podiums, displaying dozens of newspaper clippings about his activist history. He was very proud of it, and at several junctures told me how well known he was, important, and thus, how I was a "nobody." Such egocentricity was new to me, and I didn't really know how to respond, so I didn't.

The issues of *God → life → choice → sex* versus the *sex → choice → life →/God* reality, percolated under it all, even before I made this explicit theological observation. Bill also raised the question of male dominance in society. Here, first hand, I ran into a man who decried a "male dominance" that would not allow women to have "sexual freedom," on the one hand, yet who exploited such "freedom," being free himself from the consequences of pregnancy, on the other.

One of his favorite illustrations was to take an acorn out of his jacket pocket, and say that it was small, and no more a tree than an embryo is a human life – disregarding the fact that such an acorn is unfertilized apart from its proper soil, de facto haploid with no future otherwise. Had I been quick enough in my thoughts, I could have injected some fun: "What would you do if all of a sudden, the acorn in your pocket sprouted? I guess someone surreptitiously put some moist soil in with it." He also said to the audience, "If I put a pencil dot on the wall – a "fertilized" human egg is a quarter of

180

that size – you can believe that that is a person, but don't you make me believe it," as reported in the North Adams Transcript. This is a secular achievement ethic, the opposite of *nephesh*.

Two moments in the debate stick in my mind. During the question and answer period, one gentleman congratulated me while also being quite cruel in his language toward Bill Baird. So I rebuked him, saying that such an attitude does not serve the pro-life ethic. I was surprised at my spontaneous boldness, and wondered immediately if I would alienate the man and other pro-life advocates as well. Afterward, he gave me a handshake and thanked me.

Also during the question and answer period, Bill asked the college audience, for a show of hands on who supports a "woman's right to an abortion." Most the audience sided with him.

In retrospect, had I had the presence of mind, I could have had some fun. I could have responded by also taking a poll: "How many people here believe that the act of human abortion is an intrinsic good, and can tell me why?" I doubt but a few would raise their hands and give it a try. And then I would have said: "How is then, Mr. Baird, that most people support what they know cannot be defined as a good act?"

The United Church of Christ, Ware, 1985

A month later Mr. Baird was scheduled to address a group of ministers in the United Church of Christ (UCC), meeting at a church in Ware, western Massachusetts. I was contacted by a woman minister with the UCC who identified herself as "pro-choice," but was vitally interested in having both sides heard in this meeting. She asked if I were interested, and I said yes.

When she asked Bill Baird, he said no, that he wanted a more "intimate" and "collegial" meeting with the clergy. She was deeply chagrined and apologetic, indeed, embarrassed. In her best effort at salvage, she persuaded the clergy association to invite me to their next month's meeting on May 14.

Perhaps 35 UCC ministers were in attendance, I gave an address, and took questions in a morning meeting scheduled to end at noon, followed by a luncheon. The clear if not vast majority of the clergy were "pro-choice," in favor of legalized abortion in some capacity. I do not recall the specific nature of my talk, but it was biblical in focus. The question and answer period was energetic, and still going strong when the noon hour arrived.

In the hallway right afterward, en route downstairs to the luncheon, one clergyman stopped me, looked at me intently and said, in reference to the question and answer period, "You sure think fast on your feet, don't you?" His gaze was unsettling, and indeed, an unmistakable spirit of darkness was striking. I answered, "Well, I don't know how fast I think on my feet, but I do know that I seek to do my thinking before I stand up." His intensity remained, and he said, while first looking at me, and as he then turned away, "Oh you're slick, really slick."

When I went downstairs, to a nice spread prepared by women in the church, I wandered over to the kitchen area for some reason. As I did, one woman looked at me, then looked both ways, leaned close in, and said softly, "Are you the pro-life minister who spoke today?" I said yes. Then she said, "Well, all of us in the pews are on your side."

WEZE Radio, Boston, 1989

My third interface with Bill Baird was in 1989, on WEZE Christian radio in Boston.

The host of the show, Jeanine Graf, was on vacation for a week, and she invited a Jewish friend, an agnostic, to host her show in her absence. True hospitality, especially on a Christian radio station. So he invited Bill Baird and I to debate the abortion subject.

At one juncture Bill was insistent on trying to have me call him a murderer (of the unborn), so he could rationalize an accusatory mode against me. But I would not do so. Finally, I said to him, "Bill, are you familiar with Jesus's words in the Sermon on the Mount, where he says that calling someone a fool is equivalent to murdering him?" He said yes. I continued, "Bill, I drive in Boston traffic, so I qualify." That ended the interchange.

An interesting reality came to the fore in how the host joined with Baird in arguing against me, thus violating his role. In the middle of it, I thought how strange it was for a Christian radio station to have a decidedly non-Christian host side with another non-Christian against a Christian guest. When the show was over, I wondered what value it had. But then the station heard from many listeners who thought it was the best show they had heard. Why? Because they heard a Christian ganged up on, but who responded with graciousness, not anger or condemning attitudes (by God's grace I would add). This aha is the point when I first began to envision the concept of the Mars Hill Forum series, which I began in 1993.

Bill Baird was also pressing the issue of how abortion would be prosecuted if made illegal. Would I call for the death penalty? I said, no, I was not interested in punitive measures, and gave some biblical background on the difference between premeditated murder and manslaughter. I was only seeking the proactive of life for mother and child alike. I also identified the reality of male chauvinism and the culpability of the abortionist. The first reality is to hold men accountable for the well-being of the children they conceive, and for their mothers too. And when the culture becomes pro-life enough to legally protect woman and their unborn equally, the legislative process can judge best how to hold now illegal abortionists liable.

The Lonely Pro-Abortion Warrior, 1990

My fourth interface with Bill Baird was at a pro-abortion rally at the Boston State House in the spring of 1990 (of which I write about in Chapter Eight), just a block from my office at the time. Planned Parenthood of Massachusetts was lobbying for a pro-abortion legislative purpose, and they had 200 supporters there. I had eleven supporters of the New England Christian Action Council (NECAC), on very short notice in the middle of work week, present with our positively provocative signs from the Sacred Assemblies for the Unborn (again, see Chapter Eight).

Bill Baird was there, approaching the various media present, always good for an interview as the reputed "father of the abortion-rights movement." As well as our supporters, several people from the Massachusetts Citizens for Life leadership were present. In speaking with one, I learned that many people in Planned Parenthood and the larger pro-abortion movement had bad blood between themselves and Baird, but I do not recall the reasons. It seemed to be a matter of ego-turf.

After the event, I ran into Bill walking down Bowdoin Street, and we stopped and spoke for five or ten minutes. We engaged in some of the issues of debate in a conversational tone, and as such I sought for ways to touch his humanity. As we parted, he downhill, and me uphill, I remember sensing such a spirit of oppressive loneliness hovering over his person. I could only pray for God's grace to intervene.

According to his Wikipedia report in 2016, Bill Baird is now 84 years old. In the last category, *Books*, this entry is found: "In 2012 Joni Baird finished Bill Baird's biography after nearly thirteen years of research and writing. She is still seeking an interested literary agent to help get Bill Baird's biography published." The lonely pro-abortion warrior.

WEEI News Radio, Boston, 1990

My final interaction with Bill Baird was on WEEI News Radio in the spring of 1990. My friend, Jon Rodman, was the news director. I had met Jon in 1984 or 1985 when I taught a pro-life seminar at South Shore Baptist Church in Hingham, Massachusetts.

Jon asked me to do a radio debate with Bill, and the radio on-air person who hosted it was quite nervous that it would turn caustic, but it did not. Bill came with a woman who proclaimed herself the publisher of the largest "feminist" pornography magazine in the United States. Bill and I had our interchange, live, then afterward left.

WEEI at the time was on the 44th floor of the Prudential Tower in Back Bay. The three of us stepped into the elevator at the same time. And on the ride down, in the brief time for conversation, Bill said quite baldly: "I can have sex with anyone, anywhere, anytime I want," standing next to his female associate and professed pornographer, he, a father of four. The ethos of a male chauvinistically driven abortion ethos, I thought.

Governor Dummer Academy, 1985

In January, 1985, I was asked to address the weekly chapel at Governor Dummer Academy in Byfield, Massachusetts. It is the oldest private boarding school in the United States, founded in 1763, grades 9-12, currently with 450 co-educational students.

The school was in a season of rapidly moving away from any serious biblical moorings. The topic was the debate over human abortion, and in my presentation to a packed chapel of students and faculty, I used the text of Leviticus 20:1-5, making analogy between child sacrifice and human abortion.

I hit the topic head-on, and painted a candid profile of child sacrifice in the ancient world according to one archaeological report I then read – the bronze idol, with a roaring fire inside of it so that the bronze glowed with heat; with outstretched arms to receive the infant (usually a boy, often the firstborn) to be burned alive; the screaming then suffocating child, cooking flesh, the mother not allowed to utter any public grief – and this was hard enough to confront. This information was taken in stride by the audience.

But when I then described human abortion as a parallel, and in terms of the suction apparatus, dilation and curettage, saline solution etc., a sense of horror swept the audience as groans, moans and deep murmuring protests erupted. Especially from the faculty. It was a baptism for me into the debate at this threshold, making me think of reactions to Jesus when he discussed judgment on sin.

The school headmaster was not pleased, and this was later communicated to me. Yet, I described reality, and there was no room for it, it appeared, as part of the education of young people at Governor Dummer Academy. None of us like to look at images of the Holocaust of Jews and other human beings who had been utterly dehumanized and destroyed by the Nazis. Yet Auschwitz and other concentration camps, with all the tactile, graphic and photographic images in place, are preserved as a memory so that we can all learn: Never Again. When might this same reality and response come to pass concerning the Holocaust of the Unborn at the hands of a male chauvinistic abortion industry?

But the chaplain was pleased, as she wrote me on January 28, 1985: "Thank you for your time and effort in communicating results of abortion to the student body here at GDA. Much is needed in the area of moral teaching here, and you have made it one step easier."

Brown University, 1985

In early 1985 I addressed a debate at Brown University, Providence, Rhode Island. During the audience participation, a young woman posed me some of the most thoughtful questions I have ever received, from her politically "pro-choice" perspective.

After the debate, she approached me and said, "You know, John, before I came in here tonight, I hated you, even though I had never met you. You're a Christian, a man and pro-life." As she said this, I thought to myself, *Uh-oh, three strikes and you're out.*

She continued, "But you showed me more intelligence, respect and graciousness than any professor I've had in three years at Brown. Moreover, you posed to me questions I had never thought of before, and I just wanted to say thank you." She paused, took a breath and a step back, then said, "But that's not to say I'm converted yet!"

This is one of the most wonderful compliments I have ever received. This woman received a gift from me as a servant of the Gospel, and that gift was the freedom to ask questions.

University of New Hampshire, 1985

On April 3, 1985, I was invited to debate the subject of human abortion at the University of New Hampshire in Durham. My invited debate partner, a professor of philosophy, cancelled at the last moment. So there I was with 140 students and no one to debate.

No one left, and I said I would do my best to represent how an abortion-rights advocate would make the case, and how I would respond. I did do, then we opened it up for a vigorous time of questions and answers. Interestingly, in an audience that was perhaps 80 percent not on my side of the issue, nobody said I misrepresented the pro-abortion argument.

Which is to say, the Gospel is always interested in an honest definition of terms, and listening to all sides of a given debate equally. Thus the power of informed choice is possible, and informed choice always honors human life from natural origins to natural demise, and with the view toward eternal life.

During the question and answer period, one young woman was arguing for the "right" to choose abortion. When I sought to add the humanity of the unborn to the equation, she responded by saying that she still had the "power over" the fetus. She said it with such passion that the whole room became hushed, and as I was about to form an answer.

But then a Christian woman, sitting right behind the college co-ed, leaned forward and said to her, "Oh – you mean you're bigger." It broke the quiet with piercing clarity. The young women then threw her hand over her mouth, quite dramatically, in a huge aha moment. And after the event was over, she talked at length with some Christians who were there.

There were two young men sitting by themselves in the top row, and following this aha moment, one of them said, "I don't see what the problem is. If I get a woman pregnant, she can go get an abortion. What's the big deal?" As he did, seventy sets of female eyes turned and glared at him in the next aha moment of the evening (as least for the rest of us). As I moved on to

187

the next question, the two men quickly slipped out of the auditorium. Their chauvinisms, their reification of women, had been self-exposed.

University of Rhode Island, 1985

On April 16, 1985, I participated in a six-person debate on abortion, three on each side, at the University of Rhode Island (URI). The *God* → *life* → *choice* → *sex* versus *sex* → *choice* → *life* →*/God* paradigm percolated (even before my articulation of the same), along with the question of male chauvinism. And to which I also added my passion for an honest liberal arts inquiry into the subject.

One interlocutor was Dr. Bob Weisbord, professor of history. He focused on maternal deaths due to illegal abortions before *Roe*, the smallness of a fertilized egg is, not knowing whether "it" exists and has a soul, of a woman's right to abortion apart from any reference to the man who impregnated her, contraception as the answer, privacy, and opposition to anyone imposing their "morality." He also highly recommended sexual fidelity, but alas, "morality cannot be imposed," and thus the existential need is to choose the lesser of two evils, as it were.

There were over 100 people in attendance, with many good questions between the panelists, and from the audience. But too, between Dr. Weisbord and one of my co-panelists, there were some fireworks of charges and counter-charges, leading to questions over who is being "Nazi" and who is imposing morality, etc.

At one juncture I stepped into the fray, pulled away from the accusatory language, and things settled down. As I did, and as I argued for "informed choice" in advancing a true "pro-life" ethic, Dr. Weisbord looked at me, surprised, and exclaimed, "I wish Jerry Falwell were like you!" Now, this was meant to be a compliment to me, but it was also unfair to the Rev. Falwell (of Thomas Road Baptist Church, Liberty University and the Moral Majority). Falwell was moving from an older era of separatist Baptists into a culture-engaging faith, and his trajectory was far healthier than for the top-down media who criticized him.

188

Planned Parenthood, 1985

From the time I began in pro-life ministry in late 1983, I repeatedly sought communication with abortion-rights leaders, and their refusal to address honest questions was nearly always the case. Twice I wrote a certain state director for Planned Parenthood.

He responded on November 13, 1985, and here is a portion:

> Further, it is the practice of this agency to not engage in debate and/or rhetorical dialogue with persons who hold anti-choice points of view. And from your two letters, this is clearly your perspective on the matter of abortion ... But our experience indicates that there is no benefit in engaging in discussions that restate the merits of our personal or organizational beliefs. I would suspect that your views would not change after a discussion and I know that mine would not.
>
> We jealously guard our time and effort and will engage only in activities that move our cause forward.

In other words, this man, in representing Planned Parenthood, does not believe that communication and debate, with those with whom he disagrees, will advance his cause. As he uses the "anti-choice" pejorative (like the Religious Coalition for Abortion Rights), so too he displays a lack of inner confidence in his advocacy. In flight from the power of informed choice and the power to love hard questions.

Dartmouth College, 1986

The Dartmouth Area Christian Fellowship (DACF) and Campus Crusade for Christ planned for me to debate at Dartmouth College, Hanover, New Hampshire, on January 22, 1986, the thirteenth anniversary of *Roe* v. *Wade*. They made inquiries to find an interlocutor for me, beginning with the local chapter of Planned Parenthood and professors on campus, but could find no willing party.

So we decided instead to hold a forum at the Collis Common Ground, the social center of the school. And we planned to show the current and controversial film by Dr. Bernard Nathanson, *The Silent Scream*. Nathanson was a former abortionist in pre-*Roe* New York City, and personally oversaw some 60,000 human abortions. Then when he realized what he was doing, did an about face.

Nathanson's video was the first one produced for public purpose that showed an ultrasound of an unborn human being undergoing an abortion, and as crude as the ultrasound technology was at the time, the child's discernible silent scream on his or her mouth, as the womb was invaded, was uniquely compelling in its horror.

The Planned Parenthood videotape response was produced by the King County chapter (Seattle, Washington), and it had a copyright warning on it against unauthorized use except for private purposes. Not knowing how to interpret this, and not reading the warning until just before the forum, I spoke with the sponsors on how to proceed. Would we run the risk of a lawsuit? So the spokesman for the DACF campus group announced this explicit concern to the audience at the outset. We did not want to risk a lawsuit, but we deeply wanted both sides to be heard. And as we hesitated on showing it, the boos came as everyone wanted to see it, as had been advertised.

I was willing to risk such a possible lawsuit, but the sponsors were more circumspect, and we prayed about it. So we showed *The Silent Scream*, with the audience knowing our intentions and concerns. As it was showing, a young woman student approached the DACF sponsor, and said that her mother was on the board of Planned Parenthood of King County. She called her mother, received permission to show the video, and thus we did. When this announcement was made after *The Silent Scream* was completed, the audience erupted in cheers.

Thus, this unplanned drama increased the energy and interest of all present, and is one of those portraiture moments that always stick in my mind.

Afterward, I presented my additional theological comments, then took questions from the audience.

The room was full enough (maybe 100-120 students, faculty and others). I set the stage in defining creation, sin and redemption and the definitions of life and choice, theologically and biologically. During the question and answer period, I was addressing the first question posed, from a person in the front row. While doing so, I saw a young woman at the upper left, straining anxiously to keep her arm in the air. So I interrupted my answer to the first person, and said, "I see your hand, and after I finish this question, I will come to you next."

A Christian woman, sitting next to her, told me later that all night the young woman had been agitated, and when I acknowledged her eyeball-to-eyeball, her body, facial expression and demeanor greatly relaxed. This is the power to love hard questions in the ministry of the Gospel – we always seek to honor the humanity of all people equally, regardless of the issue or context. I forget the question these many years later, but it came from the depth of her soul and experience.

Harvard Medical School, 1986

On February 13, 1986, I addressed a debate at Harvard Medical School, with a colleague who is a medical doctor, Andy White. It was entitled, "Abortion: What is the Physician's Responsibility?" The abortion-rights side was represented by a physician, Dr. Marian C. Craighill, and a Unitarian minister, the Rev. Elizabeth (Betty) Ellis-Hagler of the Unitarian Universalist Association (UUA). About 80 medical students were in attendance (one-fifth the student body). During the evening, Andy and I consistently spoke of the woman and her unborn child equally. But the abortion-rights advocates kept positing a war between mother and (unwanted) child.

Dr. Craighill spoke of being "pro-choice" and not "pro-abortion," and within her own "faith tradition" she said "God is pro-choice." The paradigm of *God* → *life* → *choice* → *sex* versus *sex* → *choice* → *life* →/*God* reality again pre-percolated, always regardless of which side of the debate we may occupy. However, she did not give any biblical basis for this view.

A lead question for Dr. Craighill is whether the "life of the woman is central," where those of us who are pro-life argue (supposedly) that the "egg is superior," concerns about the crime of "wife-beating," the rape question that needs address, and how a woman is free "with her own body" to do as she pleases. Dr. Craighill also spoke of life in the womb as "potential life," the woman should always seek to nurture, but the choice remains her own up to 24 weeks of pregnancy. Dr. Craighill also said she would not "impose her morality" on others, that there are no absolutes in the medical world, and that the "quality of life" is most important.

In my comments in response, I raised the theological question of creation, sin and redemption as definitive in defining a biblical pro-life ethic, a concern for "slippery slope" arguments that dehumanize, the deeper reality of the male chauvinistic realities that equal the true anti-woman posture, the non-scientific definition of "potential life," and if it is only "potential life," that means it is also "potential non-life," or potentially something else, and if so, how so? I said that the Bible does define when biological life begins, and noted the unintended consequences of an argument based on control of our own bodies in various other circumstances (e.g. drug abuse), not to mention the fact the unborn child is not a part of the woman's body, but rather, he or she is a whole and separate body dependent on the mother's womb and body. I also asked her, "Were you once a one-celled zygote in your mother's womb?" This links origin and destiny in a continuum of reality that cannot be arbitrarily dissected.

The greatest dynamic of the evening was during the question and answer period. A medical student announced that politically he held a "pro-choice" position. He addressed Andy and I, noting how we expressed "care for both the woman and her unborn child." Then he addressed our debate opponents and noted how they only spoke about care for the woman, asking them, "Do you also have any care for the unborn?"

192

Dr. Craighill and the Rev. Ellis-Hagler looked at each other, were at a loss for words for some embarrassing moments, then Rev. Ellis-Hagler gestured to us, and said, "Well, that is their concern, not ours."

The audience, overwhelmingly "pro-choice" in sympathies, then rippled with some laughter and amazed sighs. The contrast could not be clearer: abortion-rights activists define an inequality of the strong over the weak, and accept a war; pro-life advocates define and accept the hope of true equality and reconciliation.

On February 20, I received a thank you note on the letterhead of the Christian Medical Society of Harvard Medical School:

> Although the organization of last week's debate fell to the Hamilton-Hunt Society, and we were there as spectators, rather than as planners, I nonetheless wanted to express my thanks on behalf of the Christian Medical Society to both you and Dr. White for your having participated in the debate and following discussion. We appreciate the time and effort which you were willing to devote to help educate us on the important issue of abortion. As future physicians, we will do doubt have to face squarely many matters of life and death, and I fear that our preparation for such duties is often woefully inadequate.

> I appreciated, as the Rev. Ellis-Hagler pointed out, the calm tone which you helped establish early in the discussion, and the evident effort which you made to tailor your remarks to the medical student audience. Having since talked to numerous students who attended the debate, the only "complaint" I've heard is that there just wasn't enough time to discuss so many of the issues. In the general climate of the medical school, it is so usual for us to be told, especially by the faculty, that the institution of abortion on demand has been an enlightened public health measure, or at worst a "necessary" evil in an imperfect world, that it was truly refreshing to hear you speak out against this inhumanity, in which our profession has been a major accomplice. I just admit that we in the Christian Medical Society, at least as a group, have been lax in facing the issue, and should feel convicted that it was

only by the efforts of another organization that the discussion this past week came to be. Nevertheless, I am also reassured by God's faithfulness in this matter, for it was clearly His work that such a large and open crowd turned up for the event.

Thanks again for having come to speak. If there is any way in which the Christian Medical Society can be of any assistance to you in the future, let us know. We pray, as your brothers and sisters in the Lord in this medical school, that His grace, freely granted through His Son, might continue to be with you in your life and work.

In rereading this letter for the first time after three decades, I am struck by the power of elite institutions to deceive the social order. I am blessed for how well Dr. White and I were received in our biblically rooted and scientifically directed pro-life advocacy. And as well, I am grateful to consider how many future physicians became, or were strengthened, in the honoring equally of women and their unborn as a result of the evening, thus ministering to and saving many otherwise broken, or thankfully, not to be broken lives.

The Gloucester Daily Times, 1984-1989

On February 9, 1984, the Gloucester Daily Times (Massachusetts), published a letter to the editor from me. I then lived one town over in Rockport, and my office was in Gloucester from later that year to late 1989. It was in response to an earlier letter by the statewide director of Planned Parenthood, Nicki Nichols Gamble. She argued about what it means to be "pro-choice," and my letter challenged her use of the language.

My next letter, responding to a pro-abortion editorial, was on November 25, 1985. I used to work at the Times as a local sports journalist while in seminary, and Cape Ann with its four towns is very local. Little did I know what would follow – over 100 letters to the editor on both sides of the issue, where I was at the center of it – until I moved my office to Boston in late 1989.

194

It was quite a learning curve for me, where in the face of all the issues and suffering concerning abortion, I learned to communicate, hopefully better, as time passed. I was interested in every person who challenged me, and on two or three occasions was able to meet with such people personally (with more unanswered invitations extended). In early 1985, I invited Ms. Gamble, or anyone else in her office interested, to debate the subject. And despite a second invitation, I never heard back. I sought out other abortion-rights leaders likewise, but without success.

Fuller School, 1986

So I decide to hold my own forum, and invite the public. On April 25, 1986, we held the forum at a local middle school auditorium in Gloucester, Massachusetts. We distributed flyers citywide and also in Rockport, Essex and Manchester. Some 110 people turned out, which is quite large for such a small community, largely centered around the fishing industry. Yet, the Times did not see fit to send a reporter.

When I arrived at the school that evening, I was greeted by three women protesters with placards. (This is the only time I have been protested to date.) They were not protesting me per se, but were opposing a pro-life initiative for the 1986 state ballot. It opposed taxpayer funded abortions, and I supported it, but it was not my public focus, nor was it the advertised or actual substance of the forum that evening.

I approached the women, invited them into the forum, and offered them equal time from the podium to address their concerns. One woman left, and the other two accepted my invitation but demurred to take the podium. So I gave them first shot at asking questions from the audience, and priority in the amount of time they wished for. One woman asked many questions, and we went back and forth for a good period. It was the highlight of the evening for me.

In her final statement, she said how she now agreed with me 90 percent on the subject, but still could not accept my opposition to abortion in the cases of rape and incest. My response was straightforward – if we have 90 percent agreement, let's build on it and go from there.

I stated my belief, and as she now agreed with the rest of my pro-life concerns, then a patient examination of the rape and incest issue would lead her to understand the consistency and compassion I was pursuing. However, I was not going to push the issue – I prayed that the seeds of truth she had accepted would bear fruit in due season.

Salem State College, ca. 1986

This is an event I would have forgotten about, except that in August, 2015, I was speaking at Alton Bay Christian Conference in New Hampshire, on Lake Winnipesaukee. Afterward I was approached by a man who had headed up InterVarsity Christian Fellowship (IVCF) at Salem State College in Salem, Massachusetts in the 1980s. He now works for IVCF at Harvard.

He sought to organize a debate on campus with me and an abortion advocate, but could not find a willing participant. So instead we held a forum, as per the Dartmouth model, where we showed *The Silent Scream* and Planned Parenthood's rebuttal, followed by my comments, then questions and answers.

There are two things that made an impact on him that evening. First, he met a young woman whom he later married. And second, he spoke about how upset many students on campus were ahead of time that such an event was even happening. Thus, when he entered the auditorium, he had never witnessed such a hostile audience. Then he said how amazed he was that within ninety seconds of my introductory comments, the whole audience shifted attitude completely, eager for what was to follow.

This is a reality that the Lord Jesus has woven into my character, and it traces back through my faith to my father (1918-2010) and his character. He grew up in the Great Depression in Nebraska, served as a Navy physician in World War II in the Pacific, and in 1950 founded the Connecticut Blood Bank, serving subsequently as chief of hematology at the Hartford Hospital for nearly four decades. We come from a long direct and indirect heritage of Presbyterian ministers, including many lead abolitionists (e.g., the Rev. John Thomas Rankin, 1793-1886, known as the "Manager of the Underground Railroad"). My father was in medicine for one reason – he simply loved caring for people, and so many of his patients he treated for free because they could not afford it otherwise. Thus, in this modeled character which shaped me, and in my Christian faith, I have never been interested in winning a debate to win a debate; rather, I want to see people reconciled to the love of God and one another.

As it is, only being reminded of the Salem State forum, three decades ex post facto, did my memory get jogged enough to recollect what he described. Now too, I have seen this happen in very many other contexts, private and public. This is the power of the Gospel, which the apostle Paul speaks of in Ephesians 2:14 as breaking down "the dividing wall of hostility."

The Universalist Unitarian Association, 1986

On October 23 and 28, 1986, Dr. Andy White (with whom I had addressed the earlier debate at Harvard Medical School) and I participated in two debates with the Unitarian Universalist Association (UUA). The UUA was represented by the Rev. Jerry Goddard and Ms. Mary Andrus Overley, ASCW. I had debated Rev. Goddard once on the radio, and also later visited with him in his church office, where we discussed, among other things, abortion and its impact on Social Security.

These two forums came about because of a "bull-session" I had with the Rev. Gary Smith, special assistant to the president of the UUA, at the Boston headquarters in July (adjacent to the State Capitol). I had arranged to meet with him simply out of a desire to talk about matters of religious liberty. Because of some honest rapport we established in terms of openness and the affirmation of women in order to empower them to choose life for their unborn, he informed me of a recent UUA resolution (passed by their General Assembly in Rochester, NY that June). This resolution ("for study" by local UUA congregations) restated their long-standing belief that women have full option to choose abortion.

197

But, in a unique effort for a "pro-choice" group, they said: "Whereas the current polarized environment is not conducive to open discussion and we as a religious body are in a position to explore moral arguments, encourage public discussion and promote consensus on shared values; therefore ... Be it finally resolved: that individual UUs, congregations and the UUA open discussion with those of different mind and seek opportunities for consensus from our shared values." Thus, an openness to communication and hard questions.

In view of this resolution, I took the initiative. The Unitarian Universalists pride themselves on open-mindedness (I know, as I was raised in a UUA church prior to my conversion in 1967).

In the two debates, it was mostly the "moral arguments" that had focus, and I set the table concerning the defining questions of life and choice, along with the attendant reality of male chauvinism. In Springfield (the UUA church in Longmeadow) the crowd responded well to us, and Andy and I felt some heart and minds were opened, even in the face of some open hostility.

With the Rev. Goddard, we felt like we were coming up against an "existential brick wall," as he did not deal with much of our argument, but dismissed it in order to focus on other concerns I saw as quite secondary.

Thus, in the Boston (Arlington Street Church) debate, we focused on two primary issues, and left with a good sense of having won substantial ground. First, we established a positive and scientific definition of human life beginning at conception, but Rev. Goddard continually fudged at this point with only negative assertions. Then at one point, during the audience interaction, Dr. White's father introduced himself as a "simple man with a simple question." He noted how silly the "acorn" argument is (referenced that evening by Jerry Goddard, and as we have seen with Bill Baird). It must first be planted in the ground in order for any suitable analogy. Rev. Goddard simply changed the subject.

Second, we defined constitutional liberties which he denied us. He said that it was illegitimate for us to seek the legal ban of any abortions beyond the

Roe v. *Wade* decision, that such equals an "imposing" upon society of a narrow view. He did not even grant us the right if we won the vast majority of this country's opinion. And when we turned his logic back on him, it was clear that in truth he was and is imposing his own religious non-definition of human life on us and the unborn, without any appeal to scientific criteria.

Clearly he was not open or honest at these points. At the end of the evening, he said to me, "I'm worn out." To which I replied, with a smile, "Well, I'm just getting warmed up." Andy commented to me later that when someone defends an intellectually dishonest position, it wears them out when challenged.

Despite the "brick wall," Rev. Goddard did affirm many things we do in the empowering of women to choose life for their unborn. But at the bottom line, it was a challenge of opposing worldviews. We believe in the sanctity of all human life, in a personal God, in eternal life. Rev. Goddard is an existentialist who believes life is a cosmic accident of a material and godless universe, that there is no eternal life, no purpose for it all. And this is where the real battle over abortion lies, the Gospel v. opposing worldviews, and their contrary spiritual domains. We must proclaim Jesus, and seek to get behind the "brick walls" and touch human hearts with God's love and hope.

With Ms. Andrus Overley, a social worker, it was a different matter. Though she affirmed the legal option of abortion in her opening statement, she did not once seek to articulate or defend it in the open forum. Rather, she sought to focus on areas of mutual agreement in terms of openness of dialogue, the affirmation of life-empowering options for women facing crisis pregnancies, and the renunciation of violence or harassment on either side.

Temple University, 1987

A dear friend of mine, David Buffum, from seminary and years in the same local church, was head of residential life at Messiah College's inner city campus in North Philadelphia, across from Temple University, in the 1980s. He also taught a class in ethics, and had me teach a series for his class each year for several years. He arranged for me to debate the Rev. Barbara

Chaapel, Director of Public Information at Princeton Theological Seminary, on February 18, 1987, at Temple.

One or two weeks prior, I received a phone call from some woman in New Jersey or Pennsylvania, calling the offices of the NECAC, asking for any written publications by the ministry. She gave her name, but I forget what it was. So I sent along some newsletters, and one unpublished position paper. During the debate with the Rev. Chaapel, she worked in some material and questions concerning Genesis 1-3. They were of such a specific nature, that in that moment, I realized it was a friend of hers who had called me for the material. And this is fine. Scouting me out ahead of time.

But it is too bad that Barbara herself did not have the temerity to call, identify herself, and ask for the material to help her in preparing for the debate. I would have been glad to oblige, and also to chat with her to any extent that she wished, here ahead of time. And the reason is simple. As soon as I began my various debates over abortion, I could see that my goal was not to "win" a debate per se, to engage in the pursuit of gotcha moments. In fact, over the years, friends have often said to me something like: "You could have nailed (him or her) at this point." And my response would be, "It is not my goal to nail anyone on a debating point, for Jesus has been nailed to the cross already not to win a debate, but to reconcile us to his love."

In other words, my goal is to win the relationship, to let genuinely and mutually instructive aha moments happen as they may happen. This is not to say I would not make my case as persuasively as possible, but would do so always in an open-ended way, allowing my interlocutor to hopefully own some new questions or perspectives. Understatement is far more powerful at honest persuasion than is overstatement or backing someone into an ethical or intellectual cul-de-sac.

The evening was titled "The Debate over Abortion," and some 100 people attended. I addressed the questions concerning the definition of human life, and the nature of informed choice and male chauvinism, among others. This I did in the context of the *God → Life → Choice → Sex* versus *sex → choice*

200

$\rightarrow$ *life* $\rightarrow$*/God* paradigm, as by this time it was firming up in my public presentations.

The Rev. Chaapel began with postulating a war between society and the woman, and ignored the reality of male chauvinism as I identified it. She also said that to be a "person" God says "you have to choose between right and wrong." Now, this is a non-sequitur, for life precedes choice by all definitions and in all reality. She did not define proactively what a "person" is biblically, as I have in terms of *nephesh*. Nor did she define right and wrong relative to human abortion. As she constructed her argument, I could see where she had read my material and was trying to weave through it in order to challenge it. But she was doing so in a pot shot manner, and not with a structured theology of taking the text on its own terms.

Taylor University, 1989

In 1989, as I debated a Universalist minister at Taylor University in Upland, Indiana, a student asked him, "Do you think sex outside of marriage is a good thing?" The minister, who had supported the need for legalized abortion for some thirty years (concerned with "back alley abortions"), was caught off guard. He took a deep breath, was about to answer, took another deep breath, did not answer again, shifted weight between his feet, and finally answered something like, "Well, generally speaking, no!"

From that point, his attitude perceptibly changed. By the time it came for his concluding remarks, he essentially conceded the debate by refusing to give a final rebuttal, indicating respect for the argument I had made and the attitude in which it was couched. He then concluded, saying to me, "Thank you and God bless you!" Once he was challenged to speak out against sexual promiscuity, he de facto rejected the reversal motif of *Sex* $\rightarrow$ *Choice* $\rightarrow$ *Life* $\rightarrow$*/ God*.

Cornell University, 1989

In early March, 1989, as referenced earlier, I was invited to address a debate at Cornell University in Ithaca, New York, addressing a CPC banquet

201

on a Thursday night. It was scheduled in conjunction with a large abortion-rights rally in the Arts Quad the next, and I attended. Two or three thousand students were there, attracted from some twenty colleges in the Northeast.

The two main speakers were Professor Carl Sagan (author of the book and popular PBS series, *Cosmos*), and Betty Friedan, former and first president of the National Organization for Women (NOW).

As I listened to Dr. Sagan, I so much wanted to interact with him. He defined human life according to brain waves (secular achievement ethic v. biblical *nephesh*). One local paper reported: " 'I am a proponent of life,' Sagan told the charged crowd. He then called right-to-life activists 'well-intentioned,' but said the right-to-life argument is inconsistent" in terms of nuclear disarmament and caring for the poor (allegedly).

Several years later I invited him to address what would have been my first in the Mars Hill Forum series, and he was interested. But then he fell ill with terminal cancer, and before he died, sent me a signed copy of his final book, *The Demon-Haunted World: Science as Candle in the Dark*. Deep biblical imagery at the center of Biblical Theology 101.

The Friday evening debate was with Dr. Daryl Bem, chairman of the department of psychology (and later head of Planned Parenthood of Tompkins County). It proved to be a gracious interchange. His argument employed a psychological strategy to reverse the debate expectation – saying he was more pro-life than was I because he advocated birth control to prevent more "unwanted pregnancies." I answered otherwise, linking fidelity in marriage to the holistic pro-life position, something countermanded by the contraceptive ideology, also challenging his cited research with contrary data. The *God → life → choice → sex* versus *sex → choice → life →/God* rubric was on full display as other issues percolated as well.

At one juncture during the question and answer portion, he was exerting great intellectual energy in trying to answer a question from the audience. He had earlier denied that biological human life begins at conception, and in his answer to a different question was just about to admit the biology of conception, then abruptly switched tack when he realized it, but without a cogent argument.

It hit me as I watched him – so much intellectual energy can be spent trying to rationalize what the human soul knows is untrue, that clarity is lost and intellectual ability eventually avoids and does not pursue hard questions. They are often hard, not due to their intrinsic nature, but because the answers challenge deeply held presuppositions and chosen identities. Even for the most brilliant people, the biblical love of hard questions can prove a stumbling block.

Wellesley College, 1989

At Wellesley College, Wellesley, Massachusetts, in March of 1989, I was invited to debate feminist attorney, Jamie Sabino. She had worked against my 1988 pro-life referendum in Massachusetts (Chapter Six). It was an audience of some 120 filling a room at this women's college.

When I as a minister asked Ms. Sabino the attorney a legal question concerning the status of the unborn, citing *Roe*'s key clause, she said that she did not understand it, and thus visibly and quickly lost the audience. The very pretense of ignorance in the "I don't know" argument of the *Roe* Court on display, the intrinsic opposition to the power of informed choice. There was no willingness to look at foundational realities such as the Declaration of Independence and the Fifth and Fourteenth Amendments. As consistently is the case, the paradigm of *God → life → choice → sex* versus *sex → choice → life →/God* percolated, with the question of male chauvinism front and center as usual.

The University of New Hampshire, 1989

In October, 1989, I addressed a most dynamic debate, at the University of New Hampshire (UNH) in Durham, to a packed auditorium of some 400 students and faculty. I will give it a fuller review in Chapter Nine concerning the demonic presence that exploded publicly after the debate.

Here I will make one observation, parallel to a moment at the 1986 Harvard Medical School debate. There, the physician and minister supporting legalized abortion, were questioned by a student, "Do you also have any care for the unborn?" They were speechless for some embarrassing moments until they said that the concern for the unborn belonged to my partner and I. They essentially silenced themselves.

At UNH, like URI, I was involved in a panel of three on each side of the debate. During a time of dialogue, I asked the panel of abortion advocates: "Is there anything intrinsically good in the act of human abortion?" They hesitated for perhaps ten embarrassing seconds. Then one woman said, "Well, we're not used to the format yet ..." and proceeded to avoid the question, because they knew that human abortion is intrinsically an act of destruction. And we were already 45 minutes into the format.

Ithaca College, 1990

A debate was set up for me by a student at Ithaca College in Ithaca, New York, on April 13, 1990. My interlocutor was Shelley Drazen, chair of the Tompkins County Coalition for Reproductive Choice. She was well known for her passionate rhetoric and activism.

The sponsor, in preparing the event, advertised it with posters across campus: *Abortion: Get beyond the slogans! The Good Friday/Friday the 13th Debate*. Now the date afforded this double entendre, but Shelley was furious. She thought it was intended to pit Good Friday on the one hand, versus the sadistically violent movie of 1980 called "Friday the 13th" (which produced a franchise of sequels), aligning her such gratuitous violence. Now I had not seen the movie, nor do I have any interest in such a genre.

So Shelley threatened to cancel, and we spoke by phone. She was mollified in understanding that I had nothing to do with the title selection, and too, I had just spoken with the sponsor accordingly – no need for provocation, intentional or non-intentional. Now, had someone set me up with a similarly perceived provocation from the other side, I would have been that much

204

more eager to address such a debate, and show the beauty of the Gospel in contrast.

So the debate happened, more than 200 were in attendance, and Shelley could not help but mention the controversy of the event title up front. It had unsettled her deeply, and this I was able to address in a satisfactory manner. Then, in my opening comments I explicitly stated that there are only four issues with which we ever have to deal. One man glared at me as if to say, "Don't take me for a fool. I know there are far more than four issues. I am an educated man." I let the statement stand for a moment, then said: "God, life, choice and sex." He did not challenge me after I defined what I meant.

At the end of the evening, I made a quip, as I often do in letting people know about materials I have available: "For those interested in my propaganda, see me after the debate." Immediately afterward, a man rushed up to me: "I knew it! I knew it! You are a propagandist!" So I asked him how he defines the nature of propaganda. He said, "Lies! Damned lies!" So I said, "No. It means to propagate. My wife and I have propagated four children, and I also seek to propagate the Gospel."

New York University, 1990

In 1990, I addressed a forum at New York University, in the East Village of Manhattan. Again, my sponsors sought to find an interlocutor to debate, but proved unable. So I addressed the modest audience myself, and like Salem State in 1986, as I walked in, the hostility was palpable. Yet, within ninety seconds, the attitude changed readily.

In this season I had two formats I used in speaking solo to skeptical audiences. First would be the posing five central questions up front, and they would tune in readily. Then I would propose my best answers in quick summary form, then ask for their toughest questions. Here are the questions, and I gave brief cognate information to buttress my reasons for posing them:

1. What are the boundaries of choice?
2. Is not all law based on a prior definition of human life?

3. Is there any known legal example in all American law, apart from *Roe*, based on a non-consensus as to the central fact of the case?
4. Are there any known facts to dispute the biological reality that each individual human life begins at the point of conception?
5. How can feminist ethics be reconciled with human abortion?

The second format defined six terms up front, and I would ask 1) if they were honestly defined and salient, and b) for any questions or comments:

1. Definition of liberal arts inquiry.
2. Definition of conception.
3. Definition of abortion.
4. Definition of abortion as the ultimate male chauvinism.
5. Definition of the abortion debate as a religious war.
6. Definition of Christian ethics in a pluralistic society.

During the forum that evening, there were two women sitting about halfway up the auditorium, and they were having a hushed, animated, but noticeable and somewhat distracting (to others) conversation the whole time. During the questions and answers, one of them was trying to raise her hand to ask a question, but her friend was resisting her attempt – until the question was posed, and the friend departed the auditorium. I forget what the question was, but in my spirit I prayed for the woman who left – who knows what pain she has been through? And all the dynamics of their friendship and debate over the subject that led both of them to be there that night?

The College of William & Mary, 1992

On January 23, 1992 (a day after the nineteenth anniversary of *Roe* v. *Wade*), I addressed a debate at The College of William & Mary, Williamsburg, Virginia. My interlocutor was Grace Sparks, executive director of Planned Parenthood of Virginia. The title was: *Will the New Supreme Court Abort Roe vs. Wade? Abortion Debate – Bring Your Toughest Questions*. There were some 500 in attendance. Our sponsors, the *Off Campus Student Council and Debate Society*, hosted a nice dinner for Grace and I ahead of time.

206

Up front I organized my comments within the rubric of *God → life → choice → sex* versus *sex → choice → life →/God*. And as usual, the issue of male chauvinism came up as central. Grace is a gracious person, and her issues, among others, centered on how, as per *Roe*, it is a matter of "potential life," and to define "life" or "personhood" concretely violates choices within the nature of "religious pluralism." This is a unique argument, that somehow choice does not allow a concrete definition of terms – the opposite of the biblical power of informed choice. The issue of rape and incest was raised, but once I addressed it, the subject changed. Grace emphasized that, indeed, "I'd like to see no abortions." But of course, our different views of the boundaries of healthy human sexuality …

At the very end of the evening, I stepped into it. In answering a question, I sought to give an illustration of my desire to communicate with and receive the toughest questions from anyone on any subject. I then mentioned the context of the debate over homosexuality, and how at Harvard I had studied with many professed lesbians, and the very positive communications that resulted.

The audience erupted in howls and protests across the auditorium. I was not prepared for this. One woman was incensed, and said it was unfair in a debate for me to bring up a new topic at the end. So I sought to reiterate the point of my illustration, not as a new debate topic, but an example of the wide applicability of the ethics I had sought to employ in the face of the abortion debate.

The answer helped calm thing down, but boy, what a way to end the evening as the ripples continued. The homosexual rights movement was significantly gearing up in the universities at that time, but since I was not publically addressing it as a subject, I was somewhat impervious to its extent and depth. And this is even as I met many lesbians, in particular, in the pro-abortion movement in front of the abortion centers (see Chapter Eight). It proves that the *God → life → choice → sex* versus *sex → choice → life →/God* reality dominates in this debate as well, and where the suffering of so many girls, women and boys, under the tyranny of male chauvinism, drives much pain.

207

Republican Party Platform Hearings, 1992

On May 26, 1992, in Salt Lake City, Utah, there were competing protests on the abortion debate on the streets outside the Republican Party Platform Hearings downtown, heavy with media coverage. I was in town teaching a seminar, preaching and speaking at a pro-life consortium. At street-level, I had opportunity to speak awhile with a national abortion-rights political leader in the Democratic Party. At one juncture I appealed explicitly to the POSH Ls of the image of God that I first expressed at Brown University in 1989 (peace, order, stability and hope; to live, to love, to laugh, and to learn). Then I asked her: "Are you seeking these same qualities, and if so, how does human abortion serve this end?" She looked at me with widened eyes, took a step back and said, "Oh, you're good – really good." And there she ended the conversation, refusing as well later invitations to address a Mars Hill Forum.

I also met Kate Michelman at this time, president of the National Abortion Rights Action League (NARAL), from Washington, D.C., who as a Democrat, was trying to get a hearing at the Republican event, not admitted, and was outside as well. I approached her, had a nice conversation, and invited her to address a forum with me, and this came to pass three years later at Georgetown University.

Ridgefield High School, 1993

In the spring of 1993, I gave the keynote address to some 1,000 students (including faculty) at Ridgefield High School, Ridgefield, Connecticut. The occasion was "Clergy Awareness Day," and there were nineteen such religious leaders there in eclectic diversity.

My subject was religious liberty, but the two questions from the floor at the end of my address both dealt with abortion. In response to one of them, I diagnosed the Playboy mentality of human abortion; namely, that if a woman gets pregnant by a chauvinist, he sends her off to the abortion center to get "fixed," that is, aborted, to be returned to him like a broken toy that has been repaired, and thus, a toy which can be played with again.

When I said this, so many of the boys in the crowd groaned that the whole auditorium reverberated with a "gnashing of teeth," and as many of their girlfriends similarly stared them down and questioned them as well.

And in this moment, I saw, up close and in painful depth, the breeding ground for the sexual promiscuity and male chauvinism that undergirds the abortion ethos. Also, in consideration of how many political leaders are men who know they have "fooled around," they have no moral mettle to resist the demands of political feminists. The abolition of male chauvinism, repentance of it where any of us have been guilty, and the honoring of marriage, is key to reversing the reversal.

Because of such a visceral and disruptive response to my words, the principal then cut the assembly short. Afterward, over lunch, this Jewish principal was sitting next to the invited rabbi and myself. The rabbi casually mentioned to him as a fellow Jew, "I am amazed that so few people in my congregation know the meaning of *shalom*. They think it only means 'peace,' and is merely a form of greeting."

The principal appeared caught off guard, so I interjected: "*Shalom* means integrity and wholeness, of which peace is a cognate." The rabbi turned to me in amazement and quipped, "How is it that a *goy* [a Gentile] knows what *shalom* means when my Jewish congregants do not!" (Now, too, I grew up in West Hartford, with the largest Jewish population in any municipality in Connecticut, a block from Beth Israel, and so many of our family friends were Jewish; but still, I did not know what *shalom* really meant until I studied Hebrew.)

I subsequently addressed a Mars Hill Forum with this rabbi, on the topic: "Jewish and Christian Dialogue: The Binding of Isaac – Issues of Human Sacrifice and Biblical Interpretation." We had a delightful conversation.

Yale Law School, 1994

In Chapters One and Two, I referenced the Rev. Katherine Hancock Ragsdale, president of the Religious Coalition of Abortion Rights (RCAR).

Our first forum was at Yale Law School, sponsored by several campus organizations, February 25, 1994, entitled: *Abortion: A Human Right or an Act of Human Destruction?*

RCAR actually takes no formal theological position. In 1993, they changed their name to the Religious Coalition for Reproductive Choice (RCRC), to move away from a perceived negative to a perceived positive. In its mission statement in January, 1994, we read:

> The purpose of the Religious Coalition for Reproductive Choice is to ensure that every woman is free to make decisions about when to have children according to her own conscience and religious beliefs, without government interference. The Coalition's primary role is educating the public to make clear that abortion can be a moral, ethical, and religious responsible decision.

> Comprised of national mainline Christian, Jewish and other religious organizations, the Coalition works to educate and mobilize the religious community to create a public opinion that is conducive to pro-choice policymaking, and that affirms women as moral policymakers. Because women of color are disproportionately affected by restrictive laws and policies, the Coalition places particular emphasis on developing broad-based participation and leadership.

In other words, the reality of the *God → life → choice → sex* versus *sex → choice → life →/God* conflict is firmly in place. These "mainline" religions forsake biblical theology, and RCAR includes the Unitarian Universalists and the secular humanist American Ethical Union accordingly. Their unity is simply individual choice with no government interference against it. They want the government to affirm this idolatry of choice, while saying that the same government has no place to define and protect human life as per the nature of the Declaration and constitutional history.

RCAR references women yearning for the freedom to make their own "moral" decisions, which they should do as with all of us, but sadly, in choosing abortion they only yield further to the male chauvinism they seek to

210

flee. RCAR says women "of color" need a voice in such "choice," but RCAR does not address the overwhelming reality of how abortion nearly triples the comparative ratio of abortion among Black Americans.

Katherine reflected the RCRC materials in her presentation, but tried also to make a biblical case that the fetus cannot make a choice, and thus is not fully human. She could not counter the *nephesh* reality, and too, the scientific reality that the human fetus is wired for life, and fully resists abortive invasions. Choice?

The Rev. Ragsdale's three major points are these: 1) there is no consensus as to the biological origins of human life (thus, the pretension to ignorance per Cain, the enemies of Jesus and the *Roe* Court); 2) there is no biblical witness, namely, it is silent on the matter of human abortion (choosing a negative to counter the complete positive of the biblical witness for life and how the Scriptures define the humanity of the unborn as the prior level; and 3) her definition of a one-way separation of church and state, where the state may define the freedom for abortion choice, but not for the freedom of the unborn to live.

Katherine also brought up the issues of rape and incest, to which I gave response. Thus, in our subsequent forum in Chevy Chase, January 21, 1996, I was able to start with the subject. She neither challenged me accordingly, nor added anything else different from Yale Law School. She only did her best to avoid sound biblical exegesis.

The State University of New York at Buffalo, 1994

On April 21, 1994, at the State University of New York (SUNY) at Buffalo, in Amherst, I addressed the second of my three Mars Hill Forums with Dr. Paul Kurtz. He taught philosophy at SUNY Buffalo, and also founded and headed the world's largest secular humanist organization there in Amherst. In his presentations and many books, e.g., *The Forbidden Fruit: The Ethics of Secularism*, he supports "abortion rights" and "sexual freedom." So once I asked him if he knew the Hebrew translation, context, purpose, theology and/or ethics of the language of the "forbidden fruit" in

211

Genesis 2. He did not. Indeed, he found it a useful stand-alone clause, in my understanding, suitable too for those who reject the biblical text due to post-biblical understandings, and reactions to poor teaching or hypocrisy in the church.

Sometime after the forum, I wrote him a letter. In it I made observation that his reason for rejecting the God of the Bible was because he reverses the *God → Life → Choice → Sex* paradigm. His response? "I appreciate the many fine points you raise in your letter." No challenge to my diagnosis.

"Sexual Politics," 1994

In 1994, I met with a Protestant minister, "conservative" in his theology but "liberal" in his politics, who headed up the Connecticut Council of Churches. He was concerned that I focused too much on what he termed "sexual politics," and not enough on the poor.

I mentioned the reality where 70-90 percent of all men incarcerated for serious crime grow up de facto or functionally without a father. It is the male chauvinism of such sexual irresponsibility that leaves pregnant women and mothers of newborns to fend for themselves. And if the child is not aborted in the womb, he or she is aborted in the power for healthy life choices by the crippling absence of fatherhood.

Fatherless boys thus seek ersatz "families" in the inner cities, which outsiders call "gangs." Without the socializing influence of present and loving fathers, they seek identity with other fatherless boys; and in the ghettos with limited employment opportunities, they easily fall into drug use, then drug selling; and then to protect their "gang" and drug-selling turfs, they buy guns, shoot each other, kill and maim innocent bystanders in drive-by shootings, and thus contribute to social chaos and multiple human misery.

The misery they were given by sexually promiscuous and absent fathers is what they export at large to the culture around them. And the fatherless girls become sexual adjuncts and toys of the male "gang" members, and/or become prostitutes to support their drug habits. Thus, many die young, alone, aborted, forsaken and miserable. And most of this evil can be directly traced back to sexual infidelities, especially in terms of male chauvinism. Traced back to the reversal order of *Sex → Choice → Life →/ God.*

As I made this argument, I asked my minister friend: Does abortion-on-demand, the potential legalization of homosexual "marriage" (as of 1994), laws such as no-fault divorce, and Aid to Families with Dependent Children (AFDC), strengthen or weaken the marriage covenant and family? [AFDC is where, at that time, women, and especially teenage girls who would take advantage of it, could get more money from the government to live on if they had children out of wedlock, than if they were married.] Is not the violence in the ghettos traced to a sexually promiscuous male chauvinism in particular? Do not "sexual politics" address the core of this issue? And if we want to address social and racial justice, is not the honoring of the marriage covenant the linchpin?

He did not disagree. Again, the reality of *God → Life → Choice → Sex* and its *sex → choice → life →/God* reversal, and the pervasive evil of male chauvinism.

The United States Coast Guard Academy, NARAL, and Senator Dodd's Office, 1994

On May 20, 1994, I was invited to give the banquet address at an annual fundraiser for the Pregnancy Support Center (PSC) of Southeastern Connecticut. The venue was the United States Coast Guard Academy in New London.

A woman named Jean Rexford, who worked with both Planned Parenthood's state offices in New Haven, and the state chapter of the National Abortion Rights Action League (NARAL), had been tracking and slandering me for quite a while at this juncture – but I was not yet aware of it. As it turns out, she had heard me give an invited address at the founding convention of the Christian Coalition in Connecticut in June, 1993, where my pro-life advocacy was front and center. She also later heard me, in September, 1995, address a forum at the Unitarian Universalist Church in

213

West Hartford, the church in which I grew up. My guest was the president of the UUA, John Buehrens. Our topic was religious liberty, but the abortion question came up as well. Ms. Rexford was deeply scared of my advocacy, saying so publicly at the University of Connecticut the next day, even calling me "the most dangerous man in Connecticut."

In this season, Rexford contacted various newspapers, from the Nantucket Beacon, the Hartford Courant, the Hartford Jewish Ledger, now the New London Day, then the New York Times and finally to the Waterbury Republican-American. She insinuated (at the least) that I was a violent man, in trying the to get the newspapers to libel me, that I was plotting to harm people's civil rights. She even contacted an attorney, Charlene LaVoie, a "community lawyer" who worked for Ralph Nader, to accordingly investigate a "warfare prayer" meeting I hosted in Winsted. But it was for prayer only, aiming at tearing down demonic strongholds that actually harm all people's unalienable rights; likewise, to pray for the protection of the unborn. But Rexford deliberately twisted the language to say we were plotting temporal harm against various (unnamed) political leaders and others. When later I learned of Rexford's conspiracy, I contacted all the newspaper writers, her and LaVoie (including use of certified and return receipt signed mail), they all silenced themselves in due course, and stopped the slander and libel.

At Rexford's initiative, NARAL contacted the office of U.S. Senator Christopher Dodd, asking that the fundraiser at the Academy be canceled for illegitimate use of federal property. (A fun word about Chris Dodd. We grew up in the exact same house on Concord Street in West Hartford. His father, U.S. Senator Thomas Dodd, sold the house to my father in December, 1959. Chris Dodd was then fifteen and I was six. So, as he moved out, I moved in, and yes, this is the closet our politics ever came. I did try on two occasions to visit with him in his office, but no interest).

So Dodd's office put pressure on the Academy and the PSC, and the fundraising component of the banquet was removed. The day prior, on May 19, 1994, the New London Day had an article by Steven Slosberg reporting on NARAL's protest, and in it, he also sought to advance Rexford's slanderous/libelous campaign against me. It is still remarkable to consider how much hatred certain elitists have for women and their unborn. All a cognate to male chauvinism.

Smith College, 1994

In November, 1994, at a Mars Hill Forum at Smith College, Northampton, Massachusetts, with Patricia Ireland, president of the National Organization for Women (NOW), most the audience was sympathetic to a pagan feminist worldview. Probably more so than in any other venue. I shared earlier about Patricia's positive response to my definition of the power to give in the marriage relationship, and here as so consistently, the reality of the *God* → *life* → *choice* → *sex* versus *sex* → *choice* → *life* →*/God* paradigm percolates naturally.

The topic for the evening was *Feminism and the Bible: Do They Share Any Common Ground?* Abortion was not a specific subject per se. But in Patricia's questions of me, she asked specifically about violence at abortion centers, and thus the abortion subject took prominence. In the process, I alluded to human abortion in its male chauvinistic realities, from my diagnosis that abortion is the opposite of the power to give. I also told her about my 1989 face-to-face meeting with the founder of Operation Rescue, Randall Terry. I challenged his theology, opposing coercion of the human will, illegally or otherwise, and he thereafter cut off all communication (see Chapter Seven). Patricia was surprised at my consistent ethics.

With the television lights so bright in my face, I could not see the audience very well past the first few rows. And given my natural concentration on the subject at hand, and my focus on Patricia's person as the one with whom I was communicating, I was not so much aware of how the audience was responding. Christians in the audience, especially among the Smith students who were members of Campus Crusade for Christ, later told me how amazed they were to watch fellow students nodding their heads to my words – women whom they knew to be feminist, pro-abortion, lesbian and/or pagan.

215

At the end of the audience participation time a woman challenged me on how I could respect women's dignity while opposing abortion. We were running out of time, and I only had a few seconds to give answer.

So I said (taken from the videotape): "I think that if I had the time to address the abortion issue straight ahead, you would find that I would argue that abortion rips off women as much as it rips off the unborn, and allows male chauvinists to run free." Before I completed the final clause, the auditorium of some 550 people broke into enthusiastic and sustained applause of 17 seconds (timed from the tape; with one discernible loud "boo" in its midst). I was astonished, and there I sat, there Patricia Ireland sat and there the dean of students, as moderator, sat – all equally surprised.

Aha moments percolate at a certain pace for me, and it is not necessary to identify them all. But this one is as huge as I know. Thus, I did what I rarely do – listen or view tapings of myself – here in order to recollect my words and the response exactly.

This was not supposed to happen. There I was – a white heterosexual male, an evangelical pro-life minister. Six strikes against me on a "politically correct" campus. The image of God had been touched in these women. They knew the male chauvinistic reality of human abortion, from direct personal experience, and/or through the testimony of women friends. And perhaps for the first time, they heard a man diagnose it. I was not there passing judgment on women, but as a man I was submitting my gender to judgment first.

If the reality of human abortion as the ultimate male chauvinism can win an audience at Smith College which came to hear one of their heroines, it can win the whole culture. And with the successful presentation of this argument in politics and culture, biblical literacy and concomitant character, we can demonstrate that it is Christian pro-lifers who truly respect all women equally, rooted in the mutual nature of covenantal marriage. Thus the "pro-choice," that is, the idolatry of choice consensus in this nation will fall apart. The few extreme pro-abortion partisans will be marginalized in their own choices, and we will be able to build the moral consensus necessary to win the legal protection for women and their unborn equally.

216

At a 1998 forum with Patricia at the Chautauqua Institution, Chautauqua, in northwest New York on Lake Erie, I mentioned this response at Smith College over breakfast. Patricia said, "Well, you had the audience stacked with your supporters." I answered, saying that perhaps 60-80 people there were known by the sponsors to be Christian and/or pro-life. The overwhelming audience were Smith students and faculty. Then I said, "If I could stack Smith College with my supporters, I could also elect every member of the U.S. Congress." (Maybe we should try.)

Georgetown University and C-Span, 1995

On April 11, 1995, I hosted Kate Michelman, president of the National Abortion Rights Action League (NARAL) – whom I had met in Salt Lake City three years prior – in a Mars Hill Forum at Georgetown University in Washington, D.C. It was carried live on C-Span, and was entitled: *Abortion, Blockade and Gunfire: Who Are the Peacemakers?*

However, with just five minutes before the start of the forum, one of Kate's assistants tried to change the agreed-to ground rules, so as to cut out the one-on-one interchange between Kate and myself. But I said no – the personal interaction is central for the purposes of honest communication.

The centrality of male chauvinism proved to be central, and the driving force for this the nation's leading pro-abortion activist. Kate testified that evening, as she did so often in public, of the trials and humiliation she suffered when her ex-husband left her in 1970 with three young daughters to raise alone, and as it turns out, pregnant. She secured an abortion "for survival" pre-*Roe*), and has defended that prerogative ever since – being in the estimation of many, the most effective single-issue lobbyist on Capitol Hill from 1983-2004. She did her best to minimize the one-on-one interaction time between us that evening by cutting into it with her lengthened opening statement.

But some good interaction did occur. At one point in the question and answer period, Kate was beginning to lambast "anti-choice" fanatics. Then she looked at me, sitting at next to her at the table, reached out and touched me on the shoulder and said, "But not you, John." Her whole countenance then changed. By profiling the true ethics and power of informed choice, the biblical witness can minister to the hearts and minds of those who have been violated by the male chauvinisms of the abortion ethos (thus, the *God → life → choice → sex* paradigm versus the *sex → choice → life →/God* reversal percolates as usual, along with attendant male chauvinisms).

At the end of the evening there were still many people in the audience waiting in line to ask questions. Under the constraints of the time limit, the moderator made a passing comment that Kate and I would have future opportunity to continue the dialogue. Kate interjected with a passionate, "No!" She was not free to embrace a genuine love of hard questions in that context anymore, though in a live interview on CBN News right afterward, she was most gracious.

In my opening statement that evening, I made an argument that she never challenged, identifying five levels of violence surrounding the abortion debate. I listed them in reverse order:

5. The violence of return gunfire (where a few abortion-rights supporters have fired guns, but to no one's injury).

4. The violence of gunfire (e.g., John Salvi and Paul Hill killing abortionists or employees of abortion centers; as well as, implicitly, the violence of bombings [even though many bombings had proven to be inside jobs of the abortion centers looking for insurance money]).

3. The violence of blockade (the violating of time and space, and its implicit paving of the way for an escalation to more severe forms of violence).

2. The violence of human abortion (its deliberate destruction of unborn human life).

1. The violence of male chauvinism (its sexual idolatry which then coerces most abortion decisions into being).

218

And thus, no to all forms of violation of the innocent.

The reality of the violence of male chauvinism, as the catalyst to a host of subsequent evils, is uncontested. This Kate did not counter. Her testimony about having been abandoned by her ex-husband has always been effective as winning sympathy for her plight. And I honor that testimony from the outset. The answer however, is not to pass that violence on to the unborn.

After the forum, I wrote Kate briefly. She had stated how her husband's abandonment forced her to abort their fourth child. I gently suggested that if we do not forgive those who betray us, we will forever be embittered, and thus, slaves to their sins. Our unforgiveness allows them still to control us. In order to be free, we need to unilaterally exercise the power to forgive, as Jesus forgives his enemies and all humanity on the cross (Luke 23:34), as Stephen forgives his killers even as they stone him to death (Acts 7:60).

Dartmouth College, 1996

As mentioned in Chapter One, I once addressed a forum with Ann Stone, chairman for Republicans for Choice, at Dartmouth College, Hanover, New Hampshire, February 13, 1996.

I met Ann at the Salt Lake City Republican Party Platform hearings in May, 1992, and she was always glad to communicate. My prepared outline for Dartmouth was rooted in the *God → Life → Choice → Sex* paradigm, a critique of *Roe* accordingly, and a detailed review of the hell of rape and incest, it also being the quintessence of male chauvinism.

Ann's response was wonderful. She is instinctively pro-life, but her belief is that the government has no place in the matter – that there are times when a woman has no other choice. Thus, she does not embrace an idolatry of choice as does RCAR and the whole pro-abortion movement. To be cornered into choosing abortion is truly undesirable.

At the time, I was fashioning proposed language for the Republican Party Platform, which I have since codified in a different context, and write about

219

elsewhere: "All human life is made in God's image, is of equal value in God's sight, and for its entire natural duration, is to be protected by due process of law as the first order of human government."

Ann accepted this language during the forum. Why? Because the language of "entire natural duration" allows for debate. She is free to argue that such natural duration does not begin at fertilization, and I am free to argue it does. Truth always rises to the top, and the biblical confidence in the freedom to ask hard questions, and to honor the humanity of those who believe otherwise, is virtually unlimited in its extent, and attractiveness to the human soul.

I communicated with Ann a number of times over these years, even once visiting her office in Arlington, Virginia. She was engaged in crisis pregnancy work, and her associate, in looking at the questions we use in front of the abortion centers (see Chapter Eight), mused and said, "Classy."

The Temple of Music and Art, Tucson, 1996

As of yet, I have never visited Tucson, Arizona. A forum was scheduled there for April 29, 1996 at The Temple of Music and Art, with my guest being, for a second time, Patricia Ireland, president of NOW. Our topic was: *Human Abortion: Should it Be Kept Legal?* But it was cancelled.

As it turns out, the event was being sponsored by the Crisis Pregnancy Centers of Tucson, selling tickets at $8.00 to help cover costs, including Patricia's substantial honorarium. When the local chapter of NOW learned they had to buy tickets from a pro-life organization, they were furious, went online in the early days of the effective internet, and it went viral. They refused to give a dime to anything remotely pro-life, even though the Centers were hosting their national president. The opposite of the power of informed choice, the opposite of the power to love hard questions.

Patricia was being protested by her support base, and this was not good for intramural politics and keeping her job. So she rescinded her participation, and to a substantial financial loss on our part. But, in the Gospel, we have the power to forgive the debts of others, celebrated in the Lord's Prayer. We are free to honor those who, though being outside the Gospel, are due financial remuneration in a free market economy (see Romans 13:6-14). So I was free to reschedule with Patricia, and this we did.

The State University of New York at Buffalo, 1997

In a similar vein to my 1989 debate at Wellesley College, on April 8, 1997, I addressed a Mars Hill Forum at the State University of New York (SUNY) at Buffalo with Lucinda Findley, a graduate of Yale Law School, an abortion-rights attorney, and professor of law, who argued the defense in a nationally profiled case in the U.S. Supreme Court, *Schenck v. Pro-Choice Network*, addressing "buffer zones" around abortion centers. The forum was entitled: *Why is Abortion Such a Big Deal?* At one juncture when I was quoting the *Roe* Court's non-consensus language concerning "when life begins," Attorney Findley said she was unfamiliar with that portion of *Roe*.

I was flabbergasted. Here we have a top-notch lawyer who has argued at the U.S. Supreme Court concerning "protections" for legalized abortion. Yet she shows either true ignorance concerning the central fact in the abortion debate, or else she has so deeply imbibed the *Roe* mindset, that she cannot see such a pretension of ignorance, or cannot remember when she embraced the "I don't know" rationale.

I noticed a remarkable phenomenon in the audience of some 220 students, that during the question and answer period, none of them once challenged anything I said. They all grilled Professor Findley. On a very secular campus, no less. We know there was a solid contingent of Christians present at this forum (perhaps one-third of the audience), but what does that say about the confidence of the abortion-rights position among college students, where sexual promiscuity is the rule, and on Professor Findley's own campus? It seemed that their sentiments were less confident or vocal than among students a decade or two prior.

221

The Christian Broadcasting Network, 1997

The forum with Patricia Ireland, president of NOW, cancelled in Tuscon a year prior, came to pass at the Founder's Inn, Virginia Beach, Virginia, on April 22, 1997. This is the conference center and hotel built by the Christian Broadcasting Network (CBN) on its own property, with conference space available to rent. I had spoken in the past at CBN Chapel following a 1991 television appearance, was on their show right after the 1995 Georgetown forum with Kate Michelman, and had also spoken at the adjacent Regent University, with friends on the faculty. So, it was not hard to advertise the event locally, and some 250 people turned out.

My opening address highlighted the *God → life → choice → sex* paradigm as the necessary locus to look at the abortion debate, giving the parallel to the Declaration of Independence, and observing that "choice" depends on the prior definition of "life" in theology, law and science. I then outlined the six pillars of biblical power for how I conduct myself, and how accordingly I lobby for the equal protection of women and their unborn. Under the pillar of hard questions, I addressed, among others, the question of rape and incest.

Patricia's many concerns, and consistent with the idolatry of choice, centered on avoiding the definition of human life, while laboring under the ever present concern for male chauvinism but also playing into it at the same time by allowing the abortion ethos.

One point of dynamic debate came as Patricia said that pro-life advocates have "no right" to try and win the legal protection of the unborn. To do so would be to force our morality and definition of human life on everyone else. So I asked her: "And whose definition of life is now law?" She stopped for some disquieting moments, having no answer.

Trinity College, 2000

I hosted (now the Rev.) Debra Haffner at a forum at Trinity College, Hartford, Connecticut, September 28, 2000, sponsored by InterVarsity Christian Fellowship, in concert with the chaplain's office. Debra is the former president of the Sexuality Information and Education Council of the United States (SIECUS), which works assiduously to advance a libertine sexual ethos in public education, including support for legalized human abortion. Debra grew up Jewish, became Unitarian, and was later ordained in the UUA.

The topic for the evening was: *What is Sexual Morality and Justice?* A large range of topics are subsumed accordingly. In my opening comments, among other factors, I defined the *God* → *life* → *choice* → *sex* versus *sex* → *choice* → *life* →/*God* paradigm. When I mentioned human abortion in this context of "sexual morality and justice," I spoke of the injustice of the male chauvinism that drives the abortion ethos. Debra never challenged this.

In her opening address, Debra did speak of "God," so I later asked her who "God" is. She could not answer, and was unable to provide a definition of terms necessary for informed choice. For the evening, the subject of unalienable rights dominated the question and answer period, namely: What is life, who qualifies, and why and how should it be protected?

The room was originally set up with seventy chairs, but some 100 people crammed in. During the question and answer period, we had a fire alarm, and all of us had to spill out onto the quad in a cool drizzle. As we were exiting, Debra quipped about how many people would return. It was another ten or fifteen minutes before we were allowed, but nearly everyone did return. It was a dynamic event, and was concluded by the chaplain while many were still waiting to ask questions.

I have been in touch with Debra a number of times across the years, and hosted her once on a radio show. She is always gracious, even as we are legions apart on biblical theology and sexual mores.

Boston College, 2000

I once crossed paths, at some conference, with Francis Kissling, president of Catholics for a Free Choice in Washington, D.C. I invited her to address a forum during a subsequent phone conversation where she quizzed me as to its purpose, and she said yes. It was arranged for the Boston College (BC – a Jesuit institution) on November 3, 2000: *Should Religion Be a Part of the Abortion Debate?*

As a Protestant, I was given great hospitality at one of the nation's leading Roman Catholic institutions, being entrusted to advocate and defend a biblical pro-life ethic in the face of the most vociferous critic of the Church in this regard. There was no love lost between them – so BC, and the chaplain, the Rev. Ron Tacelli, who served as moderator, took a real risk in allowing such a forum, and for that, they are to be honored.

In my opening address, I spoke of the POSH Ls of the image of God, and important places of theological interface between Roman Catholicism and evangelical Protestantism. I highlighted the *God → life → choice → sex* versus the *sex → choice → life →/God* paradigm, addressed "abortion as the ultimate male chauvinism," and gave a detailed review of the hard question concerning rape and incest.

Ms. Kissling followed with her opening address, which was disappointing. Instead of making a proactive argument for "Catholics for a free choice," she immediately sought to rebut me. This she attempted, not in addressing any concerns I defined, but in trying to change the subject away from what I had said.

She did not challenge my definition of theological and biological humanity, said she agreed with my definition of male chauvinism, adding, "Not all men are bad ... in fact, some of them are good friends." Yet all night she lambasted the male priesthood in its leadership of the Catholic Church, and it was painfully obvious to the audience that she has deep anger here.

Now, here again, I give great credit to Rev. Tacelli and the college. It is precisely this kind of assault they feared might happen, sharing this with me ahead of time – they knew Ms. Kissling far better than did I. But given my conversation with her ahead of time, and my optimistic attitude, I accepted her assurances ahead of time that she was interested in genuine conversation and hard questions in all directions. I was betrayed, for as it turns out, she was longing to speak at a place like BC in order to lambast the male priesthood, and here it is, a Protestant minister unwittingly, but warned nonetheless, opens the door ...

But too, as judged by the question and answer period, she fooled no one. After I presented an initial question, Ms. Kissling gave a lengthy and evasive answer, turning it into an unrelated question, and as I attempted to answer that question, she interrupted me and complained that I was exercising a typical "male" strategy of reshaping the discussion so that she could not ask me questions (!). Her continued interruptions frustrated the Rev. Tacelli as he sought to moderate a real discussion, not a one-way tirade. At one juncture when she interrupted, she told me that I was not allowed to answer the question at hand the way I was choosing to answer it (!).

At the conclusion of the evening, I raised the question about the nature of the human soul, as had been discussed earlier, and promised to send her my exegesis on *nephesh*. She had also sought to use Exodus 21:22-25 to discount the humanity of the unborn, as with the Rev. Katherine Hancock Ragsdale and others, rooted in the work of Harvard feminist scholar Elisabeth Schüssler Fiorenza (my post-grad thesis at Harvard addressed one of her books). I also promised to send Ms. Kissling my exegesis as rooted in Meredith Kline's groundbreaking work. I followed up after the forum in providing these promised resources, but even after further communication, I did not hear back from her.

This is one of two forums I have addressed over the years where I had to clearly conclude that my interlocutor had no real interest in any modicum of honest communication. Yet, her intransigence was obvious to the well-attended event, and thus the power of informed choice was well served.

University of Connecticut Medical School, 2006

Sponsored by the Christian Medical Fellowship, I was invited to address a forum at the University of Connecticut Medical School in Farmington on February 3, 2006. This was utterly unique, as my interlocutor, Dr. Janice

Lee, was an abortionist and medical director at the Hartford Gyn Center, and also sometimes participated in the Christian Medical Fellowship.

I organized my presentation in concert with the overwhelming reality of male chauvinism encountered everywhere since the early 1980s; the *God → life → choice → sex* versus the *sex → choice → life →/God* paradigm hewn out of the 1986 encounter with the national Religious Coalition for Abortion Rights; the POSH Ls of the image of God as first articulated at Brown University in 1989; the give or take reality vis-à-vis marriage defined at Smith College in 1994; and followed by two proposals which find maturity in the final chapter of this book.

Dr. Lee presented more of a visceral profile, with no reference to structured biblical theology or biological science: "It is not a decision of intellectual reasoning or theology – it is a decision of the heart;" "I will never know if God is he or she;" a prayer to God: "if you don't want me doing this, let me know, or otherwise show me …;" and "Anglican theology calls for limited family size and the use of birth control." She brought up the "reproductive rights needed for women," horror stories, repudiating violence against "abortion providers," and the belief that all aborted babies go straight to heaven (thus assuaging her conscience, it was clear).

I did ask Dr. Lee: "Can you imagine Jesus performing an abortion?' She could not find the words to say yes.

University of Richmond, 2009

In my fourth forum with the Rev. Barry Lynn, Esq., director of Americans United for the Separation of Church and State (AU), we addressed abortion as a subject to itself. It was sponsored at the University of Richmond, Richmond, Virginia, on March 23, 2009: *Women, Choice and Abortion: What are the Issues?*

In my opening comments, I addressed the give versus take options in marriage and all human relationships, the male chauvinism of human abortion, the *God → life → choice → sex* paradigm versus the *sex → choice*

226

$\rightarrow$ *life* $\rightarrow$*/God* reversal, that choices can only be made by those who are first alive, biological definitions, and the simple slogan summary: *You have the power to choose life* (see Chapter Eight).

Barry is a friend, and he has always enjoyed addressing a Mars Hill Forum. He had earlier said publicly that in these forums, real thinking happens, and not the usual petty politicking he experiences otherwise.

In his opening address he spoke of the Constitution, theology and the "ramifications of protecting fetal life." He believes that abortion is a religious issue that can exercise unwarranted influence on government policies; "every child should be a wanted child" (idolatry of choice); biological life cannot be precisely defined (per the pretension of ignorance in *Roe*); the fetus "may be a living thing" (nix *nephesh*); that no one can claim "divine truth" (for which there can be real abuse, but also, in the final analysis, contra revelation and the power of informed choice); and thus, "viability" is where the law should begin to affirm some rights for the unborn (secular achievement ethic).

Endnote

Thus, this is some of the "lived biblical theology" I have pursued in the face of the abortion debate across the years.

1. The *God* $\rightarrow$ *life* $\rightarrow$ *choice* $\rightarrow$ *sex* versus *sex* $\rightarrow$ *choice* $\rightarrow$ *life* $\rightarrow$*/God* paradigm undergirds all.
2. The power of informed choice is set in contrast to the pretension of ignorance.
3. The attendant male chauvinisms drive the abortion industry.

◆ ◆ ◆

Chapter Six

In Massachusetts Politics

While taking a shower in early 1987, and in prayer, a simple idea came. I had no idea it would hit the mark with such theological and political precision, that huge and powerful opposition would be mobilized on short notice, and put me, and my growing family, through subsequent unrelenting years of hell.

Namely, the idea was to place a multiple-choice question on the Massachusetts ballot that sought a consensus on the biological origins of individual human life, redressing the *Roe* v. *Wade* Court's pretension of ignorance.

1987 Survey

Step one was to conduct a survey asking such a question. I organized a number of groups with standards on how to seek an honest response, and we even biased the sample against pro-life sentiments. So in a demographic admixture statewide, with 45 percent done on university campuses, we asked people when they thought an individual biological human life began, giving four options.

Of the 902 people who answered, the breakdown is as follows:

1. Conception: 637 (70.6%).
2. Viability: 124 (13.7%).
3. Birth: 120 (13.3%).
4. Other: 21 (2.3%)

We made sure the responses were spontaneous, which is to say, we passed out no information regarding the science of conception beforehand. Now we did so afterward, and a large portion of those who did not answer "conception" were willing to rethink their answers. But these numbers were not recorded.

On the campuses, "conception" ran about 61 per cent, and in the cities and towns it ran about 82 per cent. When a Catholic priest friend of mine noted these results, he mentioned how remarkable it is that those who have not been to college know how children are conceived, but among the college educated, it is more of a "mystery." I responded and said: "It is not so much a mystery to the well-educated concerning the conception of human life; rather it is their increased ability to avoid the obvious by talking around it, and their willingness to feign ignorance in order to justify sexual promiscuity."

Boston NOW

During this survey process, I had one of my "supervised ministry" students from Gordon-Conwell Theological Seminary, David, reach out to a range of "pro-choice" advocates. Interviewees were asked ahead of time for a 45-minute visit and give response to a 14-question survey. Of the questions, for example, they were asked where any common ground might exist in how terms are defined, what ethical conduct is appropriate in the debate, and what role religion should or should not play.

Among others, David was able to interview the director of counseling for Planned Parenthood in Cambridge. She was very courteous, professional in demeanor, and her answers were straightforward.

He also tried to contact the offices of Boston NOW to set up a visit with their director. There was no response, so on April 1, 1987, David visited their offices on Commonwealth Avenue near Boston University.

Only the receptionist was in, and he sought to engage in at least some brief conversation. She asked to look at the questionnaire, and when she saw the motto on the NECAC letterhead, "biblically committed to protecting the unborn," she laughed. She said she had no time to talk with him, that "her time was limited and she preferred spending it with pro-choice students." David said he was "pro-choice" in language he was prepared to define, and a graduate student, but nonetheless she sought to end the conversation.

Then he asked her if she could take just a few seconds to answer a multiple-choice survey on the biological origins of an individual human life. When she saw it, said, "This scares me. This scares me more than the other one." She asked for our fact sheet on the matter, said she disagreed with some of it, and as David asked her what points they were, she would not respond.

1988 Ballot Question

Our goal was to place this non-binding multiple-choice question on as many ballots as possible statewide:

In **biological terms**, when does an individual human life begin?

Mark a cross X in the square next to the answer you prefer. Only vote for one.

[   ] A. Conception.
[   ] B. Viability.
[   ] C. Birth.
[   ] D. Write-in: specify a different biological term _____.

Massachusetts allowed legally non-binding referenda to be placed on the ballots, either per state representative district (160 in the state) or per state senatorial district (40 in the state), if enough registered voters petitioned for it. A question can be petitioned to appear on the ballot of just one district, or many.

We chose to organize per representative district, which required 200 validated signatures each. I was a complete novice at political organizing when I began. The laws governing these referenda also limit the time available to gather the signatures, to several months, in the spring and early summer of the election year. Nonetheless, we got a grass-roots organization going, with almost no money (we were only able to raise some $18,000 total for the political committee that sponsored it).

230

We were active in most of the districts of the Commonwealth, and by the deadline, we qualified in 105 of them. Had there been another three or four weeks, I believe we could have had 155 districts qualify, and perhaps in the other five as well (the only districts where we did not yet have volunteers). A year after the fact, I learned that this was the largest public policy referendum drive in Massachusetts history. The largest prior effort qualified in 61 districts.

As we gathered the signatures, I had many reports from the representative districts that an average of one-third of those who signed the petitions considered themselves politically "pro-choice," and they signed because they thought it was a fair question. All such petition signatures, with name, street address, and town or city, have to be validated, checking to see if they are active registered voters. About 70 percent on average are validated. We had such a well-disciplined group of volunteers, that our validation rate was 93 percent. We turned in many forms that were 100 percent validated (55 lines per sheet), and a member of Secretary of State's office said he had never before seen that happen.

When the petitions were turned into the Secretary's office on August 3, 1988, one member of the staff was astonished. He said to me privately, "How did you gather so many signatures without us knowing about it?" I then said, "Well, I signed out all the petition forms in the spring from your office." He was still miffed, in that he had heard nothing about it, whether in terms of publicity or media reports, during the process of the signature collections. So I said, "Well, do you go to church or listen to Christian radio?" He sighed.

We were so grass-roots that we were off the radar screen of the Massachusetts political establishment. We walked and did not fly. Then he asked, "Well, how did you gather so many signatures from all these districts? How many paid signature gatherers did you employ?" This was news to me. I did not know, at that time, that there is such a thing as people who could and would be paid to collect signatures for a ballot initiative.

So I told him so. His eyes widened, "Then how did you gather the signatures?" I told him we had about 900 volunteers, from a committed core on outward. He was blown away, and said it was the largest grass-roots volunteer effort in the state he had ever seen.

This part of the story is worth retelling for one simple reason – pro-life Christians are the most grass-roots political force in the nation. We can do, with little money, what other political partisans cannot do with large financial resources. As well, in the process of gathering the signatures, our volunteers were consistently strengthened in their faith and pro-life convictions, as they shared with people on the streets, and saw many "pro-choice" people open up to the Christian and political witness.

Yet the volunteers were only asking about the ballot question itself, and not proactively bringing the Gospel into it (as we were told by the local organizers). Rather, it was the potential signatories who brought up the subject, indicating a deep instinct among all people that a pro-life position naturally flows from a biblical worldview. Our volunteers found the question's simplicity, and its theological and political precision so compelling, that their confidence grew easily. They learned by street-level experience how powerful this question can be at reversing the reversal in the abortion debate today, in changing its language.

In preparing for this initiative, I was informed that the sitting Attorney General would do his best to keep it off the ballot. James Shannon was a former board member of Planned Parenthood League of Massachusetts (PPLM) and as staunchly pro-abortion as any. Also, coincidentally, Governor Michael Dukakis was then running for president, and for years he held the position that he "doesn't know" when an individual human life begins, using *Roe*'s logic as cover. The Attorney General had a constitutional duty under Massachusetts law to review all "public policy questions" to see if they are truly concerns of public policy. When I was researching this, I came across a public policy petition in the earlier part of the century where a group of people had gathered enough signatures, asking the authorities to require a certain man to paint his barn, because it was an eyesore (or something like that). The Attorney General blocked it – it was not a matter of public policy.

The day after the validated petitions were submitted, August 4, 1988, I wrote Mr. Shannon. I outlined for him the nature and rationale of our question and stated up front that I knew him to be in favor of legalized abortion. I also said how we were following *Roe*'s language and the 1981 U.S. Senate hearings as precedent for seeking to determine if there is or is not a consensus on the biological origins of an individual human life. As well, I outlined why we chose the multiple-choice format, its precedence in a 1970 state ballot initiative, and why we did not include an "I don't know" option. I explained that we wanted a positive response to the question, not a negative one, thus we did not choose a yes/no format either.

This was pure folly on my part – erring on the side of innocent intent sans wisdom (cf. Matthew 10:16). I was eager to make my case, but I should have awaited the Attorney General's response.

On August 17, I received a phone call from an Assistant Attorney General, Paul Lazour. He wanted a legal brief from me arguing my case. This is remarkable as I look back, for I am not an attorney, and did not realize how unusual this request was. Why ask for a legal brief unless there is a predisposition on the Attorney General's part to block the question? For otherwise there is no reason for one. Also, it would give the Attorney General more advance knowledge of my position before he wrote his decision. But I was roped in, as I trustingly and naïvely thought they were interested in engaging in the real argument.

Also, in the phone call, Mr. Lazour asked if I were willing to consider the possibility of adding two further options to the multiple-choice question. The first option he offered was "I don't know," and the second option was, "No, I do not want to so instruct my legislator."

When I heard this, I was convinced that intellectually and politically, the Attorney General's office was scared. The Civil Liberties Union of Massachusetts (CLUM) had already written his office, urging him to block the question from the ballot. Also, back on August 4, the day after I had submitted the petitions, I had to return to the Secretary of State's office to photocopy one petition sheet that had been overlooked. When I walked in

233

that morning, I was surprised to see about one dozen women pouring over all our petition sheets. I spoke briefly with one, being clueless to who she was and why she was there.

I was a political novice, and assumed this was some standard procedure, and that these women were employees of the Secretary of State's office. Only later did I learn that they were volunteers from the Boston chapter of NOW. The word about the petitions had apparently spread very quickly, from within the Secretary of State or Attorney General's office, to the entire abortion-rights establishment in the state.

We also learned later, that within hours, they had mobilized to oppose this petition drive they had previously known nothing about. Of this we were apprised from a third party who coincidentally learned of it from a first-hand inside source. It turns out that the "pro-choice" elitists were deeply afraid of this question, and thus de facto, fearful of the power of informed choice and "the consent of the governed."

Once when I was in front of Preterm abortion center two years later (see Chapter Eight), talking with an impassioned activist from NOW, she told me that she was one of this group at the Secretary of State's office that day, and that they were checking for false signatures. It appears that they were so astonished and frightened by our success at gathering signatures, that there "must" have been fraud involved. This NOW activist in fact told me how they discovered much fraud among our petitions, so I asked her if NOW ever challenged even one of the validated signatures. At this she changed the topic. Not one signature had ever been challenged.

But whereas our theological, intellectual, and ethical homework, and political organizing, were in place for the petition drive, we were not prepared a) financially, b) legally in terms of fending off the power of bully politics, and c) most importantly, in terms of intercessory prayer.

In Luke 14:28-33, Jesus gives two parables where I learned the downside in this process:

Suppose one of you wants to build a tower. Will he not first sit down and count the cost for completion? Perchance, as he sets the foundation and is not strong enough to finish it, everyone who sees it will mock him, saying, "This man began to build but was unable to complete it."

Or suppose a king considers going to war against another king. Will he not first sit down, and consider whether he is powerful enough with ten thousand to oppose the one coming against him with twenty thousand? If he is not, he will send an ambassador while the other is still far away, and ask for terms of peace. Accordingly, any of you who does not set apart everything of himself, is not powerful enough to be my disciple.

Since I came to know Jesus, I have never hesitated to give up everything in order to follow him. But there was a wisdom I lacked in what I sought to do in Massachusetts in 1988. Whereas I succeeded well, by God's grace, in imparting the vision for the multiple-choice ballot question at the grass-roots, I came up empty handed in trying to get responses from key pro-life politicians. We were financially marginal at every step, and not wise to the realities of political partisans who will be as dishonest as necessary to maintain their power.

But especially, I was completely unprepared for the demonic assault that began immediately after the presentation of the petitions to the Secretary of State's office. We had very little organized intercessory prayer in place (ad hoc at best), and thus we were made vulnerable to the political bullying of the question off the ballot, and the subsequent corporate bankruptcy of the NECAC. The spiritual dimensions were remarkable, as we will see in Chapter Nine.

I did not count the cost in terms of our financial ability to build this "tower," to apply the words of Jesus's first parable above. Had I been wiser, I would have just organized the petition drive in a half-dozen representative districts on the North Shore where I then lived. Thus, I would not have exhaustingly and anxiously worked up to the deadline to organize the whole state.

Rather I could have collected the signatures in those several districts in short order, and had the time to focus on prayer and fund-raising. And I would have been able to patiently learn the political territory ahead of time, and had I done so, we could have won against the vested-interest and well-connected political assault that came our way. Then we could have done the rest of the state the next election cycle, with success already in place. I bit off more than I could chew. In terms of Jesus's second parable above, the battle is applicable to spiritual warfare in part, and I was ignorant to the army opposing me in the heavenlies. We must know our enemy's strengths and weaknesses before engaging in war, and our enemy is the devil and his demons.

But the Attorney General's office was scared when Mr. Lazour called me on August 17, 1988. When he proposed the extra options, I knew we held the moral and intellectual high ground. I answered by saying a) how can I legally change the petitions ex post facto? (which he knows is the case), that nearly 26,000 registered voters had signed; and b) even if I could do so, I would not. But I still said I would get back to him, which I did in a letter the following week.

I prepared a "legal brief" of sorts (something I learned formally how to do later) for the Attorney General, and in my letter to Mr. Lazour, I specified how it was the very "I don't know" posture of *Roe* which we were challenging, as well as challenging the use of negative responses such as the second option he offered us. On the Attorney General's part, this was all calculated as he prepared to rationalize the blocking of our question. He knew that his position in support of *Roe* was based on its morally and intellectually anemic pretension of ignorance, and that this question exposed the central lie of *Roe*.

Now it might have been funny to see the abortion-rights partisans organize a political campaign against our ballot question, saying, "Vote: I don't know!" They would be thus advertising their commitment to ignorance for all to see. However, an "I don't know" posture is democratically and constitutionally invalid in the sense that we cannot elect an "I don't know" to public office, and we cannot vote an "I don't know" statute into law. If we do

236

not know for whom or what to vote, then we simply do not vote – this is the democratic way to register our uncertainty or dissatisfaction with the options. We then trust in the system where among those who do decide, a candidate will be elected or an issue decided. I was committed to honest and democratically informed choice.

When James Shannon handed down his opinion on September 2, 1988, he said that our question was not properly a "question of public policy," because a) it was not phrased as a proper form of "instruction," and b) multiple-choice questions were not permissible.

It is thus clear to me that the Attorney General acted in egregiously bad faith. If his opinion were truly a legal one, and not motivated by political bias, then:

1. why did his office offer me a phrase with the words, "instruct my legislator," if in fact he believed it were not a proper form of "instruction" to begin with;
2. why did his office seek a legal brief from me ahead of his decision, unless he were plotting to block the initiative, and he wanted to gain an exact preview on how to preempt my argument; and
3. why did his office offer me two additional choices if in fact he believed that multiple-choice were invalid?

Thus, I needed to appeal his decision, and to present a full legal brief making my argument. Accordingly, with no money in hand, I sought legal counsel to file lawsuit against the Commonwealth. I did all the research myself, and we heard through the grapevine that the Attorney General expected us to win in court. They put a number of Assistant Attorneys General on the case against me, and pulled together an amalgam of legalese in the September 2 opinion to deny us our civil rights.

We appealed directly to the Massachusetts Supreme Judicial Court (SJC). Had I known better, we would have started at Suffolk County Superior Court in Boston (this will be detailed as to why as we proceed). In my legal brief, I answered the Attorney General's September 2 opinion and argued that our

237

proposed question was a) fully "an instruction on a matter of public policy," b) it provides for the "affirmative no" in a comprehensive manner, and c) multiple-choice has both constitutional warrant and specific precedent. In order to grasp how morally and intellectually deficient the abortion-rights position is, it is helpful to walk through my argument that the Attorney General did not face head-on – all he could do was employ the power of his office self-aggrandizingly against us.

The Legal Argument

Here then is the substance of my 1988 and 1996 legal briefs (we tried a repetition these eight years later), interwoven with some emendations and editing to make it as accessible as possible for my purposes here:

A. Definition of Public Policy

Any discussion of "public policy" is rooted in the Massachusetts Constitution, beginning with Part 1, Article 5:

> All power residing originally in the people, and being derived from them, the several magistrates and officers of government, vested with authority, whether legislative, executive, or judicial, are their substitutes and agents, and are at all times accountable to them.

This Article is explicit: we the people are self-governed, and as such it is we who define the terms of how and through whom to make public policy – the nature of representation in a democratic republic. This is congruent with a) the "Declaration of the Rights of the Inhabitants of the Commonwealth of Massachusetts," and b) the Declaration of Independence and its definition of unalienable rights and "the consent of the governed." Thus, the Massachusetts Attorney General is an agent of the "original power" of its citizens, and his power must therefore be in service to the citizens, and not in censorship of them. (It is a question of the power to give versus the power to take.)

Part 1, Article 7 of the Massachusetts Constitution is likewise broad:

238

Government is instituted for the Common Good; for the protection, safety, prosperity and happiness of the people; and not for the profit, honor, or private interest of any one man, family or Class of men:

Therefore the people alone have the incontestable, unalienable, and indefeasible right to institute government; and to reform, alter, or totally change the same, when their protection, safety, prosperity and happiness require it.

In order for the Attorney General to define the proposed question as inimical to public policy, he had to show a) that the initiative was not of the people, and b) that it did not address issues of protection, safety, prosperity and/or happiness. In both cases, he did not do so. Mr. Shannon was in fact in opposition to Article 7, as the common good of the petitioners was not in view, but his political "private interest" was in focus.

Also, his opinion opposed the constitutional "original power" of the people. It was in direct conflict with *Yankee Atomic Electric Company v. Secretary of the Commonwealth*, 403 Mass. 203 (1988). In this case dealing with a nuclear waste ballot question. Chief Justice Hennessey stated:

(W)hen certifying petitions as to proper form, the Attorney General is not to be a censor; people should be allowed to speak and act freely through the initiative process. *Id.* at 211.

Here the Chief Justice commended Mr. Shannon in his official status for not acting as a censor. But in the case of my question, Mr. Shannon did act as a censor. He censored my public policy concerns under the pretext of "form." As well, *Yankee* deals with the initiative petition process for legally-binding matters, and its guidelines are stricter than those concerning the legally non-binding public policy petition we initiated. Cf. Op. Atty. Gen., Sept. 4, 1984, p. 76. Thus, Mr. Shannon's censorship in regard to our question is that much more egregious.

Mr. Shannon's opposition to the "original power" of the people is also seen in his September 2, 1988 opinion:

239

These failings also destroy the ability of voters to provide instruction through this question. Voters facing this question are not told that they are instructing their legislator, and cannot be certain what public policy, if any, will be affected by their vote" (p. 9).

Mr. Shannon here assumed the "original power" of the people for himself, not allowing the freedom of the people to determine the public policy implications of a question they had petitioned for the ballot. As I had evidenced to him in my brief, our question so clearly instructed public policy matters, for example, with respect to laws on abortion, fetal research, tort, liability, homicide and prenatal care programs, that it was disingenuous for him to suggest otherwise. Mr. Shannon impugned the integrity of the "original power" of the people, apart from which he holds no authority.

Articles 5 and 7 state that the rights to define and initiate concerns of public policy are reserved to the people. Article 19 of Part 1 of the Massachusetts Constitution defines this further:

> The people have a right, in an orderly and peaceable manner, to assemble to consult upon the common good; give instruction to their representatives, and to request of the legislative body, by the way of addresses, petitions, or remonstrances, redress of the wrongs done them, and of the grievances they suffer.

Mr. Shannon's opinion did not provide any constitutional definition of the "original power" of the people, so his argument from the onset was deficient, and the definitions he brought to Article 19 were likewise deficient. In other words, whereas his opinion speaks of the traditionally "broad view ... of what constitutes an appropriate question of public policy" (Op. Atty. Gen. Sept. 2, 1988, p. 2), he instead applied an unconstitutionally narrow reasoning to the word "instruction" in this context, as a pretense for dismissing our proposed question. Instead of rooting his concerns in the Constitution first, from which to then understand the applicability of the General Laws, Shannon reversed the process and, as we will further see, used unrelated case law to obscure certain General Laws, to obscure and repudiate the Constitutional rights of the people for "original power."

240

In Article 19, the language is very broad. Both the "common good" and "instruction" are inherently inclusive terms, assuming etymological breadth and full dictionary options of usage. Also, the words "addresses, petitions, or remonstrances" equal a chain of interfacing definitions, syntactically structured for breadth of intent, and not for the narrowness of restrictions per Shannon's opinion. My proposed question addressed the legislators through means of petition to give a clear declaration as to whether the "non-consensus" tenet of *Roe* is sustainable. If the voters were to demonstrate that there is a consensus for "conception," then the instruction to the legislators is clear – protect the lives of unborn human beings under due process of law.

This instruction is so clear, that the Attorney General and the abortion-rights establishment did everything they could to block the question. The Boston chapter of NOW immediately mobilized to scrutinize the signatures, the CLUM wrote the Attorney General in opposition to the proposed question, Planned Parenthood filed an *amicus* opposing it, and the Boston Globe editorialized against it.

All this concerted energy was invested to oppose our question for one simple reason – it poses perhaps the most important single form of instruction about the abortion debate possible: defining a consensus as to the biological origins of individual human life, and to thus establish a democratic consensus that the central tenet of *Roe* is in error, and therefore in need of public policy and/or judicial review.

Mr. Shannon then contradicted his own narrowness of definition:

> Prior opinions of the Attorney General and case law have not
> precisely defined what constitutes "public policy" and the nature of the
> concept does not readily lend itself to an exact definition … (public
> policy includes matters of 'community common sense and common
> conscience applied to matters of public morals, public health, public
> safety, public welfare, and the like') [ibid. p. 3].

Note how the Attorney General follows in the footsteps of the *Roe* Court. *Roe* admitted that the Constitution does not define "privacy" and "person" in

241

so many words, so too Shannon says the same about the opinions of the prior Attorneys General and Massachusetts case law relative to the terms "public policy," and as we will see, "instruction." Those who pretend ignorance when they cannot make a positive case for their views, will then fish in a sea, even a penumbra, of broad definitions for narrow ones to suit their purposes. Then they will accuse us who honor the context of broad constitutional definitions and freedoms as being "narrow."

(It is just like the accusation of unbelievers that the Gospel is narrow and negative in its view of freedom, when indeed its *akol tokel* is the most embracive and positive definition of freedom in human history. It is the pagan definitions that are narrow, negative and indeed, equal slavery.)

Shannon steps into *Roe*'s mold of serving the reversal. The common sense consensus on "conception" and its automatic application to the moral and legal status of the unborn is obvious *prima facie*. But Shannon on the one hand said there is inexactitude in defining what public policy is, and on the other hand is exact in excluding our public policy question as outside his inexactitude, even though it is well within his inexact definitions. This is a double-minded standard rooted in moral and intellectual dishonesty.

As an immediate example of this narrowness of terms, we can look at this section of Shannon's opinion:

> Generally, it can be said that matters of public policy involve determinations of what governmental action is desirable or necessary for the public interest, as opposed to individual concerns, and as contrasted to statements of fact. Cf. *Borden, Inc. v. Commissioner of Public Health*, 388 Mass. 707, 721 (1983) [distinguishing between facts, regulations and public policy]" (ibid.).

Later in his opinion, Shannon said that our question calls for a "descriptive" answer as opposed to an "instruction" (as he defines it). This is a subtle way to say that our question is seeking irrelevant "facts," and not seeking to instruct legislators on matters of public policy. In his citing of *Borden*, he maintained that there is a distinction between "facts, regulations and public policy," to thus portray our question as being opposed to a matter of public policy. This was eisegetical fishing.

A review of *Borden* shows a) there is no such distinction as Shannon alleged, and b) the substance and terms of that case, where applicable, actually sustained our case. It is clear to me that his argument was disingenuous, as was his attempt at narrowness. *Borden*'s concern with "facts" was limited to whether or not federally established facts for the hazardous nature of formaldehyde and cognate substances can be retested in court, so as to allow producers to buy time and make hassles for those consumers seeking repurchase satisfaction. The agreed to "fact" of its hazardous nature must not needlessly be retested in court, because its established factual nature has already instructed the formation of public policy banning the substance's specified use.

In my proposed question, we did not seek a needless reiteration of established fact for ulterior purposes. Rather, we sought to establish what *Borden* defended presuppositionally, namely, an original fact upon which public policy is instructed. It already was an established fact that formaldehyde was hazardous, and the laws defended in *Borden* were based on such a fact. There has been no democratic attempt in Massachusetts or elsewhere to establish the central fact of the abortion debate, to redress this flaw in *Roe*, and we only sought to exercise our "original power" to petition for a redress by means of the non-binding public policy ballot initiative.

Shannon also cited *Griffin v. United States*, 500 F.2d 1059, 1066 n.16 (3rd Cir. 1974) to disqualify our proper concern with "fact." However, the same interdependence between scientific facts and public policy is also found here, consistent with that in *Borden* which also states, "(a) regulation is essentially an expression of public policy," e.g., "facts" also express public policy, contra Shannon's opinion. Op. Atty. Gen., Sept. 4, 1984, p. 377. Thus, the very sources Shannon cites actually contradict his narrow definition of public policy employed to block our proposed question. It may also be noted that his opinion with regard to *Borden* distinguished between the public interest and individual concerns, as does the Massachusetts Constitution. But not so here – Shannon effectively placed his individual concerns in opposition to

243

the public interest of 25,835 voters, thus clearly reversing reality to suit his ends by implying that my proposed question was not one of public interest.

Thus far in my argument against the Attorney General's position, I had noted the proper definition of "public policy" rooted in the Commonwealth's Constitution, Part 1, Articles 5, 7 and 19, and how our proposed question qualifies. Then I turned to the Massachusetts General Laws, where the relevant part as cited by Shannon is in G.L. c. 53, § 19:

> ... asking for the submission to the voters ... of any question of instructions to the senator or representative from that district, and stating the substance thereof, the attorney general shall upon the request of the state secretary determine whether or not such question is one of public policy ...

At this point, the General Laws use two key terms, "instruction(s)" and "public policy." We will see how Shannon employs "instruction" in an atomistic fashion to obscure the public policy nature of our question. But before the formal definition of "instruction," there is the need to further embody the definition of "public policy."

The Attorney General's opinion also maintained two other qualifications for what equals an instruction concerning public policy:

> In addition, the proposed question must be fit for legislative action ... The instruction contained in each public policy question must be consistent with the powers of the Legislature and subject to legislative action or attention (Op. Atty. Gen. Sept. 2, 1988, p. 4).

In further qualifying this opinion, he continued:

> Indeed, a review of prior public policy questions placed on the ballot reveals that such questions consistently have proposed specific legislation or resolutions contemplating a particular governmental action (ibid. p. 5).

I argued that a) our question is fit for specific legislative action or attention, b) it is consistent with the powers of the Legislature and c) Shannon's opinion did not seek a constitutionally broad definition of public policy congruent with the "original power" of the people. Rather, it sought a restrictive definition with the singular aim of blocking the public policy concerns of the proposed question. I also noted that the nature of specificity, in addressing legislative action, belongs to the people's initiative. I chose a simple and understated question because everyone knows its public policy implications, and also I did not wish to obscure such simplicity with needless or redundant language. In fact, part of the Attorney General's statutory duties with respect to ballot initiatives is to be sure they are as simply stated as possible, and my question was as simple as can be.

There are three opinions of prior Attorneys General which specifically applied to my concerns. First, Op. Atty. Gen., Aug. 16, 1939, p. 99:

> The provisions of said sections 19 and 21 dealing with instructions on public policy questions should be broadly construed, so that the representatives of the people in the Senate and in the House of Representatives may be informed, so far as a vote can show it, of the sentiment of voters in their respective districts.

> The general intent of the Legislature in enacting said sections 19 and 21 was to afford an opportunity to the voters to apprise their senators and representatives of their sentiments upon important public policy questions. (Cf. 1955 Op. Atty. Gen. 51, where the words "public policy" are not limited or qualified in any way, and are to be construed broadly).

Second is Op. Atty. Gen., Sept. 29, 1978, No. 8:

> Under prior opinions of the Attorney General, it has been determined that the term "public policy" as used in section 19 should not be given a restrictive meaning. (Cf. 1974/75 Op. Atty. Gen. No. 22 at 63; 1974/75 Op. Atty. Gen. No. 11 at 54; 1968/69 Op. Atty. Gen. No. 5 at 37; and 1966/67 Op. Atty. Gen. Nos. 34 and 77).

And third is Op. Atty. Gen., Sept. 4, 1984, pp. 75-76:

> I am of the opinion that the term "public policy" as used in G.L. c. 53, § 19, should not be given an overly restrictive meaning ... each question must concern an important public matter ... On the basis of an unbroken line of precedent, I adopt the broader view and conclude that the question is one of public policy ... [In addressing the problem that the Legislature cannot act contrary to the common defense of the nation]: I find it crucial, however, that the petition as filed instruct(s) the Representatives to vote not in favor of legislation but in favor of a resolution. Because it is within the prerogative of the Legislature to memorialize Congress to declare Northampton a nuclear free zone, I have concluded that the question, as rephrased, is one of public policy within the meaning of G.L. c. 53 § 19 ...

> Public Policy questions, unlike initiative petitions, are not restricted to providing instructions only on questions of law making; instead they extend to any question of important public concern that may appropriately receive attention or action by the General Court. Under the provisions of the Massachusetts Constitution, Pt. 1, article 19, the people of the Commonwealth have the right to provide instructions to legislators. This power is not expressly or implicitly restricted to any particular type of legislative action, nor does G.L. c. 53 § 19, contain any such restrictions. Accordingly, public policy questions may concern subjects excluded from the popular initiative so long as they remain subjects for some type of action by the Legislature.

The language here is overwhelming in its vindication of the broad interpretation of public policy according to the "original power" of the people. It cites "an unbroken line of precedent." It is clear in the opposition to any restrictive impulses, while making certain that the broad question is a fit subject for legislative attention or action.

When I originally filed complaint against the Attorney General's opinion of September 2, 1988, I cited three bills then pending before the General Court (cf. SJ 88-363; 4898, pp. 13-14). H. 2650 called for a memorialization of the

246

U.S. Congress to establish the rights of the unborn. H. 3396 sought to prohibit the use of state funds to pay for an abortion resulting from rape. And S. 411 sought to loosen Massachusetts restrictions on fetal experimentation. In each of these bills, a consensus on the biological origins of individual human life would have provided clear instruction to legislators on the sentiments of the people, regarding the humanity of the unborn, when deciding these issues.

My proposed question had strict parallel to the 1984 Northampton question which the Attorney General ratified. Namely, the declaration of a nuclear free zone does not tell legislators what to do in specific, but rather it properly assumes that the legislators would receive it as a sentiment of the voters, if passed, and would thus be most applicable if the Massachusetts Legislature (known as the General Court) wished to consider a "memorialization" of the U.S. Congress. My question did exactly the same for H. 2650 (1988), which memorialized the U.S. Congress to protect the unborn – plus it applied to much more as well.

Any cursory review of legislative attention or action in the Commonwealth would reveal many bills addressing issues where the definition of biological humanity is crucial. Question 1 on the 1986 ballot dealt with state funding of abortion. In Op. Atty. Gen., Sept. 24, 1976, p. 89, the Attorney General ratified a public policy question which sought to instruct legislators to ratify a Human Life Amendment to the U.S. Constitution. In 1972 there were two different public policy questions, both dealing with attempts to repeal pre-*Roe* restrictions on abortions (appearing on the ballots of 14 representative districts). Also in 1972, another public policy question appeared on the ballot of 9th Plymouth representative district. It reads:

> Shall the Representative from this District be instructed to approve the passage of an anti-abortion amendment to the Constitution of the Commonwealth which would guarantee the right to life, from the moment of conception, to every human being?

Here the terms of "conception" and "human being" are central. My proposed question was in the center of what it means to instruct legislators as

247

to a matter of public policy, and with specificity. And especially, I argued in my brief how the question uniquely redresses *Roe*.

In a nutshell, when it came to a question of what "public policy" is, I argued that we who had petitioned for the question were exercising our "original power" according to the Massachusetts Constitution, Part 1, Articles 5, 7 and 19, and the General Laws, chapter 53, §19. Attorney General James Shannon never engaged the debate on these terms, choosing instead to use opinions of prior Attorneys General and unrelated case law, and out of context to boot, to oppose our "original power." Shannon's fear to engage the discussion at the level of the Massachusetts Constitution is similar to the refusal to engage in any question concerning origins. (Human abortion opposes the order of creation, and embraces the reversal.)

For me this was a wake-up call to my political naïvetè – little did I expect such intellectual dishonesty. I had yet to learn the shrewdness of a serpent to complement the innocence of a dove.

B. Definition of Instruction(s)

Shannon's contention that my proposed question was not one of "public policy" hinged on his unconstitutionally narrow definition of the word "instruction." This word proved to be his hinge-point of being legalistic for the purpose of denying the purpose and nature of the laws to begin with. His "opinion" constitutes a letter to the Secretary of State on all the proposed public policy questions in a given election year. He thus stated:

> I have determined that one of the proposed questions transmitted by you is not properly an "instruction [ ] ... [by the people] ... to their representatives [ ]." Massachusetts Constitution, Part 1, art. 19 ... Both the form and content of this question are unprecedented and fatally deficient. Accordingly, it is my opinion that it would be inappropriate for the submitted question to appear on the November ballot as a public policy question (Op. Atty. Gen. Sept. 2, 1988, pp. 7-8).

In the legal brief, I had already evidenced the public policy nature of the question – its "content." Shannon's argument rested on his criticism of its "form." Though he cited the Massachusetts Constitution, he nowhere defined its use of language – he made no attempt to exegete it on its own terms. As well, his complaint about lack of precedent was disingenuous. The broad freedom of "original power" will certainly, in the course of history, address new questions (e.g., [at the time] genetic cloning), and the "original power" of the people assumes their prerogative to suit the form to the content in a way they best see fit. Also, the subject matter of our proposed question has overwhelming precedence, and its multiple-choice form has precedence, as I will note.

On the face of it, Article 19 is generic in the use of "instructions," not restrictive, and G.L. c. 53, § 19 assumes the same, as already noted. Its choice of language expresses breadth of intent in the phrase, "any question of instructions." The "any" is openly inclusive, not exclusive, and "instructions" as a plural form, reflects the same.

The *Random House Dictionary* (op. cit.) provides the range of meanings for "instruction":

1. The act or practice of instructing or teaching; education. 2. knowledge or information imparted. 3. an item of such knowledge or information. 4. Usually, instructions, orders or corrections ... 5. the act of furnishing with authoritative directions ...

Article 19 and G.L. c. 53, § 19 assume that "any" of these forms of instruction are intended as part of the people's "original power." My proposed question involved all these five definitions, and the second and third in particular contravened Shannon's opinion.

Shannon continued as he gives his definition of what an "instruction" is in his September 2, 1988 opinion:

> On its face, the beginning of life question does not provide a
> representative with any instruction or direction regarding governmental

249

action. Indeed, it does not indicate whether any governmental action at all is contemplated by the proposed question. In addition, the proposed question fails to notify voters what public policy, if any, would be changed or established by a representative seeking to follow their instruction. Providing instruction to a representative is fundamental to properly posing "a question of public policy" under Massachusetts law. See discussion, *supra*. The proposed question fails to do this. This purely abstract, descriptive question conflicts with the long legacy of past public policy questions and the unambiguous intent of article 19 and chapter 53, which is to provide instructions to the Legislature (pp. 41-42).

In six capacities, I challenged this argument.

First, as already argued, the question does provide clear instruction – there is no doubt as to the impact of the question if "conception" were ratified by a majority of the voters. And if "conception" fails, then supporters of *Roe* would be strengthened. I was willing to take this risk because of my prior commitment to democratically informed choice, and because of the necessity of redressing *Roe*'s non-consensus argument – which for the first time in U.S. history, based an interpretation of law on a statement of ignorance as to the central fact of the case. If truly there were no consensus, then the *Roe v. Wade* (and *Doe v. Bolton*) Court should have remanded the cases back to Texas and Georgia, or it should have thrown it out, leaving them in the hands of the several states. This is why my question elicited such concerted opposition, including the Attorney General who used to sit on the board of PPLM (he resigned only because it became an election issue in 1986, because of his potential conflict of interests in ruling on matters concerning abortion – and indeed his bias came through against my public policy question two years later).

Second, Shannon's specific concern was with a standard phrase employed in other public policy questions, "Shall the Representative from this district be instructed to vote for …?" This is an appropriate phrase, but it is merely one example of how the "original power" of the people is exercised – the freedom to choose the form of instruction. Shannon's opinion denied me and the other petitioners such a freedom of choice as guaranteed by the Massachusetts Constitution. Also, in 1990, I initiated another public policy question that changed the wording to include "so that the Senator from this district may be instructed to vote for legislation that protects such human life ...?" Nonetheless, Shannon also blocked that question, revealing that his concern was not with his narrow use of "instruction(s)," but with the multiple-choice format, which I will address shortly.

Third, Shannon's attempt to call the question abstract was without foundation. He created whatever abstractness there is by not quoting the exact question, by rephrasing it, per *Roe*, as "when does life begin?" This phrasing lends itself to philosophical and theological questions capable of abstraction. This is precisely why I emphasized the words, "biological terms," and specified the adjectival noun, "individual," in order to remove all abstraction. It was a concrete question with concrete public policy implications.

Fourth, Shannon used the word "descriptive" to disqualify the question as undescriptive. I evidenced the dishonest use of language here, citing his false dichotomy between facts and their relationship to public policy vis-à-vis *Borden*.

Fifth, it is curious how Shannon said our question conflicts with the "unambiguous intent of article 19 and chapter 53," in that he never defined the terms therein. Instead, he placed an eisegetical review of case law ahead of the Constitution and General Laws, and in so doing, he was in conflict with the unambiguous intent of Part 1, Articles 5, 7 and 19 of the Massachusetts Constitution, and G.L. c. 53, § 19, which is rooted in "original power," as I consistently demonstrated.

And sixth, when Shannon wrongly maintained that my question did not have "any" governmental action in view, he was also in opposition to Op. Atty. Gen., Sept. 4, 1984, pp. 75-76, already cited in regard to the nuclear free zone public policy question in Northampton. The General Court was forbidden by U.S. law from taking that instruction and putting it into law, but it was a valid question because of the possibility of a resolution

251

memorializing the U.S. Congress. In the case of my question, it is a clear instruction toward a memorialization of the U.S. Congress for a Human Life Amendment, not to mention the many specific governmental actions of the General Court for which the question does provide instructions, as also evidenced in my brief.

Thus, it was clear that my proposed question was fully within the original meaning of the word "instruction(s)" as used in the Massachusetts Constitution, Part 1, Article 19 and in G.L. c. 53, § 19.

C. The Affirmative No and Multiple-Choice

I do not believe that questions about "public policy" and "instructions" were Shannon's real concern – just a pretext to build a case against what he really feared – the power of informed choice. His real fear was a positive multiple-choice question. The language of "pro-choice" is a ruse for abortion-rights supporters to cloak their true intents.

In his September 2, 1988 opinion, he stated:

> Moreover, voters are instructed to respond through a set of choices that does not allow for affirmatively voting that no instruction on this issue be given. The question's failure to allow voters to reject entirely any instruction to their legislator on the subject of the question appears to be unprecedented in the history of public policy questions (pp. 42-43).

Shannon's purpose here was to build a syllogism to disallow our use of multiple-choice: namely, if the question does not provide for an "affirmative no," and if the question appears to be unprecedented, therefore the use of the multiple-choice format is wrong. This syllogism was false and it was a reversal of reality. The truth is that the multiple-choice format provided for the "affirmative no" in the most comprehensive fashion possible, and it is with striking precedent.

First, the "affirmative no," as Shannon used it, applies specifically to the yes/no format, and he twisted its deeper purpose against multiple-choice. For example, if someone were to vote "no" to the nuclear free zone question, it is most likely due to his saying "yes" to federal nuclear deterrent policies for the common defense.

Second, the "affirmative no" is not automatically provided for even in the yes/no format. Someone can vote "no" because they do not understand the question, or because they are simply negative to any change in the status quo. Thus, they employ a "no" as a pure "negative" and actually affirm nothing. Affirmation of an opinion is what public policy questions seek to elicit – this is the defining or deeper purpose in view.

Third, multiple-choice is multiple affirmation, and includes a wider range of "affirmative no" as well. The three positive choices and write-in option allow voters to say no to one term by saying yes to another – they negate by an affirmation. But affirmation is the key – an "affirmative" basis for the "no." If one does not agree with conception as the answer, he or she can choose implantation, nidation, quickening, viability, birth, or otherwise.

And fourth, in multiple-choice, a "no" or "I don't know" option added to it would not be affirmative – it would be purely negative. The "no" Shannon called for with regard to my proposed question would have affirmed nothing, and this is why it did not belong in a multiple-choice format. Shannon sought to impose such a negation on multiple-choice in order to destroy its affirmative power, opposing the constitutional purpose for the "affirmative no," which is to provide affirmative instructions to the legislature.

As well, in both yes/no and multiple-choice questions, there is the "no instruction" option for the undecided, uncertain or uncaring. Namely, they can leave the ballot blank. This is the case when voting for candidates for public office. The write-in option is always available, and so too the option not to vote if no satisfactory choice is possible.

I argued that Mr. Shannon knew this, for he offered me two additional choices, both pure negatives, through his Assistant Attorney General on

August 17, 1988. The first "choice" offered was "I don't know," and the second was, "No, I do not want to so instruct my legislator." Shannon knowingly offered these in bad faith, because he had already received my August 4 letter explaining how the multiple-choice format was chosen explicitly to challenge *Roe*'s "I don't know" posture. Where in all U.S. legal history has "I don't know" been the basis for interpreting law prior to *Roe*? Can an "I don't know" be elected to public office or written as a law? As well, Shannon stated in his opinion that his office cannot "materially alter the substance of the question" to bring it in line with his stated objections, for to do so would violate the signature requirements of G.L. c. 53, § 19. Yet he had asked us to do precisely that on August 17.

In other words, Shannon, consistent with the *Roe* rationale he supports, wished to deny the people their right for positive choices, because he knows that *Roe* supporters have no positive term they can agree on or support. They need a "negative no" because they do not have an "affirmative no" or any positive position on the question. By denying our prerogative to frame the question as a positive multiple-choice, he sought by fiat to keep the question from being discussed through public ballot in any fashion that might actually redress the people's concerns about *Roe*.

Shannon revealed his true agenda, buried in a footnote:

> A review of past questions reveals no Massachusetts ballot question that offered multiple choices with no opportunity for a voter to reject the entire proposition, except for a question regarding the Vietnam War that was placed on the ballot by a Special Act of the General Court. Chapter 588 of the Acts of 1970. This 1970 question is inapposite here because it was not placed on the ballot as a public policy question under article 19 and G.L. c. 53. In analyzing public policy questions, it bears noting that the applicable statutes assume that a question may be 'negativized', G.L. c. 53, § 22, and militate against multiple choices by requiring that a response receive a majority of all votes cast to constitute an instruction. G.L. c. 53, § 22. (Op. Atty. Gen. Sept. 2, 1988, p. 10, n.8).

First, Shannon contrived the linkage of multiple-choice and the "negative" option in order to disallow multiple-choice as I defined it above. Second, the Vietnam multiple-choice question confirms Shannon's bad faith directive in that it provided no negative or so-called "affirmative no" choice – only three positive choices were provided. And especially, the Vietnam question is not inapposite – rather it ratifies our "original power" to also employ multiple-choice. The very power of the General Court (Massachusetts Legislature) to make a Special Act for the ballot is derived from the people, according to Part 1, Articles 5, 7 and 19 of the Constitution. As such, if the 1970 General Court can employ multiple-choice on a non-binding ballot question, how can the Attorney General prohibit we the people from doing the same?

Third, the uniqueness of the Vietnam question is worth looking at. That same year, a public policy petition placed Question 5 on the senatorial district ballots in the 1st Essex and 2nd Middlesex districts. It was in a yes/no format, but the General Court felt that the nature of the question required multiple-choice in order to fully instruct the legislators, so they passed a Special Act for a state-wide multiple-choice question. The results bear this out: 59 percent of the voters in the two senatorial districts answered "yes," the United States should immediately pull out of Vietnam. The General Court gave three options as to Vietnam policy: a) immediate withdrawal, b) gradual withdrawal or c) win a complete military victory. The results gave the option "b" of "gradual withdrawal" a 52.5 percent majority, and the "immediate withdrawal" option, pace the yes/no senatorial district option, dropped to 33 percent, a 26 percent reduction. Thus, the multiple-choice format produced a true sentiment that was obscured by the yes/no format.

Our multiple-choice question would also have produced a significant and therefore instructive difference, over and against a yes/no format. Shannon argued that a question on a "theory of when life begins" is permissible if we were to observe his restrictions, i.e., reduction to the "standard" phrasing in a yes/no format (Op. Atty. Gen. Sept. 2, 1988, p. 10, n. 9). But this would allow the "non-consensus" rationale of *Roe* to hide behind a purely negative "no" answer, and therefore Shannon affronted the "original power" of the people.

Fourth, his one-sentence declaration of inapposition between a voter initiated public policy question, and one initiated by the General Court, is remarkably flimsy, it is a specter without substance – and it equals the entire substance of his fears. Everything he has argued prior to and subsequent to this point is meant to run cover for this one sentence.

Fifth, Shannon said that multiple-choice was inapposite because G.L. c. 53, § 22 assumes a question may be "negativized." This is wrong. The statute says that a majority of votes must be gained in order to constitute an instruction. This requirement may make the multiple-choice format a more difficult means to gain a "majority," but neither the multiple-choice or yes/no format guarantees that an instruction will be given. The risk that "no instruction" would be given was undertaken by the 1970 General Court, and in fact, the second option did receive a majority.

Shannon, in his disingenuous opposition to our ballot initiative, imposed an ex post facto restrictiveness upon the General Laws. And to do so, he further denied the "original power" of the people by saying that the Legislature's initiative in multiple-choice is irrelevant, despite the fact they receive their power to do so from we the people's "original power" to compose various instructions, petitions and remonstrances to our elected officials – "broadly construed." This broad construction includes the freedom of the people to compose a multiple-choice question, and as evidenced by the General Court doing so in 1970.

And sixth, Shannon said that "(t)he instruction contained in each public policy question must be consistent with the powers of the Legislature ..." (Op. Atty. Gen. Sept. 2, 1988, p. 4). How could our multiple-choice format possibly be inconsistent with our elected Legislature, when they too saw fit to pose a multiple-choice question?

Our case was based simply and honestly on the clear understanding of the Massachusetts Constitution, Part 1, Articles 5, 7 and 19, and G.L. c. 53, § 19 – on the "original power" of we the people. We had given evidence by exegeting the texts themselves, with specific reference to our proposed question. Mr. Shannon had only referred to the Constitution and General

Laws vaguely, without defining any of their terms as we have, and he did not respond to our specific definitions. His conduct evidenced an opposition to true definitions of terms, an opposition to the power of informed choice.

Bad Faith and Dropping the Ball

Thus the argument was laid out, and it was never challenged head-on. Rather, in my political naïvetè I assumed there would be an honest response. I did not realize how deeply scared the abortion-rights establishment was of the question. And though the response was rooted in bad faith, I expected my day in court – but did not get it.

In hiring an attorney, I consulted with him to know how to present my argument, and what channels to proceed with to challenge the Attorney General in court. He helped me considerably, and was proud to file my lawsuit with the argument it made. When he received a copy at his office of an *amicus*, or "friend of the court" legal brief from the Planned Parenthood League of Massachusetts, supporting the Attorney General against our public policy question – he knew how deeply the proposed question struck their nerve.

However, my attorney was not specially trained in this type of law, and he did not do two basic steps necessary to present the lawsuit. According to the laws governing "public policy questions" in Massachusetts, if the Attorney General writes an opinion against a question, he can only be challenged in court if it is proved that he acted in "bad faith." As well, legally non-binding public policy questions are last in the order of petition filings, with legally binding questions taking precedence. What this means is that it's constitutionality is decided upon only weeks before the November election. There is a very narrow window (about four weeks) in which to prove the "bad faith" charge, take the Attorney General to court, and gain a ruling before the November ballots are printed in early October.

Thus, step one would have been to gain a hearing before the Suffolk County Superior Court (as earlier noted), argue the reasons why the Attorney General acted in "bad faith," and gain a favorable ruling. Then, step two was to take the case to the Supreme Judicial Court and argue it on its merits – to argue the case I have outlined here. But we never got that opportunity.

I was intellectually aware we needed to show that the Attorney General had ruled in "bad faith." But I did not know the legal procedure and simply believed that my argument would evidence the "bad faith." And my attorney was unaware of this specific procedural need. I also know now there was extraordinary witchcraft coming against our lawsuit of the Attorney General, and who knows how it may have helped cause this oversight.

What we did was simply file suit with the SJC, and after clearing procedural elements, they ruled they could not hear the case because we did not formally argue and evidence the "bad faith" first in Superior Court. Then, when we re-petitioned the same question in two representative districts in 1996 (with some original petitioners that still lived in the state), we learned that we had no ability to accuse "bad faith" after the 1988 ruling had been handed down. No redress in the system.

It was here that a member of the Supreme Judicial Court told us what we should have done in 1988 in terms of process (filing first a "bad faith" charge against the Attorney General in Superior Court). Thus, the only means remaining for the question in Massachusetts is through the Legislature, and this would require another statewide effort, and the re-creation of a network that became dispirited following the 1988 blocking of the question – and that season is now ancient history.

I was also told by political insiders that we had the best case to prove "bad faith" in state history. As I have already noted, Shannon was a former board member of the Planned Parenthood League of Massachusetts, who had to resign that position when he ran for Attorney General in 1986, because potential conflicts of interest questions were raised. Due to my August 4, 1988 letter to him, he knew why we phrased the question as a multiple-choice as opposed to a yes/no format, in our desire to redress the "I don't know" posture of *Roe*. Yet, when he had an Assistant Attorney General contact me on August 17 with the possible addition of an "I don't know" and

"No, I do not want to so instruct my legislator" answers, he was doing so in bad faith, for he already knew our position.

Had he truly been convinced that a multiple-choice question was invalid, he would have simply ruled so. Rather, he tried to get us to include an "I don't know" option because that is the abortion-rights argument, and he feared a question that did not allow the pretension of ignorance to be chosen. He knew our use of multiple-choice was constitutionally valid. And his whole legal argument was a smokescreen to hide this reality as best he could. As well, why would we be requested to present a legal brief before the Attorney General's ruling? This reflects to me a "bad faith" predisposition to rule against it, and to learn our argument ahead of time. Oh, was I politically naïve.

As well, we saw plenty of indications of likely collusion between the Attorney General's office, NOW, CLUM and PPLM to defeat our question. Had there been the opportunity to take sworn depositions on this matter, I would have liked to traced what phones calls began, from whom to the NOW volunteers on the evening we filed our petitions. As well, it seemed to us that the CLUM letter, Planned Parenthood's *amicus* and the Attorney General's brief all shared the same database – in terms of content and structure of thought.

Religious Bigotry

Now we could have asked a question: Does an individual biological human life begin at conception? Yes or no. And with a yes/no format, the Attorney General said he would have approved it. And likely, we would have won by a 60-40 margin. But I did not want the abortion-rights people to argue a negative. I wanted to see what positive point they were willing to argue – I wanted a positive informed choice. I wanted to honestly define the terms of the debate.

For example, had it been a yes/no question, they could have conducted a campaign saying something like, "Vote No on Question #3 – Keep Church and State Separate!" Or, "Vote No on Question #3 – Say No to Religious

259

Intolerance!" Or, "Vote No on Question #3 – Don't Let Zealots Impose Their Religion on You!" Or, "Vote No on Question #3 – Don't Let the Anti-Choice Fanatics Destroy a Woman's Freedom to Choose!" And etc.

Jesus said to the Pharisees at one point:

> Every kingdom divided against itself will be laid waste, and every city or household divided against itself will not stand. If *Satan* casts out *Satan*, he is divided against himself. How then can his kingdom stand? … He who is not with me is against me, and he who does not gather with me scatters" (Matthew 12:25-26; 30).

The abortion-rights movement is likewise divided against itself. Its philosophical unity is only in the power to confuse and negate, to take and destroy, whereas we pro-life Christians should be united in the power to give and the ethics and power of informed choice, which lay at the root of the proposed multiple-choice question.

My question would not have allowed the abortion-rights movement to unite in negation, but would have exposed their inability to unite in any positive fashion. They could not have said, "Vote Viability," because they disagree among themselves and cannot make a positive argument for it. The same for "Vote Implantation," "Vote Quickening," "Vote Birth" or "Vote 3 Days After Birth." And if they wanted to be esoteric: "Vote Nidation" (the point past when twinning is no longer possible, 7-14 days after conception).

The only thing they could have done in the face of such a public policy question was to tell people not to vote – which would have increased our percentage of consensus. They could conduct no campaign against it. And my campaign would have been one very simple slogan: "Conception is it." We would have then passed out full-color flyers on the science of conception and fetal development.

In other words, I marshaled all I could to make it multiple positive choice, for in so doing we would have been in the driver's seat. It would have taken the oxygen out of the "pro-choice" movement in their public relations campaign, having thus to dance around their opposition to the language of choice in service to human life. Their idolatry of "choice," their prostitution of truly informed choice at the altar of unborn death, would have been widely revealed.

When I suggest how the abortion-rights establishment might have conducted a campaign on a yes/no question based on their religious bigotry, we have already noted the anti-biblical nature of *Roe*. But in the 1988 Massachusetts question, we saw it in bold relief. On August 12, the Civil Liberties Union of Massachusetts wrote the Attorney General, asking, ahead of time, that our question not be approved. The letter stated:

> First, the ballot question, as worded, does not pose a question of public policy but instead a question which implicates, for many individuals, religious views concerning the point at which human life begins.

> In our view the government has no proper role making inquiries into its citizen's views on religious matters, even if those views are expressed in the form of an anonymous ballot. Although the proposed ballot question is couched as a question of "biological" fact, casting the question in those terms cannot conceal the reality that is constitutes, in effect, a poll of the voter's beliefs on a religious matter.

Also, Planned Parenthood, in their *amicus*, stated (in strikingly parallel language):

> There is yet another problem with the proposed question. To many people, the question will necessarily be read to ask 'in [religious] terms, when does an individual life begin.' But if the question is viewed as an inquiry into the voters' religious beliefs, it is equally improper as a ballot question. The separation of church and state mandated by the federal and state constitutions require that voters not be polled as to their religious beliefs, and that their representatives not be instructed to vote to adopt one religious belief of doctrine over another (pp. 9-10).

261

This is remarkable. Even though my question specifically emphasized "biological terms," the religious bigotry of these two organizations came to the surface. They knew I headed up a Christian pro-life organization. They had to cast it as a religious question, not biological. Just like the satraps had to plot against Daniel (chapter 6), not on legal grounds, where he was faultless, but in a bigotry against "the law of his God," Able, the CLUM and PPLM believe, to thus incite opposition.

In arguing that our question was really a "religious" one, and using the straw figure of "for many people," and the "if" clause that serves prejudicial ill-definition in order to obfuscate, and that "religious" questions may not be asked, what they end up saying is that the science of biology is religious. Therefore, scientific questions are precluded from the ballot because scientific concerns are really religious (!). Or, religious people and groups are not allowed to ask public policy questions. What this means, if consistently applied, is that religious people (especially those, maybe only those, who take the Bible seriously) are not allowed to participate in matters of public policy except as "secular" citizens – only if they are willing to deny their "religious" convictions.

This logic also says that since "biology" is "religious" in matters of human abortion, the door is opened to oppose any public discussion of an issue on the grounds that it may be "religious." This is an extraordinary affront against the Declaration of Independence, the opposite of the "no religious test" of article VI of the Constitution, and the opposite of the First Amendment. It is an attempt at political tyranny and opposite to the six pillars of biblical power and honest politics. It reveals a hatred of the Gospel, and we need God's grace to serve a reversal of this reversal. As well, Only Genesis has a positive view of science and the scientific method, and we see the pagan religious ethics in the CLUM and PPLM's opposition to my question.

Strategy

The time is overripe to address this question nationwide. It is time to take this multiple-choice question and a) present it to the U.S. Congress for a roll-call vote, b) likewise state legislatures, and c) to place it on as many state ballots as possible. This will be dynamic and revealing a vote as we have ever seen on this issue.

This process would accomplish the following:

1. It would demonstrate the consensus that exists at the grass-roots, and cannot then be swept under the rug politically as were the results of the 1981 U.S. Senate Subcommittee hearings.
2. It would use the power of democratically informed choice to define the central fact of the case deliberately ignored by *Roe*.
3. It would reverse the reversal, serve the true *God → life → choice → sex* order of creation and thus redeem the language of choice to protect unborn human life, instead of destroying the unborn as does the idolatry of *Sex → Choice → Life →/ God*.
4. Thus, we will demonstrate that: "pro-life" = pro-informed choice; that "pro-choice" = anti-informed choice, because "pro-choice" is really pro-abortion. Those who oppose such a referendum would paint themselves as anti-democratic, and we will have defined and taken the true high ground.
5. It is legally non-binding, only seeks consensus, and therefore it requires nothing in terms of legal change. If there is truly no consensus as often claimed by abortion-rights ideologues, then they can rest easy. There would be no changes in the law, and their full democratic participation has been enfranchised. If there is a consensus, there are also no required legal changes. But we would then have a level playing field based on this establishment of fact, from which we can try to win the hearts and minds of the culture and thus change the law. And the full democratic participation of abortion-rights advocates is enfranchised every step of the way. But neither the ancient serpent, theologically in the Garden of Eden, nor pro-abortion partisans, in the current political landscape, are interested in a level playing field. They only want dominance ceded to them.
6. Many "pro-choicers" will see it as an honest question, and we will be in position to begin to win the "middle ground."

7. It allows the "personally opposed but …" people to have the genuine privacy of the ballot box to express their convictions. I believe most will answer "conception," and emerge with more confidence in their pro-life instincts as part of the true cultural majority. This will strengthen the winning of this "middle ground."

8. No unified opposition is possible, as the framing of the question redresses the dishonesty of *Roe*. Since abortion-rights partisans are based on *Roe*'s "I don't know" posture, they cannot affirm any positive definition apart from conception, for they know "conception is it." They are a house divided, and have no ability to unite around nidation, implantation, quickening, viability, birth or otherwise. They know that once the question gets on the ballot, they will have forfeited their public image of "pro-choice," and their anti-informed choice position will be laid bare. Their pretension of ignorance will be their strongest suit. Why otherwise did the Massachusetts Attorney General, the CLUM, PPLM and NOW so fear the question?

9. It is a biological issue at question, and not an item of religious creed. The only religious issue in this process, and a crucially important one, is whether or not a person's religious or philosophical worldview allows him or her to embrace a scientifically accurate definition of terms. This will demonstrate that: "pro-life" = an accurate scientific definition of terms; and "pro-choice" = a fear of an accurate scientific definition of terms.

10. At this juncture lobbying should begin for a federal law that requires all abortion providers to offer an ultrasound of the unborn fetus to their patients, with a list of abortion alternative services also provided – thus providing a true reality of informed choice.

11. Also, laws should be advanced that require all biological fathers to be responsible for the well-being of women they have impregnated, and children thus conceived.

12. Once accurate definition of terms, once the biological definition of individual humanity, are proven in the public domain, then and only then can the real debate begin, and the other issues be addressed – such as male chauvinism, promiscuity, poverty, population, rape and incest, women's health, deformity, racism, etc. With a consensus in place that "conception is it," then the campaign that "abortion is the

ultimate male chauvinism" – one that impregnates the abortion ethos and industry – takes center stage. The dignity of women and their unborn are parallel. The idea of abortion as a woman's "right" or "freedom" must be demythologized if we are ever to win the legal protection of the unborn.

13. In practical terms, we have to succeed well enough in the process to make human abortion heinous and undesirable to most of the culture, and this too means regaining a cultural embrace of the goodness of man and woman in marriage, and thus, the social opprobrium toward sex outside marriage. Our work is cut out for us.

14. The voters in the states that demonstrate such a consensus will then have both the political and moral authority to call upon their state legislatures and the U.S. Congress to look at the abortion debate with such a consensus in view. This is the sole manner which paves the way for the U.S. Congress to muster the two-thirds majority to call for a Human Life Amendment to the U.S. Constitution, and for the three-fourths of the State Legislatures needed to ratify it. With such a consensus on the biology of conception and the male chauvinism of human abortion in place, current lawmakers can be held accountable or face being replaced. Pro-life Christians in this process will have taken the high moral and political ground at every turn as we have testified to and modeled the ethics and power of informed choice in the face of those who do not. And the unborn will have been honored as image-bearers of God.

15. In all this we will honestly and successfully change the language of the abortion debate, and gain the driver's seat to win the equal legal protection for women and their unborn.

In Sum

In our forum together at Georgetown and on C-Span, I asked Kate Michelman if we pro-lifers have the right to win legal protection for the unborn through constitutional process. She tried to deflect the question but then said "no," some rights such as abortion are above the law: "Just as you said John, 'liberty and property.' " But I had been arguing "life, liberty and property ..." She excised "life," which is the nature of human abortion.

265

Just like Patricia Ireland, Kate and others who are idolaters of "pro-choice" fear the power of informed choice, for by definition it serves the humanity of all, including the unborn. Yet, their idolatry has been in the driver's seat all these years, and had there been a biblically literate church sufficient to challenge this, we could have reversed such idolatry a long time ago. The time is overripe for the believing church to arise.

♦ ♦ ♦

Chapter Seven

The Idolatry of Operation Rescue

In 1986, Randall Terry seized the imagination of many committed pro-life activists, as he chained himself to a sink at an abortion facility in protest. Then his new group, Operation Rescue (OR), hit the national spotlight in November, 1987, when some 350 fellow activists from across the country joined with him to block access to an abortion center in Cherry Hill, New Jersey. Some 200 were arrested, and the movement followed for some four tumultuous years until the blockades were blocked due to intrinsic and extrinsic variables. Terry's motto was facile: "If you believe abortion is murder, act like it's murder."

Terry published a book by the same name shortly thereafter, and in it he made a case for civil disobedience, citing biblical reasons as it were, arguing that all abortion centers could be shut down if he could marshal enough fellow blockaders. I encountered this idea two-years earlier in Philadelphia, and rejected it *prima facie* (in accord with deeply held and tested biblical assumptions), but too, I was always open to being persuaded by a better biblical argument.

Thus, I wrote Terry in early 1989 to pose some biblical questions about his strategy, and was able to arrange a meeting with him on April 1 in South Boston. But he was unreceptive to my concerns, and thereafter shunned all further discussion about the issue. I have concluded his entire approach is opposite to Biblical Theology 101 and all that flows from it. The very idea of blockade is predicated on coercive tactics hatched in secret against police authorities and pro-abortion organizations. Terry's position, as he articulates it in his book, and in the meeting I had with him, effectively places politics ahead of the Gospel.

Now, my interest is to be positive and biblical in what I do – and this is how I will address the larger topic. But since Terry's leadership led to the most arrests of any civil disobedience movement in U.S. history (some reports exceed 100,000), and galvanized public attention, it needs honest redress.

As well, and importantly, the many well-intentioned Christians who did participate in blockade, did so with good motive. Still, all of us need to be biblically critical in our thinking about this subject. Pro-life Christians participated in Operation Rescue largely because there was a vacuum in vision. There was, and still is, very little political success in moving toward the legal protection of the unborn. And though Crisis Pregnancy Centers (CPCs, aka Pregnancy Resource Centers, PRCs) were and are doing excellent work, they can only reach a small portion of abortion-minded women. In 1986-1987 it seemed that the possibility of persuasion within the political process was remote, so the violence of blockade came to be embraced by a number of pro-life advocates. As it was embraced, it was a public confession that they were forfeiting the power of persuasion en masse. They had admitted defeat in the court of public opinion.

When I began to raise questions about the tactic of blockade, many friends who had joined Operation Rescue asked me to reconsider. One person told me that half the OR volunteers in Boston were evangelicals whom I had recruited into the pro-life cause. So I went to hear one Operation Rescue speaker with an open mind, but my questions only sharpened. And then I wrote Randall Terry after reading his book.

Idolatry Revealed

In my meeting with him, several items stand out. First, Terry criticized me for not taking the "risk" of arrest, assuming, I guess, this must be the reason why I said no to blockade. I responded in part by stating the true risk is that of loving your enemies, as I sought to do on college campuses in the face of this debate.

Second, in my proactive understanding which would preclude vigilante actions such as blockade, I defined the power of informed choice, and asked him if God forces people into eternal life. He said no. Then I asked him why he was trying to force women into choosing life for their unborn. His response was straightforward, "We're talking about saving babies here, not saving souls," and then he said that I did not understand the nature of choice.

Here is where I see an idolatry of "pro-life" most clearly. Politics are in place ahead of the Gospel. This thinking actually reverses the biblical order of creation seen in *God → life → choice → sex*, serving instead its reversal, *sex → choice → life →/God*. This idolatry of "pro-life" serves the idolatries of sexual promiscuity and "pro-choice" by giving such advocates more self-justifying energy to maintain their sins if we were in any way coercive. If the living and preaching of the Good News is not our ultimate and defining purpose, then we labor in vain to protect the unborn. If the saving of the unborn from abortion is not a subcategory of the doctrine of salvation, does this not upend biblical faith?

In his book, Terry called for the "rescuing" of the unborn by any means possible. He said to me that Jesus would not stand by and let innocent children die, and thus we must physically intervene by means of blockade or otherwise. On what basis I asked. This he argued without any example from the life of Jesus, and as we have seen and will see, this is contrary to how Jesus lived and taught.

I also asked him: "Why then did God not only 'stand by' when Herod slaughtered the innocent boys, but also called for the death of children in the pagan nations that sought Israel's destruction?" No answer. (And I larger question about which I write elsewhere.) Also, why did Jeremiah take the leaders of Jerusalem out to the Valley of Ben Hinnom where child sacrifice was happening daily, prophesy against it, yet he did not take the law into his own hands to stop it? Rather he called on King Zedekiah to stop shedding such innocent blood, and honor the Law of Moses.

Then third, and critically, I asked Terry if he believed, like me, that all Scripture is defined interpretively by the doctrines of creation, sin and redemption outlined in Genesis 1-3. He said yes. Then I asked, "Can you then show me where you root your strategy of blockade in these doctrines?" He answered quickly, "Well, how do I know that your strategy is rooted in these doctrines?" He then dismissed the subject and refused to entertain the question again.

Within several years after its inauguration, Operation Rescue was not only a failure, but it hardened the hearts of many people against the Gospel, and provided a windfall for abortion-rights groups. Sadly, Terry proved to be a perfect foil for them to demonize and raise money by fear, since his language against abortion advocates was so condemning. His face and name were splashed on Planned Parenthood fund-raising letters to motivate their donor base to give more (and very successfully), and likewise with the American Civil Liberties Union (ACLU).

In the early 1990s, I had lunch in New York City with the then executive director of the ACLU, Ira Glasser, and gained an inside perspective on how they succeeded so well in their fund-raising, with Terry and Operation Rescue to vilify. Could that ever be said of Jesus? In contrast (and this is after our own work at New England's largest abortion center, 1989-1991), Ira did not oppose how we conducted ourselves. Chapter Eight will detail its past success, and enormous potential for the present on forward – all rigorously biblical.

(I have also addressed two forums with the then president of the ACLU, in 1997 and 2005, Nadine Strossen, at Gordon-Conwell Theological Seminary in South Hamilton, Massachusetts, and the Harvard Club in New York City. Though the topic was not abortion, it came up briefly at one juncture, and she says, pace *Roe*, that if the unborn can be shown to be "persons" within the language of the Fourteenth Amendment, then legal protection must be afforded. An honest advocacy, unlike the presidents of NARAL and NOW in public forums.)

Also, it allowed pro-abortion groups to lump CPCs in with OR in their public rhetoric. And for anyone who participated in the blockade of an abortion center, it reduced their ability to participate in political dialogue, for they had already forfeited that arena by their vigilante actions. Thus, I contend it was a large net loss both for the pro-life witness in this culture, and for those Christians and churches who participated in or supported it.

Later, Terry became an unsuccessful candidate for the U.S. Congress in 1998 (in upstate New York), but in order to do so, he had to sign a consent decree with the National Organization for Women, making legal promise never again to be involved with blockade or cognate violative actions. He signed the decree in order to avoid further lawsuits against his former actions and make himself more "politically viable," and in particular, to avoid the loss of his campaign funds to those lawsuits. Therefore, what moral or intellectual integrity does this represent, if truly he believed the strategy of blockade were biblical?

So much energy, time, money and resources were expended on OR. I knew people who spent hundreds and even thousands of dollars to travel around the country to participate in various blockade efforts, who also had to pay court fees and who lost much income from the time they spent in jail. As well, there were practical deficits the strategy could not avoid. Especially, it took great personal and financial sacrifice to organize a blockade, and its sustainability was limited. For up to several hours at a time they could block an abortion center before being hauled away to jail. And as best I recall, I do not believe that OR in Massachusetts was able to block access to an abortion center on even a dozen occasions, before they were too worn out to continue.

I am biblically convinced that if a woman, with or without the pressure of a boyfriend or other party, is blocked from an abortion appointment, she will often become more adamant in following through with the abortion at the next possibility. Some women were dissuaded on their abortion plans by OR, but I am convinced they could have been, and many more likewise dissuaded by a biblically wise and peaceful presence, women whose hearts were otherwise hardened by the violative strategy of blockade.

And when a woman's heart does become hardened by the tactic of blockade, she is much less likely to seek out pro-lifers later if she were dealing with post-abortion trauma. She is not likely to seek out people who were blocking her or yelling at her. But for women who walk past a peaceful witness and secure an abortion, if later they do have regrets, they are far more likely to seek out pro-life counselors.

271

A Former NOW Activist

To cite one example where blockade harmed the witness of the Gospel, I once received a letter from Amy Tracy, who used to be in a high profile position with NOW in Washington, D.C., working closely with Patricia Ireland. She had since become Christian, and saw the video of the 1994 forum with Patricia at Smith College. She wrote:

> First, I am so glad that the Lord raised up a "normal" Christian to present a positive vision of Christianity to folks like Patricia. You stood up for truth with grace and humility, without compromising your position. I noticed that your style and peaceful presence rattled Patricia more than any of your arguments.

> In that forum Patricia spoke of her experience with Christians. Like her, I experienced real violence at the hands of the anti-abortion and anti-gay activists. In the five years I wrestled with O.R., the 'Lambs of God' and similar groups I rarely, if ever saw the Christ I know.

> Likewise, in the heat of the battle, I sometimes responded to their hostility and fear with violent behavior. But I never claimed to be non-violent per se (though I did theoretically believe in it). Nor did I claim to be "Christ-like" or "holy." My words matched my actions. Not that this should excuse my behavior.

> As a brand new Christian, I harbored a lot of anger toward the Christians who I felt had grossly misrepresented Christ. Why hadn't anyone ever told me about the hope, the joy or the freedom! I knew nothing of God's promise of love beyond comprehension. What role had their self-righteous anger and arguments played in drawing me closer to Christ? If anything they drove me further away from the God who was tangibly wooing me. Three months into my Christian walk, I called my pastor wanting to know whether I really had to spend eternity with these folks.

> The Lord helped me bury the resentment …

This is a gracious and remarkable letter, and its value to me is in the context of her comments, as we glean from her perspective of Operation Rescue when she was an abortion-rights activist. Amy testifies to God's love drawing her even in the face of Christians who behaved hatefully toward her. But do we want God to work in spite of us, or through us? And at what point do we cross the line into false teachings?

And in truth, it is false ethics that are more dangerous than false teachings per se, and in my experience I now see overwhelming evidence that the reason people teach falsely, is that they bend teachings to suit their sinful egos. That is very different from the humble who may stray into a false understanding – we all do it. But are we willing to be corrected? If we really believe it is the Holy Spirit who convicts people of sin and righteousness, then we will put aside the folly of trying to argue or pressure people into eternal life. The real goal and courage is to love our enemies and witness the power of God's Spirit convert the soul.

This backdrop to the origins and nature of Operation Rescue sets us up to now look at the biblical realities vis-à-vis civil disobedience and obedience.

Civil Disobedience

The Definition of "Rescue"

The name "Operation Rescue" is derived from Proverbs 24:11-12, which Terry used as an all-encompassing hermeneutic:

> Snatch away those being led away to death; withhold those tottering toward slaughter. If you say, "Lo, we knew nothing about this," does not he who measures the mind and will discern it? Does not he who guards your soul know it? Will he not return to each man according to what he has done?

Many translations render the first word here as "rescue," and hence, the name "Operation Rescue." Fine word. But in these pages, I do my own translations from the Hebrew and Greek Scriptures. In so doing, I tend toward the most basic and literal, not trying for a polished rendering into smooth English. In Hebrew, for example, it is context that defines the best translation of a word; whereas in Greek, there can be so many different words for the same root idea, thus helping to define context. In most English translations, we lose much of the theological power of underlying Hebrew and Greek word usage. It is lost for the sake of smooth English syntax, and we are all the poorer for it.

In v. 12 for example, we see some very important words in the Hebrew Bible come together: *lev* (the totality of mind, will and heart, the inner self); *shamar* (to guard, e.g., its first biblical usage in Genesis 2:15, for Adam to guard the Garden, viz., the protection of and later rescue of all human life); and *nephesh* (soul, life, person, as we have reviewed in depth already here). And for example, in some of my Greek translations ahead in these pages, the term *dunamis* (power) is so often under translated.

Proverbs 24:11-12 is a powerful passage, and we in the church should be committed to do everything possible to "snatch away," to "rescue" the unborn and any others who are in harm's way. The question is how to do it, and whether our hermeneutic (interpretation) is exegetically or eisegetically based.

The Book of Proverbs is composed mostly by Solomon, at a time of national peace in Israel, in the tenth century B.C. It presupposes a king and people who both submit to the Mosaic covenant. There is agreement on *Yahweh Elohim* as the true King, and the goodness of the moral and social order he ordains, ultimately rooted in the nature of the biblical order of creation. Thus, presuppositionally, the call to "snatch away" or "rescue" occurs within the law, not outside.

Thus a proverb – as a pithy statement about right and wrong with the freedom to use hyperbole – given in this setting, is universally received as generally true. But it only applies within the nation of Israel. The Israelites are not being called to go to Carthage, Greece or Assyria, and intervene against the practice of child sacrifice. They are called to intervene in their own nation against covenant breakers, in concert with the authority of the

274

king, consistent with the biblical theocracy as a covenantal community of choice. Thus, if an Israelite sees a family taking their child to a place of human sacrifice, the Israelite is to act congruent with the law, and/or notify the king or his appointed officers to intervene and rescue the child. Moreover, the parents are held accountable, and any high places for such sacrifice are to be duly destroyed. This is what reforming kings such as Josiah are ordained by *Yahweh* to do (see (2 Kings 22-23).

In the assumptive context of such social order, we can look at two other proverbs: "It is not good for a soul to have knowledge without completeness, and hasten to sin by foot (19:2); and, "Scornful men stir up a city, but wise men turn back anger" (29:8).

In Jesus's first coming, the Jewish Zealot party is eager for him to lead an armed rebellion against Rome. They want deliverance now, and do not understand the difference between the two comings of the Messiah. One of Jesus's disciples belongs to this party, and is called "Simon the Zealot." Even after Jesus's resurrection, his disciples are eager for the physical kingdom of Jerusalem to be restored at that very moment, not grasping the eschatological history that has yet to unfold, not grasping the goal of the New Jerusalem.

The ethos of Operation Rescue seeks to force the "theocracy" of the Second Coming upon a people who have not chosen it. Here the biblical illiteracy and idolatry of Operation Rescue is profiled in spades – quick to run to the sin of imposition and thus roil a city. Such actions are contrary to the power of informed choice which defines the nature of Israel's theocracy from ca. 1446 to 586 B.C., and the nature of the eternal theocracy to be governed by King Jesus – also, as always, a community of choice. Coercion of the mind, will and heart of any person violates the eternal Gospel.

Zealotry without knowledge is hasty and it misses the way, and this is the fruit of the blockade strategy. Blockade and its articulation oftentimes mocked believers who disagreed with it, mocked the image of God within unbelievers, put stumbling blocks to the faith in front of many, and stirred up cities as few others have done in the United States in the twentieth century. Wisdom will turn away anger, and not miss the most effective ways to win the legal protection of the unborn within a constitutional and democratic republic.

Snatch Away from Within the Womb?

In Proverbs 24:11, the verb for "rescue" is *natsal*, and it is in the hiphil form (*hatsel*). The basic meaning is to "deliver," and in the hiphil form, "to cause deliverance." It can be accurately translated here as "to snatch away." So the language is very strong, yet we have a basic problem with its applicability to the unborn. How can we snatch away a child who is inside the womb? We have no power to atomistically rescue the unborn.

The only rescue that can be effected involves the mother as well, which means the need to deal with the power of informed choice and her heart, mind and willpower – it requires the engagement of her power to give to her unborn child. There are two ways of affecting her will – by the pagan ethics of coercion or by the biblical ethics of informed choice. If she is physically blocked from an abortion appointment, but her will is unconverted, then she will find another means to abort her child. And of course, the ugly specter of male chauvinism hangs over her as a vulture, and this needs address. If her informed choice is won, then the unborn child has been rescued.

The Parallel to Child Sacrifice

As well, if *hatsel* is applicable to our culture and the blockade of abortion centers as Terry argues, what is the closest analogy in Scripture by which we can make comparison? It is the matter of child sacrifice, and Terry is correct in his book when he shows the parallel between the sacrifice of children to the pagan god *Molech*, and human abortion today. But, if he is also correct in his blockade strategy for the unborn, can a parallel use of "rescue" be found in the Hebrew Scriptures with respect to blocking Israelites or others from sacrificing their children to *Molech*, *Ba'al*, *Chemosh* or other pagan gods? No.

The Mosaic prohibitions against child sacrifice are first found in Leviticus 18:21 and 20:1-5. The theocratic punishment for so doing, or even turning away when others do it, is the death penalty. Human sacrifice is regarded as a sexual perversion, as the structure of Leviticus 18 emphasizes. So too human abortion. The subject of Leviticus 18:1-30 is unlawful sexual relations. It opens with the command not to follow Egyptian and Canaanite customs, and concludes with the same command, with the caveat that if Israel does so, the land will "vomit" them out just as it did the pagan nations beforehand. It is predicated on the assumption of the moral order of *God → life → choice → sex*.

In its lists of sexual perversions, the first subject addressed is that of incest, followed by the subjects of fornication, adultery, child sacrifice, homosexuality and bestiality. It seems a logical order of increasing perversion, or to put it another way, of concentric circles of deviance away from the center of one man, one woman, one lifetime as ordained in the order of creation. After child sacrifice is then proscribed, homosexuality and bestiality are outlawed.

Homosexuality and bestiality do not produce children, so there is a logic where the prohibition of child sacrifice is placed – after prohibited sexual relations which can procreate, and prior to those which cannot. It is also the only subject in this chapter that does not address a sexual relationship per se. Child sacrifice is a perversion of true sexuality, where the offspring of a legitimate or illegitimate union is sacrificed to false gods. The reason for the sacrifice is due to the fears of pagans in the face of destructive gods and goddesses. They believe that to secure good crops, peace, fertility and material blessings, they need to sacrifice at various levels to the capricious deities, bargaining for their "protection" and forbearance of destruction. The costliest form is child sacrifice, and ironically, many times it is prescribed for future fertility.

Today, the ethos of human abortion is rationalized, by its elitist proponents, for food (for the poor who cannot "afford" to have a child), peace (in the case of fractured sexual relations), future fertility (have a baby when "you're ready") educational goals (don't sacrifice your "future" for a child) and material prosperity (have your act together in terms of job, house, savings and retirement before you have a child).

Jeremiah and His Prophecy in the Valley of Hell

As Judah, the final remnant of the Israelite nation, is veering toward the Babylonian exile, Jeremiah prophesies against their practice of child sacrifice to the Canaanite god *Ba'al* (19:1-15). In this text we have the most thorough profile of a prophet's words with regard to this practice in the Bible. Jeremiah is called to address the elders of the people and the priests in the Valley of Ben Hinnom, where the trash dump burns day and night, and where child sacrifice is multiplying in the final days of Jerusalem and Judah. This happens as the nation makes a remarkably quick descent into pagan folly, after the reforming kingship of Josiah and his full fidelity to the covenant. Nations readily prosper or fail depending on leadership.

Child sacrifice is a practice completely foreign to the nature of *Yahweh Elohim*. Thus, Jeremiah prophesies the destruction of the city so long as it remains "stiff-necked" in its rebellion to the Word of *Yahweh*, including a descent into literal cannibalism. He breaks a Topheth jar (in which the charred remains of the children were buried) in judgment, and as a symbol for the shattered city coming.

If the strategy of blockade were applicable anywhere in the Bible, per Terry's argument, it would be here. More than a constitutional and democratic republic, this is theocratic Israel, where the laws are given directly by *Yahweh Elohim*, and the king is charged with enforcing them. But too, the redress available to dissenting citizens is not vigilante action, or even to rewrite the laws within Israel or Judah if they do not like them. But it is the freedom to emigrate to another nation that more closely resembles their priorities. And many of the surrounding pagan nations endorse the practice of child sacrifice. The Israelites originally agree with Joshua that *Yahweh*'s laws are good, and they agree with the stipulations of the Mosaic covenant. Jeremiah is the final prophet, reminding the remnant Judah of these stipulations.

Jeremiah has friends in high places in Jerusalem, friends at the palace court and within the priesthood (see 26:24; 38:7; 39:14). So though as a prophet he has the opposition of the king and the religious elitists, he is not alone. He would have little problem rounding up a good remnant of faithful Jews, who if persuaded that it were called for by *Yahweh*, would provide a blockade to the Valley of Ben Hinnom where the child sacrifices are occurring regularly and with increasing frequency. Moreover, unlike the status of the unborn still within their mother's womb, Jeremiah would have the physical ability to "snatch away" the little boys or girls from their parent's arms en route to Ben Hinnom. He could actually have a literal "Operation Rescue." But he does not do so. If blockade were truly applicable from Terry's appropriated language of *hatsel* in Proverbs 24:11, then it would have been in evidence at this very moment at Ben Hinnom. It is not.

The reality of my critique is ratified by Jeremiah's use of the exact same words in Jeremiah 22:1-3, "snatch away" (*hatsel*). He is addressing King Zedekiah, holding him accountable to rescue the oppressed, and to do no violence to the alien, orphan and widow, nor to "pour out blood." The "pouring out of blood" is language that includes reference to child sacrifice.

Jeremiah doesn't even consider becoming a vigilante, that is, to take the law into his own hands, as he works through civil government even as it is uncivil. He calls the king to be faithful to the covenant, and to his role in civil government. Whereas Zedekiah is turning away from the enforcement of the Mosaic laws, Jeremiah knows that the restoration of civil order is not accomplished by a resort to civil disorder, by a condescension to the tactics of the ancient serpent. Civil order is restored by a successful appeal to a higher civil order. And if the people do not respond to such an appeal, then *Yahweh* will bring his judgment by his means. In the application of the power of informed choice at this juncture, this means the destruction of the city, the siege, famine, cannibalism and other horrors Judah brings on itself.

In the waning days of the covenantal theocracy, the Jews have completely syncretized their religion, mixing devotion to *Yahweh* with devotion to a host of foreign gods. The height of their idolatry is child sacrifice to *Molech* and *Ba'al*. Outside the Potsherd Gate of Jerusalem, is the Valley of Ben Hinnom, where the city's trash is dumped. The trash pile is continually burning, with the smoke always rising from its heaps. It is here that the child sacrifices take place, in specially constructed fireplaces known as "places of Topheth." The

279

gods of *Ba'al* and *Molech* are used in parallel terms in the Hebrew Scriptures, *Molech* as an Ammonite god, and *Ba'al* as a Canaanite god.

As detailed earlier, the bronze idol of the Ammonite *Molech* is truly horrific in the actual process of child sacrifice. During the ceremony, both among the Ammonites and in other child-sacrificing cultures, a religious fervor with demonic trances is induced, accompanied by heavy drumming that helps to drown out the screams of the infant as he is burned alive. The mothers of the sacrificed children are often coerced, and in some cultures they are not allowed to utter one word, or sob one tear, or they would also be killed.

The parallels to human abortion are compelling at every ethical level, with the distinction that the screams of the unborn cannot be heard. Human abortion is evil, but a coercive response to a coercive evil only entrenches the evil more securely. Redemption reverses the reversal; it does not mimic the ethical stratagems of evil. Male chauvinism is not to be answered with a competing male chauvinism.

The Valley of Ben Hinnom is shortened in common parlance to the "Valley of Hinnom," which in the Hebrew is *ge'hinnom*. In the New Testament, it is translated by the Greek *gehenna,* thus transliterated into the English, and it is used as a word for "hell" by Jesus. Thus, and as his Jewish hearers well understood, Jesus describes the nature of hell as a place of burning that never ceases, a place of fire where people choose to come and worship a false god who demands human sacrifice. It is a place that confirms the chosen identity of the idolaters and murderers, one that leads to temporal Babylonian exile, and at the end of Revelation, eternal chosen exile into the awaiting abyss of the Babylonian harlot. These are the ethics of the ancient serpent, his very chosen abode. To speak of the hell of human sacrifice and human abortion is to be biblically literate. The Valley of Hell.

So in Jeremiah 19 we see the parallel to human abortion, yet we see no blockade, even though Jeremiah has the political power to pull it off (at least once), and the technical ability to actually snatch the child and run away with him or her. But to the end, Jeremiah lobbies for the king to stop the evil. Had

Jeremiah tried to rescue the children himself, the culture at large would have undoubtedly ended their tolerance of him. He would likely have been stoned to death, and his prophetic ministry ended well before *Yahweh*'s appointed time. King Zedekiah stays in power partly because he continually oscillates between the idolatrous will of the people and the word of *Yahweh*. He does not embrace the courage to lead the people and put his life on the line, trusting in *Yahweh* to protect him if he were to be faithful to the covenant.

When an elitist regime introduces idolatries to the common people, as a means to maintain control over them, eventually a monster is created that demands the obeisance of the political elitists as well. It comes to the point where they are controlled by the idolatrous appetite of the people they have fed. Thus Jeremiah prophesies both to the people, their elders and priests, and to the king himself. As we thus see, the strategy of blockade is not employed in a theocracy as a means of rescue. Nor is it applied in a pagan nation. The United States has both a biblical heritage and the freedom for pagan religion to exist freely within it at the same time. There is no biblical precedent for the coercive practice of blockade as a means to rescue the unborn from the death of abortion.

In Terry's book, he does not deal with the question of Jeremiah with regard to child sacrifice. Neither does he look at Daniel as we will shortly. In both cases, it is the king's responsibility to lead the nation in the abolition of human sacrifice. King Josiah and other Hebrew kings do so, because they are persuaded by *Yahweh* to do what is right, not because they are coerced by means of a vigilante "civil disobedience."

A Biblical Review

Terry lists a number of incidents of civil disobedience in facile points of analogy to his strategy of blockade. It is good to review these texts, and to demonstrate the fact that vigilante action is never once undertaken by *Yahweh Elohim*'s people, by disciples of Jesus the Messiah, at his command or by his permission.

Starting in the Hebrew Bible, another way of putting it is that in all situations of civil disobedience, it is by *Yahweh*'s covenant people who are:

1. politically disenfranchised;
2. forced into belief and actions contrary the Law of Moses;
3. who have no legal recourse to assert their rights of religious liberty;
4. they take no vigilante actions to change unjust laws; and
5. in all the places where the Law of Moses is not being honored on their behalf, they work within the law.

The Courage of the Hebrew Midwives

The first place of civil disobedience is in Exodus 1:6-22 with the Hebrew midwives, who refuse to obey Pharaoh and kill the newborn Hebrew males.

The beginning of Exodus starts with the theme of the preservation of the Messianic lineage. Following the commands to Adam and Noah to be fruitful and multiply, the Hebrews are doing exactly that. As *Yahweh* has promised that Abraham and his people will be a blessing to all nations, so Joseph is a blessing to Egypt, rescuing them from the seven-year famine, even strengthening the hand of the Pharaoh in the process. Joseph manifests the power to give, with no strings attached. Though he has been falsely imprisoned to begin with, he serves Pharaoh wholeheartedly when *Yahweh Elohim* brings about his deliverance.

Yet the ancient serpent, working in proxy, is warring against the faithful lineage. Instead of a historical record regarding Joseph and his family being maintained, a new king arises some years later, ignorant of the debt he and Egypt owes the Hebrews. Being a servant to the devil's ethics of the power to take, he sees in the multiplying Israelites not a resource for blessings, but a threat that does not exist.

This is how sin warps the view of reality – distrust instead of trust, even when trust is powerfully earned. The Egyptian king does not consider that the Israelites might be his allies in time of war, or even cultivate the possibility, consistent with who they are as a people. Also, if the Egyptians are fearful they would leave Egypt, the Israelites, while still free, must also have been an economic asset to the nation by their intrinsic sabbatical ethic with its attendant productivity. A racial bigotry now comes into place. So the king plots "shrewdly" to contain the perceived threat, but his shrewdness is folly, as the Israelites only increase that much more, and in the process, he embitters them against himself.

As his folly is evident, he seeks a program of infanticide against the Hebrew boys, seeking to reduce their potential military might in the future. He tries to enlist the Hebrew midwives as his agents, and runs into firm resistance. He runs into faithful Israelite women, who in their position of political weakness, act shrewdly with a moral innocence that trumps his attempt at shrewdness with its moral evil. They are innocent as doves and shrewd as serpents in defeating the agenda of the ancient serpent.

Shiprah and Puah deflect the Pharaoh's intent by stating a fact – the vigor of the Hebrew women in giving birth. They are more vigorous because of a) faith in *Yahweh* that produces strength in sexual fidelity, in contrast to the wasting realities of cultic sexual promiscuity ordained by the Egyptian goddess *Isis*; b) the sabbatical work and rest ethic; and c) because of the physical rigor developed in hard slave labor, in contrast to a softer existence, by comparison, for wealthy Egyptian women in particular, but also to those of all economic stations.

But still, the midwives do not comply with the king's edict. The text says that "they let the boys live." To what exactly does this refer? Do they 1) supervise births where they let the boys live? Do they 2) supervise so as to shrewdly not be present at the moment of birth? Or do they 3) give word to the Hebrew women, or other midwives, not to notify them of the approach of the time of birth, but only afterward – to then serve the mother and child accordingly? For indeed, the Pharaoh could have responded: "Well, if they gave birth before you arrived, why did you not kill the boys when you did arrive?"

Pharaoh knows what he is up against, and he knows he is not going to prevail against such a shrewdness – rooted in a culture of life – designed to resist him.

Accordingly, what we have with the civil disobedience of the midwives is a matter of faith in *Yahweh*, a holy fear of *Elohim*. They are being commanded by Pharaoh to actively disobey *Yahweh Elohim*, to participate in an act of destruction. If as Jews or Christians we were ordered by the government to actively participate in an abortion, or even as a nurse ordered by a hospital to attend and/or assist an abortion, similar disobedience is called for, with attendant trials embraced. But in the United States, we have (had) political and legal redress (but now, consistently being eroded).

In ancient Egypt, the midwives do not have such redress – they are slaves, they are politically disenfranchised. And yet in their disobedience, they disobey only in terms of beliefs or actions being forced on them that run against their faith in *Yahweh Elohim*. They do not lift a vigilante finger to challenge the Pharaoh's hold on political power and his arbitrary laws, as morally illegitimate as it is. No vigilante actions.

Partly because of this ethically consistent witness, when the time for deliverance comes through Moses, many Egyptian people side with the Hebrews – knowing that their own sufferings are a direct result of Pharaoh's actions against them. And the Pharaoh has no cause to accuse the Israelites of having plotted politically or militarily against him. (Nor can they plot militarily, since the Egyptians denied them any arms, which, by the way, is why the United States has the Second Amendment – to protect the First Amendment, to preclude the possibility of a tyranny.) The midwives are above reproach in all they do, and rewarded with their own children as a result.

Preserving the Life of One Hebrew Infant

The second act of civil disobedience in the Bible immediately follows in Exodus 2:1-10, with the birth of Moses.

When the mother of Moses hides him from the edict to kill newborn Hebrew males, she acts both shrewdly and innocently. In his defense before the Sanhedrin in Acts 7, Stephen states that the Pharaoh successfully forced his forefathers to throw the newborns out to die (v. 19), perhaps this having occurred after he failed in his plan with the midwives.

And it must have had a measure of success, since Moses's mother is concerned that a three-month old boy would be "discovered." As well, Moses's mother perhaps has an interior threat against her son to be concerned about, the complicity of fearful Israelites (but not the complicity of Moses's father, cf. the reference below to Hebrews 11:23). Miriam (Moses's older sister) is also there when the Pharaoh's daughter discovers the child in the basket among the reeds in the Nile, and Moses's mother plays on the needfulness (*nephesh*) as true strength, thus catalyzing mercifulness in the Pharaoh's daughter to rescue him.

Augmented by *Yahweh*'s divine intervention, Moses's mother sees him adopted by the Pharaoh's daughter (who uses her royal position to serve such civil disobedience), and she herself is hired as his nurse. She gets paid to raise her son instead of seeing him killed, paid by the very family whose head, the Pharaoh, wants her son killed. She raises him in his infancy and roots him in his Hebrew identity. The reversal of the reversal. Thus, Moses is raised in the power, education and wealth of the oppressive nation (cf. Acts 7:22), adopted as a grandson to the Pharaoh and thus in royal succession, and is positioned remarkably to be Israel's deliverer.

The Pharaoh likely knows his daughter has adopted a Hebrew boy, but is confident that by training him in the Egyptian culture, he will believe, live and act as a pagan Egyptian. The writer of Hebrews speaks of the faith his parents have in hiding Moses, seeing his special nature, "and they were not afraid of the king's edict" (11:23). So the variables are exactly the same as with the Hebrew midwives, applied to a specific and important case. We see civil disobedience based on keeping faith not to disobey *Yahweh*, by people who as slaves have no unalienable rights in the land in which they live, but who also engage in no vigilante action to change the unjust laws.

Moses as Vigilante: Hard Lesson to Learn

In his book, Randall Terry records these two instances above, arguing they are in service to his vigilante theology – despite the substance of the text as it proves to be – but he does not address the third case of civil disobedience, which immediately follows in Exodus 2:11-15a.

Here is Moses, he who has the political power to try and persuade the Pharaoh if he had chosen (cf. Acts 7:22, where Stephen speaks of Moses being "taught in all the wisdom of the Egyptians and was powerful in words and action"). But instead, as an adult when he goes to visit his people, he takes the law into his own hands. Seeing an Egyptian beating a Hebrew man, Moses kills him and buries him in the sand. Whether he could have been successful with Pharaoh is questionable, but in either event, Moses did not seek *Yahweh*'s counsel on how to seek justice for his fellow Hebrews.

Moses may think his motivations are solid, and, he has been raised up by *Yahweh Elohim* to deliver the Hebrew people. But his actions are folly, rooted in human reaction, not the leading of *Yahweh*. He lives in the darkness of the moment, seeking to conceal his actions. As he then tries to arbitrate between two Hebrew men fighting, being concerned that they not be divided among themselves while being simultaneously oppressed by Egypt, he encounters cold reality. The Hebrew man who is in the wrong blurts out that Moses had killed the Egyptian – challenging his prerogative to judge him. It has become known.

Moses is dressed as Egyptian royalty, but probably recognized as a Hebrew. Likely his parents have let it be known how their son has been adopted into the Pharaoh's line, but his affection for his own people may not be understood, especially in such a setting. One or several Israelites must have seen Moses furtively kill the Egyptian, but with no knowledge as to why. Thus he can be regarded as a rogue vigilante, with neither rhyme nor reason apart from the arbitrary exercise of self-aggrandizing power. And certainly the Hebrew man in the wrong is not concerned for why Moses killed the Egyptian – he is just interested in not being held accountable for hitting the other Hebrew. He blurts out an effective counter thrust, and succeeds.

The fruit of Moses's vigilante action is fear for his life, as Pharaoh seeks to kill him, and thus, forty years of exile in the Midianite wilderness. The fruit of Operation Rescue has been the nastiness of the opposition it engendered, and the exile of the pro-life witness from many sections of the culture for some years. *Yahweh* humbles Moses in the wilderness, and prepares in him the necessary character for him to trust in *Yahweh* when he is sent as the deliverer, and not by human, military and coercive means. *Yahweh* is King, governs the later demands given to Pharaoh to let the Hebrew people go, and *Yahweh* does so consistent with the ethics and power of informed choice, a vision Moses does not have when he kills the Egyptian. It would be lovely to see the pro-life movement learn the same lesson in the wake of the error and failure of blockade.

The Courage of a Pagan Prostitute

The fourth instance of civil disobedience is with Rahab the prostitute, in hiding the Hebrew spies Joshua 2:1-16, and Terry also cites this case.

The first element in the story is to note that Jericho is dedicated to destruction by *Yahweh*, as one of the Canaanite cities whose evil has reached its full measure, and as Abraham is told 400 years earlier. Their own triad of sorcery, sacred prostitution and child sacrifice has reached its unrepentant limits, and now *Yahweh* is using Israel as his agent of judgment against them.

Rahab is a prostitute and innkeeper, and earns a good living at it, perhaps as a Madame as well, having a privileged home inside the city wall. Perhaps she is a prostitute out of survival instinct – the only way she knows to provide for her parents and siblings in a pagan city, unmarried, as the text does not mention a husband (cf. Deborah in Judges 4:4). She is familiar with the power and goodness of *Yahweh* to Israel, and like the rest of her nation, has heard reports of the exodus.

But unlike the rest of her fellow Canaanites, she then deduces that *Yahweh* is the one true Creator, and her gods are false. As a prostitute and innkeeper, and as one to whom the king would send direct notice, she likely knows all the city's intramural politics and power-play schemes. She likely knows its gossip thoroughly, and perhaps in such a position, hears of the reputation of *Yahweh*, and sees his goodness compared to the pagan deities that enslave her.

Two Hebrew spies, scouting out Jericho for the Israelite invasion, come to her inn, and she knowingly hosts them. When the king learns about it, he sends a message for Rahab to give them up. Instead she creates a ruse to save the spies. In her shrewd disobedience, she is now choosing to pursue the moral innocence of the Mosaic law, and thus hides the spies. This she does by means of intrigue, and knows enough secrets to barter for personal power (undoubtedly having many in political power as her patrons). But she also has no unalienable rights, and is de facto in the position of the politically disenfranchised. Her life is in jeopardy when the king's messengers come to her, and chargeable with treason.

She has no legal redress to help reform the city, for even though all her fellow Canaanites know the power and reputation of *Yahweh*, they are still committed to their false gods. Thus, in their fear of the Israelites, they do not consider repentance as she does. Rahab is disobeying for the sake of belief, for choosing the Messianic lineage against the seed of the ancient serpent. And she is disobeying a city doomed to destruction (choosing *akol tokel* over *moth tamuth*). There is no point of comparison here for the United States today, where legal redress and reform are possible. The only modern comparison is Nazi Germany, which we will review momentarily.

Rahab's shrewdness, in pursuit of moral innocence, is interesting to consider – for she engages in her civil disobedience with no upbringing to be a truth-teller. I am not certain whether she lies to the king's messengers, or whether she is utterly shrewd, choosing her words carefully so as not to be caught in a lie, either on the spot or later if confronted again. She has chosen her allegiance even before the king hears of the two spies, having hidden the Hebrew men in advance of his message.

So she says, "Yes," the men have visited. True. When she says she does not know where they have come from, she could be employing a double entendre where the messengers think she is saying she does not know they are Israelites. Perhaps she is saying that she does not know the exact location from which they come into the city, before learning they are Hebrew spies. Then they could have left for the roof at dusk, when it is time for the city gates to close, thus leading the messengers to think they have left the city. But in truth Rahab tells the spies to go to the roof and hides them there.

Or this is a point of direct lying she cannot get around, but is able to obfuscate it well enough for the moment. She then gives advice for them to pursue the men quickly, counting on her ruse to lead them out into the country in pursuit of phantoms. Rahab is shrewd, and she does not tell them the information they are looking for. But she knows the city is under the judgment of *Yahweh*, and as a pagan seeking to evade paganism, she does what she can do to choose life (not unlike Jacob struggling with *Yahweh* for the blessing in Genesis 32:22-32). As a pagan she does her best from within her terror to choose the truth, to choose allegiance with *Yahweh*'s covenant people. And indeed, she becomes a foremother to the Messiah she has chosen, Jesus.

Also, since Jericho is in a state of war against the Israelites, and spies are involved, civil disobedience is a different matter than for citizens within the due process of laws of a nation. Rahab is a traitor to the "city-state" (*polis* in the Greek, from which we derive "politics") and its false gods, and is willing to risk death if caught. And the Hebrew spies run the same risk.

There is no analogy here with reference to the United States today and its premise of unalienable rights. As Christians in a nation founded on biblical ethics, we are called in civil matters to be truth-tellers, and when civil disobedience is required to maintain the integrity of our confession of faith, we do not play games. We are held to higher standards as a covenant people, than was Rahab before she knew the covenant.

Courage in Nazi Germany

In Nazi Germany, Lutheran pastor and theologian Dietrich Bonhoeffer participates in the 1944 conspiracy to assassinate Adolf Hitler. It fails, and Bonhoeffer is hung just before the Allies liberate Berlin in the spring of 1945. He resists coming to this point for years, being instinctively committed to working through civil order, pace Lutheran theology. But Bonhoeffer comes to recognize that there is no civil order left to work through in a dictatorship that has a perverted populist support, at least until the war turns against Germany, and there is no ability for a redress of his grievances.

Even Nero, as emperor in Rome, had more checks on him through the Roman Senate than does Hitler with the Reichstag. But since Hitler's seizure of the Reichstag in 1933, he gradually builds into the nation's psyche an idolatry of himself, of the Third Reich and the military machine he is building, to the point where he is an absolute despot. With his systematic murder of over twelve million people, including the holocaust of six million Jews, Bonhoeffer makes the decision to choose political revolution. In so doing, he puts aside all expectations of mercy or fair treatment under the Nazi regime, and embraces his death courageously. He has forsaken his political allegiance with Hitler's Germany completely. At this point of choosing allegiance, we see analogy with Rahab.

The American Revolution

There is a lively argument as to the appropriateness of the American Revolution. Could we have succeeded in the pursuit of civil liberties without revolt against England? When Paul and Peter call us to obey the governing authorities, where do we draw the line? (I will look at these passages shortly.) I am not certain how to answer this question, for I cannot compare the tyranny of King George III to that of Adolf Hitler, despite all the entreaties the king and his predecessors refused as the Colonists sought to have his de facto covenantal promises kept.

The signers of the Declaration did appeal to an authority greater than state or church, to the Creator himself, that which even King George III had to acknowledge, as they sought moral justification in the sight of God for what they were doing – historically quite unique. The fruit of the American Revolution thus leads to a much greater grasp of biblical liberty than was the case in England in 1776, but still, a Christian people (at the time) revolting (with justification) against a "Christian" nation? A central reason why I am grateful for the American Revolution is that it is the fruit of the Reformation where the power of the church to control the state, and vice versa, is finally discarded.

When Emperor Constantine legalizes Christianity in 313 A.D., the Roman Empire stops persecuting Christians, but his successors later start persecuting pagans, and the century does not close before Emperor Theodosius enacts laws that later leads Emperor Justinian to eventually force all the pagans in the Roman Empire to convert to Christianity, as well as the Jews, under penalty of the sword if they do not comply. This is the moral death of the church's witness, as extreme a violation of the power to give and the power of informed choice as possible. In a simplified diagnosis and in terms of political order, it takes the antecedents to and the flower of the Reformation to begin this reversal of this reversal, and the American Revolution to complete it in terms of a political covenant.

Regardless of unanswered questions in my own mind at this stage, it is clear to me that the only reason I would ever participate in any civil disobedience is if the Bill of Rights were abolished sufficiently enough by a coercive and constitutionally illegitimate State power, and the moral grounds for political revolution were in place – where I am ready to forswear any claims to civil rights under the current political regime. It would have to be analogous to Rahab or Bonhoeffer. Yet I am persuaded there is a better way.

Weak Analogies

Operation Rescue is an acknowledgment, by those who articulated its vision, that the power of persuasion is something they did not possess in the process of a constitutional and democratic republic. Not only was eisegesis employed in the definition of "rescue," but other weak analogies were in place.

For example, it was said that in blocking the abortion centers, they were doing the same as disobeying a "No Trespassing" sign in order to save a child from a burning building. This is the context of Proverbs 24:11-12 when such rescue is affirmed by the operative covenantal law. But this analogy is facile, and by definition, all analogies or secondary or tertiary arguments to begin with. There is a great difference today. This society, in its current laws, is persuaded that the born child is a human being protected under the law, whereas they do not regard the unborn that way. It will allow for the breaking of a "No Trespassing" sign for the born, but not for the unborn. Regardless of the illegitimacy of the laws allowing human abortion, a rationale for civil disobedience cannot rest on such a false analogy.

In OR, when protesters were arrested, often they passively resisted by going limp. Yet this is no different than active resistance, as it violates the police officers who are thus forced to drag them away, and only increased the backlash, in which some police departments engaged. It is completely the opposite of how Jesus faced his arrest. When Judas comes with the mob to seize him, Jesus is already prepared. Just before this moment, he awakes his disciples in order to greet the betrayer as he arrives (Matthew 26:45-46). Jesus is in full self-control – a fruit of the Holy Spirit (Galatians 5:23). He is willing to embrace his arrest and death head-on, because he knows he is doing the will of the Father. Jesus employs active embrace of his arrest, and does not engage in any form of active or passive resistance.

The point here is that various members of OR consistently protested their treatment at the hands of the police (and there was some nasty treatment), and many of them protested the civil and criminal penalties the courts levied against them. Thus, they did not meet the criteria of a Rahab or Bonhoeffer who forsake their citizenships as they embrace political disobedience or revolution. And until such a threshold is crossed, civil obedience is the godly means of serving justice. The ethos of blockade cannot have it both ways – civil disobedience and resistance to its consequences.

Thus, this I understand as the only basis for present civil disobedience:

1. When a false confession or false action is required of us, in opposition to the Bill of Rights, and where no concomitant action is taken to force a change in such false laws;
2. And/or possibly, if all redress of grievances were abolished and the political culture were as evil as a Nazi Germany, thus making war an actual good as it saves human lives and set people free from tyranny.

In the meantime, persuasion by civil means is the right and effective way, and even persuasion in the face of tyranny. I cannot help but to think that God would have given the nation's founders a shrewdness and moral innocence to have won independence from Great Britain without the recourse to war, had the theological groundwork been sufficient, known, embraced and lived. As angels of *Yahweh* win victories for Israel at certain times without recourse to a war initiative on the nation's part, why not now for any people who call on his Name?

A Jewish Queen in a Pagan Land

Another place where some have argued for civil disobedience is found is in the Book of Esther. When King Ahasuerus (Hebrew name; his Greek name Xerxes is more well-known) rules Persia and the upper Nile region (486-465 B.C.), God sovereignly brings a Jewess, Esther, to be his queen. A political sycophant named Haman arranges for the king to allow the destruction of the Jewish people living in exile there, but Haman does not know Esther is Jewish. Esther's cousin Mordecai has been a father to her after her parent's death, and has also been key in helping her become queen. Mordecai sends word to Esther to bring the situation to the king's attention, to intercede for the protection of the Jews (Esther 4:9-17).

Though the queen, Esther is still politically disenfranchised, with no unalienable rights. The king has totalitarian authority. She needs to approach him to intercede on behalf of the Jews, but to do so goes "against the law" unless the king grants exception. Thus Esther is still acting in civil obedience as she approaches him. She is willing to die if need be, but fasts ahead of time in preparing for success.

Esther thus goes before Xerxes, the golden scepter is lifted and she gains audience. Clearly, the king holds her in high esteem and recognizes that she would not "break the law" without cause. Her reputation precedes her ability to succeed in this risk. As well, when she gains the king's audience, she acts with extraordinary shrewdness and wisdom in having Haman's plot exposed. *Yahweh* is also sovereign in drawing the king's attention to the chronicles of his reign, where Mordecai's faithful service to him is recorded where he had earlier exposed a plot to assassinate the king. Thus, as Haman's plot against Mordecai and his people is exposed, Haman is hanged, and the Jews are allowed to defend themselves ahead of the enactment of Haman's plot.

This summarizes the whole book, and our biblical literacy is well served by reading it in detail. As we do, we can see how the art of persuasion, based on a reputation above reproach, serves in the deliverance of the Jews from a holocaust. The tactics and rhetoric of blockade only serve the opposite, and have entrenched the resistance of those whose god desires the holocaust of the unborn. To grasp how to make it first the Gospel, then politics …, biblical literacy is essential. We need to know the whole canon, and see how the competition between earthly and heavenly citizenships plays out across all its pages.

Daniel and the Abolition of Child Sacrifice in a Pagan Empire

Civil disobedience is also a major theme in the Book of Daniel, but once again based on a higher view of *Yahweh Elohim*'s sovereignty, and as well, in tandem with the power of civil obedience. The balance between the two teaches us much. Vigilante action is a repudiation of this sovereignty.

In Daniel 1, he and his three friends have been deported from Jerusalem to Babylon in 605 B.C., the first of two deportations that precede the final destruction of the city and final exile of 586 B.C. These four young men, members of the Judahite royalty and likely in their teens, are selected to be trained as servants to King Nebuchadnezzar's palace, with their God-given nature of physical and intellectual prowess being easily noted.

294

They are already well versed in the Hebrew Scriptures, and refuse to defile themselves with Babylonian food that does not meet kosher standards as outlined in Leviticus, and perhaps is also too rich for bodily health. Daniel takes the lead in acting on this conviction, and his three friends follow suit. In other words, though slaves in a pagan land, they choose to keep not only their moral separation from pagan religion, but their cultural separation as well. The Hebrew cultural law exists to protect the eternal moral law within it for the sake of the Messianic lineage. They are free to be in the pagan world, but not of it. They are free to take on Babylonian names as necessary, and love their pagan neighbors, but maintain their Jewish names and identities as well.

Thus, when presented with a required diet that would defile them, Daniel shows shrewdness and tact. His character has already won him favor in the sight of the chief official, Ashpenaz, who is responsible for their training, and who is thus willing to go along with Daniel's proposal to eat only food that comes from seeds (from *zera*, the literal Hebrew), and drink only water.

Daniel's shrewdness is evident as he asks the guard to test him and the other three on the proposed meatless diet. If they pass the test, then the chief official's fears are alleviated, and he does not have anything to fear from the king. And if not, Daniel implicitly lets the official know he will not resist the diet again. Daniel could propose such an "if" clause because he knows *Yahweh Elohim* will honor his own Name, and honor Daniel and his friends who do not have to compromise with a diet dedicated to pagan deities. Daniel's Hebrew name means "*Elohim* is (my) Judge," and he acts accordingly. (In the Book of Daniel, written in a pagan land and likely interfacing with official records, *Elohim* is used, since *Yahweh* is falsely used by the pagans who view him as a tribal deity, and not the one true Creator.)

The fruit of this "civil obedience" and diplomatic skill is such that Daniel and his three friends surpass all the other young pagan men training with them, gaining a reputation for being ten times wiser than all the court sorcerers – of men many years older. How often are Christians viewed similarly by the pagans and secularists of our age? And how foreign is

Daniel's orb of influence in contrast to that of Operation Rescue? Daniel's wisdom is then tested in chapter two.

This chapter continues the theme of the difference between the true God and false gods, as four of *Yahweh Elohim*'s faithful remnant live in a foreign land. The Jewish nation is exiled in 586 B.C. because they were told this would happen if they persisted in serving false gods, and *Yahweh Elohim* also tells them that a pagan nation would rule over them. But in time a remnant will return to Jerusalem – having learned that *Yahweh Elohim* is sovereign the whole time, whether over a rebellious chosen people or a pagan nation.

In chapter 1, we see the ethical and intellectual power of the faithful Hebrew men, in contrast with their pagan peers, and with the nation's leading wise men. In chapter 2, the same contrast intensifies as Nebuchadnezzar is not willing to suffer fools and sycophants. He has a terrible dream, and requires the sorcerers and their cohort to prove themselves by revealing to him the nature of the dream before giving an interpretation. They protest that no sorcerer can know such things, only the "gods" can, and the gods do not "dwell among flesh."

In a similar contrast between Elijah and the prophets of *Ba'al* on Mount Carmel, the true God, *Yahweh*, answers with fire (1 Kings 18). It is an ethical as well as a supernatural issue. Ethics refers to relationships, and *Yahweh* has a living relationship with his servants. The false gods who are no gods, but are demons in masquerade, give no real power to the Babylonian sorcerers. The sorcerers know their gods are essentially hostile demonic forces at best. These "gods" must be manipulated through religious ritual and sacrifices, in contrast to the living *Elohim* whom Daniel knows.

The sorcerers engage largely in a game of tricks, and Nebuchadnezzar knows it. So the decree is issued for their execution, and Daniel and his three friends fall under its swath (though they were not present at the meeting when the sorcerers were found wanting). Daniel acts wisely and with tact, and asks why such a harsh decree is given, learns why, and thus asks for time to see if he can interpret Nebuchadnezzar's dream. Thus, Daniel and his friends pray to *Elohim*, they are answered, and he tells the king his dream and its interpretation.

His exercise of the power to give with no strings attached is evidenced as his actions then also directly save the lives of the pagan sorcerers, and he is then appointed over them by Nebuchadnezzar. His actions are the opposite of the vigilante, the opposite spirit to those who attack the persons of abortionists instead of embracing the power to love enemies.

The Babylonian sorcerers (from many nations with many different gods – but they are all ultimately syncretists) know that it is Daniel's God who saves them, not their own gods. The dynamics are interesting from this point forward – in their stubbornness they are like the unrepentant citizens of Jericho, and intensely jealous. Daniel is salting the leading pagan nation of the time with the Good News of *Elohim*'s nature, instead of becoming a pagan due to the influence of having been taught Babylonian astrology.

Because of Daniel's character and wisdom, he wins the king of the most powerful regional nation to give praise to the true God. He is given unprecedented authority as a believer in a pagan land. A reversal of the reversal as he is set in charge of the cadre of these sorcerers. Daniel reflects the power to give with no strings attached, willing like Joseph to serve a pagan nation (Egypt, Genesis 39ff) for its internal blessings – the seed of Abraham's blessings to all nations. Blessings come to Babylon under Daniel, even though Nebuchadnezzar is still imprisoned in his pagan beliefs. On the one hand, when the power of *Elohim* is evident, and Daniel as the servant of *Elohim* is seen publicly as above reproach, Nebuchadnezzar gives honor to *Elohim*. But then, on the other, the king turns back to his pagan deities in a flash, and this is what happens in Daniel 3, where the civil disobedience of Hananiah, Mishael and Azariah (their Babylonian names being Shadrach, Meshach and Abednego) comes to the fore. Nebuchadnezzar only knows of God's power through Daniel thus far.

Here we encounter the story of Shadrach, Meshach and Abednego refusing to bow down to an idol. Nebuchadnezzar decides to set up an image representing the god Nabu, after whom he himself is named. The text indicates that not only are the royal officials required to attend the dedication ceremony to his idol, but all the people as well. Babylon is the greatest empire of that time in the near east, and Nebuchadnezzar has an inflated view of himself as world ruler. And in commanding "all the peoples, nations and men of every language" to worship the image, he is using the idol worship to reinforce his personal political claims to power.

Shadrach, Meshach and Abednego arouse the jealousy of the other royal officials because of their natural refusal to worship the idol. The officials report this to Nebuchadnezzar and frame it as a direct affront against the king himself, arousing his fury. The way Nebuchadnezzar then addresses them reflects an initial disbelief on his part, and a respect he holds for them and for Daniel. Is it true? he muses, and then gives them a reprieve from the original order, a special second chance. When his "attitude" toward them changes after their subsequent refusal, we glean how he originally regards them with respect. He expects them to cede to his wishes because they are not vigilantes. This attitude change may as well reflect a demonic insurgence within him, revealing its presence, along with the easily irritated temper of a despot who expects unflinching obedience.

Shadrach, Meshach and Abednego know the king knows their character, and thus they should not have to explain their faith to him. As well, this language likely reflects the fact that they know they are in excellent stead with the king for the quality of their service as administrators over the province of Babylon, and they know he knows they are not seeking to affront him at all. But he is trapped by his own idolatry, and it manifests when his demonic fury erupts in the face of their understated confidence.

They are prepared for true civil disobedience, but not with any spirit of defiance against the king. They are men above reproach first, and this moral and spiritual authority is what energizes true civil disobedience when required. God's deliverance comes in response, as they are preserved in the furnace of fire, and as an angel joins with them. In Nebuchadnezzar's response after they are delivered by *Elohim*, he readily recognizes his error and thus the integrity of the three Jewish men.

298

These are a radical people, and it is such a radical remnant that are needed today to be salt and light in American politics and culture. When death holds no tyranny over our decision to follow Jesus, then the sycophants to the ancient serpent, in their various elitist positions, are powerless to mute the Gospel.

In this power contest, there is no flavor of human egos clashing against human egos. The three Hebrew men are politically powerless against the king's edict, with no legal redress. Though in high political positions, they nonetheless serve at the pleasure of a pagan king. They take no vigilante action against the idolatry. Instead, the power of informed choice is woven deeply into Hebrew their souls, bearing witness thus.

Their power of civil obedience, established at the outset of the Book of Daniel, empowers their successful civil disobedience when it is required of them. Operation Rescue reflects an opposite ethical understanding, where it proposes to coerce a pagan spirit into submission (a theological oxymoron).

In chapter 4, King Nebuchadnezzar has another dream for which he seeks Daniel's interpretation. The first dream that Daniel interprets in chapter 2 prophesies the eventual destruction of Babylon. In this second dream, it prophesies specific judgment on Nebuchadnezzar himself. The entire chapter simply records a letter from Nebuchadnezzar, published after the fact for his whole kingdom to receive.

Daniel is given the Babylonian name of Belteshazzar when he begins his training ("Bel, protect his life," where Bel is the name for the Babylonian god *Marduk*, and possibly parallel to the Canaanite god *Ba'al*). Yet he lives per his Hebrew name, "*Elohim* is (my) Judge," and is thus vindicated at every turn.

In Nebuchadnezzar's letter, he speaks of a disturbing dream, and seeks out all the various sorcerers for an interpretation, but none could interpret. Finally, Daniel presents himself and gives interpretation.

The way Daniel treats Nebuchadnezzar is instructive for the balance between civil obedience and civil disobedience. Daniel and his three friends never engage in vigilante action to oppose pagan Babylonian worship, nor the pagan zenith of child sacrifice as (likely still) permitted in certain of its provinces. They are at rest in their spirits, as their character gives witness to their faith in *Yahweh*. To take the law into our own hands is the surest sign of stating that we believe God is not sovereign.

When Daniel is given the interpretation to Nebuchadnezzar's dream, he shows honor to the king's position, even though it is pagan and totalitarian by definition. In so doing he places confidence in the broken remains of the image of *Elohim* within him, knowing that the mere criticism of sin is not the way to salt or reform the nation. Now, Daniel wishes that the dream applies not to the king, but to his adversaries. This does not reflect on Daniel's part a hatred toward the adversaries of Nebuchadnezzar, but rather it reflects an acknowledgment that *Elohim* has judgment to pour out on sinners, specifically upon those who destroy Jerusalem.

This also reflects Daniel's witness for the salvation of Nebuchadnezzar's soul. He wishes for Nebuchadnezzar not to be the one who is so judged. Daniel of course knows that it is the king of Babylon who has so earned *Elohim*'s wrath. He delivers the word of *Yahweh* as Jonah does to Ninevah (see the book of Jonah), and with hope that Nebuchadnezzar's judgment can still be averted. So, after Daniel interprets the dream, in diplomatic understatement he calls Nebuchadnezzar to renounce his sins and evil ways by doing what is right and by being kind to the oppressed.

This is the same witness Jeremiah gives King Zedekiah, in the same season back in Judah, in the specific context of opposing child sacrifice in the waning days of Jerusalem before 586 B.C. (cf. Jeremiah 19; 22:1-5, earlier referenced). Thus, Daniel's witness against child sacrifice percolates to the surface at this point as part of an all-inclusive calling of the king to righteousness. Child sacrifice is not part of Babylonian religion, but Babylon governs various peoples that practice it.

When Nebuchadnezzar regains his sanity and returns from his seven-year exile living as an animal, he receives greater prosperity yet, and he praises the King of the heavens who has humbled and taught him who really rules. The ethical outworking of this can only mean that Nebuchadnezzar has renounced his sins and also addressed child sacrifice wherever in his empire it occurs (e.g., Assyria).

Who rules in the king's stead during the seven years of his exile? Daniel, still an exile in his high positions of political authority, is likely in charge, since Nebuchadnezzar had earlier put him in charge of both the province of Babylon and over the Babylonian wise men. He is de facto prime minister to begin with, with access to the royal seal by which to conduct business in the name of the king. This would equal a certain legal abolition of any child sacrifice within the empire, and Nebuchadnezzar would then continue the abolition as his position is restored. This likely abolition of child sacrifice is thus not through vigilante action, but is a cognate to the power of civil obedience coupled with the power of true spiritual authority.

In chapter 5, the Book of Daniel jumps to 539 B.C., 23 years after the death of Nebuchadnezzar. King Belshazzar is now on the throne. He has forgotten the lesson *Elohim* had taught Nebuchadnezzar, and compounds it even worse by profaning the gold goblets taken from the temple in Jerusalem, and using them for his own pagan banquet where he "praised the gods of gold and silver, of bronze, iron, wood and stone" (v. 4).

In the face of such a dualistic and syncretistic paganism where the articles dedicated to the true God are used in praise of false gods, *Elohim* pronounces judgment against him in the sign of the handwriting on the wall. Belshazzar dies that night and Darius the Mede becomes king, as the Medes now conquer the Babylonians. We thus come to chapter 6.

As Daniel is taken as an exile to Babylon in 605 B.C., as a "young man," he is probably 15-20 years old. The events of chapter 6 take place in 539 B.C. or shortly thereafter, which means Daniel is now as old as 85. His wisdom and reputation are remarkable, and he has survived the reigns of several kings. Thus, when Darius the Mede (aka Cyrus) takes control of

301

Babylon, Daniel is a fixture, and his qualities are so evident to Darius, that he plans to set the whole Babylonian kingdom under Daniel's charge.

What would have happened had the ethos of vigilante action been in place in the lives of Daniel and his three friends? They would have long since been put to death. But because they know *Yahweh Elohim*'s sovereign power to give and the derivative power of informed choice, they truly salt a pagan nation, and accomplish a prophetic reversal of the reversal. Nebuchadnezzar is humbled and he praises the King of the heavens, and in all likelihood, any child sacrifice is officially opposed for that season. This same witness is magnified with Darius.

Here too we see the reality of self-aggrandizing elitist power. The other administrators and the satraps are jealous of Daniel because of his incorruptibility, and because he is a Jew who does not buy into their polytheistic justifications for self-serving power. They are sycophants, wanting to be the king's trusted advisors. But when the chips are down, Nebuchadnezzar calls on the unassuming Daniel. Darius also sees this quality of character in Daniel. Most of the administrators and satraps are also likely much younger than Daniel, and frustrated by the knowledge of his long years of incorruptibility. Because of his ethical nature, they are unable to overthrow his honest political power by human machinations. Daniel's character unmasks the true reality of the contest. They have to challenge the "law of his God" openly. Daniel cannot be dismissed, so the contest is one of spiritual power.

Thus, two administrators and 120 satraps in Babylon manipulate King Darius, in recommending to him an edict forbidding prayers to any god or man for thirty days. Daniel is not consulted, and of course would not agree. They know that Darius, in issuing such a decree, is bound by the legal system of the Medes and Persians and unable to rescind it. Darius is a slave to a legal system that has no room at this juncture to correct errors, no room for the power to forgive and be forgiven. The elitists know this and play it exactly in order to entrap Daniel.

Daniel's response, in civil disobedience for proper cause, is to define the power contest on his own terms – he prays to *Yahweh Elohim*, with thanksgiving, openly and publicly, as he has always done before. No political machinations, nor even an appeal to Darius. As he is thankful to *Elohim* in the face of this trial, it is the basis for him to seek and receive *Yahweh Elohim*'s help. How does vigilante action accomplish such a trust in God's sovereignty?

When Darius realizes he has been deceived, and is nonetheless a slave to a decision into which he has been tricked, he tries in futility to rescue Daniel. Even he does not have benefit of unalienable rights to redress an evil plot among his subordinates. His only option is then to trust in a God he does not know. And the reason Darius is willing to do this is because of Daniel's reputation for integrity. So *Elohim* sends an angel to protect Daniel in the lion's den, the decree is fulfilled, and Darius then sends the conspirators with their families to the lion's den instead. Just like when Haman plots against the Jews, he falls into the very trap he made for Mordecai.

Miscellany: The "Civil Disobedience" of Ehud, Gideon, and Uriah

Three other people in the Hebrew Bible are worth noting via-à-vis civil disobedience. First is Ehud (Judges 3:12-30), who assassinates a pagan king when pretending to bring him tribute. But this is not within a civil government, but in a war between nations, as other examples indicate, and as our understanding of Israelite holy war as ordained by *Yahweh* (which I write about elsewhere).

Second is Gideon (Judges 6), where he disobeys the local government as he destroys the altar to *Ba'al* and the *Asherah* pole. This can be read as an act of political revolution, because of the social (not to mention religious) reform it is aimed at. However, Gideon is raised up by *Yahweh* as a judge in Israel. He is called to restore true law within that setting, to enforce the covenant stipulations to which the nation had agreed with Moses and Joshua.

And third, in 2 Samuel 11, Uriah presents a remarkable example of a man who "disobeys" his king as he refuses David's instruction to go to his home and sleep with his wife while on a brief military leave manipulated by king. David is trying to cover over his own sin of adultery with Uriah's wife, Bathsheba, who is pregnant by him, trying to somehow make it look like she becomes pregnant by her husband Uriah.

Uriah, unaware of the king's ploy, instinctively acts out of a deeper faithfulness to the Mosaic covenant (and as a Hittite), out of concern for the well-being of the ark of the covenant. He refuses to mix civilian and military matters (cf. 2 Timothy 2:3-4). He refuses the king directly, and yet he is the righteous one, putting David to shame morally. He does so on the basis of the criteria for civil disobedience – he does not submit to a directive where he has to compromise his faith in *Yahweh*. He does not engage in any vigilante action to oppose David's will. As well, David does not command him, using kingly authority, to act a certain way, for this is a personal matter outside the king's prerogative. Thus, David is suggesting a course of action Uriah knows is not a legal command, but actually a "benefit" being given to him. A different context than questions of civil disobedience.

Miscellany: The Civil Obedience of David, Obadiah, Ezra, Nehemiah, Esther and Jeremiah

Apart from the acts of civil disobedience and obedience, as they interface, which we have examined in the Hebrew Bible, six other brief examples can be mentioned.

First is 1 Samuel 16 through 2 Samuel 1, where we can trace much detail concerning David's rise to become king of Israel. He is anointed after Saul has proved unfaithful, and yet David radically obeys Saul and honors his kingship. Even as Saul repeatedly tries to kill David, he still honors him. When David finally has to flee for his life (proper civil disobedience), he refuses to seek Saul's life (civil obedience), sparing him on two occasions when he could have done otherwise, and he refuses to take any vigilante action to overthrow his government. Indeed, he later executes the opportunistic Amalekite who claims to have killed Saul. David trusts in *Yahweh*'s sovereignty and timing.

Second, in 1 Kings 18:1-15, we see Obadiah, who obeys his evil master Ahab, in the fulfillment of his official duties; while at the same time hiding 100 prophets of *Yahweh* from Jezebel's murderous intents. Because of his position in the civil order, he is able to aid the prophet Elijah. In both these cases, it may be seen as "civil disobedience" to the evil Ahab and Jezebel, but in reality, it is civil obedience to the Law of Moses. It is a literal fulfillment of Proverbs 24:11-12, snatching away the prophets from being dragged to the slaughter by Jezebel. It is embraced to protect the faith, the Messianic lineage, but no vigilante action is undertaken to overthrow wicked political authority. The sovereignty of *Yahweh* is assumed and honored.

Third, in Ezra 4-6, we see diplomatic wisdom and tact when dealing with the pagan nations who seek to conspire against the rebuilding of Jerusalem. Ezra and those with him do not take the law into their own hands, as political exiles in their occupied homeland. The enemies of the Jews write King Artaxerxes (ruled 465-424 B.C.) to have the Jews compelled to stop their rebuilding, and this ploy succeeds until Darius (not the Darius in Daniel, aka Cyrus) comes to power. Ezra and those with him do not rebel. Darius then counters Artaxerxes's order, the rebuilding begins again, and in due course, is completed.

Fourth, in the Book of Nehemiah, as the appointed governor, Nehemiah also works through civil authority under Artaxerxes to gain the original permission to rebuild Jerusalem and its temple – the permission that is later rescinded when the enemies of the Jews complain. Fifth, in Esther 2:19-23, Mordecai, Esther's uncle and father-figure, living under Xerxes, saves the king's life by uncovering and reporting an assassination plot against the king. It is this act of civil obedience that the Lord later uses to assist in Esther's plea against Haman's plot.

And sixth, in Jeremiah 38:24-28, Jeremiah obeys the oscillating and fearful King Zedekiah in the final hours before the destruction of Jerusalem. Zedekiah thus saves Jeremiah from other court officials who want to kill the prophet. Zedekiah has Jeremiah use a partial truth (cf. 37:15, 20), but not to give the whole truth to the officials (cf. 38:14-23). Jeremiah obeys the king, in a balance of the innocence of a dove, and shrewdness of a serpent (cf. Matthew 10:16), in a spirit similar to that of the midwives in Egypt.

Theologically speaking, all acts of civil obedience we see, and will yet see, ultimately root themselves in the confidence of knowing how to invest trust into the *nephesh* of the untrustworthy, to know how to respect the broken remains of *Yahweh Elohim*'s image within them, so as to win genuine favor.

One other observation can be made in the Hebrew Bible vis-à-vis civil obedience and disobedience. During the seasons of Israel and Judah's obedience and disobedience to the Law of Moses, the "consent of the governed" tacitly operates (rooted first in Joshua 24:14-27; see then 1 Samuel 9). Namely, kings often act in concert with the people's sins because they do not have the courage to risk their lives in enforcing the covenant stipulations. And when kings do act faithfully, such as with a Hezekiah or Josiah, the people readily consent, consistent with the courage of their king's convictions and actions. The power of true leadership. Thus, deeper than law and its enforcement is the matter of the human will, and whether or not the people want truth. When they reap the fruit of their *moth tamuth* and cry out to *Yahweh* for deliverance, he sends them a righteous judge or king. Reform of evil politics comes not with vigilante action, but with honest prayers and just action based thereupon.

The Courage of the Magi

In the New Testament, there are several places where the issue of civil disobedience comes into play. First is in the interface of the Magi and King Herod in Matthew 2:1-23.

Herod the Great seeks to deceptively use the Magi to learn the whereabouts of the infant Christ in order to kill him. But as the Magi are warned in a dream not to return to Herod after their visit with the infant King, Herod is furious, and begins his search and slaughter, as a puppet of the devil's agenda. Herod sees the infant Jewish king, the "anointed one," as a political rival in the temporal arena. The Lord appears to Joseph in a dream, and he, Mary and Jesus proactively flee to Egypt.

306

The argument raised here is that the Magi disobey Herod in a fashion that can be analogous to blockading an abortion center. There are two salient factors.

First, the disobedience has nothing to do with recognized civil authorities. The Magi (possibly tracing back to Daniel) are from the region of ancient Babylonia (modern Kurdistan), and are not under the Herod's political jurisdiction.

Second, the analogy of blockade to protect the unborn is made by some who also make the analogy of Jesus's vulnerability as a boy under the age of two. But note how God handles the situation. In telling Joseph to escape to Egypt until the danger is over, and upon Joseph's return, he settles in a region where Herod's son, Archelaus, has no authority, and therefore no ability to carry out his father's designs. God is free to have Joseph use human energy to avoid evil, in obedience to his instructions, but this is the very opposite of vigilante action. Just as vigilante action would have led to Moses, Jeremiah and Daniel being put to death – thus cutting off their superior witness – so too it would have led to the death of Joseph, Mary and Jesus, as it were. Joseph and Mary act to protect their son, and are not involved in coercing others to get them to change their minds. A successful "rescue" of the unborn is when the mother is persuaded to honor the life of her child.

Also, with the Magi and with Joseph, they are politically disenfranchised, have no legal means of redress, and act only to protect their faith in the Messiah. They employ no means to change the laws of the land by vigilante action.

The Courage of the Apostles in Face of the Sanhedrin

For Randall Terry, Acts 4-5 forms a cornerstone of his Operation Rescue rationalization. In both chapters, the apostles obey God instead of man.

In Acts 4, Peter and John are hauled before the Sanhedrin (the Jewish Ruling Council, with representative interests), and are "commanded entirely not to speak or teach in the name of Jesus" (v. 18). They are being persecuted for the healing of the crippled beggar, and in so doing they lay the blame for the crucifixion of Jesus at the feet of the religious elitists. In 4:19-20, they answer the Sanhedrin's command: "Judge for yourselves before God whether we should listen to you rather than God's judgment. For we have no power but to speak about what we have seen and heard."

The Sanhedrin is a religious body, restricted by the occupying Roman authorities to legislating only in religious matters, which by definition cannot affect the social and political order (but able, in concert with and subjugation to the Roman authorities, to jail people on "religious" matters if interpreted to be a civil threat to Rome's authority, then submitted to Roman authority for final arbitration).

As well, the Sanhedrin threatens but cannot punish them as severely as they wish because of the power of the miracle, and how it has won the allegiance of the people. Peter and John are thus released, and thereafter in public prayer they cite Psalm 2:1-2 with its Messianic implications in the light of such persecution, they pray for further boldness, signs and wonders in the name of Jesus, and their meeting place is shaken with the presence of the Holy Spirit.

So here is the context for Randall Terry proclaiming obedience to God and not man. But the passage has nothing to do with disobeying political authorities, or with vigilante action. If the Sanhedrin had political authority, the apostles would have had the right to disobey, because they were being commanded not to preach the Gospel. But in so doing, the apostles would still have no truck with any vigilante attempt to overturn the Sanhedrin's authority or Roman political authority, to force them to change law.

This is again a matter consistent with the Hebrew midwives and Daniel, where they would not be forced into renouncing belief in *Yahweh Elohim*, nor into disbelieving actions.

In Acts 5:12-42, we have the text Randall Terry quotes most.

The apostles, in their ministry, are meeting in Solomon's Colonnade inside the walls of the temple court, miracles are happening and their numbers continue to grow. The high priests, their circle, and the wealthy Sadducees are jealous. So they have the apostles arrested, but an angel delivers them from jail overnight, and they return to teach in the temple courts. They are thus escorted willingly to appear before the Sanhedrin to be cross-examined. They are ordered again not to teach in the name of Jesus, to which they answer, "It is necessary that we obey God, not man."

But too, as in Acts 4, we are looking at an example of religious authority, not political, and Terry's analogy severely misses the mark. There is no vigilante action to resist or change Roman law as classic eisegesis seeks to implicate.

As well, because their character, actions and words are above reproach, the apostles have moral authority to disobey in the proper context, and they gain supernatural deliverance in accord with *Yahweh Elohim*'s larger purposes. Vigilantes lack such moral authority and spiritual power, as Moses learns when he kills the Egyptian man. He thus has no supernatural deliverance, but instead has to flee for his life into the desert.

In the ministry of Moses and Daniel, we see the confirmation of their witness to the Lord with signs and wonders. And here again with the apostles. In looking at issues of church and state, and at discernments concerning the line necessary to be crossed before civil disobedience is even theoretically possible, too often we neglect this supernatural dimension. I believe that those who are serving God in this arena need the same power of the Holy Spirit if we are to succeed.

The proper witness of the apostles also wins the positive response of the respected rabbi Gamaliel (5:33-40), and his advice to the Sanhedrin. He is the most well-known Jewish teacher of his era, under whom Saul (Paul) is educated. When we exemplify a lived biblical theology, we can see the unity of the church come to pass, win the respect of friends and enemies alike, convert many of the fence-sitters, and even convert some of the enemies. But the tactic of blockade sharply divided the church, and only gave pretext for the abortion-rights establishment to slander the pro-life movement at large.

Summary: Biblical Criteria for Civil Disobedience

Thus, our only basis for civil disobedience, per the Bible, is:

1. when we are being forced to deny the Lord Jesus by word or deed;
2. when we are politically disenfranchised, having lost unalienable rights, and
3. only insofar as necessary to keep our integrity, never by means of vigilante action to change evil laws.

All three criteria must be met. Operation Rescue fails. We instead work within the law through love, a sound mind and the power of the Holy Spirit.

The disenfranchised Hebrew midwives protect the Messianic lineage, but engage in no political resistance.

Moses changes the situation of the Israelites being tyrannized by Egyptian law, not by taking vigilante action against it, but through the civil order of approaching and prophetically providing Pharaoh a way out.

Rahab, in choosing to rebel against a pagan polity where she has no legal redress of grievances, sides with the Law of Moses, and is willing to die for it.

Esther risks her life by going through civil order, and thus thwarts an evil law.

Jeremiah works through civil order, and even though it is not heeded, he refuses to fall into the idolatry of taking the law into his own hands. His witness is crucial for the exiles in Babylon, and the preparation for the Messiah.

Daniel, Hananiah, Mishael and Azariah all do the same, evil laws are removed, and good laws made in their place.

The apostles resist religious idolaters who oppose their preaching in the Name of Jesus, but engage in no vigilante thoughts or action.

Civil obedience is more radical than civil disobedience when seeking to transform culture. Civil obedience per biblical ethics is courageous, whereas civil disobedience per vigilante action is by definition cowardly, even in spite of the best motivations. Such civil obedience is effective, whereas vigilante action is not. Thus, we have basis to understand why civil obedience is prescribed for Hebrews and Christians in the Bible.

True civil disobedience, in its limited arenas of permissibility, it not a prescribed teaching. It is a necessary reaction, but only insofar as rooted in a prior redemptive proactivity. Reactively, we disobey when called to deny Christ, but we do not initiate such conflict, and we engage in no vigilante action. We initiate in accordance with an appeal to the image of God; we initiate a radical ethos of civil obedience.

Simply put:

1. civil obedience is prescribed for the church as a proactive ethic in culture;
2. civil disobedience is only permitted in circumscribed capacities in reaction to evil laws or authorities which seek to force us to disobey the Gospel in word or deed;
3. vigilante action is never permitted.

Prescribed Civil Obedience

Paul's Witness

So far, we have examined civil obedience in the context of proper civil disobedience, where it is a necessary reaction to evil. In separate context, we can now look in the New Testament, at passages that Randall Terry does not address in his construction of the blockade rationale.

In Romans 13:1-7, Paul calls for submission to the governing authorities, as no authority exists apart from God having established it. Paul defines a covenant of submission to civil order, one to which Christians unilaterally assign themselves in response to faith in God. The question is not how evil a government might be, but rather it is a question of how we can answer and overcome such evil on God's terms. In fact, when Paul and Peter call for submission to the governing authorities, they are referring to the Roman Empire then headed by Caesar Nero (who ruled from 54-68 A.D.).

Not only is Nero an aggressive persecutor of Jews and Christians, but among many horrors he commits, he also rapes his niece, she becomes pregnant, and then he forces her through an abortion that kills her. Paul is radical in applying the ethics of the Sermon on the Mount. This means countering taking with giving, cursing with blessing, hate with love, and potential domination with submission to true law, as the best means to neutralize the dominating powers. This is exactly what Esther and Daniel accomplish.

In Romans 12, Paul calls the believers to a radical nonconformity, and in so doing, he sets the stage for chapter 13. We are not to be conformed to this world, but to be transformative instead. Paul gives detail, and sums this up under the rubric of loving our enemies especially, and thus overcoming evil with good. This is the predicate for honoring government.

Thus, when we arrive in chapter 13, the readers in Rome, where Nero rules, know the radical nonconformity to which they are being called. The Roman Christians, many of whom are soon to face martyrdom under Nero, are called to obey a higher law of civil order than Nero knows. Thus the Gospel flourishes even more. During the several centuries of on and off-again persecution of the Christians by the Roman government, eventually the Christian fearlessness of death brings the tyrannical government to its knees – and with no vigilante action.

In this period, the Christians seek an end to abortion within the sphere of civil obedience to Roman laws. And in the practical ability of rescuing exposed infants (most of whom were girls), they go against the Roman *paterfamilias* customs allowing exposure, but this is not a matter of formal Roman law.

At the deeper level, regardless of our success in persuading rulers of righteousness – Jeremiah does not succeed with Zedekiah, whereas Daniel succeeds with Nebuchadnezzar (aided by signs and wonders) – our citizenship is ultimately not of this world. So we succeed when we persuade evil rulers to turn to God, and we also succeed when they do not repent, but instead put us to death.

Paul also lives out his ethics of civil obedience, and as a result, spreads the Gospel powerfully. When he returns to Jerusalem (Acts 21ff), and is illegally arrested, Paul does not suffer a loss of patience and joy in his spirit. When he and Silas are in prison earlier, their praises set them free from their chains, and it leads the jailer to Christ (Acts 16:16ff). When Peter is imprisoned earlier, the angel of the Lord leads him out of jail (Acts 5:17ff). Signs and wonders when needed, and a willingness to die for the sake of the Gospel, when ordained by God.

In Jerusalem, Paul uses his citizenship rights to appeal to Caesar. Before that, when he reacts to the ill-treatment of the high priest Ananias, Paul then humbles himself when he is told that he is insulting God's high priest. He had not known who it was when Ananias had his official strike him, and when informed, he submits to the authority of the office even though its occupant is a mockery to it (23:1-11). Then Paul, in a position of submission, wisely discerns the competing presences of the Pharisees and the Sadducees, and thus states how he is on trial before them due to his "hope in the resurrection of the dead." This exposes the house divided in the Sanhedrin, and in the ensuing squabble between the Pharisees and Sadducees, Paul is rescued by the Roman soldiers.

From this point, Paul is delivered by God from an assassination plot by the religious elitists (23:12-22), he bears witness to the Gospel before the Roman governor Felix, his successor Festus, then King Agrippa (25:1-26:32), then to the Romans on the ship that is taking him to Rome as a prisoner (27:1-44), to the people on Malta where he is shipwrecked, with signs and wonders continuing to follow his ministry (28:1-10), and then to Claudius Caesar's very household (28:11ff; Claudius's rule preceded that of Nero's, from 41-54 A.D.).

Because of Paul's ethics of civil obedience, he is rescued from the Jewish religious elitists who try kill him. He does not give pretext for the Roman authorities to put him to death for a civil rebellion, when illegally arrested and denied his rights as a Roman citizen. He winds up in the middle of the capitol city of the Roman Empire, and salts the whole empire with the Good News as a result of the concentric influences that go out from there. When it comes time for his martyrdom at the hands of the Romans (ca. 67 A.D. during Nero's reign), he has completed his course and is ready. His trust in God's sovereignty is the key to it all. It is God's sovereignty over pagan nations which gives him the freedom for the radical nonconformity of a unilateral civil obedience from the position of a persecuted man. The reversal of the reversal.

Paul also defines civil obedience in 1 Timothy 2:1-4, where we are called to pray for those in authority in order that "all men might be saved."

The Case of Philemon

Paul's diplomatic skill within the rule of law is also seen in his letter to Philemon. Onesimus, Philemon's slave, is a runaway who meets Paul in prison (for some unknown charge) and becomes a Christian. Onesimus is liable for the death penalty under Roman law if Philemon were to seek it. Paul arranges for Onesimus to return to Philemon, rooted in a new and profound mutual citizenship and fellowship in the kingdom of God they now share, thus putting aside the Roman law punishment option. Chattel slavery is overcome by prior biblical reality, and seeds are planted for legal abolition. There is no hint of vigilante action on Paul's part – his instincts for wisdom, and his kingdom of God agenda, are far too well-honed for that.

Peter's Witness

In 1 Peter we have two sections where the matter of civil obedience is at play: 2:9-17 and 4:12-19.

In 2:9-17, Peter is writing to Christians undergoing persecution, to those who have no unalienable rights in the political order in which they live. They are ultimately aliens in this world, as they aim for their eternal citizenship. They are thus called to be a "holy nation," set apart and above reproach in their conduct in the sight of the pagans. This they do while submitting to political authority, living as free people, able thus to put to silence the ignorant talk of foolish people.

In 4:15-17, Peter says that Christians should not be criminals or "busybodies," since judgment begins with the household of God. The word for "busybody" is the Greek *allotrioepiskopos*, which literally means "to oversee or rule that which belongs to others." In the political context this refers to Christians seeking to take the law into their own hands in any capacity – literally. This is thus an explicit rebuttal of any Christian possibility of participating in vigilante action, a rebuke to Operation Rescue's *raison d'etre*.

Extra-Biblical Analogies

Thus, for me the biblical material is clear in defining the balance between civil disobedience and civil obedience. "No" to vigilante action in any form, and "yes" to ministering to the broken remains of God's image among sinful governing authorities with attitudes and actions that are above reproach.

Much of the argument for the civil disobedience of blockade in Operation Rescue, has been based on analogies of other examples of civil disobedience such as the Underground Railroad, Henry David Thoreau, Mahatma Gandhi and Martin Luther King, Jr. The problem here is that analogy is always a secondary or tertiary form of argument, and only has validity here if it has prior biblical warrant. Thus, to make use of such analogies can place politics ahead of the Gospel. Thoreau is a transcendentalist who specifically rejects

315

biblical authority, and Gandhi is a Hindu who specifically rejects biblical authority although he tries to syncretize certain elements of the Sermon on the Mount into his Hindu worldview.

But when it comes to the question of the Underground Railroad and Martin Luther King, Jr., we have biblical concerns at the forefront. One of my ancestral relatives is the Rev. John Thomas Rankin (1793-1886), as referenced earlier, a Presbyterian minister who was known as the "Manager of the Underground Railroad." (I am a direct descendant of his grandfather, the Rev. Adam Rankin.)

John Rankin flees Kentucky as a slave holding state, and from his church across the Ohio River (in Ripley, then later in Ironton, Ohio), he is a key link for runaway slaves to Canada from the South, and serves in this capacity for 44 years in the nineteenth century, where he and his seven sons personally escort some 2,000 runaway slaves to liberty in Canada.

The Rankin lineage from Scotland was deeply involved in the abolitionist movement, and the Rev. Andrew Rankin (a more distant relative) is the founder of the nation's first college for Black Americans, following the Civil War, Howard University in Washington, D.C., and after whom their Rankin Chapel is named. The linkage of concern for blacks who were denied their humanity and civil rights in the 1857 *Dred Scott* U.S. Supreme Court decision, and for the unborn who are denied the same in the 1973 *Roe v. Wade* ruling, is as compelling as it can be. I did not choose this lineage, but I warmly embrace it with thanksgiving.

The laws challenged by the Underground Railroad have to do with competing state laws, not with a federal law. Some states allow slavery, others do not. Thus, especially after the federal Fugitive Slave Act of 1850, the workers in the Underground Railroad face a more complex question of interpreting what civil obedience and civil disobedience actually are. And many do not care to discern the difference as I do presently, given their theological and political understandings of the time. They are wedded to the good words in Deuteronomy 23:15-16 commanding refuge be given to foreign runaway slaves. Applicable between the states within genuine federalism? I believe so.

Beforehand the abolitionists have no such legal restrictions, and in a nation rooted in the consent of the governed, they have redress of grievances. So they go about their business, willing to suffer if caught. John Rankin has a $100,000 bounty on his head in those days (close to $3,000,000 today) from slave-owners in Kentucky and neighboring southern states, and his seven sons had $10,000 bounties each (close to $300,000 today). Never once do any of them suffer the slightest harm.

As well, we can ask the question: What would have happened in the ante-bellum South if a person with Moses's spiritual authority simply said, "Let my people go"? Had there been a biblical faith sufficient enough to trust in God's supernatural deliverance as he did for the Hebrews from Egypt, I believe God would have responded accordingly.

In the Civil Rights movement, beginning with the publicity surrounding Rosa Parks and her refusal to yield a seat in the bus, we have similar issues at play, where she is not disobeying federal law, but is acting in accordance with it against local bigotries. And Martin Luther King, Jr. works within the framework of civil obedience in all he does.

Idolatry

I believe the biblical evidence is univocal – no to the idolatry of vigilante action, and yes to the proactive power of the Holy Spirit everywhere present in a Biblical Theology 101.

The idolatry of Operation Rescue is rooted in a facile theology, an exercise in eisegetical proof texting. It was meant to stir up anger, and as a result proved unsustainable to the human soul, and a gross disservice to the equality of women and their unborn.

◆ ◆ ◆

Chapter Eight

At New England's Largest Abortion Center

At the onset of Operation Rescue, I was in the middle of very productive pro-life work in churches and on campuses, was also aware of picketing at abortion centers, and visited some who were doing so on one occasion. At large, those who picketed were an admixture ranging from low key to high strung people as they sought to protest human abortion. So I knew the Gospel needed to be there, at the Potsherd Gate as it were (reference forthcoming), where the innocent were being killed. But seeing the reactive nature of much picketing, I knew I had to do my biblical homework well.

In this season too, I had a number of evangelical pro-life advocate friends join Operation Rescue, and they sought to persuade me likewise. I had a deep visceral reaction to the idea, but too, was willing to be listen to the argument. This led first to addressing a forum on the subject at Gordon-Conwell Theological Seminary with a fellow graduate (it was a very good and thoughtful biblical exchange – we have always been friends who hold mutual respect). And second, to my April 1, 1989 meeting with Randall Terry. At that juncture I was already fashioning my own proactive strategy, and as it turns out, just two months away from its inauguration.

Sacred Assemblies for the Unborn

Thus, on June 3, 1989, I initiated a Christian witness at New England's largest abortion center, Preterm, in Brookline, Massachusetts, adjacent to Boston, which later I called the Sacred Assemblies for the Unborn (SAU). Preterm was then performing in excess of 10,000 abortions a year. Over a two-year period, we maintained a weekly presence on Saturday mornings with several early exceptions. Usually we had from a dozen to three dozen people; on a number of occasions we had 50 or more, and several occasions we had large turnouts, including our first time with some 225 participating. Activists from the Boston chapter of the National Organization for Women (NOW) were also there for the first nine months in equal numbers, but afterward called it off because, according to one of their leaders, we "were persuading too many of them."

The Strategy

In these assemblies, we had several points of strategy. First was a visible presence augmented by banners and signs. Second was a peaceful and conversational presence, where we sought to engage pro-abortion protestors, police, passersby, "escorts," guards and others in honest dialogue. Third was worship, including song and prayer in various capacities. And fourth was the eventual development of the Jeremiah 19 Liturgy. It all involved a specific embrace of spiritual warfare, where we were seeking to break the demonic forces present (see Chapter Nine), and to see the Spirit of God touch the hearts and minds of all those involved with Preterm in any capacity, especially the women coming for abortions.

In the first element of our strategy, we had two large banners, each about six feet in width, and three-and-a-half feet in height. One banner was at the front of Preterm, on the sidewalk on Beacon Street, and the other on the side street near the rear entrance and parking lot.

The banners had white block letters against a green background (like a highway sign), and easily visible from quite a distance:

YOU HAVE THE POWER TO CHOOSE LIFE.

When I first set to composing the words of the banner in 1989, I was not sure exactly what I wanted to say, except that I had "the ethics of choice" and "informed choice" in mind. But how do we translate them into the metaethics of language in the marketplace of ideas and sentiments? That is, being sure people understand what we mean with certain language. From the Greek, *meta* means that which surrounds, and *ethikos* means how we treat people ("ethics"). So all language connotes more than immediately meets the mind's eye.

319

So I set about to trying to sum up the concept in as few words as possible, trying to incorporate this language and explain it at the same time. I thus arrived at a phrase of 37 words (I do not know where in my files, if at all, these words might still exist).

When I called the friend who was working in concert with the company making the banner, and relayed to her my choice of the 37 words, she was incredulous. "John, you can't put a dissertation on a banner. It has to be simple."

"But Ruth," I replied, "This is not a dissertation. I have worked very hard to make it as simple as it is." No go. Ruth explained that the banner could have no more than five words, so that it could be read and grasped in a moment's notice. Otherwise its effectiveness would be moot.

The following exercise, as I reduced it to the seven final words, *you have the power to choose life* (seven passed muster with her), was a most valuable experience. One of the greatest tasks for a sound theology is to communicate the fruit of a biblical education in language that the wider culture can readily grasp, and in contexts where they are most likely to have interest in paying attention. This I tried to do with the 37 words, but that was more serviceable as an introduction or summation when teaching a class, not for a banner. The challenge is to be able to know the simplicity of the order of creation, then to engage the complexity of the reversal, and to finally be able to extrude the simplicity into the language of the reversal of the reversal.

The two polarities usually in evidence are a) to keep the simplicity and avoid the complexity, with such a gospel viewed as "simplistic" to the well-educated and culturally competent; or b) to deal with the complexities so much that the simplicity is lost, and such a gospel is viewed as complicated and unreal to those who need to know that Jesus loves them. Only the proper ordering of creation, sin and redemption maintains the true balance.

Even so, to know the simplicity, to delve into the complexity, and to emerge with simple truth able to address complex social sins, is another matter. It involves a lifetime of being a disciple. At that moment in the spring of 1989, I needed to learn this lesson thoroughly. And I am grateful to God for what emerged. I learned how to capture the substance of the ethics of choice with language that was simpler and which touched the motivation of the human heart. I also was trying to do two things at the same time with the banner. First was to reach out to abortion-minded women and truly enable them to intelligently and emotionally reconsider at the same split moment. Second was to employ such language that the abortion-rights advocates could not slander, and thus perhaps, touch their souls too.

Before and during my studies at Gordon-Conwell, and as I entered pro-life ministry, I began to grasp the biblical "ethics of choice," as I came to express it. From my studies at Harvard where I encountered the feminism expressed by abused women, I came to articulate the power to give. Both of these streams – not yet fully integrated into the theological paradigms I have since defined – came together as I sought to choose the words for the banner. It was language for chauvinized women – whether they were protestors on hand to oppose our witness, or whether they were en route to having their uteri vacuumed out – *you have the power to choose life*.

The first six words equal the centerpiece of feminist sympathies: *you have the power to choose*. And pagan feminist thinking believes the concept of the power to choose is their formulation of an identity in stark opposition to a biblical worldview. Unfortunately, too much of the church has forfeited this territory to the pagan feminists – the language of "power" in the face of the gender wars at large, and the language of "choice" in face of the abortion debate in specific.

Biblically, most of us pro-life Christians have instincts that are otherwise, but we do not possess the theological perspective or language to express ourselves better. The reality today is that elitists in politics, academia and the media easily intimidate the pro-life instincts of many people. It is time to reverse this reversal of *sex* $\rightarrow$ *choice* $\rightarrow$ *life* $\rightarrow$/*God* and regain the wisdom of *God* $\rightarrow$ *life* $\rightarrow$ *choice* $\rightarrow$ *sex*.

Such a banner, or sign, in its simplicity, reverses the fiction that biblically rooted pro-life advocates wish to impose their will on others. The words *you have* underscore the language of acknowledgment and gift, of the power to give. We are stating what both the abortion-rights activists and the abortion-minded women *have* to begin with – they possess something which we acknowledge a priori. It is something neither God, nor we, desire nor will take away, consistent with the power of informed choice. Already, the ministry of "first the Gospel" is being communicated. Our power to live in the light places our agenda on the table for all to examine and critique, and its ethics are thus self-evident.

The words, *you have the power*, also strengthen this language of acknowledgment, for in adding *power*, feminist yearnings find resonance. This is to touch and resonate with the POSH Ls (peace, order, stability and hope; to live, to love, to laugh, to learn) of the image of God in a false context, so as to redeem them for true context. This is further symphonized with the language of choice: *you have the power to choose*. These six words are as central to all "feminist" theories as any summation can make. We know that the abortion choice is largely the result of male chauvinisms, and many feminists and abortion-rights activists are in painful reaction to having been so violated.

Thus, these six words minister to the *nephesh* of the broken remains of the *imago dei* within them, as the POSH Ls are touched. Ironically, as these six words are read by the abortion-minded women, especially those being pressured by a boyfriend or other male, these "feminist" words begin to work the reversal of the "feminist" reversal support for human abortion. It gives a moment of breathing space for such women to stop and reconsider – "Am I exercising the power of my own choice, or am I being bullied into something I really don't want to go through with?"

When the final four-letter word is added to the phrase, *you have the power to choose life*, the de facto feminist ethic of misinformed choice is revealed. The power of informed choice requires accurate definition of terms, it requires an acknowledgment of reality. When "life" is put in, the object of "pro-choice" is no longer amorphous. It takes on flesh, it becomes real in its consequences. The power to choose? The power to choose what? Are all choices equal (e.g., dualism), or are some good and some evil? Back to the Garden and *akol tokel* versus *moth tamuth*.

Does "pro-choice" as a political slogan refer to all unrestricted choices, such as a male's "choice" to force or dominate, or should the choices of the chauvinist be opposed, since they are evil choices? Or does the "pro-choice" slogan represent a deception where the only choice considered "sacred" is that of human abortion when "wanted" or "needed?" In order to reverse the reversal, "choice" must be defined accurately so as to be redeemed.

The fruit of this banner in 1989-1991 at New England's largest abortion center was dramatic.

We also had some signs (24" by 36"). First we had the slogan signs per the banner, white on green. And second we had question signs, black letters against a yellow background. In 1989, we had ten questions (now it is twelve – #3 and #12 have since been added, with several also slightly edited, 18" x 24"). They are also designed to be clearly visible against any surrounding. These read:

1. **AREN'T YOU GLAD YOU WEREN'T ABORTED?**
2. **WHY DO YOU FEEL NO CHOICE BUT ABORTION?**
3. **IS IT YOUR CHOICE, OR HIS CHOICE, FOR YOU TO ABORT?**
4. **HOW DOES HUMAN ABORTION ADD TO YOUR OWN DIGNITY?**
5. **MIGHT YOU REGRET THIS ABORTION SOMEDAY?**
6. **CAN ANYTHING GOOD BE SAID ABOUT HUMAN ABORTION?**
7. **DOES GOOD CHOICE NURTURE OR DESTROY HUMAN LIFE?**
8. **WHY DOES THE HUMAN FETUS FIGHT TO STAY ALIVE?**
9. **WHY DOES "FEMINISM" ABORT UNBORN GIRLS?**
10. **WHICH COMES FIRST? YOUR LIFE OR THE POWER OF CHOICE?**

11. **CAN YOU IMAGINE JESUS PERFORMING AN ABORTION? WHY NOT?**
12. **IS THE ABORTION INDUSTRY RACIST?**

More recently, I have considered adding: **Question #13: Is Abortion Marketed on the Backs of Raped Women? Question #14: Why Do the Top-Down Media Love Human Abortion? Question #15: Why Do Top-Down Politicians Love Human Abortion?** And: **Question #16: What are the Definitions of God, Life, Choice and Sex?**

The questions were all designed to be intelligent and thought-provoking, not accusatory. In a two-year period of Saturdays, we saw 200 or more women turn away from their abortion appointments. And hundreds, even one or several thousand honest discussions, resulted with the abortion-rights activists, and others who were there.

The Power of the Banner

On September 30, 1989, I was not present at Preterm, placing one of my seminary students in charge (I had four students from Gordon-Conwell doing supervised ministry with me that fall). I received a detailed report from several witnesses to one of the most signal examples of the power of this slogan. At the rear entrance, two volunteers were holding up the banner, with other pro-life volunteers also present. One was Sue O'Connell, a volunteer who with her husband would travel nearly 100 miles from Amherst, Massachusetts, and they were as regular as any of our volunteers. That morning, Sue's eight-year old daughter, Kelly, was also with her. From the parking lot, people coming to Preterm would then enter the rear door.

There were about eight "escorts" positioned by the door, some dozens of feet away from Sue and Kelly, each wearing aprons designating their escort status. These were women and men, serving as volunteers to Preterm, to "guard" (reversal of *shamar*) incoming "clients" from being harassed by "anti-choice zealots." Since the parking lot was private property, our volunteers never went onto it from their public sidewalk positions.

This particular morning, a college-age woman walked down the street and was preparing to cross the lot to the rear door. As she did, she stopped, looked at the banner and pondered its words. Sue offered her some printed literature, and the young woman was preparing to receive it. But during those moments, the eight escorts saw what was happening and quickly came up and surrounded her, creating a human blockade around her with arms linked. This was a common practice these escorts developed to shield women when trying to break through an Operation Rescue blockade. Blockade against blockade, force against force, human angst against human angst.

So it was tragicomical to witness their intensity of forming such a blockade where there was no physical interference to these women as they entered the abortion center. But they had a deeper fear – that abortion-minded women might intelligently reconsider their choice, and seek some informed input from a different perspective. Thus, the escorts started shouting and chanting so as to prevent these women from hearing anything Sue might say, and also prevent any printed literature from coming her way. They forced this young woman into the rear doors of Preterm by such a surrounding tactic, being careful not to physically touch her and run afoul of the law.

Another witness to the event told me that as much as he opposed the tactic of blockade, the sight of the woman being hustled inside made him so frustrated that he emotionally wanted to physically intervene. As he wrestled with these thoughts, eight-year old Kelly O'Connell started praying out loud and with the strength of child-like faith, as she rebuked the devil, his deceit and his influence upon that young woman, and commanded that she would come out of Preterm, in the name of Jesus. And within minutes the woman did, shaken in countenance, making her way back to Sue and the others, where she received some materials (for a local CPC) and went her way. A triumph for the biblical power of informed choice. By God's grace, not by answering coercion and lawlessness with opposing coercion and lawlessness – but by answering in the prayer undergirding our strategy.

Thus the banner, in its summation of biblical theology, *you have the power to choose life*, has a power that abortion-rights activists are unable to answer. When *Yahweh* says to Cain that he must overcome his sin, and when Moses and Joshua tell the Israelites to choose between life and death, between *Yahweh* and the false gods, he is saying that they "have the power" to do so. Not the intrinsic ability within sinful humanity to overcome evil, but the broken remains of *Yahweh Elohim*'s image within them are sufficient by his grace to discern truth from falsehood, and to say "help me Lord" (*nephesh*), at which point he sends his help. By acknowledging this "power" within hurting people, we serve the reversal of the reversal, and redeem the language of choice to serve human life, not to destroy it.

The Power of the Questions

Our signs also prove effective at having women stop and reconsider their intentions, and effective at catalyzing conversations with the abortion-rights activists. I conceived of them the day before our first assembly, and they remained almost unchanged for our entire two years at Preterm, and as we moved from cardboard signs to more durable materials.

After being there several times over the summer, on September 9, 1989, we began to be present every Saturday, and the numbers of people equaled about 40 on each side. I saw some of the fruit of how deeply these signs affected the abortion-rights activists. A woman representing the "Reproductive Rights Network" ("R2N2" as her signs also said) had taken the time to make six signs, each numbered correspondingly to our signs. In each case the given sign sought to answer a given question we had posed.

I was delighted. She was trying to have other abortion-rights activists hold up her signs, but almost without success. So I went to strike up a conversation with her, and thanked her for having taken the time to answer our questions in such a fashion. I asked her if she were interested in talking about her answers, but she was very tense, distrustful, and did not want to talk. I prayed for her – much soul pain just below the surface.

Yet she could not resist asking me some questions, and as I answered, she relaxed somewhat. I then asked her if I could copy down the words from her signs, and she was hesitant, and then allowed me to do so, as long as I did not harm any of her signs. So I sat on the sidewalk and copied their words down:

326

Question #1: *Aren't you glad you weren't aborted?*

Answer #1: My mother is pro-choice and I am glad that she was not forced to bear an unwanted child.

Question #2: *Why do you feel no choice but abortion?*

No Answer.

Question #3: *How does human abortion add to your own dignity?*

Answer #3: The right to abortion adds to every woman's dignity because it allows women to control their lives. No religion can be allowed to limit or dictate choice!

Question #4: *Might you regret this abortion someday?*

Answer #4: No. Women who have been able to obtain abortions maintain that it was the right decision. They have put a lot of thought into exercising their right.

Question #5: *Can anything good be said about human abortion?*

No Answer.

Question #6: *Does good choice nurture life, or destroy life?*

Answer #6: Good choice nurtures the lives of women.

Question #7: *Why does the human fetus fight to stay alive?*

Answer #7: A fetus is not a human being. It is dependent on a woman's life and cannot survive outside her womb.

Question #8: If feminism = human care, why destroy the unborn human?

Answer #8: Feminism = freedom from oppression and harassment. Help women exercise their right to accessible, legal abortion. Save women's lives.

Question #9: *Is not all law based on a prior definition of human life?*

No Answer.

Question #10: *Can you imagine Jesus performing an abortion? Why not?*

No Answer.

When I composed our signs, I had certain words underlined, words which were meant to quickly touch a point of response of the image of God in the readers. As well, the signs made no negative statements about or caricatures of any people, groups or political affiliations, but instead sought to get women to think in terms of their own dignity and power to make the right choice.

In reviewing this woman's selective responses, I had opportunity to reflect upon words which she had carefully chosen, and cared about deeply enough to commit to public language. And in her words, I see a reflection of the motivating pain behind the abortion-rights movement – the nature of male chauvinism.

In my first question, the emphasis was on the word "you," seeking for women to think about their own humanity, their possession of life and gratefulness for it. With the R2N2 woman's response, I see aversion to the question. She did not say she was not glad to be alive (unaborted), but rather focused on her mother's dignity being preserved in resistance to being "forced." The R2N2 woman must have been hurting enough to deflect the purpose of the question, and perhaps her mother's own prior struggles.

The R2N2 woman did not answer the second question concerning feeling "no choice" but abortion." Perhaps she did not have time to prepare answers to all ten, and she chose the six in which she felt most interested, or for which she felt best able to give some answer. Or perhaps she, like many abortion-rights activists, is a woman who once had an abortion, one where she felt no choice as the father of the child refused any responsibility. Then in her pain at such chauvinistic treatment, she conflates an attempt to rationalize some dignity on her part by saying she had a choice to have an abortion, although her boyfriend actually gave her no choice. Maybe this was not the case with the R2N2 woman, but her answers indicate much pain, and such a scenario I have proposed is true for too many other women.

In her answer to question #3, the argument that "the right to abortion" adds dignity because "it allows women to control their lives," again seems to be a reaction against the chauvinistic treatment by men. And then her answer reflects an emphatic fear of impositional religion, which is a subject not even in view in this question. As well, all our signs, along with the banner, along with our non-blockade presence, equal the opposite of limiting or dictating choice.

Even yet, though we try our best to succeed at the metaethics of language, some people have been violated too much by organized religion to see through their own pain to the substance of what we are trying to say. Our mere presence is interpreted viscerally on their part as a shoving of unwelcome religion down their throats. At times like this, gentleness in spirit, infused by prayer, and augmented by eyeball-to-eyeball respect for her dignity as an image-bearer of God, is all the more important as we seek to hurdle these obstacles. As she relaxed a bit in my brief conversation with her, hopefully this was due to something of the goodness of the true Gospel touching her.

In the R2N2 woman's answer to question #4, the "no" answer seems defensive as much as it does personal. Most women do regret their abortions, modestly or completely, and the reality of post-abortion trauma is real and pervasive. And for many who say they do not regret it, a legitimate question is raised as to what extent a denial mechanism is in place to help salve the emotional pain. This woman may have had an abortion herself, and put much thought into it, though her sign put it in the third person. (And my experience leads me to view this as the likely scenario.) Having done so, no regrets are possible without an identity crisis such as the subconscious might suggest. And whereas she might have put much thought into it, many women being hurried off to an abortion appointment have not, and they are the ones that such a sign can reach at the last moment.

Question #5 went unanswered. Human abortion is an act of intrinsic destruction, and very hard to rationalize as "anything good." This is the very question I posed to the pro-abortion panel at the University of New Hampshire debate that fall – one that also stumped them. In the ten question signs, the choice of what words were underlined sought an overall balance in focus, and this is the only one that actually focuses on the word "abortion" itself. In so doing, it focuses on the human nature of its object. It is all in an attempt to help focus on the humanity of the unborn child, which only in the touching of the mother's humanity, can we help to serve his or her rescue.

The answer to question #6 is again selective and defensive. It gives a true statement, but perhaps a false implication. Namely, the choice of human abortion does not serve womanhood's intrinsic nature, and only rarely is it necessary to actually save her life from an otherwise septic condition coincidental with pregnancy. If such rare cases were the sole focus of "abortion-rights," there would be no political turmoil. The underlying relationship between the definitions of "life" and "choice" are in focus. Choice cannot first exist apart from life, and good choice does not deliberately destroy human life.

In the answer to question #7, the denial of the unborn child's humanity is the only recourse. And too, as already noted, the Latin word *foetus* simply means "young one" in the personal and human sense. And yes, the fetus is dependent on mom's womb, and indeed we are all dependent daily on the womb of the earth's ecosphere for daily survival. The R2N2 woman could have been asked, rhetorically in response, "And upon whom is a woman's life dependent? Her mother, father and the ecosphere, et al. and etc.? Who is not in some sense always dependent on others?" The theology of *nephesh*. And the R2N2 woman avoids the question of the fight. Namely, regardless of the semantics employed to dehumanize the unborn, we are all genetically programmed from our conceptions to be eager for life, to fight to live.

This eagerness is pre-conscious, and it energizes our self-awareness as it comes into full flower. The abortionist's scalpel must literally chase the unborn child inside his or her sanctuary in order to kill. The unborn child instinctively fights to stay alive, a point of identification which may help some abortion-minded women reconsider. But for the R2N2 woman, her pain of being hurt by religiously chauvinistic imposition may have been too great for her to be willing to so identify with the unborn – even an unborn child as she was once herself.

The answer to question #8 is revealing. In the prior seven questions, I focused principally on the women coming in for an abortion appointment, seeking to empower them to choose life. Question #8 is aimed at the "feminists" present, asking them to consider the meaning of their own self-defining term of "feminism." Feminist theory in its many permutations says specifically that if the world were run by women, and not by (chauvinistic) men, then we would have a more peaceful and ecologically friendly planet. Feminism is thus advertised as equaling "human care," and I sought in this question to link that assertion with caring for the unborn human.

The R2N2 woman avoided this linkage and stated that feminism equals freedom from harassment. Amen – and only the power of informed choice can provide such freedom. But only because of the prior reality of *Yahweh*'s power to give. Here the sheer positive definition of human freedom is clear, a "freedom for." The highest view of freedom outside of the foundation in Genesis 1-2 is a negative freedom, a "freedom from" violation. But until violation is understood, both "freedom from" and a "freedom for" are not possible. Unless the order of creation, the reversal and the reversal of the reversal are understood, true freedom cannot be grasped.

Question #9 is designed as the one legal question, for any lawyers, government officials or even police officers who might take notice of it. It is such a simple assumed reality that it is readily overlooked except by those committed to a constitutional federalism. Why have any law at all except to

331

define and protect human life as the starting assumption? As I describe my strategy for winning the legal protection for women and their unborn, the centrality of this question is front and center.

Finally, question #10 addresses a theological concern, and the only one which I simultaneously answer, in this case with a rhetorical question. Given the R2N2 woman's response to question #3 where she imports the question of religion, this might seem like a question that would spark a response on her part. The reason it did not, I suppose, is that it is one thing to castigate "religion" as an institution or force that oppresses people, and another thing to castigate Jesus as a person.

In all of history, very few if any people ever say anything negative about Jesus as a person, other than the religious and political elitists who oppose him in his day – and as they do so knowingly without just cause. Even such elitists today are most hesitant to do so. His reputation is so singular, and also, who can honestly imagine the Son of God, who healed the lame and the blind, delivered the demonized and raised the dead – who could imagine him giving countenance to the surgical or chemical destruction of an unborn human child, on the ostensible grounds of the "right to choose"?

Once when I was holding this sign at Preterm, a woman abortion-rights supporter approached me and said how she resented me "forcing" religion on her. I asked her how I was doing this, and she pointed to my sign: *Can you imagine Jesus performing an abortion? Why not?* I then asked how the sign "forced" religion on her, and she said that the mere introduction of the name of Jesus into such a political issue equals such a "forcing."

She was receptive to dialogue, so I explained how the posing of the question was exactly that – a question. It requires nothing of her and makes no demands of her attention or action. It is one of ten questions we are posing, and the only one with explicit theological content. In fact, she is free not to read it or any of the other questions, and I am exercising my freedom of political expression in the use of such a sign, just as the abortion-rights supporters are doing with their own signs. She is at Preterm by her own volition, and no force is being applied to her to make her read the signs.

As well, I noted that the question only has as much influence on people's thoughts and actions to the degree that they regard Jesus as someone whose person and teachings matter to them. If they believe Jesus is Lord and Savior, then the question raises a critical issue; if they regard Jesus as a mere human teacher, then the question raises concerns proportionate to how they view his teachings; if they do not give a whit about Jesus, then the question means nothing.

I explained that many women coming in for an abortion have been raised with some sort of Christian teaching, and that my question might affect them positively as they intelligently and emotionally reconsider their plans – this equals the power of informed choice, the opposite of forcing religion on someone. For those abortion-minded women who do not care about what Jesus might think of abortion, the sign poses no force against their decision. Then I briefly profiled the nature of the power of informed choice, and her freedom to disregard the question if Jesus means nothing to her.

Her response was lovely. She apologized for having misinterpreted the purpose of the sign, and thanked me for my explanation. I left it there. I did not probe about her opinion of Jesus Christ, nor was it appropriate at that juncture. She had received enough substance already, worthy of reflection.

Street-Level Engagement

When we first arrived at Preterm on June 3, 1989, it was the result of much groundwork, prayer, many letters, phone calls and a good number of seminars I taught in the metro Boston area. Near all the people we recruited had never before been to an abortion center or engaged in any activism. They trusted the biblical vision I sought to articulate. As I arrived, there were also several people from Operation Rescue present, including a man holding up a sign with a bloody picture of an aborted child. I was bold – for he had every right as we had to be there, and on his own terms – and asked him to put the sign away. I told him how it can be confused by women being pushed into abortions, as though it were an accusation against them, since it is the devil who condemns. We were there to be radically positive and redemptive. He accepted my perspective and put the sign away.

333

We had about 225 people "come down" (a clause I always used, since I "came down" from the North Shore, north to south as it were). Many were there for part of the morning, and some for all of it (7 a.m. to noon). The abortion-rights supporters were present in roughly equal number.

Boston NOW and their allies were organized in para-military fashion. They had cell-phones (which then were expensive and comparatively rare) and walkie-talkies. They also had a very distinct hierarchal structure, where we could identify their chapter president who was in charge, Ellen Convisser, and various "lieutenants" (as I called them) underneath her, coordinating other NOW members, and the larger core of college students (metro Boston has some 600,000 undergraduate and graduate students). The NOW recruits had been told that we were Nazi-types, and were in reality trying to catch them off guard and "rush" to blockade access to Preterm at an unguarded moment. Thus, psychologically, most of their recruits were poised the whole time, awaiting a "rush" that never came.

Biblical Excursus

This hierarchal structure of Boston NOW merits a biblical excursus in Ephesians 6:10-20, which contains the most comprehensive statement of spiritual warfare in the New Testament:

> Henceforth, be strengthened in the Lord and in the power of his strength. Clothe yourselves in the full armor of God so that you can powerfully stand against the schemes of the devil. For we do not struggle against flesh and blood, but against the chief rulers, against the authorities, against the world rulers of darkness, against the spiritual forces of evil in the heavenlies. Therefore, take up the full armor of God in order that you can powerfully resist the evil day, to be able to stand your ground, and after you have worked out everything, to stand.

> Stand firm accordingly, girding your loins with the truth, clothed with the breastplate of righteousness, and with your feet bound underneath with the readiness of the Gospel of peace. In all things, take up the

shield of faith, powerful in quenching all the burning arrows of the evil one. Receive the helmet bringing salvation, and the sword of the Spirit, which is the active word of God. And with all kinds of prayers and entreaties, pray at all appointed times in the Spirit. And keep alert in your prayers, praying at all appointed times for all the saints.

Pray also on my behalf, that words may be given whenever I open my mouth, so that with boldness I will make known the mystery of the gospel, for which I am an ambassador in chains, that I may speak with necessary freedom.

The "armor" of God is the metaphor (cf. Isaiah 59:17) for a real war; which is to say, that just as physical armor is needed for a physical war, spiritual armor is needed for a spiritual war. And that armor is inescapably ethical in nature. The ethical precedes and defines the spiritual. The devil schemes, he plots, he manipulates; he strategizes to outwit, outflank and destroy the saints of God. We must be wise as serpents in our strategic placements, and innocent as doves in our character and conduct. And as we read in v. 13, "after you have worked out everything," then to stand prepared, we see how we must out strategize and outflank the devil. And in Christ we have all the wisdom and armor so to do.

The contrast is clear, as Boston NOW had its hierarchy in their defined battle (in Chapter Nine we will more deeply identify the demonic realities in the background), here at the prior reality, Paul profiles the hierarchal nature of the heavenly conflict in terms of the demonic component. He identifies "chief rulers" (Greek root: *archon*), "authorities" (*exousia*), "world powers" (*kosmokrator*) of darkness, and "spiritual forces of evil" (*pneuma* and *poneria*) in the heavenlies. The "heavenlies" is identified as the "dark world," the spiritual domain and trafficking world of demons.

First, the word *archon* is rooted in *arche*, which means "beginning," and in the sense of determining order. An *archon* is one who is invested with power from the beginning, at the top – a king, chief, ruler, prince, magistrate. The word "hierarchy" comes from the Greek roots *ieros* for "sacred," "holy" or "priestly," and *archon* for "chief rulers." Thus, its concept etymologically precedes any sense of human political organization, and refers to an organization in the heavenlies of rulers that begins with the first or chief ruler, and then works its way through those of descending rank and power.

The word "hierarchy" refers first to *Yahweh Elohim*'s order, with himself as the eternal King, based on the power to give, and then to the ranks among the angels in service to God and the image-bearers of God. *Satan*, as a fallen angel, mimics the concept of hierarchy, based on the power to take, and undoubtedly taking angels of established rank and power with him in his rebellion. Now, in his masquerade, he sets up his own hierarchy with himself at the top, aspiring to mimic the mountain of God but cannot rise greater than the abyss, so his "*satanic* counsel" is an "abysmal court" (terms more fully defined elsewhere). Thus, Paul speaks specifically of the hierarchy of "world powers" of darkness, of "spiritual forces of evil" – the hierarchy of the devil with his fallen angels. Paul starts with the chief powers in his list here, and the concept of hierarchal ranks.

Second, the word *exousia* is rooted in *exesti*, which simply refers to the idea of what is "possible" and "permitted," what is "doable." Thus, *exousia* specifically refers to the concept of "power," "authority" and "ability." Third, the word *kosmokrator* is rooted in *kosmos*, for "order" and the "material world" or "material universe," specifically as that world or order which is lower than and distinct from the heavenly world. The lower register in contrast to the higher.

Third, the word *krateo* (from *kratos*), refers to "superior strength" or "force" able to "vanquish" opponents. In other words, these *kosmoskratoras* (plural form) are demons who operate in the human political world in order to vanquish their enemies. These are the demons who work to inspire sorcery at the right hand of power, who seek to inspire and energize totalitarian despots in the goal of killing first the Messianic lineage, and now the believers in the Messiah.

And fourth is the *pneumatika tes ponerias,* or "spiritual forces of evil." This is a general reference to "evil spirits," and as such, to any lower class or rank of demons than already defined. Not the officer class as it were, but the enlisted.

In sum, Paul defines a hierarchy of demons:

1. *Satan* (*ha'satan*), the "accuser" or "slanderer"; the devil himself (the *diabolos* for "traitor" or "slanderer"); then underneath him:
2. the chief demons (the *archas*, plural of *archon*);
3. powerful demons of the next rank (the *exousias*);
4. powerful demons whose specified task is to dominate the human political order (the *kosmokratoras*), to destroy opponents; and
5. lower ranked demons (the *pneumatika tes ponerias*).

Paul outlines a well-organized and scheming army of demonic opposition. Thus he describes the need of the church in terms of the language of the Roman soldier. We need the soldier's protection of the loins, a belt as it were, as the truth that holds our armor in place, and also protects life-giving power. The "breastplate of righteousness" is the confidence we have in our hearts that Christ is our righteousness (contra the folly of human ego), and it protects our chest and vital organs. Our "feet bound underneath" with the readiness that comes from the Gospel of peace, which is our mission. The "shield of faith" adds a mobile layer over the breastplate of righteousness and over the rest of the body, to proactively be wielded in response to the blows of swords and burning arrows coming our way. And the "helmet of salvation" protects the head, the mind, the control of the whole body; and with the assurance of the gift of salvation we have by trusting in Jesus, we do not fall prey to fear or doubt about our calling while on the battlefield.

The "sword of the Spirit" is our one offensive weapon, to cut down the enemy as Jesus dispenses with the devil in the temptation in the wilderness; it is the power of the "active word (*rema*) of God," the power of biblical literacy. And finally, we are to "pray at all appointed times in the Spirit," interceding for ourselves and one another. This is warfare prayer in the broadest and most inclusive sense, which of course, cannot find analogy in the Roman soldier's armor, for here we transcend the human analogy into an arena deep in the heavenlies. Since *Satan* and his demons are limited

337

creatures, they do not have access to the inner thoughts of our mind – they can only attack our thinking processes from without, and they measure our thinking by our words and actions.

Back to the Streets

Excursus noted, we now return to the NOW lieutenants in June, 1989. They were frantic as they moved about the perimeter of the crowd, watching for any "signal" on our part, preparing for the expected fiction that would indicate the coming "rush." After the first dozen of us arrived early, formed a circle and started singing hymns and worship songs, the NOW people surrounded us and started their loud decibel chants and slogans, e.g., "Racist, sexist, anti-gay, born-again bigots go away!" But the wear and tear on their vocal chords was demanding.

As numbers grew on both sides, this continued for an hour-and-a-half, and as the lungs of the NOW chanters weakened, it proved that singing praises to God is far healthier and enduring. During this time, a detail of Brookline police officers that was sent to keep opposing sides apart, gradually relaxed their sense of urgency, and across the following two years, increasingly cut back then cut out their foot patrol presence.

After NOW et al. tired of their chants, we later brought our worship to a close for a time. It was hot and sunny, on its way to temperatures exceeding 90 degrees. We were equipped with plenty of ice-cold spring water, and NOW apparently was not. We began to distribute it to Christian and pagan alike, and in the process it naturally served an important priority, which was to engage the NOW activists in honest dialogue at street-side.

Most of the NOW activists, especially the college students, were grateful for the water. I was told of one encounter, however, that was as tragic as it was comical. As one of our volunteers was passing out the cups of water, a woman reached out to take it, then hesitated and looked at the person offering the water, and queried, "Which side are you on?" When she learned his Christian identity, she refused the water. But she was the exception as it turns out.

Very quickly, dozens of ad hoc conversations broke out, involving groups of two, several or many more people from both sides engaged with each other in discussion about our presence, abortion and the Gospel. Prior to that June 3, I had come down once myself to gain a sense of the territory, and had engaged in conversation with some pro-life picketers whom I knew.

One man was a member of Operation Rescue who respected my work on college campuses. When I spoke to him about my strategy to engage the abortion-rights activists in honest dialogue at street-level, he told me how impossible it was for such a goal to be realized. He profiled for me their antagonistic nature, and how what I do on the campuses is great, but in front of an abortion center it is a different reality. But I felt otherwise, and to see it come to pass was a joy.

At its height that Saturday, some 100-200 people from both sides were simultaneously involved, and the din of conversation was so great, that it competed well with the street noises and passing trolleys, cars, buses and trucks – almost like the din which precedes an event in a concert hall when the lobby is packed with people awaiting the opening of the doors. It was exceedingly fruitful, as I participated in various discussions, received feedback from conversations others had, and in the intervening times, circled about to gain a larger perspective.

After one such circling, as I made my way back to the center of the discussions nearest the doors of Preterm, I stopped to look around and give an ear. As I did, I noticed the president of Boston NOW, Ellen Convisser, about ten feet away. As I did, a sudden panic came over her as she observed what was going on about her. She then spoke to one of her "lieutenants," and said, "What's happening here? We are not in control. We must put a stop to this!"

She then gave instructions to have the conversations forcibly broken up, and the lieutenants and others actually grabbed their own people, pushing or pulling them away from our people, and commanded them to cease talking with us. Even yet, most of the NOW recruits ignored these commands and continued their conversations.

In fact, the then president of the national Christian Action Council (CAC) Tom Glessner, M.D., was present with us that morning. He was in the midst of a delightful discussion with some NOW activists at that juncture, when he witnessed this happen to him. I believe the discussion continued.

NOW Lieutenants

So, for our first several times down to Preterm, we saw large numbers and much interaction with NOW recruits, and increasing frustration on the part of the NOW leadership and its lieutenants. They were not "in control" in their censorship of informed choice. We had the godly self-control based on the power to give, the power to live in the light, the power of informed choice, the power to love hard questions, the power to love enemies and the power to forgive.

In one of these early assemblies, one of our volunteers heard one of the NOW recruits ask one of the lieutenants how to respond to our slogan, *you have the power to choose life*. The NOW leader responded, "Well, that's their language, and we tell our people not to use it anymore." They forfeited the language of choice, and thus we saw the reversal of the reversal. They tacitly acknowledged that their "pro-choice" rhetoric is dishonest, and that the power to give and the power of informed choice, as rolled into our slogan, redeems the language of choice to protect the unborn.

It was very frustrating for these lieutenants. There was one young woman in particular with NOW, with whom I crossed paths often across several initial Saturdays. We never spoke, but she knew who I was. Her energy level was very high. One time we had a remarkable morning at Preterm, where worship was powerful, witness was engaging and where we noted seven women turning away from their abortion appointments.

Afterward, I saw her sitting on the sidewalk as most people had left, her head buried in her hands. Perhaps at this juncture she realized we were not going to rush Preterm to blockade it, but rather were doing exactly what we set out to do – communicate as honestly as possible in the face of such a painful debate. As we were gathering up our signs, and in my only interaction with her, I stopped as I walked past. She looked at me, and I said spontaneously, "God bless you." She replied, "Yes, I need it." In that moment I saw the Holy Spirit working on her heart, as she had come to know what our true agenda was – to show equal love to women and their unborn, to show the power to love enemies, to state with conviction: *you have the power to choose life.*

"Peacekeepers," the Fear of Dialogue, and Forfeiture

Part of Boston NOW's paramilitary organization was the presence of "peacekeepers" who wore purple armbands to identify themselves.

I was once engaged in a conversation with such a "peacekeeper" named Erica, and a man who was also wearing a purple arm band approached her and said, "You are not allowed to talk with them if you are wearing a peacekeeper arm band." Erica questioned the policy, and after he did not change his mind, took off her arm band and we continued the conversation.

I then said to the man, who would not face me, "Oh, you mean that dialogue is not a part of peacekeeping?" Stone silence on his part, but he listened intently to the dialogue that Erica and I continued, standing nearby the whole time.

Their fear of dialogue and honest questions came to the point where by March of 1990, we were told by some of the escorts that the word had gone out from Boston NOW to stop recruiting people to come and counter-protest our presence. They forfeited territory where prior they controlled the language of the debate. Especially in the face of Operation Rescue as a foil. No longer. Our substance foiled their search for a new foil.

The word was that we were persuading too many of them, especially among the college recruits. Now persuasion involves many levels, from a salting influence of helping to remove false stereotypes, to complete conversion to Jesus Christ. What I took this to mean was mostly in the "salting" capacity, the rototilling then scattering of the seed. It was clear to us from the outset that Boston NOW and their allied organizations tried hard to portray us as bigots, anti-democratic, homophobes, Nazis and such.

But from our initial Sacred Assembly, this false stereotype was shattered. In the din of conversations catalyzed that day, I remember overhearing one abortion-rights advocate exclaim in wonder, as she was observing the event, "Why, these people are nice!" The reversal of the reversal, and the devil fears such redemptive power. Indeed, as a cognate, a friend overheard a NOW activist say that day, in horror, to one of her comrades, "These people are more dangerous than Operation Rescue. They're going for our minds!" Well, the whole soul, including the mind, will and emotions.

Thus, from March 1990, until we ceased activity with the bankruptcy of the NECAC in June 1991, there was no organized opposition to our presence at Preterm apart from a few exceptions. There were only the few escorts and occasional others. We won the territory spiritually, and were able to concentrate more on worship.

A Marxist-Leninist

That morning in June, 1989, the largest banner from among abortion-rights activists said, "Oppose the oppression of working women." Below it was the larger main slogan: "Fight the Reaganite Anti-Abortion Movement!" On the bottom it said, "Marxist-Leninist Party." When the man in charge of the banner learned I was the organizer of the Sacred Assembly, he made his way over to me, introduced himself as secretary for the Marxist-Leninist Party of Boston, and wondered with open hostility if I were a "Reaganite anti-choice clone." From there he lectured me for 20-30 minutes, in language laden with Marxist nomenclature and assumptions.

He was a large man, and as I listened to him, I found many points where I could have easily raised objections. But instead I remained silent on those divisive points and affirmed with nods or brief words the various places where I did agree. Toward the end of this time, he suddenly realized that I was listening to him – and was visibly shocked. His presumed stereotype of me was wrong, and he perceived the respect I gave him as an individual.

342

Our conversation was interrupted by some exigency as we stood among so many people on the sidewalk and street. Sometime later, he approached me again, but this time with an eagerness for a true exchange of ideas. We talked, and I made my arguments for a biblical worldview and its pro-life perspectives, and soon he was beginning to ask me question after question. Again the conversation was interrupted.

At the end of the morning, he approached me a third time and said, "I have just one more question." I forget the exact question he posed, but it had something to do with how Christians should conduct themselves in political disputes, and my answer was simple and straightforward. Then he broke into a big smile, shook my hand with the strength of a rail-splitter, said "thank you," and left.

The Power of Not Having an Answer

As referenced earlier, that fall I had four students from Gordon-Conwell Theological Seminary doing supervised ministry under me. One student, Andy Davis, now a pastor with a Ph.D. in Church History, was in charge on a given Saturday in October. Andy was holding a sign next to several abortion-rights activists, each holding their signs, and he sought to initiate conversation. One college-age woman conversed with him for some 45 minutes, but in a distant fashion, and since NOW had told their recruits not to engage in conversation with us, in fear (still) of a sudden rush on our part to physically block access to the abortion center. This we were theologically opposed to doing, but NOW did not yet trust this to be the case. In other words, this woman was committed to being there since we were there, and perhaps the conversation helped her pass the time.

At one point she asked Andy a question, and Andy said something like, "That is a good question, and I really don't know the answer. I'll have to get back to you." This freedom to admit when we do not know the answer highlights the integrity of the power to love hard questions – in this case, it was not having the right answer per se as much as having a genuine and humble love that made the difference. This woman was astonished at his honesty, and then entered into a warm and truly probing discussion, and two of her friends joined in as well. For the next 45 minutes, they discussed one question: Who is Jesus Christ?

Andy communicated across the chasm. More remarkably yet, this woman returned to Preterm five months later looking for him. He was not there, so she asked the seminary student in charge that day, Bill Wilder, how she could contact him, and Bill provided the information. Bill is now a Ph.D. in New Testament, heading up a vital university ministry center. Her statement went something like this, "Where is that fellow I talked with in October? He asked me a couple of questions that have been bugging me ever since, and I need to talk with him." Bill provided the contact information.

The Jeremiah 19 Liturgy

By the spring of 1990, just as the word went out from Boston NOW headquarters to dissuade any more counter-protest of us, I developed a more concerted worship strategy. This revolved around what I called *The Jeremiah 19 Liturgy*, and we were able to use it on various occasions. Our worship in song was a central element of the strategy; and service to the ministry of the sidewalk counselors was the fourth element (those who were there prior and after our presence, who seek to reach out one-to-one to women entering Preterm for an abortion).

Essentially, we began with guitarists who led us in contemporary choruses and classic hymns – choosing songs where the theology was strong, the melodies delightful and the appeal wide in terms of the cross-section of the believing churches.

When we did not have a guitarist on hand, we sang a cappella. In the best scenario, especially through March 1990, before the "word" was given by NOW to its supporters to desert their posts, there were always people worshiping in song and prayer, while others were conversing with abortion-rights advocates, while sidewalk counselors were doing their work, and while the banner was being displayed and the signs with their questions being held. Some people only engaged in the worship element, and never held a sign or engaged in conversation with the abortion-rights advocates. Some people

344

concentrated on the signs and witness elements. People participated at the level they chose. And at singular times, we would gather as a whole group for worship, with the signs being held in the assembly, the banners being maintained at curbside and at the rear entrance.

Here is the liturgy:

> **Leader:** We gather here today to seek God's mercy, to stop the killing of the unborn in this place. Hear the words of the prophet Jeremiah:

> **People:** This is what *Yahweh* says: "Go and buy an earthen flask, and with some elders and priests, go out to the Valley of Ben Hinnom, at the opening of the Potsherd Gate. There proclaim the words I speak to you."

> **Leader:** The Valley of Ben Hinnom in 600 B.C. was used for places of Topheth, where infant children were burned alive to the Canaanite god *Ba'al*. Topheth means a fireplace for child sacrifice. Today we stand in front of an abortion center [or *political institution*] where human life is destroyed [or *mocked*]. It is a modern, updated Topheth shrine.

> **People:** So hear the words of *Yahweh*, O kings of Judah and inhabitants of Jerusalem; this is what *Yahweh* of armies, the *Elohim* of Israel says: "Behold, I am bringing evil on this place, that which will make the ears of all who hear of it tingle."

> **Leader:** Judah faced *Yahweh*'s judgment in 586 B.C. with the destruction of Jerusalem and the temple they made into an idol, and thus the destruction of the nation, followed by their exile to Babylon. To the extent that this nation sanctions and continues the practice of human abortion, we invite *Yahweh*'s judgment.

> **People:** "For they have deserted me and made this place strange; they have burned sacrifices in it to other gods, unknown to their fathers and the kings of Judah, and they have filled this place with the blood of the innocent."

345

Leader: In the idolatry of *Ba'al*, the Hebrew people were seduced into believing that by burning their infant children alive they could gain fertility, peace and prosperity. Today we see an "idolatry of choice" where "choice" becomes a false god used to destroy unborn human life, instead of true choice which nurtures all human life. And it is overwhelmingly rooted in the choice of men who get women pregnant, only to then flee responsibility and true manhood.

In a life disrupted by a crisis pregnancy, human abortion is sold as a means to regain a lost sense of peace, order, stability and hope. But human abortion does not restore these shattered remains of God's image. Rather, it only fractures a woman's life more deeply yet, and lets the man off the hook. This is idolatry, and we Christians are just as vulnerable to idolatry apart from God's grace.

People: "They have built the high places of *Ba'al* to burn their sons in the fire as a holocaust to *Ba'al*, something I did not command nor speak, nor did it come to my mind. So behold, the days are coming, proclaims *Yahweh*, when this place will no longer be called Topheth or the Valley of Ben Hinnom, but the Valley of Slaughter."

Leader: Here, at a modern Topheth shrine, we have a signpost to our own nation's judgment, of our own pending Valley of Slaughter. The victimizers become the victims, and one day human abortion will be remembered not as a woman's freedom or empowerment, but of her and her nation's slaughter. A slaughter not only of the unborn, but of women's dignity and men's dignity as life-nurturing humans.

People: "I will lay waste the counsel of Judah and Jerusalem in this place. They will fall by the sword in the face of their enemies, by the hands of those who seek their souls, and I will give their carcasses as food to the creatures of the air and the beasts of the earth. I will devastate this city and make it an object of hissing; all who pass by its heights will be appalled and will hiss because of all its wounds. I will cause them to eat the flesh of their sons and the flesh of their daughters, and men will be caused to eat the flesh of each other during the stress

346

of the siege poured out on them by the enemies who seek their souls."

Leader: Jerusalem's idolatrous sacrifice of her infant children led to a literal cannibalism. This nation's destruction of her unborn progeny cries out for a modern equivalent. All the hallmarks of Sodom's lawlessness only grow – sexual anarchy that leads to social anarchy and the trampling of the poor and needy.

The harvesting and cloning of human embryos for research and transplants is its own form of human cannibalism. And why do we presume that we are above the descent into literal cannibalism one day? From the ground beneath our feet there cries out the blood of millions of unborn U.S. citizens. We will reap what we have sown, apart from God's mercy which triumphs over judgment for those who seek him.

People: Then break the flask in the eyes of those whom you brought, and say to them, "This is what *Yahweh* of armies says: I will cause the people and this city to be broken just like the vessel is smashed and cannot be repaired."

Leader: The jar Jeremiah used was similar to those used to bury the charred remains of the sacrificed children. And the parents truly wept as they buried them. This is the terror of idolatry. But today, the idolatry of human abortion hides the terrible act of its destruction within the machinery of the suction apparatus, at the edge of the scalpel or through the assault of toxic chemicals. There are no coffins, no tombstones, and too often the grief remains hidden and festering.

As surely as Jeremiah's breaking of the symbolic clay jar signaled *Yahweh*'s impending judgment, we believe *Yahweh Elohim*, the Lord Jesus, pronounces judgment upon the sites and apparatus of human abortion, upon its political and economic enablers, and upon those who cling to its idolatry while mocking the Lord and Giver of life. As Jerusalem became like Topheth, so too will the ethos of human abortion kill the culture that enshrines it.

Therefore, I break this jar as a prayer for *Yahweh Elohim* to bring an end to the evil of human abortion, and the male chauvinisms that undergird it. We thus proclaim God's love to the women and their unborn children so victimized. I also break this jar as a symbol to break the powers of darkness which govern the abortion mind-set. In the name of Jesus Messiah, *Yahweh Elohim* incarnate, let it be.

[break jar]

People: "In Topheth they will be buried until there is no more room to be buried. This is what I will cause to happen to this place and to those who dwell there, declares *Yahweh*. I will make this city like Topheth. The dwelling place in Jerusalem and the houses of the kings of Judah will become unclean in this place of Topheth, all the houses where they made sacrifices of incense on the roofs to all the armies of the heavens and poured out drink offerings to other gods."

Leader: When Jeremiah broke the clay jar, he declared that he was not the Judge. He trusted *Yahweh Elohim* as the only righteous Judge, and faithfully called on King Zedekiah and the other leaders to put an end to the shedding of innocent blood. To do so, they had to first put away the sins of sorcery and worshiping the stars, also of sacred prostitution, which together leads to human sacrifice.

Likewise, we trust in the one true Creator and the power of honest persuasion in the public arena. No people are our enemies, even those who perform or support human abortion. Only the devil and his demonic host are our enemies. Thus we appeal to men to become true men and honor all women as equals and complements, and we appeal to the hearts and minds of all people of good will – stop the killing,

People: Thus we affirm:

• Yes to the marriage of one man and one woman for one lifetime.
• Yes to loving and faithful fatherhood.
• Yes to women and their unborn.

- Yes to the image of God in all people – born and unborn.
- Yes to the power to give in face of the pretension to take.
- Yes to informed choice which serves human life.
- Yes to the power to bless in face of the pretension to curse.
- Yes to the power of love in face of the pretension to hate.
- Yes to the Good News of Jesus the Messiah.

People: Jeremiah then came from Topheth, where *Yahweh* had sent him to prophesy, and stood in the court of *Yahweh*'s house and said to all the people, "This is what *Yahweh* of armies, the *Elohim* of Israel, says: 'Behold, I am going to bring on this city and the villages around it every evil I spoke against them, because they were stiff-necked and would not listen to my words.' "

Leader: We are all stiff-necked apart from God's grace, and we who are believers welcome the deepest and most challenging questions from abortion supporters, in the prayer that they are seeking the same grace in the midst of their broken lives.

People: Jeremiah also says, "Behold. I am setting before your faces the way of life and the way of death." And Moses says, "Choose life." So listen to the words of Jeremiah spoken to King Zedekiah: "This is what *Yahweh* says: Do justice and righteousness. Snatch away the one who has been robbed from the hand of his oppressor. Do no violence, do not oppress the sojourner, the orphan or the widow, and do not pour out innocent blood."

Leader: Jeremiah promised peace for Israel if King Zedekiah were to obey. The same promise is before us today, if we as a nation, beginning with our leaders, would turn away from the slaughter of unborn human children. Forgiveness is offered to all who seek it, and it is complete in its healing of past sorrow and guilt for those who dare to believe.

People: We say to all who would listen:

- You have the power to choose life, if you dare to believe it and ask God for it.
- If you do not have this power, what power and choice do you have?
- If you have power and choice, why not use it?
- Courageous and compelling choice always nurtures human life, and in Jesus Christ, such courage, power and choice is uniquely available.

Amen.

The Liturgy in Practice

We used the liturgy perhaps a dozen times, and it was powerful. On June 16, 1990, we had an SAU with about 50-60 Christians present, mostly from one church, including some fifteen young children. About a dozen abortion-rights activists were also present, in one of their rarer appearances those days, and these were people mostly from ACT-UP ("AIDS Coalition to Unleash Power"), the militant homosexual group. During that morning I was able to share Christ with one of the ACT-UP leaders for about two hours.

When it came time for gathering and reciting the liturgy, some six or eight of the abortion-rights activists stood by observing. One of them was trying to mock it with taunts and laughter, but her compatriots did not follow suit. Instead they were listening attentively to each word. When the jar was smashed on the sidewalk, as on the other occasions when we conducted the liturgy, its symbolic power merged with true spiritual power. There was complete quiet for several moments before I continued with the liturgy, and the one mocking woman was also self-silenced, not to resume her taunts again. The children were specially intrigued as well.

In the smashing of the jar we are imitating Jeremiah's use of the symbol as *Yahweh* commands him. In the smashing dynamic, the visual encounter with this destruction conveys to the mind the larger prospect of the destruction of a city or nation, as Babylon in particular ravages Jerusalem and Judah in 586 B.C. It causes people to become more pensive in considering God's prerogative and promise to judge sin – and such reflection is on the side of the angels. The catalyzing of thought is our radical goal, necessary before actions can be reformed.

This we witnessed here and in other instances, though this may have only been one of several times when there were any abortion-rights activists present apart from the escorts. Thus I was eager to gauge their response, as I would love to see hundreds of counter-protestors every time we were to be present at an abortion center. I am eager for them to encounter the Word of God in all its truth and beauty, and I know how such a liturgy conveys God's judgment upon human abortion while extending mercy to those who would repent.

After the liturgy concluded that morning, we began to sing a praise song, and I squatted and began picking up the pieces of the broken jar. Within moments at least six of the children, ages two to seven, were all around me, spontaneously picking up whatever pieces they could find, reverently and in absolute quiet, and placing them into my hand.

The strength of childlikeness had been catalyzed to crush the works of the devil. After the song, I addressed the group for two minutes, conscious that I also had the undivided attention of the abortion-rights activists. I spoke of what a profound parable this seemed to me:

> Here we are, in front of an abortion center where adults use technology to break little humans into pieces. And here we are, observing little children, who in seeing brokenness, respond with shock, and instinctively desire to pick up the broken pieces and put them back together.

I spoke of Jesus's words in Matthew 18, how we must become as little children in order to enter the kingdom of the heavens. As I did, I looked straight at the abortion-rights activists, and I saw the convicting power of the Holy Spirit begin to penetrate past the pain and defenses. The natural reaction of the little children speaks reams about the nature of the Good News, of *shalom* coming into a broken world through the work of the

Messiah. "Come to me all you who toil and are burdened, and I will give you rest."

The Jeremiah 19 Liturgy portrays the judgment graphically and in biblical order, so that the mercy which triumphs over the judgment can be grasped (see James 2:8-13). In this one moment of time, of theological *kairos* (a specific and significant moment in time), the liturgy served the proclamation of the Gospel to people who would not be willing to stop long enough to otherwise consider it. We need to see this power released as often and as widely as possible. An abortion center is a place where the devil tramples hopes and dreams, a place where the Gospel sorely needs to be lived and proclaimed.

The Fear of Pro-Life

From this season, let me share several related anecdotes.

The Boston Globe

In the 1980s, the media covered Operation Rescue in depth, partly because it made good sound bites for the abortion-rights activists in their condemnation of the blockade and other violative tactics. But even in so doing, and in focusing the issue away from the nature of human abortion itself, they still biased their coverage highly.

For example, I say no to blockade and its cognate tactics. Nonetheless, the OR participants, almost without exception in some 100,000 arrests, only engaged in passive resistance. And they deserve respect for this restraint. But the television news would show clips of people pressing against a police blockade trying to forcibly break through it, and yelling vulgarities. The news would run these clips in a context where the casual observer would identify these people with Operation Rescue. Yet in reality it was the abortion-rights activists behaving this way. The sad reality is that this bias is part of the fruit invariably reaped by blockade tactics – it brings out the worst in others as they react and become more self-justified.

But the media ignored us as much as possible, in the Sacred Assemblies for the Unborn. I believe this because they could not make a negative caricature out of what we were doing, and because we were going for their minds too. We defined the terms and language of the event, and they could not stomach it. At our first assembly, it was the only time, with one exception, that I noticed any media present, a Boston Globe reporter, Adrian Walker, and she spent much of her time just looking at our questions. But in her brief article the next day, combined with focus on another event that same day, there was no focus on the substance of the issues these questions raised. The only focus was on our non-blockade presence as being distinct from that of OR.

I remember the night before the June, 1989 event, realizing that the media's likely strategy was to try and portray a division among pro-lifers – to try to get us to do some finger-pointing against OR, and to use such accusations to profile an intramural squabble. I could imagine their headline: "Pro-life Leader Condemns Operation Rescue," or "Anti-Abortion Movement Splits," etc. And since I disagreed deeply with the tactic of blockade, and was trying to present an alternative – which I would have been delighted to have accomplished before OR came on the scene – I did not know how I would answer such a question.

My agenda was positive, yet due to OR's prominence, and due to the fact that I wanted to honor the pro-life commitment of most of its recruits while not endorsing their tactics, I faced a quandary. Not being able to come up with a simple sound-bite answer ahead of time, I took Mark 13:11 seriously (understanding the different exact context), and trusted that if such a question were posed, then the Holy Spirit would give me the right words:

> And whenever you are handed over (to trial), do not be anxious
> beforehand about what to say. Just say what is given you in the hour,
> for it is not you speaking, but the Holy Spirit.

The next morning, in the brief interview the Globe reporter had with me, she cut to the chase: "What is the difference between your group and Operation Rescue?" And indeed, the Holy Spirit gave me words in simplicity and power I had not composed beforehand: "The difference is simple:

Operation Rescue believes the time has arrived for civil disobedience, and we do not believe it has yet arrived."

A parallel passage to Mark 13 is in Luke 21, and adds the following words of Jesus: "For I will give you a mouth of wisdom that none of those who oppose you will be powerful enough to resist or speak against" (v. 15).

This happened here and it happens elsewhere. But only by depending wholly on the grace of God in Christ Jesus. I did not have to get into the nature of civil obedience and civil disobedience, and the criteria for a justifiable political revolution. A simple answer to a simple question. The reporter had no further questions on this subject, and in the brief sub-article the next day in the Globe, it was muted. No negative headline came to pass.

WGBH at the State Capitol

In the spring of 1990, there were two simultaneous pro-abortion events close to my downtown Boston office. First, the Boston chapter of NOW encouraged college students to skip classes and attend a rally for "abortion-rights" on the Boston Common. And second, Planned Parenthood was having a rally for "abortion-rights" in front of the State Capitol.

So, in the middle of the week, and on short notice, I was able to pull together eleven people to take our slogan and question signs, first to the NOW rally, then to the Planned Parenthood rally. With the NOW activists and college students we had some good conversations. With the Planned parenthood demonstrators (adults with professionally vested interests), it was a different story.

There were two hundred of them at Beacon and Park, in the conclave of the steps to the Capitol. We stood in their midst with our signs, and everyone was looking at them, or trying not to look at them, and all the media focused on them – the four commercial television stations plus WGBH Public Television, and a host of radio stations. And many of our people got elbows in the ribs or other unfriendly bodily contact at this, a heavily advertised public rally where "all are welcome."

I was interviewed on camera for 45-50 minutes by a senior reporter for WGBH, who went from professional distance to intellectual curiosity and respect, to genuine warmth. I was not her stereotype of a pro-life activist, son of a physician, ex-Unitarian, father of four, and post-grad student at Harvard. She told me that I was going to be the "Newsmaker" interview for the 10:00 p.m. news. At 9:45, she called our home, was emotionally stressed, and said that the segment could not air because there were "problems in the taping room."

She had been overruled I am sure, for they had a boatload of videotape, and the phone call did not come until very shortly before airtime. I surmise that her boss could not splice the tapes to make me say something I was not saying (I do not use stereotypical language or clichés, and I always speak of women and their unborn equally), or make me appear as an angry or clueless chauvinist in some capacity. And too, the signs speak for themselves.

At 11:00 p.m. we looked for coverage on the other four television stations, and were able to come across two reports. In the one which we saw in full, it said that there were 200 people on each side of the debate (we were only eleven plus several other pro-lifers who happened to be there). But the funny part was this – the television angle shot, designed to show the size of the crowd so as to flatter Planned Parenthood was taken from ground level, aiming through the people to the speaker with the Capitol in the background. We could see all the poles of our signs, but not the signs themselves. The pro-abortion media is deathly afraid of the power to love hard questions.

Running for Governor

At this same event, I crossed paths with Bill Weld. He was running for governor and was working the crowd. And I joined a discussion he was having with a friend of mine who headed up InterVarsity Christian Fellowship at Brown University. In the course of the three-way discussion, I made mention the biological humanity of the unborn, and that it begins at the moment of conception. So he quizzed me directly, asking me if I could prove it, with an incisive focus. So I gave a brief and succinct overview of the haploid spermatozoon fertilizing the haploid ovum, and producing a diploid cell which equals a biologically discrete and whole human being. As I did, I saw a spiritual darkness palpably descend upon him, he said not a word, and immediately turned away and began to seek votes elsewhere. Weld succeeded in his run for governor, as a Republican against Boston University president, and Democrat, John Silber, and Weld won by a narrow margin that was supplied by pro-abortion and pro-homosexual advocates.

The President of NOW

In 1990 or 1991, the president of the national NOW, Molly Yard, addressed a rally at Stage Fort Park in Gloucester, Massachusetts, and we learned of it a day-and-a-half beforehand. I then lived one town over, in Manchester, and along with Rockport (where I lived for nine prior years), and Essex, these four municipalities equals what is called Cape Ann, on the North Shore of Boston jutting out into the Atlantic Ocean.

Molly Yard was on a national bus tour to "rally" support for abortion-rights. The tour brought her to Stage Fort Park, and its beautiful vista of Gloucester harbor and the ocean. It was a blustery day, and about 100 supporters for NOW showed up, and with an ad hoc phone-tree on short notice, we saw 80 pro-lifers turn out. We simply stood around the perimeter, with one banner and the signs, and said nothing.

I was not the only organizer of the event (the local leader of the Birthright center was the other), but I asked our people to quietly stand, be gracious, receive any opportunity to speak with NOW partisans that might happen, listen to the NOW event and learn from it. One deeply committed Christian woman was so excited because she had never been to such an event. It multiplied her confidence in the Gospel to hear the president of NOW speak – to experience first-hand the intellectual, moral and political paucity of the abortion-rights argument, and also to witness the anti-Christian nature of the abortion-rights argument.

I was holding one of the poles that held up the banner, bracing it continually against the wind. Our presence unsettled the NOW organizers and Molly Yard specially, not being disruptive. We were only exercising our

First Amendment liberties to be in attendance at a public event on public land, and we respected the fact that they organized the meeting and wished to address their supporters and others.

Some NOW supporters turned and looked at our signs, but most refused (at least noticeably). Had I organized an event for my Christian and pro-life purposes, and NOW or other protesters of my advocacy were to show up in similar fashion, I would be overjoyed that they cared enough to be there with a contrary vantage-point. I would have invited their leader or leaders to the podium to give me their questions directly.

In the middle of her talk, Molly Yard got frustrated, and looked straight at me and the banner, and yelled, "You say that we have the power to choose life? You're damned right we do – women's lives!" And her people gave a cheer that was not wholehearted.

The banner does not just affirm unborn human life, but it affirms women's lives and all lives, in its simple inclusiveness. The understatement of our presence and this slogan made it hard for her and her supporters to demonize us. She needed us to exclude women somehow – but we do not. I clearly sensed that she was dissatisfied at the response of the crowd, and how she was thus deflated a bit as she continued her speech. And we never said a word. The visual power to love hard questions.

The Attorney General and the "Bubble Zone"

In early 1991, the Attorney General James Shannon, announced intention to recommend laws to create a "bubble zone" around abortion facilities (there were three major ones in the Boston area at the time, on Beacon Street in Brookline, Preterm, Repro and Planned Parenthood). This was the first such initiative in the nation which sought to restrict pro-lifers from getting close enough to communicate with abortion-minded women. Sadly, this came pass largely in a reaction to Operation Rescue.

Shannon, of course, blocked our 1988 referendum by sheer political muscle and intrigue, aided by our inexperience. He knew he screwed us. When I saw the report of his intentions, I wrote him a letter, sent by certified mail. He also knew our reputation at Preterm, where we were never bothered by the law (the Brookline police publicly commended us) or even accused by any partisan for our conduct. In my letter, I told him that if he were to give a legal opinion in favor of such bubble zones, I would file lawsuit. He backed off this initiative shortly thereafter, but never answered me formally.

But alas, we were just months away from corporate bankruptcy, being thereafter unable to continue our work at Preterm. We had been driven into the ground by witchcraft and demonic powers that began to assault us when we filed our petitions in 1988, and intensified in front of the abortion centers. This reality has been a crushing reality ever since, even in the writing of this book. And that leads us to the next chapter.

The South Bronx

Many years later I was able to organize another SAU, in April, 2014, at the Planned Parenthood center in the South Bronx, New York City. It was a spiritual struggle to make it happen, that which has made it nearly impossible since 1991. There were ten of us on a fairly chilly Saturday morning.

Now, this was an entirely different world than that at Preterm in the heyday of the activist debate. The discernible response was very positive among the many passersby (heavy traffic on the road and sidewalk there), with only one exception. Planned Parenthood serves a mostly minority population in the South Bronx, indeed, in service to the very high ratio of abortions among Black Americans.

Not long after we arrived, an emissary from Planned Parenthood (inside the larger office building) came and asked us how long we were going to be there. And they returned once or twice later to ask us again. We could see, on several or more occasions, young women walking toward us, then turning away or walking past, and judging by their body language, they were nervous to begin with. I have no doubt that the visuals of these signs alone continue to be enormous in impact.

In Sum

The Sacred Assemblies for the Unborn (SAU) ratify the *God* → *life* → *choice* → *sex* versus *sex* → *choice* → *life* →*/God* reversal in the teeth of public activism. It also highlights the realities of the power of informed choice in the true definition of terms, and defining the driving reality of male chauvinism in the abortion ethos.

They celebrate the power to love hard questions at ground zero of society's linchpin sin, to love all our neighbors equally rooted in God's love, and accordingly, pace the power of informed choice, separates out the "pro-choice" and the "pro-abortion" among themselves. The former open up to one degree or another, whereas the latter refuse, and choose to silence themselves instead.

If enough of the remnant church were to employ this strategy consistent with a lived biblical theology, and we could be present at all abortion centers nationwide, we would hugely cut the abortion rate. And this is prior to winning the legal protection of women and their unborn. It also means the need for multiplied support for the Crisis Pregnancy Centers (and cognates) that minister to the hurting, and to the reform of the whole culture vis-à-vis the faithfulness of men to women in marriage.

Then, on outward. Can you imagine how we can change the language of the abortion debate if these signs, in concert with prayer, worship and conversation with skeptics, were found on every university campus nationwide? And the opportunities to minister Jesus to such a broken world? Or in the presence of pro-abortion politicians? Let's do it.

◆ ◆ ◆

Chapter Nine

Encounters with Sorcery at the Right Hand of Power

My baptism into the realities of opposition witchcraft and demonic assaults began on August 3, 1988, when we submitted our pro-life petitions to the Massachusetts Secretary of State.

Earlier we noted how, in John 1:5, the darkness of the devil can neither comprehend nor overcome (*katalambano*) the light of Jesus. I know this, yet too, my family and I have been through a literal hell from 1988 to the present because I stepped on the devil's tail without knowing it at the time. How to make sense of all this?

Let me first go back sixteen years prior, when I may have inadvertently crossed paths with *Satan* himself.

Light and Dark in St. Michael's Chapel

I was raised in the Unitarian Universalist church. My father, a Nebraska native of Presbyterian stock, with a long line of abolitionist ministers, served in the Pacific as a Navy Physician at the end of World War II. He married my mother, a Los Angeles girl, after returning stateside, and they moved to Connecticut to do his residency.

He could not endure the Presbyterian church he settled in, finding it "insufferably judgmental." So he went to the Congregational Church in town, very large, and nationally feted in "liberal" theological circles. But, alas, the minister was caught in adultery, a huge scandal ensued, and my father moved on to the Unitarian Universalist Church in town. There he found the minister to be a) "intelligent and worth listening to," and b) faithful to his wife.

My father was a theist (he wrestled with the Trinity and theodicy, the question of suffering), but he did not know that my Sunday School teachers were agnostic. They were very skeptical of the Bible and taught me the same. To be skeptical is good, if in pursuit of the truth, but these skepticisms struck me as explaining away too much, or protesting too hard. Thus I became a skeptic of the skepticisms I was taught. So though I was a self-conscious agnostic (in the positive sense of not knowing but wanting to know) by the summer of 1967 at age fourteen, I had always been amazed by the universe and my own existence in it. That September I began ninth grade ("third form") at South Kent School, a small boarding school for boys in the Housatonic highlands of western Connecticut. South Kent had a daily chapel schedule pace the Episcopal liturgy.

Chapel was required, but I determined not to participate, saying to myself, "I don't believe this stuff." So I did not sing, recite, pray, genuflect or take communion. But that proved a "dangerous" thing to do. For while other students were participating, outwardly, at one level or another, I ended up occupying my mind reading the words of the liturgy and hymns, as they were recited and sung. I was interested in the possible existence of God.

On November 1, I was standing outside the chapel in the interlude before walking down the hill to dinner. As the air pricked my spine, I felt alive. It was delightfully cold, and in those rural hills the Milky Way was exceptionally clear that evening – like a white paint stroke against a black canvas. I considered its awesome grandeur and beauty, and then I posed to myself this sequence of thought:

If there is a God, then he must have made all this for a purpose, and that purpose must include my existence, and it must include the reason I am asking this question. And if this is true, then I need to get plugged into him.

I wanted to know either way, and I was convinced that if there were a God, then it would be most natural to become rooted in my origins. But I wanted verification. The "if" clauses were real.

This was a commitment to myself, in the sight of the universe, in the sight of a possible God. It was in fact a prayer to an unknown God.

One or several evenings later I was the first student into chapel, taking my assigned seating in the small balcony. As I sat down, and looked forward in the empty sanctuary, I said under my breath, "Good evening God." Immediately I retorted to myself, "Wait a minute John. You don't even know if there is a God. How can you say 'good evening' to him?"

But also immediately I became aware of a reality that was prior to and deeper than the intellect, of a truth that held the answer to any and all of my questions. There was a God, I knew deep within me, and I knew that I had just lied to myself by saying I did not know, even though it was only now that I knew I knew. My heart knew before my mind knew, but as part of the whole that my mind was now grasping. I had yet to speak it (see Romans 10:9-10).

In this moment, God's presence ratified the reality of my belief as I simultaneously discerned a Presence literally hovering over me, filling the entire balcony. And critically, this Presence was waiting for my response – a powerful, warm, inviting and embracing cloud. This all happened within a moment's time, and I realized that I did believe. No sooner had I exhaled my agnostic retort, did I then inhale and say, "Yes I do (believe)." As I did, this literal presence of God descended upon and filled my entire being – mind, body, spirit and emotions.

Now I knew nothing at the time of the Spirit "brooding" or "hovering" over the waters in Genesis 1:2, nor of the divine name and nature of *Yahweh Elohim*'s presence and glory, as experienced by the Israelites in the exodus community with the tabernacle (e.g., Exodus 40:34-38), and later in Solomon's temple (1 Kings 8:6-12). Yet the grace of God came into my life that November evening, as he but gently crossed my path with a touch of his presence. I asked an intellectual question in view of an awesome universe, and was answered by the presence of the awesome Creator. Light came into darkness.

In remarkable contrast, I had an experience in that same chapel four-and-a-half years later, in the spring of 1972 (I enjoyed the third form/ninth grade so much I took it twice). The chapel's name, interestingly, is St. Michael's, named after the warring angel who defeats *Satan* in Revelation 12:7-9.

362

I was up late one evening in the dining room of the Old Building doing some work when a friend burst in, horrified, on me and several other seniors. He described to us in halting breaths how he had been waiting in the chapel for another friend to finish some work in the adjacent library. As he was, the communion bells rang out three times from the balcony. Thinking he was being spoofed by someone, he called out for the prankster to reveal himself. Silence. So he climbed the wooden stairs to the balcony, searched it, and nobody was there. There was no place to hide apart from where he searched, no other stairs, and all footsteps in that small chapel were most audible. A sense of abiding and evil darkness overtook him, and he fled in horror down the hill to the Old Building.

I was the only one of the several seniors there who took him seriously (or was willing to admit it). But too, I more recently learned that the friend he was waiting for had a similar experience some weeks earlier. He was in the chapel late one evening, keeping track of some under-formers in an adjacent building. Then the chapel bell rang three times, no one on the campus heard it, and a dark and foreboding sense of evil came in.

In my young faith, I believed there was nothing to fear, so I suggested we return to the chapel and investigate. It was just past midnight, and as we came within 20-30 feet of the chapel, we both looked into the windows. What we saw was a darkness that was blacker than black against the diffused light of nearby buildings, pulsating, alive, extraordinarily evil and very angry at our presence. Another step and we stopped, having come against a terribly tangible but invisible wall of air that was thicker than thick, impenetrable and driving us back. All my critical faculties were alert, and the experience was as real as anything I have known with the five senses. My friend and I turned and fled. I prayed until 4:00 a.m., trying to understand it.

This story has been shared with various others over the years, including the headmaster some forty years after the fact. He had no doubt as to its reality (he lived fifty yards away at the time).

One clue to what was happening is that the "witching hour" is known to happen when, especially, covens of witches, those into the deepest witchcraft, regularly meet to do their rituals and to curse their enemies (Friday midnight to Saturday 3:00 a.m.), especially Christians. They also prefer certain special days and seasons on their pagan calendars, related ultimately to astrological factors. This evil presence was gathering just before midnight when my friend was initially spoofed, and it may have been proximate to May Day, one such pagan holiday, but at the time I did not know to consider this element. As well, the Housatonic Highlands of western Connecticut, and especially the adjoining Berkshire Hills of Massachusetts, are well-known for concentrations of such activity.

I was blown away by the experience at the time. The very chapel where the supernatural presence of *Yahweh Elohim* descended on me in 1967 was the very chapel where this demonic presence bearing the mark of *Satan* himself assaulted my friend and me in 1972. The contest of the darkness seeking to displace the Light. And as it turns out, there is a history to the graveyard behind St. Michael's Chapel, and who is buried there – the widow of the reputed Jack the Ripper, exiled and alone, had lived nearby, and was taken care of by members of the school community.

For the next sixteen years this subject was not in focus. I enjoyed the intellectual discipline at seminary, and had no expectations of spiritual warfare as I entered pro-life ministry.

Now to fast forward to some later biblical understandings, that I only began to formulate after what I ran into in 1988.

Sorcery at the Right Hand of Power

In the biblical contest between light and dark, there are three domains – physics, ethics and spiritual warfare. In the former, light exists atomically, and darkness has no such existence, thus by definition, darkness flees the presence of light. In the middle category, when we live openly and in accountability, those who hide their intentions and action flee our presence. And in the latter, Jesus is the Light of the world, *Satan* is the prince of darkness, thus the devil flees the presence of Jesus.

Yet the devil is able to take opportunity of any and every sphere where we allow any measure of ethical and spiritual darkness into our lives.

Throughout the Bible, *Satan*'s agenda is to pervert political power so that it can subvert the Messianic promise, seeking to find darkness in the human soul in which to establish a beachhead. Accordingly, "sorcery at the right hand of power" reflects a reality where demonic counsel seeks access to political power in order shut down unalienable rights for all people equally, to shut down religious, political and economic liberty. Such liberty is uniquely the gift God, revealed fully in the biblical order of creation on forward in Scripture; and wherever such liberty flourishes, the Gospel flourishes, and vice versa. (In the hierarchy of demonic powers Paul identifies in Ephesians 6, these would specifically be the *kosmoskratoras*, or if you will, the "cosmoscrats," serving the higher evil powers all the way up to *Satan*.)

Elsewhere I write about the origin and nature of the devil. For here, my purpose is to serve a biblical strategy to win the legal protection of women and their unborn equally. Thus, I will focus on the interface of spiritual warfare as applicable to this context.

The theme of sorcery at the right hand of power can be itemized in ten select biblical texts. The theme percolates across the whole Bible, including:

1. the Egyptian sorcerers advising Pharaoh against Moses and Aaron;
2. the pagan prophet Bala'am's hired opposition to the Israelites during the Exodus;
3. the Sidonian queen and witch Jezebel's influence over King Ahab against Elijah, and against the other prophets whom she killed or sought to kill;
4. the witch at Endor being sought out for counsel by King Saul;
5. the Babylonian sorcerers in their counsel to Nebuchadnezzar in opposing Daniel;
6. the Amalekite and political opportunist Haman's advice to King Xerxes, in opposing Mordecai and Esther, in the plot to kill all the Jews in the Medo-Persian empire;

7. the high priest Caiaphas in his counsel to the Sanhedrin to seek to have King Herod kill Jesus;
8. the other religious and political elitists of Jesus behaving as children of the devil and "sons of hell" in their plots to kill Jesus;
9. the Jewish sorcerer Elymas in his counsel to the governor of Cyprus, seeking to turn him away from the apostle Paul's preaching; and
10. in the Book of Revelation, the spirit of Bala'am against the church at Pergamum, alongside the false prophetess Jezebel in the church at Thyatira.

Let's take a brief look at each.

Moses and the Egyptian Sorcerers

When Moses first attempts to rescue the Israelites from Pharaoh's enslavement, he does so in an act of murder, and has to flee for his life (see Exodus 2:11ff). Forty years later, when *Yahweh* calls him to do it by the power of the Spirit, the humility of his exile allows him to be used of the Lord. His confrontation turns out not to be a matter of human strength – as though he could raise up a human army to overcome Pharaoh's military might. No, the contest is in the spiritual domains, in the war between demons and holy angels. And the means of the devil is to have proxies, most particularly, sorcerers at the right hand of power.

Pharaoh is supported by such occultic power, and this is the real battle Moses faces. The first time Moses and Aaron confront Pharaoh with the words from *Yahweh*, "Let my people go" (Exodus 5:1), the whole conflict is handled in terms of human strength – Pharaoh multiplying the workload for the Israelites.

The second time, the spiritual contest is engaged. In Exodus 7:8-13, the Egyptian sorcerers mimic a miracle performed by Moses and Aaron, making their staffs become snakes – but the staff of Aaron swallows up their staffs.

Though Aaron's staff is superior, we see how Pharaoh relies on the wise men, sorcerers and magicians (all referring to the interfacing names

366

describing counselors trained in pagan religion and occultic power). This is sorcery at the right hand of power, where the devil has one defining goal, namely, the killing of the Messianic lineage. The word "occult" means that which is hidden or obscured, that which is not in the light; and exactly the nature of the "flaming blades" (the literal Hebrew *hashim*, in Exodus 7:11, occurring in the plural, with its supernatural warrior imagery) or otherwise rendered, "secret arts" of the Egyptian magicians.

In their fifth visit to Pharaoh in Exodus 8:16-19, we have the last stand of the occultic power, where the Egyptian sorcerers cannot mimic the miracle performed by Moses and Aaron. They have to say to Pharaoh, "This is the finger of *Elohim*."

Yet despite the obvious superiority of *Yahweh* and his delegates, the devil is unrelenting in his agenda. He directly and indirectly seeks to influence political leaders in order to kill the Messianic lineage. They live in the darkness, and they rely on occultic arts or secret counsel in order to oppose the good.

The Saga of Bala'am

In Numbers 22-24, Balak, king of Moab, seeks to use sorcery to curse Moses and the Israelites at the outset of- their exodus from slavery in Egypt. He sends emissaries to Bala'am, a sorcerer from Babylon, offering him "the fee for divination." Balak and Bala'am are syncretists, viewing all gods as local and tribalistic in nature, and that through divination, these gods can be bought for venal purposes.

Bala'am treats *Elohim* of Israel this way, but *Yahweh Elohim* will not be bought, and tells him not to curse Israel. Thus Bala'am refuses Balak's initial offer. But Balak then sends more distinguished emissaries, with a greater financial lure. Here Bala'am resorts to his manipulative ways of sorcery, seeking to see "what else" *Yahweh* might say.

In Genesis 18, *Yahweh Elohim* allows Abraham to repeatedly intercede on behalf of those in Sodom and Gomorrah, in a conversational reality of how

Yahweh Elohim treats us as his image bearers, created to govern wisely. Bala'am is at the other extreme in his purposes, yet too he is given the same freedom in *Yahweh*'s sight. Thus, to educate Bala'am in the truth, *Yahweh Elohim* affirms Bala'am's request and allows him to go with the emissaries, "but only do what I speak to you."

However, as Bala'am departs the next morning, he is opposed by the angel of *Yahweh*, whom he does not see, but whom his donkey sees. And here we read the well-known story of *Yahweh* speaking through the donkey to restrain the sorcerer's recklessness. Namely, we reap what we sow, and we may press the Lord for something, which he gives us only to show us reality and hopefully lead us to repentance.

So Bala'am is able to continue on. But in each of the three times he tries to curse Israel in Balak's presence, *Yahweh* only allows him to bless Israel more each time. Balak is furious, yet Bala'am, as constrained by *Yahweh*, gives another oracle that promises the Messiah, followed by oracles concerning the Amalekites and Kenites. He then goes "his own way" without any payment.

However, even though *Yahweh Elohim* restrains Bala'am and reverses Balak's intention to curse Israel, the sorcerer does not trade in his old ways. He then gains his income by organizing a strategy to seduce the Israelite men via Moabite women into sexual promiscuity and idolatry (see Numbers 25:1ff in concert with 2 Peter 2:15 and Revelation 2:14).

Saul and the Witch at Endor

From the time of Joshua, the successor of Moses, Israel is led by a series of judges. They are local men (or a woman in the case of Deborah) who follow the Law of Moses where *Yahweh* is King. Among the judges there are those who are faithful to *Yahweh* and the Law, and those who are unfaithful. The final judge is Samuel (see the whole book of 1 Samuel), the epitome of a good judge like Joshua. But his sons squander his leadership, and in the vacuum, Israel starts to call for a human king in the pagan sense.

Thus, they reject *Yahweh*, and Saul becomes king. He proves venal and self-serving, but he does rid Israel of all the mediums and spiritists consistent with the Law. Then, near the end of his life, he is fearful of the Philistine army, he has been repeatedly rebuked by Samuel before his death, and also rebuked by David's example. The gathering storm of judgment is approaching his soul, he has walled himself off from hearing from *Yahweh*, and in his desperation he disguises himself and seeks out a medium, a witch, looking for advice on how to keep his political power (1 Samuel 28).

Saul finds a witch in Endor who is in hiding from his edict. She is fearful, but heeds his request to call up Samuel. When Samuel shows up, by *Yahweh*'s intervention, the witch shrieks. She knows her ruse is foiled (not expecting the real Samuel to show up), she realizes who Saul is, and in the end Samuel rebukes Saul again. In other words, Saul rebukes sorcery at the right hand of power initially, but he also rebukes *Yahweh*'s prophet, and at his desperate end, uses sorcery to try and call for Samuel's help beyond the grave. Saul's death soon follows – sorcery at the right hand of power does not bring life.

The Saga of Ahab and Jezebel

Between 1 Kings 16 and 2 Kings 19, we have the remarkable saga of Ahab and Jezebel. Following Israel's rebellion against Solomon's son Rehoboam (see 1 Kings 12), the Israelites are divided into the southern and northern kingdoms. The southern kingdom is known as Judah, with the capital of King David's city, Jerusalem. The northern kingdom is known as Israel, with the capital at Samaria. Among the kings of the north, most are unfaithful to the Law of Moses, and increasingly so.

The Assyrians destroy the northern kingdom in 721 B.C., all the people are scattered among the Gentile nations, and among their descendants are the Samaritans. Among the kings of the south, many are unfaithful to the Law of Moses, but some are faithful or very faithful. And following the destruction of Jerusalem and Judah by the Babylonians in 586 B.C., the remnant is the Jews (Judahites), out of whom Jesus comes.

Ahab is a northern king, and he is introduced in 1 Kings 16:28-33 as more evil than his father. He marries a pagan queen, Jezebel, who leads him to worship the Canaanite god *Ba'al*.

As *Yahweh* instructs Moses, the reason for the existence of Israel is its nature to be a nation "set apart" (the meaning of the word "holy," *qadosh* in the Hebrew and *hagios* in the Greek) to *Yahweh Elohim*. Thus, they are to be set apart from pagan nations and their religions which only pollute the truth with their devotion to sorcery, sacred prostitution and, at the extreme, child sacrifice.

Thus, it is a great evil for Ahab to marry a pagan queen, who turns out herself to be a sorceress, guilty of "witchcraft" (2 Kings 9:22). The devil is working on the destruction of the Messianic remnant, and here by bringing sorcery to the right hand of power in the person of Jezebel.

Yet *Yahweh* always sends his prophets to provide godly counsel at the right hand of power. This is what Moses offers Pharaoh. And in the days of Ahab and Jezebel, *Yahweh* sends many prophets to hold Ahab accountable, especially Elijah.

Jezebel's influence is seen in 1 Kings 18 as she has an agenda to "cut off *Yahweh*'s prophets," and yet Obadiah, who serves in the court of Ahab, rescues 100 of these prophets at his own cost and risk. In the storyline that follows, Elijah's counsel is rejected by Ahab, except momentarily, when he gets scared. Elijah is the thorn in the side to Jezebel. He challenges the 450 pagan prophets of *Ba'al*, and the 400 pagan prophets of *Asherah* "who eat at Jezebel's table." In other words, these are 850 sorcerers in service to a lead witch who manipulates the king of Israel. Sorcery at the right hand of power.

Elijah is powerfully successful in this challenge, as *Yahweh* shows up in dynamic power on Mount Carmel. Yet afterward, when Jezebel threatens to kill him, he flees. The devil is the prince of darkness, so how and why does the prophet of the light flee darkness? Only because Elijah believes a lie about Jezebel's power, which is to say, allowing some darkness of fear to enter his soul. Whereas darkness by definition has no existence and power, we give it power when we do not live fully in the light ourselves.

As the story unfolds, Jezebel urges Ahab onto great evil, Elijah rebukes him, and Ahab repents briefly. But then he refuses the counsel of *Yahweh*'s prophet, Micaiah, and this leads to his death. Jezebel outlives Ahab, but ultimately dies an ugly death of her own doing.

Daniel and the Sorcerers of Babylon

The Book of Daniel is remarkable in many ways, and as we have already reviewed. The devil is delighted that the city of Jerusalem, its temple to *Yahweh* and the remnant nation of Judah, are under assault by the Babylonian empire prior to and especially from the beginning of King Nebuchadnezzar's reign in 605 B.C. The complete destruction occurs in 586 B.C. In 605, he deports a portion of the Judahite nobility to Babylon, "young men," with the purpose of training them in the religion, culture and politics of Babylon.

Thus, the relentless demonic war against the Messianic lineage continues. The devil's goal is to actually co-opt some of *Yahweh*'s prophets into becoming themselves sorcerers at the right hand of power, a "fifth column" to help destroy the Messianic lineage. It backfires.

Daniel and his three friends, Hananiah, Mishael and Azariah (better known by their given Babylonian names, Shadrach, Meshach and Abednego) are among those deported. They excel, especially Daniel, in all they do, maintaining fidelity to the Law of Moses while learning "all kinds of literature and learning" (1:17). This includes the practices of sorcery. In other words, they are gifted to learn about the nasty "flaming blades," the "secret arts" of pagan religion, and yet they are not seduced by it. Indeed, as light dispels the darkness, they are in control, even though they are slaves.

But as it turns out, these slaves – through *Yahweh*'s redemptive power to use human weakness in the face of demonic strength – end up in high ruling positions within Babylon, helping to preserve the Messianic remnant. A reversal of the reversal.

In chapter 2, when the "magicians (or engravers), conjurers (or enchanters), sorcerers (or magicians) and astrologers (or magicians)" – all interfacing terms, they behave like sycophants, desperately clinging to their elitist positions, their positions of sorcery at the right hand of power. Daniel then becomes the "godly counsel at the right hand of power," revealing then giving the interpretation.

In chapter 3, the same sorcerers try to have Daniel's three friends killed, but they are rescued by an angel of God and vindicated.

In chapter 4, Daniel again interprets a dream for the king, one that leads to his judgment. During King Nebuchadnezzar's seven-year exile of madness, demonically driven no doubt, Daniel the slave becomes the de facto ruler of the Babylonian empire. Here we see the reversal of the reversal, the power to give and the power to live in the light overtaking the power to take and the power of the occult. And as a result, Nebuchadnezzar repents of his sins and proclaims Daniel's God to be the true God.

In chapter 10, the demonic powers are behind political evil (see the "prince of Persia" and "prince of Greece" language in 10:13, 20). This is the contest between light and darkness, between sorcery at the right hand of power and God's power to raise up godly counsel at the right hand of power. In the United States today, or in other nations too, how many truly Spirit-filled counselors or prophets are even known to those in high political power? Who in the church would be called on today as Nebuchadnezzar calls on Daniel?

Esther, Mordecai and Haman

The relentless war of the devil against the Messianic lineage continues. In the Book of Esther, ca. 460 B.C., about 80 years after the end of the Babylonian empire and some 70 or so years after the passing of Daniel, the devil attempts to wipe out all the remnant Jews in the Medo-Persian empire (which means about half of worldwide Jewry at the time), again through a chosen proxy.

The story begins with how *Yahweh* raises up godly counsel at the right hand of power – as a Jewess named Hadassah, who goes by her Persian name Esther, becomes queen, the wife of King Xerxes. Her cousin Mordecai raised her after her parents died.

Mordecai, who holds a high position in the civil service, overhears an assassination plot against the king, and informs Esther. The plot is foiled, and Mordecai's role is recorded "in the book of annals in the presence of the king" (2:23).

Yet in an apparent disjunctive, King Xerxes thereafter elevates a previously unknown man, an Amalekite named Haman, to "a seat of honor higher than that of all the chieftians" (3:1). The king then commands all his officials to bow down to Haman, but Mordecai, a Jew who knows the history of the Amalekite attempt to wipe out the Israelites during the Exodus, refuses to do so. This Amalekite attempt is part of the devil's unrelenting agenda. In the face of Mordecai's continued refusal, Haman becomes enraged and learns that Mordecai is a Jew.

Accordingly, Haman directly influences King Xerxes to set into motion an extravagant plot to kill all the Jews in the kingdom. Sorcery at the right hand of power. Mordecai is mortified with the news and counsels Esther to risk her life and appeal to the king. This Esther does with great tact and wisdom and succeeds in gaining the king's favor. The result is that Mordecai is publicly honored, Haman's plot is reversed, the edict to kill the Jews is thwarted, Haman is hanged on the gallows he has prepared for Mordecai, his estate goes to Esther, and Mordecai is given Haman's office. Thus, we witness the reversal of the reversal and the establishment of godly counsel at the right hand of power. The Messianic lineage is protected.

Jesus, in the Face of His Enemies

Jesus is consistently stalked and plotted against by his sworn enemies – Jewish leaders who become de facto children of the devil – the quintessence of sorcery at the right hand of power. This I write about elsewhere in depth, a summary of which we will review in Chapter Ten.

Paul, a Jewish Sorcerer and a Roman Governor

In Acts 13:1-12, we read of another conflict between a servant of the Light and sorcery at the right hand of power, as Barnabas and Saul (soon to go by his Roman name, Paul) travel to Cyprus preaching the Gospel. They are invited to an audience with the proconsul (governor), Sergius Paulus, who is "an intelligent man." But they are opposed by the governor's attendant, a Jewish sorcerer (an oxymoron), Bar-Jesus, also known as Elymas.

In this conflict, Paul identifies Elymas as "a child of the devil," that is, the offspring of the ancient serpent in Genesis 3. Thus we have great evil at play, where Elymas has forsaken the God of Israel, sold his soul to the devil, and has wormed his way into being the attendant, the right hand man to the Roman governor of Cyprus. So often, as human history shows, the power behind the throne is what drives public policy – as we have foundationally seen in the biblical profile of Jezebel and the Babylonian sorcerers.

Elymas tries to turn the governor away from the faith. The reputation of Barnabas and Paul precedes them, and Sergius Paulus wants to hear the Gospel. It is reasonable to assume that what the governor does is to instruct Elymas to invite Paul and Barnabas to his home. Elymas thus twists between a need to obey the proconsul's order, while at the same time trying to dissuade him from becoming a Christian.

We can imagine Paul and Barnabas standing there in a formal reception, with Elymas standing next to the governor, trying to give him – by body language, hints or explicit words – reasons to reject the Gospel. Then the explosion of light into the sorcerer's dark world.

Paul will have none of it. He speaks in the power of the Holy Spirit and tells this proxy deceiver that he will be blind for a season. When light is too bright for our mortal frames, we become blinded. And for Elymas this is also an act of mercy. He is explicit in his opposition to the truth, and now his blindness tests his misplaced faith. His chosen spiritual darkness now becomes a physical blindness. He is a) removed from his polluting influence of the governor, and b) as he is led about by the hand, he is given a season to consider leaving his service to the prince of darkness, and instead serve the Light of the world. Sorcery at the right hand of power crushed.

The Spirits of Bala'am and Jezebel in the Early Church

In Revelation 2:14-16, the church at Pergamum is rebuked for people in their midst who hold to the teaching of Bala'am, with the attendant idolatry and sexual immorality. In 2:18-25, the church at Thyatira is rebuked for tolerating "that woman Jezebel, who speaks of herself as a prophetess." She is an adulteress who leads people into sexual immorality and idolatry, and teaches "the deep sayings of *Satan*." In other words, sorcery within the church, which denudes any authority for the church to produce godly counsel at the right hand of power; sorcery with the same effect as what Bala'am and Jezebel did to Israel.

In All These Sagas

The devil has a cardinal purpose across history, and that is to shut down human life, made in God's image and redeemed in Jesus the Messiah, and he uses political power consistently as his proxy.

Joseph, Jesus and Paul: Warnings of Danger and Strategic Wisdom

When we read the Gospels, we see the angels of God warning Joseph to watch out for certain dangers, and we see Jesus perceiving danger and moving out of its way, while also skirting it ever so closely, until it is his timetable to go to Jerusalem. When we read Acts, we see the Holy Spirit warning Paul of certain dangers, and Paul heeds the warnings while also embracing the necessary dangers in his Spirit-led agenda to go to Jerusalem and Rome.

A robust biblical theology understands the sovereignty of the Creator, *Yahweh Elohim*, and the fullness of his investment in Adam and Eve as his image-bearers. They are given authority over the creation, under *Yahweh*, with freedom to govern accordingly. We are neither puppets of capricious deities as with pagan religion; nor are we abandoned to our own license in a cold and hostile universe as with a secular worldview. The biblical reality is that *Yahweh Elohim* is sovereign, thus we in humility are able to acknowledge our thankfulness for the gift of life with its many blessings, and worship him. The biblical reality also is that we are made free by the sovereign *Yahweh* to be fully responsible in all our actions, reaping what we sow as we experience his infinite nature of creativity and order given into our finite frames. This balance is the only basis for a healthy human psychology.

The first Adam has full authority over creation, reneges on it when he does not judge the ancient serpent, and Jesus as the second Adam restores that authority to his disciples in a still broken world. To grow in the knowledge of this authority is key to an overcoming Christian life.

Joseph

In Matthew 2:13ff, an angel appears to Joseph, warning him to flee to Egypt to protect the young Jesus, Mary and himself from the coming rampage of King Herod. Then, upon returning from Egypt after Herod's death (vv. 19ff), Joseph is warned in a dream to settle in Galilee (next to the Gentiles), and thus away from Herod's son Archelaus. He follows through in thus acting wisely.

Jesus

In the gospels, Jesus is relentlessly opposed by the religious and political elitists, as they seek to kill him. But Jesus is not going to let it happen until he is ready to die as the Passover Lamb, outside the walls of Jerusalem, on his timetable. Thus, on many occasions, he changes his travel plans so as not to allow his enemies to arrest and kill him ahead of time. This is especially the case in the gospel of John.

In John 2, Jesus comes to the feast in Jerusalem, but only in a way so as not to draw too much publicity. In John 6:15, Jesus withdraws from the crowd so as not to be forcibly made king by the people. In John 7:1ff, Jesus purposely stays away from Judea and Jerusalem, knowing that certain Jewish elitists are waiting to take his life. But then later he comes on his timetable, without the public fanfare that so often follows him. This does lead to a conflict where his enemies try to arrest him, but in the face of his authority, "no one put a hand on him" (7:44).

In John 8:59, after Jesus declares he is the I AM, and his enemies try to stone him, "Jesus concealed himself, going out of the temple." In John 10:31, his enemies try again to stone him, but he thwarts their intent with his words; then in v. 39, "again they tried to take him, but he escaped their hands." Finally, when Jesus is arrested – on his timetable en route to the cross – as he speaks the words "I AM" (*ego eimi* in the Greek, from *Ehyeh* in the Hebrew), Judas, along with the officials from the chief priests and Pharisees, and the detachment of soldiers "pulled back and fell to the ground" (John 18:6). True power is powerful when used wisely, and this we see in Jesus.

Paul

In Acts 16:6ff, Paul is warned by the Spirit of Jesus not to travel to the province of Asia and neighboring Bithynia, and instead has a vision to go to Macedonia. In Acts 18, in the face of opposition in Corinth, Paul is encouraged to stay and minister in the city, as the Lord speaks to him in a vision, "Have no fear, keep on speaking, do not be silent. For I am with you, and no one is going to attack and harm you, because I have many people in this city" (18:9-10). In the riot at Ephesus (20:23ff), Paul wants to appear before the crowd, but his friends and the local officials persuade him otherwise.

In Acts 21, Paul's friends urge him not to go to Jerusalem, and the prophet Agabus (vv. 10-11) warns him of the imprisonment that awaits him. But it is God's will for Paul to testify in both Jerusalem and Rome, so he goes, knowing the cost (see Acts 9:15-16; 23:11). As he does, he is repeatedly opposed by certain Jews from the province of Asia (where the Spirit of Jesus prevents him from going earlier), and they set up plots to ambush and kill him. Due to the Lord's earlier warning about the province of Asia, Paul makes it to Jerusalem alive, he suffers false arrest and his appeal to Caesar allows him to testify in Jerusalem, and thus he the gains the protection of the Roman soldiers to be escorted out of the way of danger, as the Jews from

377

Asia have also come to Jerusalem, are lying in wait for him. He is thus able to travel to and testify in Rome – completing his calling.

In other words, this slice in the New Testament shows us the leading of the Holy Spirit, mediated as well by angels, where God's sovereignty and human moral agency work together. We are to be led by the Spirit (John 3:8), we are to "be shrewd as snakes and as innocent as doves" (Matthew 10:16), and in the face of demonic political powers, to "work out everything" wisely and strategically (Ephesians 6:13).

Witchcraft in the Midst of Massachusetts Politics

The day I submitted the petitions for a statewide referendum on human life, August 3, 1988, to the Secretary of State's office in Boston, a torrent of witchcraft and demonic opposition came against me and my family, a reality that has long contrails. I was caught totally off guard. It continued through the 1989-1991 season of our Sacred Assembly for the Unborn at Preterm abortion center in Brookline, and I wrote down very many pages of notes to what we went through, and here are just a few highlights.

And as soon as we submitted the petitions, as we have already noted, the next day Boston NOW had a team of its members checking every signature. Their collusion with the political powers was obvious. And immediately too, the demonic assault began. We could not immediately define it, but things changed dramatically in the spiritual realms, all sorts of unexplainable hassles, and it ratcheted up to full bloom the following summer at Preterm.

Voodoo

One remarkable series of events marked this whole season. On August 9, 1989, I was up late one evening (just before midnight), finishing some work, though usually in bed much earlier. I was sitting at the kitchen table, leaned back in my chair and went into prayer. As I did, I had a clear and strong vision. In it I saw a room with crudely fastened bookshelves against a wall to the right. It was laden with books of an occultic nature, along with some cognate paraphernalia. Two windows with sheer curtains were to its left,

378

straight ahead, overlooking a busy city street. I got the sense it was a second or third floor apartment in a neighborhood near Boston University.

At a table in front of the windows, four women were seated. My perspective had me gazing over the shoulders of three of them from the near corner of the table. There was one woman to my left at one end, next to a window to her left, with the right side of her profile discernible but not distinguishable. Two women were seated next to each other to my right, their backs toward me, facing the windows. I saw the face of the fourth woman, who was seated at the end of the table closest to the bookshelves. I recognized having seen her among the abortion-rights protestors at Preterm, led by the Boston chapter of the NOW.

On the table was a crude straw figure with about 35 needles stuck into it. As I looked at the figure, the Lord spoke to me and said that the straw figure had been designed to represent me, and that these women were trying to work voodoo curses against me. I also had the sense they were amateurs at voodoo, but trying hard nonetheless, opening themselves up to whatever spiritual powers were necessary to succeed in disarming our Christian pro-life witness at Preterm.

The Lord Jesus then told me: "Command the needles to explode outward." I was surprised by the word "explode," and immediately rejoined that I was sure the Lord did not intend for the "exploding" needles to hurt any of the women. Being thus assured, I then commanded the needles "to explode outward in the name of Jesus." As I did, I saw the needles pop out of the straw figure and fall onto the table – as the vision was an ongoing event like watching a live video.

As the needles popped out, the four women fell back in their chairs, knowing that this was the power of the Lord at work through my prayers. In other words, they were somehow aware that I was praying at that exact moment, and that the power of the God of the Bible was manifest in response to my prayers. The falling back of the women were as if they were struck by a powerful blast of wind.

379

That was the end of the vision, and I sat there amazed and surprised, not knowing fully what to make of it, still processing the images that had been placed before my mind's eye. The vision was clear and real, but as always, I do not fully trust anything like this without testing it and seeing clear signs of confirmation. So I put it this vision on the "back burner" and went about my life and work.

(Now, I have had quite a few clear daytime visons from the Lord across the years, yet I have never sought them. They happen as they happen, and I seek to discern wisely and understand. And they have measurable fruit when I have confidence to act on them.)

Over the next nine days, I found myself interrupted four or five times, at various times and places, with the Lord telling me to pray – for at that given moment one or several of these women, perhaps at times with others, were cursing me again. Usually a brief prayer was sufficient, but once while driving home in the middle of the day, I was compelled to pray the final twenty minutes until a sense of breakthrough emerged.

On the evening of August 18, a Friday, I was preparing some new signs for the next morning's presence at Preterm. When I was done, I looked at my watch – exactly 12:01 a.m. Then, again, the same vision of August 9 returned, exactly the same in all details and outcome, and I understood that these four women were repeating the attempted voodoo curses again, at that very moment.

After I rebuked the curses in prayer, I was immediately flooded with a remarkable sense of God's presence and peace, went to bed and slept wonderfully. In my prior trips to Preterm I had slept poorly the prior nights, filled with anxieties and uncertainties. I needed to be up at 5:00 a.m., and instead of being exhausted, I awoke fully rested. God's Spirit had touched me after the final rebuke of the voodoo, and a victory had been won in this spiritual warfare with demonic powers.

The fruit was immediately evident. I had expected about 40 people from our Christian pro-life group to show up that Saturday, but we saw as many as

150 different supporters at some point between 7 a.m. and noon. Something had happened in the spiritual realms the night before. We had an average of 80 people at a given time, and the abortion-rights supporters were almost as many at a given time. Four or five people told me how "anointed" that morning was in terms of worship, sidewalk counseling with abortion-minded women, and our witness to the abortion-rights activists. That word "anointed" had never been used before or since at Preterm.

At least seven women chose not to follow through with their abortion appointments, and the number of women observed going into Preterm that morning was very low compared with prior Saturdays. Our people found that the abortion-rights activists had an uncharacteristic openness in the many conversations that occurred, and as well, whereas in our prior times at Preterm we noted pubic displays of witchcraft against us, we saw none that morning.

This was perhaps my first experience in "warfare prayer," that is, praying for God to break demonic powers in the hearts and minds of people, who would otherwise resist the Gospel, and instead experience a level playing field to truly consider it.

In addition, that Friday afternoon, I remember leaving my office, which at the time was in Gloucester. Being increasingly aware of the spiritual dynamics, I was impressed to pray over the office, asking God's protection. After the events of the weekend, and as I came in on Monday morning, our computer's hard disk then failed completely. It cost us not only substantial money, but also a month's worth of organizational progress. The computer technician could offer no satisfactory diagnosis as to why it failed, writing it off as a mysterious "magnetic problem." Then the next day, our brand new photocopier failed. When the service technician opened up the machine, there were no problems with the moving parts. Rather, a non-moving piece, made out of space-age plastic (as durable as steel he told me), was broken in half. No possible explanation in natural terms.

As I looked at the piece and the puzzlement on the part of the Xerox technician, and considered the equal puzzlement by the computer technician earlier, I reflected on this new level of spiritual warfare I was entering. I recalled that as I had prayed over the office Friday afternoon, I prayed over everything specifically except the computer and photocopier. I remember, when I was praying, looking at my desk, typewriter, library and other elements in one room of the office, but not focusing on the adjacent room where the computer and photocopier were located. I wondered: Had these voodooists retorted to my warfare prayer with random missiles of curses until they found something uncovered by prayer?

The Lord Jesus has given us dominion over demonic powers, and I have concluded (and as I write about elsewhere in great depth) that all our prayers equal the commissioning of angels to war against demons (e.g., Daniel 10), demons which seek to interfere with the answers to our prayers, demons that are commissioned by the various rituals and solicitations of occultists.

Demonic Interaction at the University of New Hampshire

In October, 1989, as referenced earlier, I participated in a debate over abortion at the University of New Hampshire (UNH), with three advocates on both sides, and a packed auditorium of some 400 people.

After the debate, off to the side of the podium area, I sought out the Methodist minister who represented the Religious Coalition for Abortion Rights (RCAR) – to follow-up with him on certain of the points we had debated. I had several students from Gordon-Conwell Theological Seminary with me, who with about a dozen people nearby, formed into a circle of discussion. Many students were still milling around or in the process of leaving, so there was a substantial din of background noise in the auditorium.

As I was speaking with the Methodist minister, I was interrupted by a woman who came in and stood to my left. She was an avowed pagan feminist who had questioned me from the floor during the debate format itself, and the question had led to her public embarrassment because she misunderstood something I had said, that which the rest of the audience clearly understood. Now she was loaded for bear.

In her intensity to try again to discredit me, she interrupted the conversation and told me, "Stop trying to force your religion on me." I was momentarily incredulous, for the power of informed choice had been the cornerstone of my comments that evening. At that moment I was unprepared for such vehemence, so I merely responded at the ethical and intellectual level, saying, "I am not forcing religion on anyone, only seeking to persuade people openly and honestly."

She gazed intently in response and declared, "Well, you know, my god is not your god!" At this point I gained the first glimmer that something other than intellectual or political debate was in view. A real spiritual chill, a temperature change, had been brought into the air, but before I had time to process what it meant. And without the time to process it, and being caught off guard, I sought to inject a little humor with understatement. I replied, "That's obvious." Then I continued, "Nonetheless, we both have freedom in a democratic society to try and persuade one another. You are free to try and persuade me, and I am free to try and persuade you."

Then, her voice dropped at least an octave, lower than where I can reach, raspy and caustic, like an uncontrollable volcano rising from within her soul, as she exclaimed, "Well, I don't believe in democracy!" In a normal discourse, I would have followed up and asked if she were a Marxist, and would have questioned her to see if she embraces any form of informed choice.

But this was not a normal discourse. For as she spoke these words, a literal wind was released from her person, and it caused me and the other dozen or so people in the discussion circle to fall backward one or several feet, including the pagan woman herself. The RCAR Methodist minister looked at her with surprised disgust, turned away and left, and everyone else also immediately turned away and left, in somewhat of a daze, thus ending the conversation. I did not know what to make of it, and as I drove back to Massachusetts that evening, I thought about little else.

The next day, I called the several seminary students who were there with me, to gauge their discernment. They each noted the same phenomenon, of a wind being released from the woman's person and driving us back. One student, Bill Wilder (earlier referenced), said that his momentary judgment was that he had thrown his hands into the air, and fell back in a kind of automatic gesture of disbelief at her comment. But then he realized that those with him were also falling back simultaneously, and he knew he had not stepped back but was thrust back. He also noted that as soon as the words and wind came out of her, it were as though it came out against her will, and that there was "something" in her trying to take the words back and mute the reality of the wind.

It were as though an indiscreet manifestation had been made by a demon in reaction to the Gospel, and in a manifestation it would rather have not made so publicly. I believe this public display showed the true nature of the contest for the bystanders, discredited the abortion-rights argument, and thus served the reality of *Satan*'s household being divided. The Methodist minister and others on the abortion-rights side of the issue wanted to distance themselves from her and this manifestation, as they turned away and left immediately.

A demon had been squirming within her all night, at the proclamation of the Gospel in the context of the abortion debate, in hatred of the biblical power of informed choice, in hatred of a level playing field for all ideas to be heard equally, in a hatred of *akol tokel* and embrace of *moth tamuth*.

The ancient serpent opposes the true definition of terms, the level playing field and thus the power of informed choice, from the Garden of Eden on forward. And along with his hatred of the procreation of image-bearers of God, and concerning what I was seeking to do in biblical pro-life witness, I suddenly grasped how powerful the Word of God is in the face of the devil, both ethically and at the phenomenological level.

Thus I learned at a far deeper level the centrality of the devil's scheme against the unborn: *God → life → choice → sex* versus *sex → choice → life →/God*. At UNH, I stepped on the tail of a demon, and then became markedly awakened to this reality.

384

Our House in Manchester

We then rented a house in Manchester, on the North Shore (which shortly thereafter changed its official name to "Manchester-by-the-Sea"). Beginning that August, a whole range of demonic manifestations appeared, as it were, out of nowhere.

Once in prayer, I had a strong vision, of a lightning bolt coming through "strata" in the heavenlies, from the top of a small forested hill across the nearby major street, through our house, through the backyard and into a stream in a modest wooded ravine, that connected to a pond and a further stream that emptied into the Atlantic Ocean about one mile away. The hill had a certain reputation of a history of cloistered violence (I later learned). And in our backyard our eldest son (then ten), who loved to dig for old coins and bottles, discovered some bones and was somewhat freaked. And every time he would go toward the ravine and stream he sensed spiritual darkness.

We prayed about it, and at one discernible time, I knew a breakthrough had been made. As I asked the Lord what all this meant, I sensed a "haunt" in the ravine of a three-hundred-year-old demon, and demons do haunt places where there has been violence and bloodshed. I later lined up the possibility of a connection with the 1690 Salem Witch trials, just down the coast, almost exactly three centuries prior.

In the midst of that season, we were hosting a temporarily homeless family of seven, and we were a family of five plus our daughter in utero. All this in a three-bedroom cape, but the two bedrooms on the second floor were quite large. The young son of our friends had a terrifying experience, when he saw a burning light appear above his head, and it touched his finger and burned him.

Also, there was a week when the whole house was teeming with what I sensed to be a "gathering of demons," to everyone's painful awareness. On the Friday evening before going down to Preterm, I was up late praying. It was so intense, I called some pro-life friends who were involved with us at Preterm, and asked them to pray. They contacted a number of friends and did so. At midnight, in my prayers I sensed strongly the Lord saying, "the intercession is complete." Thus, with everyone asleep, I went to the top of the stairs and prayed over the whole house, declaring the peace of the Lord Jesus. I also rebuked the demon in the ravine, commanding it to depart for good. In so doing, I felt an immediate body impacting and tangibly great peace descend. The turnaround was dramatic for everyone from that point forward. And the next day, my friends told me that in their prayers, they knew a breakthrough had occurred just before midnight.

After the family moved out, my wife and I had several days off to go to Cape Cod, while our three sons were cared for. On the way home, my wife dropped me at my office in Boston. As she drove up to the North Shore she was painfully aware of a horde of demons literally chasing her, including directed in-your-face curses by some passersby on Route 1 in Saugus. Indeed, on our 1971 Volkswagen Bus we had a rear bumper sticker: "Abortion: The Ultimate Child Abuse."

Around that same time, late afternoon, I heard the Lord clearly say to take an early train home, that my wife was in need. In an era prior to cell phones, I knew nothing of what she was going through. As I was about to leave and walk to the train at North Station, she called, begging me to come right home, deeply terrified by the demonic attack. And on the train ride, I remember sitting next to a woman dripping with the occult, who got off at Salem (not surprisingly), but more than that, there was a deeper sense of the darkness crowding against us from various angles. When I arrived at home, we prayed for a period, and the darkness lifted.

Also in that season, we all traveled by car to Ithaca, New York, where I was speaking at the CPC and addressing the debate at Cornell, as earlier described. Here I learned of some spiritual warfare of a remarkable nature, and when driving home, my wife and I were talking about it. At this point, in the back seat, our two older sons got energized. They spoke of having been up to the small forested hill not far from our house, and it being a dark and scary place, that their peers felt the same, and knew various stories dealing with theft and murder associated with the place.

386

But especially, when I told them about the lightning bolt vision, and the exact day when our prayers broke through, our eldest son got very excited. "Dad – that is why I never wanted to take out the trash at night." He had experienced the presence of supernatural evil emanating from the ravine. "But ever since [three weeks ago], the evil is gone, and I am peaceful and unafraid when I take the trash out." The timetable lined up exactly with the prayers.

Witchcraft at Repro Abortion Center Follows Me to a Debate at Gordon College

In early 1990, we had some fifty people, including a contingent from my home church (the Vineyard Christian Fellowship in Wakefield), at Repro abortion center in Brookline, not far up the road from Preterm. Operation Rescue had a rally scheduled for Preterm that day.

It was one of the most intense encounters with witchcraft ever, as several dozen openly professing witches surrounded us as we worshiped. I wondered at that moment how wise it was to have children with us, for their presence was always part of what we did. Namely, families celebrating the strength of childlikeness, as such a spiritual authority is referenced in Isaiah 11:6, those who are of the kingdom of the heavens (Matthew 18:1-6).

It was genuinely ugly, all the hatred and curses. One woman in particular seemed as demonic in her presence as few people I have encountered. Then, later that spring, I was debating a woman at Gordon College, whose name and organization I forget. But her associate was this woman I saw at Repro, and she clearly knew who I was. He demonic aura was as intense as before, bringing a discrete darkness into the event. Indeed, the audience was agitated all night in a way I have never experienced, and this at a Christian College.

Black Canopy at Preterm Pierced

In the summer of 1990, we had a remarkable experience at Preterm abortion center. A church in the central part of the state sent a team of 30 or so people on a given Saturday every month, also bringing with them a

387

number of their young children. At the end of the morning on one such time, the person leading worship (with a guitar for our sidewalk gathering) told the pastor of a vision he had been experiencing all morning. Namely, there was a black canopy of evil in the heavenlies over the abortion center and immediate neighborhood. But as our prayers and praises rose up, the canopy was being stretched toward the breaking point, as though being pushed back by various spear tips. But it did not break.

The next month, there was a different worship leader. When the group was packing up at the end of the morning, he told the pastor of a vision he experienced all morning. And he had no knowledge of the prior vision that had been shared. He saw a black canopy of evil in the heavenlies over the abortion center and immediate neighborhood. So as our prayers and praises rose up, the canopy was stretched by such an assault against its evil, then it broke. And on that day, and prior to this report being shared, we noticed a dramatic change in the heavenlies, and discrete advances in the fruit of ministry as our opposition – human and demonic – was in retreat. In those days, we usually had a large number of passersby give us the "finger" and curse us. On this Saturday, I had noticed, for some reason, and counted 36 passersby give us a "thumbs up," and only one person give us the finger.

Bankruptcy

In June, 1991, the New England Christian Action Council had to file for bankruptcy, and thus the good ministry halted abruptly. It was not my decision, but that of the board of directors. I was a risk-taker beyond their comfort zones (but being initially unaware), it backfired on the one hand, and I erred on the other. I had only one year's worth of income the next two-and-a-half-years, and ended up moving eleven times in ten years with a growing family, including being homeless for two stints. It was hell.

And I can blame no one but myself. As we noted earlier from Luke 14:28-33, Jesus gives warning not to a) build a tower unless the money is in place to finish it, and b) go to war unless sufficient army strength is in place. I failed on both counts in my "tunnel-view optimism" (as my father saw in me as a little boy). I believed, quite naïvely, that in pursuing the good, finances would follow.

And the devil aims at our weaknesses, our blindsides, just like the lion prowling at the rear of the herd (e.g., 1 Peter 5:8; also how the Amalekites attacked the Israelites right after they left Egypt, cf. Exodus 17:8ff; 1 Samuel 15), looking for the weak and infirm. So whereas I gave enormous attention to learning biblical fidelity and wisdom for the sake of pro-life ministry, I always postponed financial planning. All the while, I was thinking and living outside the box in so many ways.

Under the stresses, I procrastinated concerning two matters with my board, in a) addressing criteria put before us by a supporting church that was trying to help us get out of debt, and b) in promising stipends for some of my seminary students before confirming it with the board.

In the former, the supporting church wanted the board to become more active in the fund-raising work (I was doing all of it myself). This they put in a letter to me with a large initial gift, with substantial monthly support for the subsequent year. I knew the board could not do more than it was already, and was hesitant to share this with them, and postponed sharing the letter at the following monthly meeting, not wanting the conflict I feared, and thereafter, procrastination took hold. Had I done so, I later learned, and had the board joined in and succeeded in a certain threshold of debt clearance, the church was then planning to pay off the rest.

In the latter, I could easily have told them that I had promised the stipends foolishly, and have corrected the matter. But I procrastinated in my tunnel vision hope for greater ministry income to justify it. Both matters hit the fan simultaneously in June, 1991, and with these long procrastinations never addressed, and thus increasingly out of mind, they turned into de facto lies. The board lost faith in me, there was already increasing dysfunction as it was at many levels in the prior two years, and no doubt many demonic catalysts in this regard. The board chose to file bankruptcy was chosen. No income.

I was spiritually and psychology devastated, physically sick. I aimed always for integrity, and here fell short. And it took me too much time to put it all in context, and reacquaint myself with God's grace.

So I share this here in candor, for whereas I have seen great ministry accomplished, I am in need of the Savior as much as anybody. Spiritual warfare is real, and we are responsible agents made in God's image to know and act wisely. When Jacob (the dreamer with visions) wrestles with the angel of *Yahweh* – always striving for the blessing – his hip socket is wrenched, and he limps the rest of his life (Genesis 32:22-32). I have limped ever since June, 1991, and with all the antecedents since 1988 and the petition drive that preceded it. It has been largely surreal until more recently, and I am no longer a young man, with middle-age falling further behind in the rear-view mirror.

Who Moved the Stones?

So after a year of being unsettled, and partially homeless, we moved back to my native Connecticut in July, 1992. I just needed to make a living, and by January, 1993, I was teaching seminars and classes on biblical theology and politics across the state. But even before this came into being, the spiritual warfare landed on me afresh.

I ran into a remarkable series that began with a daytime vision in early May, 1992, up in the northwest hills of Connecticut. I saw an image of a spearhead, superimposed on a map of Connecticut, running from northwest to southeast, from the Berkshires across the Massachusetts border, the width covering much territory including the capitol city of Hartford, and aiming toward New London on Long Island Sound. As I saw the vision, the Lord said one word: "Vacuum." That was it, and the vision departed.

Some weeks later, my wife and I had a powerful occultic encounter while hiking a certain hill. Then shortly thereafter, while driving north on Route 8 just prior to Winsted, I noticed an intricate pillar of stones in the wide median strip, atop a large boulder. It was two or three feet high and involved dozens of stones. Two days later, six of us hiked the same hill for the purpose of praying for revival in Connecticut, for justice and mercy in the name of Jesus to salt society. This hill was above the spot on Route 8 where I saw the stones, and in one of my prayers, I asked the Lord if these were pagan stones in need of removal, due to their spiritual evil, and if so, would the Lord send his holy angels to tear them down?

Three days later, on June 21 (the summer solstice), they came down – with no human involvement to our knowledge. We later learned that they had been up for years. It became our conviction that these stones were marking the spiritual territory of the Berkshire Hills for pagan devotion, as the land mass rises at this juncture in northern Connecticut, and as Route 8 changes to a two0way road. This pillar of stones was partially rebuilt several times, subsequently, but kept coming down, again, without any human involvement on our part. When I drove past that spot, in 2007, the large boulder was barren, with a bird sitting atop it, and a bush growing high on its northwest side. In the meantime, I heard reports of stones going up again, but they were not in place in 2015 (it is not an angle of highway I usually drive).

A Witch and a Modest Prayer Meeting

In the spring of 1993 I had opportunity to visit with a pastor in Groton, Connecticut. He told me about a remarkable visit he had recently by a witch who approached him after a Sunday worship service. She announced herself and said that in New London County there are three covens of witches assigned to curse every pastor who resides there, and that there is at least one coven dedicated to curse every pastor statewide. She also said that the curses have three priorities: first that the pastor would fall into theological error; second, into financial ruin; and third, into sexual sin. She then left.

I found this amazing. As did my friend. Since when do witches come into the open and announce their agendas? Since the devil is described as a lion on the prowl by the apostle Peter, as just referenced, it would seem that those in the occult would only risk open terrain a) if they were utterly confident in easy pickings, or b) if they were desperate for a meal.

Then in June, I also started a modest series of "warfare prayer" meetings at St. James Episcopal Church in Winsted. We were praying for the Lord to break demonic powers in the state (especially the *kosmoskratoras*, as it is). We prayed concerning specific dynamics of Connecticut's spiritual territory, choosing Winsted because of proximity to the former pillar of stones on Route 8.

We sensed that both realities were spiritually tied into the geography of those hills, and that as the curses of the spearhead were aimed from there at the capitol in Hartford and down to New London County, we wanted to pray in the same direction, essentially for unalienable rights for all people in the state, including women and their unborn. We identified the spearhead as representing curses from the Native Americans a century prior, against the White Man's God and government, for having driven them out of the state. Their exit route coursed up the Farmington River through these very hills and valleys. We prayed for forgiveness for the State.

Slander, Stones and Intimidation by a Lawyer

In returning to Connecticut, I was not involved in any pro-life work, but the contrails from the demonic realities in Massachusetts continued. Indeed, in 1993, a statewide activist with Planned Parenthood and the National Abortion Rights Action League (NARAL) started tracking me. She got on my mailing list (incognito), and began to feed slander to quite a number of newspapers in New York, Connecticut and Massachusetts – some worked with it, and some did not.

The basic thrust is that I was a violent man due to our "warfare prayer" meetings in Winsted, a clause taken deliberately out of spiritual vertical context and applied to human lateral context. In other words, in the "warfare prayer" meetings, we were praying for the Light of Jesus to dispel the darkness of demonic power, whereas this slander was trying to say we were plotting violence against people with whom we might disagree politically. This slander had no substance to base its charges other than the deliberate misuse of spiritual language. Then, in this season, in-between truck-loads

392

while moving across town, someone erected a pillar of stones on a rock outcropping next to our new house. Checking in?

The woman who was tracking me had attended a Mars Hill Forum I had addressed at the Universalist Unitarian church in which I grew up, where my guest was the president of the UUA. The next day at the University of Connecticut, she addressed a meeting called "Keeping an Eye on the Radical Right" (though I make no such identification, as one newspaper writer noted). A friend of mine happened to see the poster just beforehand, and dropped in moments before she said, "But watch out for John Rankin. He is the most dangerous man in the state, for two reasons. First, because he is a Harvard graduate, and second, because he believes that through prayer he can kick the devil out of the state."

My friend immediately thought she was kidding about driving the devil out of the state, but also noticed that she was serious, and in linking it so closely with a Harvard education. Namely, the combination of the two is what she feared. She, of deep pro-abortion sympathies, belied her pagan occultism, being fearful of true prayer in the power and Name of Jesus. But she still had it wrong. I cannot do it, but a unified church can, as it prays accordingly.

Aside: It can be said that the three most powerful men in the Bible, apart from the Lord Jesus, are Moses, Daniel and Paul. Each of them knows a) the biblical text inside out, b) pagan religion and politics inside out, and c) are followed by the signs and wonders given by the Holy Spirit. To look at it another way – if we are smart and nasty, opponents of the Gospel can dismiss us; if on the other hand, we are dumb and nice, likewise. But if we love the Lord our God with all our heart, soul, mind and strength, love our neighbors as ourselves, and know the power of the Holy Spirit, it is another reality. It is one where we can define the terms through a lived biblical theology, we change the language of the abortion debate, and thus gain the driver's seat of the debate.

Aside over: Then, in the midst of this I learned that a lawyer in Winsted was investigating our prayer meeting on the grounds that we might be plotting to "violate the civil rights" of people. And a newspaper reporter, working in conjunction with the lawyer (I later discerned), interviewed me about our prayer meeting and asked specifically if we "pray against people." I said a clear no, yet at the end of the interview she said, "Now let me review some of the major points we covered, to be sure I understand you clearly. First, you are praying against people, right?"

The agenda was clear, so I challenged her, every reporter from these other newspapers, and the lawyer head-on. As a result, the slander stopped, and never came up again.

When those stones came down in 1992, I believe the occultic powers in Connecticut were shaken. The occultists knew their spiritual power had been muted, and as soon as they fingered me, the campaign to take me down began. Sorcery at the right hand of power?

Witchcraft at Smith College

In the forum at Smith College, November, 1994, as reviewed earlier, there is one outstanding element that was at play. Smith is part of Northampton, Massachusetts, the acknowledged witchcraft capital of the nation, some forty miles north of where I live. This is a reversal, as Northampton is where the First Great Awakening began under the preaching of Jonathan Edwards in the 18th century.

Prior to the forum, we had about 150 people in committed intercessory prayer for an event that drew about 550 people, some 60-80 of whom we knew to be biblically rooted Christians. As we have already noted, the fruit of the evening was great.

During the questions and answers, a locally well-known woman, Libby Hubbard, who went by the name "Doctress Neutopia," asked the first question. She claimed, at the time, to head up the world's largest cyberspace coven. In her question she became confused, also asking if I had read her *unpublished* manuscript that speaks of a "womanist theology" (or same such) that contradicts my theology … Her confusion was apparent to all.

394

I am convinced that the power of intercessory prayer had prohibited a demonic presence there, and thus Doctress Neutopia had no crutch to lean on. The Christians who sponsored the forum were amazed at how well-known pagans, lesbians, pro-abortion activists and other skeptics listened to the presentation of the Gospel. No demonic interference ...

I learned after the forum about the goings on in the balcony – which I could not see due to the bright television lights. An hour or so before the event, three members of the Smith Christian Fellowship went up into its highest corner, to pray over the whole of Sage Concert Hall. Later, several dozen avowed witches came up to the balcony, set up their occultic paraphernalia, and sought to work curses on me the whole evening.

Also, before the witches arrived, the video team set some lights in the balcony, along with related electronics. During the forum, one member of the team went up there because there was an interruption to both the sound and light systems, giving interference in some capacity. As he did, the pervading power of evil was so great that he fled back downstairs. All the blood had drained from his face, and he appeared "white as a ghost" to the people around him. One Christian man there, knowing what was at play, immediately went up and rebuked the demonic powers, and the electronic issues were thus rectified.

After the forum, as I left, I was aware that the intercessory prayer had driven out the demonic power, but once the prayer was no longer in place, the demons were beginning to rush back in. The Light had pierced the darkness, if but briefly. If only we in the whole church knew its authority in the Gospel, in the face of the ancient serpent ...

Intercessory Prayer and Politics

The need is for biblically literate intercessory power, seeking godly counsel at the right hand of power to displace sorcery at the right hand of power. As biblical prophets confront political evil in the Bible, they do so always with a focus on the kingdom of God, seeking to be salt and light in corrupt societies.

Here are some key biblical points of spiritual and political conflict where such prayer is an operating assumption:

- Moses is a Hebrew raised in Egyptian royalty. Later, in the name of the true King *Yahweh*, he directly challenges Pharaoh, king of Egypt: "Let my people go." Moses leads the Israelites to freedom by the power of the Holy Spirit.
- Samuel is the last faithful judge when Israel is a federation of twelve tribes under the liberty of the Law of Moses. He warns the people of the coming enslavement if they choose a pagan styled king, which they do. They thus suffer under Saul, and Samuel confronts him in the end after Saul resorts to consulting a medium.
- Elijah is opposed by the wife of Ahab, king of (northern) Israel – the Sidonian witch Jezebel. She is devoted to killing *Yahweh*'s prophets, Elijah opposes her and all the false prophets, and he calls Ahab and the nation to repentance.
- Jeremiah confronts the final evil and oscillating kings, and false prophets, in the remnant Judah during its final days. He repeatedly calls the king and the nation to repent of sorcery, sacred prostitution and child sacrifice.
- Daniel, as a Hebrew exile and slave, rises to the stature of prime minister in the court of Nebuchadnezzar, king of Babylon. He calls on the king to repent of his evil. When Nebuchadnezzar does not, he is judged, goes into exile for seven years, Daniel rules in his stead, and afterward he repents.
- John the Baptist challenges the incest of King Herod the Tetrarch, and loses his life as a result.
- Jesus calls King Herod a "fox" in the henhouse, in a passing reference en route to the cross and resurrection.
- The apostle Paul calls for us to intercede "for kings and all those in authority" so that we might live peaceful lives and advance the Gospel (1 Timothy 2:1-4).

In a different age, here in the United States in the early 21st century, we need a positive vision. Proverbs 11:14 states: "In the absence of wise counsel, nations fall." Yet before any positive vision can happen, the church needs to repent of her own sins, consistent with Solomon's prayer in 2 Chronicles 7:11-22, and Daniel's prayer in 9:1-20. Then we can pray for godly political leadership to be raised up at every level, knowing King Jesus is in control.

Daniel and his three friends, Hananiah, Mishael and Azariah, under the mortal danger of political evil, intercede in prayer. As the answer comes, securing their deliverance, Daniel proclaims how *Elohim* is in control: "He changes times and seasons, he sets up kings and deposes them" (2:21).

Mary, called to carry the Messiah in her womb, prays the same prophetic reality in the *Magnificat*: "He has scattered those who are proud in their inmost thoughts. He has brought down rulers from their thrones but has lifted up the humble" (Luke 1:52).

On this basis, we can live and preach the Gospel that advances the unalienable rights that start with life.

In Sum

The ancient serpent is angry with anything in the orders of creation and redemption. He especially despises the powers to live in the light, informed choice and hard questions – all in service to the level playing field for all ideas to be heard equally. Thus, to succeed in winning full legal for women and their unborn equally, we need to be wise to these matters, and always be on the offensive in the heavenlies.

◆ ◆ ◆

Chapter Ten

Changing the Language of the Abortion Debate

If we grasp Biblical Theology 101; the *God → life → choice → sex* versus *sex → choice → life →/God* paradigm, and how these terms are honesty or dishonestly defined; the cognate pretension of ignorance in Cain, the enemies of Jesus and in the *Roe* Court; the male chauvinism of the abortion ethos and industry; the power to love hard questions where dishonest partisans silence themselves; and all the above fleshed out in their full theological and practical life applications; then we can change the language of the abortion debate, gain the driver's seat honestly, and thus set about winning the equal legal protection for women and their unborn.

There are three essential and simultaneous tasks to accomplish, with concomitant strategies in place:

1. Winning public consensus on the biological definition of individual human life, through the power of informed choice;
2. Winning public consensus on the driving reality of male chauvinism, or more understatedly put, male irresponsibility; and
3. Placing the hardest questions in the public digest in ways that cannot be ignored by elitist political, academic, media, scientific, financial and activist culture.

Jesus, in the Face of His Enemies

But first, let's flesh out the strategic ethics necessary, and these are found in how Jesus faces his plotting enemies during Passover Week. This I write about in great depth elsewhere, and here I will give a brief summary, applicable to any debate, and critically to that over the abortion debate.

The Gospel of Matthew is the most political of the four, beginning in the first verse by declaring Jesus "the Son of David." Which is to say, he is proclaimed as the Son of the founding King in Jerusalem, and thus a threat to the political power of Herod the Great, then his son, Herod the Tetrarch.

398

In Matthew 21, as Jesus enters Jerusalem, and the praises he receives from the people include "Hosanna to the Son of David," his Messianic nature is confessed. All the religious elitists are in bed with the political elitists. They have agreed to a false separation of temple and state, where the Romans grant them their religious sphere with its influence and money, so long as they do not enter the public square and seek to advance the social justice of the Law of Moses. They can have their religion, so long as it is castrated.

Jesus exposes the parallel idolatries of Rome and the temple, and thus the estates of the religious elitists. His very nature threatens all the hypocrisies in place that trample the poor. So when he is challenged, first by the chief priests, it is because Jesus allows the children in the temple courts to proclaim him the Son of David (21:14-15).

In 21:16, the chief priests try to rebuke Jesus for this, but instead he quotes the eighth psalm that celebrates the strength of the children's praise. He stops his quote short of the next clause in the psalm, that which declares such praise will "silence the foe and vengeful," a reference to the enemies of the Messiah. Since the chief priests, and all rabbis and teachers of the law, have the entire Hebrew Scriptures memorized, they literally continue on with this clause in their heads. And they know Jesus is treating them as enemies of the Messiah who will be silenced.

Thus they are motivated not to be silenced, which means if they disprove him in fulfilling this Messianic prophecy, ergo, he cannot thus be the Messiah, and he can be dismissed as a fraud.

Thus, they concoct a strategy of questions to silence Jesus.

First, in 21:23-27, the chief priests and some of the elders of the people seek to trap him on the question of credentials, asking where he gains his authority to do what he does. They are disciples of "accredited" rabbis in the city of Jerusalem, whereas he is an itinerant and "unaccredited" preacher from the rural north, adjacent to Galilean Gentile country.

So Jesus answers with a question, typically rabbinic, where he gives them a level playing field for honest debate. Where, he asks, does John the Baptist gain his authority? To paraphrase: "Answer me and I will answer you." If the chief priests and elders say John's authority is from God, then Jesus can ask why they do not believe in John, and also believe in him, Jesus, to whom John testified. This they will not do, for John and Jesus both threaten their positions of worldly power.

If they answer that John only has self-assigned or human authority, this the chief priests and elders are fearful to say, for all the people hold that John is a prophet. As Luke's gospel points out here (20:6), they fear the people will thus stone them.

So, they say, "We don't know." The pretension of ignorance per Cain. So Jesus does not answer them, and they have nothing more to say. An aha moment, for the people at least.

Second, in 22:15-22, some disciples of the Pharisees team up with some Herodians to try and entrap Jesus on the question of paying taxes to Caesar. Now, the Pharisees are orthodox, and in some sense, awaiting the Messiah, but more on political terms that justify their own positions and pride. They hate the Herodians, turncoat Jews who support the political party of Herod, and are therefore fundamentally anti-Messianic. But they both hate Jesus more, so they form a temporary and negative alliance (per the ancient Near Eastern proverb, "the enemy of my enemy is my friend," at least until the mutual enemy is dispatched, old grievances return between former enemies, and the momentary alliance is quickly forgotten).

The double trap is this: On the one hand, if Jesus says to pay taxes, the Pharisees can call him an idolater for handling a coin that calls Caesar god, he cannot be the Messiah, and thus dismissed as a fraud; and on the other hand, if Jesus says not to pay taxes, the Herodians can charge him with sedition, and have him crucified accordingly. Gotcha, both ways, they think.

But Jesus asks for a definition of terms, the power of informed choice, as it were. Namely, whose portraiture is on the Roman coin? So they bring him a denarius, with a picture of Tiberius Caesar, and the inscription, "Tiberius Caesar, Son of the Divine Augustus." Now, we have a conflict between the true Son of God, Jesus, and a false son of god, Tiberius.

Jesus answers by telling them to give to Caesar what belongs to him, and give to God what belongs to him. In other words, Jesus is saying to the Pharisees, if Tiberius Caesar is such a fool to believe himself the son of god, let him have his coin, and see what good it does him in the presence of the true Son of God at the end of the age. And to the Herodians, he says that the real portraiture that matters is the image of God in which we are all made, so give God your heart, soul, mind and strength, and do not give it to Herod. Paying taxes is no big deal; worship God alone. They are dumbfounded and have nothing further to say. Another aha moment, for the people at least.

Third, in 22:23-33, the wealthy Sadducees, theologically heterodox if not heretical, seek to trap Jesus on the question of the resurrection and angels, for they believe in neither. Jesus says they know neither the Scriptures nor the power of God on the matter. He points out how God addresses the Sadducees, as well as for all Jews, as the God of their forefathers, Abraham, Isaac and Jacob – and God is the God of the living not the dead. Thus, implied, if there is no resurrection, then their God is also dead when he speaks of Abraham et al. in the present tense. And accordingly, the Sadducees are dead people walking. They have no answer. And thus again, an aha moment, for the people at least.

Fourth and finally, in 22:34-46, the Pharisees get together again, and one honest teacher of the law happens to pass by (so identified in Mark 12:28-33), and he sees how well Jesus has answered. So he asks him concerning the greatest commandment, Jesus answers, and the rest of the Pharisees are just standing there, nothing more to say. So Jesus asks them concerning the Christ's identity, they answer the "Son of David." He thus quizzes them on a prophecy from Psalm 110 concerning the Messiah, and as a result, we arrive at the concluding statement by Matthew summing up the whole debate: "No one was powerful enough to answer him a word, and from that day forward no one dared to question him further." The final aha moment, for the honest teacher of the law, and the people, at least.

Thus, in the face of his bitter opponents, Jesus affords them the level playing field, inviting their toughest questions. The four questions concern these arenas:

1. Credentials;
2. Church (as it were) and state;
3. Theological nitpicking; and
4. Theological grandstanding.

Jesus exposes elitism and its concern for "credentials," gives the level playing field for honest debate, loves hard questions, reveals the pretension of ignorance, employs the power of informed choice, reveals the idolatries in the debate over temple and state, exposes religious idolatry, and finally, sets things straight with true theology. This is quite comprehensive, and issues we have seen percolate all through the debate over human abortion, and beyond.

The key is this: Jesus gives his sworn enemies full hospitality to rake him over the coals with their toughest questions, the dishonest silence themselves, and the one identified honest elite is commended by Jesus (in Mark 12). If the believing church were to grasp and employ the wisdom here, we will speed along the winning of legal protection equally for women and their unborn.

This means proactively going where the toughest questions are being expressed in the court of public debate; to create an honest level playing field for all ideas to be heard equally; address the central issues; change the language honestly; and gain the driver's seat for success. Thus:

A Biblical Strategy

My starting point to change the language of the abortion debate, and set the foundation for full legal protection for women and their unborn equally, is in my home state of Connecticut which has the most stringent pro-abortion laws in the nation. To even mention the word "abortion" in any context, pro or con, in the state legislature, is virtually taboo. How do we cut through this reality with honesty? It is, as always, a matter of the true definition of terms that provides for the power of informed choice. And the theology of Jesus in the face of his enemies is thus strategically necessary. As I prepare to engage the topic in the 2017-2018 legislative session, here is my strategy, and published for all to see.

A Roadmap to End Legalized Abortion

The Informed Choice Coalition (ICC) [www.informedchoice.us]

– *Roe* v. *Wade* is based on Stated Ignorance; the Bible is based on Informed Choice –

In order to win legal protection for women and their unborn equally, we need to define life and choice honestly, and as a counterweight to stated ignorance. There are three salient realities:

1. None of us can choose apart from first being alive.
2. Biologically discrete human life begins at conception. The word "abortion" comes from the Latin *ab + oriri*, "to cut off from rising."
3. The overwhelming "choice" for human abortion resides with men who choose not to marry the women they get pregnant, with men who choose to reject fatherhood.

How do we bring these realities into honest political discourse? Connecticut has the most stringent pro-abortion laws in the nation, and within the political establishment there is fierce resistance to even broaching the subject. The headwinds are strong.

We start by recruiting enough citizens to simply call and write their own state senators and representatives according to a systematic strategy where the simple question (in steps two and three) is this: **Do you support informed choice?**

1. In **Step One**, the ICC is conducting a survey in Connecticut of all members of the 2017-2018 State Legislature, the Executive Branch, and the U.S. Congress, on two multiple-choice questions concerning human life and male irresponsibility (see below). In the process, the ICC is already recruiting an initial 150-200 volunteers statewide.

2. Political leaders who answer the questions are to be honored regardless of their views – they are being honest with their constituents.

3. Political leaders who "choose not to answer" are thus in agreement with the 1973 U.S. Supreme Court *Roe v. Wade* decision which legalized human abortion, a decision rooted in a choice not to address either of these two questions. We honor the freedom of political leaders not to give answer, but too, we are honest in naming such a reality.

4. **In *Roe*, the Justices employed a "we don't know" argument as to when "life begins." This is a statement of chosen ignorance,** just like Cain using the "I don't know" argument as to the whereabouts of his brother Abel whom he had just murdered. And this is just like some enemies of Jesus using the "we don't know" argument to avoid answering him on the source of John the Baptist's authority, as they sought pretext to have Jesus crucified.

5. This "we don't know" rationale – again, the very essence of *Roe* – is the intellectually and morally weakest form of argument in history, and can easily be overcome through the power of informed choice.

6. At a prior theological reality in Genesis 2, we are given the true definition of terms of a) good and evil, b) freedom and slavery and c) life and death. We are thus given a level playing field to choose between these parallel opposites. **A true definition of terms yields the power of informed choice**.

7. One political reality of biblical theology is this: **Informed choice serves the humanity of women and their unborn equally; misinformed choice (or worse, stated ignorance) serves human abortion which also rips women's lives apart.**

8. John Rankin will continually invite any and all abortion advocates in Connecticut to publicly challenge the suitability of these two questions.

9. John will teach seminars statewide, rooted in his book: *Changing the Language of the Abortion Debate*. And John will also begin the TEI Leadership School in January, 2017, for the deeper and empowering biblical theology to address all of life and its toughest questions.

10. At a January or February press conference in Hartford, John will announce the results of the survey, sum up this strategy for legislators, the media and the public, address the toughest questions in the debate over human abortion, and receive any and all questions.

11. **Step Two** is to pursue legislation to place these two questions on the 2018 state ballot. At this juncture we need to recruit at least 12 ICC volunteers per representative district (12 x 151 districts = 1812 volunteers statewide), who will each make phone calls and write personal letters to their state senators and representatives, asking them to **Support Informed Choice** and allow citizens to vote on these two questions on the 2018 ballot (letters are best sent via the post office, as emails are easy to ignore or delete).

12. Given the expected political opposition to even allowing the debate out of Committee, and even then, to keep it from being voted on for the ballot by the General Assembly, and even then, facing a likely gubernatorial veto: **Step Three** is to recruit as many more volunteers as possible to ratchet up the calls and letters. We can succeed.

13. When successful, **Step Four** is to recruit enough more volunteers to canvass the entire state for the actual ballot question in 2018.

14. This strategy can be imitated in the other 49 states. Even if *Roe* were to be overturned by the U.S. Supreme Court at some point, it would only remand the matter back to the States. The strategy of the **Informed Choice Coalition** is thus necessary to address this concern, as it prepares the way to win the necessary 38 state legislatures to pass a Human Life Amendment to the U.S. Constitution: "The unalienable rights of life, liberty and property belong to all people equally under the rule of law. The first order of human government is to protect human life for its entire natural duration, out of which liberty and property rights become possible." And let the debate on "entire natural duration" ensue. **Law cannot be changed until the hearts and minds of men and women are changed, and this strategy will energize such a process.** Pro-life law should then first hold men legally accountable for the lives and well-being of their unborn children.

Law cannot be changed until the hearts and minds of men and women are changed, and this strategy will energize such a process.

Human Abortion and a Process of Informed Choice

We recognize that the U.S. Constitution defines three principal arenas of unalienable human rights, and with a specific order – life, liberty and property.

The 1973 U.S. Supreme Court *Roe* v. *Wade* decision left the beginning of individual biological human life undefined. We believe this matter should be addressed. If there is no consensus on the biological beginning of individual human life, let it be shown, and the status quo of *Roe* v. *Wade* will hold and be strengthened. If, however, a clear consensus emerges, let it be instructive.

In **biological terms**, when does an individual human life begin?

Mark a cross X next to the answer you prefer. Only mark one.

A. Conception [ ].

B. Viability [ ].

C. Birth [ ].

D. Write-in [ ]: specify a different biological term _____.

It will be interesting to see how many legislators will refuse to answer the question, choosing public ignorance over informed choice, thus explicitly or implicitly supporting *Roe*. Regardless, the educational power and public debate over this question will accrue to the truth, and an overwhelming majority of those who answer will affirm that "Conception is it."

Then, this question needs to be voted on in the U.S. Congress, then referred to a public non-binding vote at the state level, then in every state. We will thus gain the driver's seat, initially framing the new language of the abortion debate:

1. **Informed choice, rooted in an honest definition of terms, serves human life; *Roe* v. *Wade* is the opposite, based on a pretension of ignorance (tracing back to Cain and the enemies of Jesus).**

Human Abortion and Male Irresponsibility

We recognize that the 1973 U.S. Supreme Court *Roe* v. *Wade* decision does not address the role of fathers or male responsibility. As well, we recognize that in the overwhelming number of abortion decisions, the man has left the relationship and refuses accountability.

To what extent is human abortion driven by male irresponsibility?

Mark a cross X next to the answer you prefer. Only mark one.

407

A. Very Much [   ].

B. Somewhat [   ].

C. Very little [   ].

Of those who give answer, the majority will likely answer "A." But those women who do not answer are de facto affirming *Roe* in their conflicted pains, or in support of other women, relative to having yielded to male chauvinism in the name of feminism. Any men with guilty consciences, and as legislators, will likely choose not to vote on the matter, thus voting for the logic and ethics of *Roe*.

Then, this question needs to be voted on in the U.S. Congress, then referred to a public non-binding vote at the state level, then in every state. We will further gain the driver's seat, also framing the new language of the abortion debate:

2. **Human abortion is the ultimate male chauvinism.**

Then we need to organize the **Sacred Assemblies for the Unborn (SAU)** at every abortion center in the United States, on all college campuses and at every other suitable venue. We will additionally gain the driver's seat, and congruent with the prior two realities, also frame the new language of the abortion debate:

3. **Pro-abortion advocates silence themselves in the presence of honest questions.**

Endgame

As we thus set the foundation for a human life amendment, on the one hand, there is, on the other, a far deeper constitutional surgery needed.

408

Namely, the need to radically reform government from the bottom-up, 1) in cutting all law by 99 percent, 2) taxes by 50 percent, 3) setting the economy ablaze as rooted in the true *oikonomos*, and 4) where the starting point is the biblical *God → Life → Choice → Sex* paradigm at the roots the Declaration of Independence. This I propose in detail elsewhere.

◆ ◆ ◆

Epilogue

A Memorial to Zephyr

(Words and Music © 1984 Beverly Rush)

Zephyr, you're the gentle wind, the silent breeze in my life. Zephyr, though a gentle wind, you brought a storm in my life.

When you blew into my life, my body felt so strange. If I could change one thing in this world, it's the day I brought you pain.

Zephyr, you're the gentle wind, the silent breeze in my life. Zephyr, though a silent sigh, you're the deepest cry of my life.

When I sought the grace of God, he took away my shame. Though the years have passed, it's not 'til today, that you've ever had a name.

Zephyr, you're the gentle wind, the silent breeze in my life. Zephyr, you're the gentle breeze, the first fruit in my life.

Now there is hope for mothers and fathers, who drink this mournful cup. Know that every child who has been forsaken, the Lord will take him up.

And love him, and hold him, and keep your treasure safe. And when you are ready, in your heart he'll find a place.

Zephyr, you're the gentle wind, the silent breeze in our lives. Zephyr, though a silent breeze, you have sung your song in our hearts.

You have sung your song in our hearts.

◆ ◆ ◆